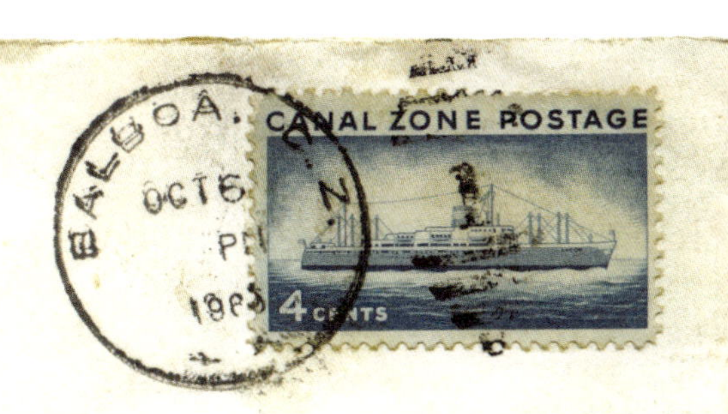

Roman Ondak
Panamska 9
821 08 Bratislava
Slovakia

To

Maja,
Adam
and Tino

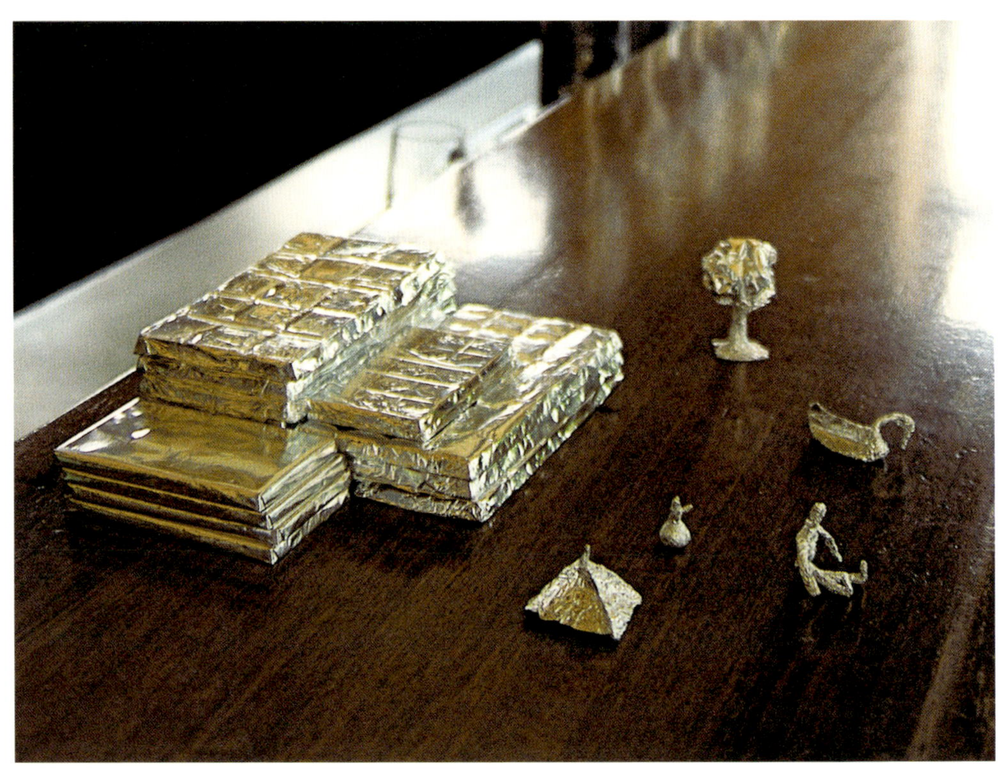

Roman Ondák

Measuring the Universe

BAWAG FOUNDATION EDITION
Christoph Keller Editions

Contributions by

Bernhart Schwenk
Jeanine Griffin
Tim Etchells
Magali Arriola

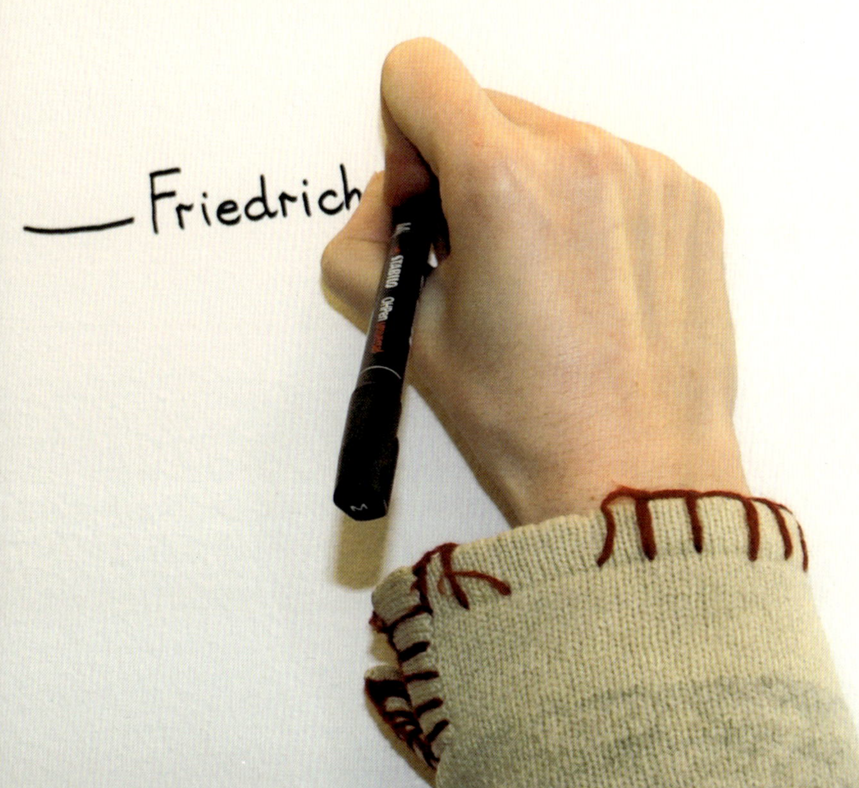

Friedrich

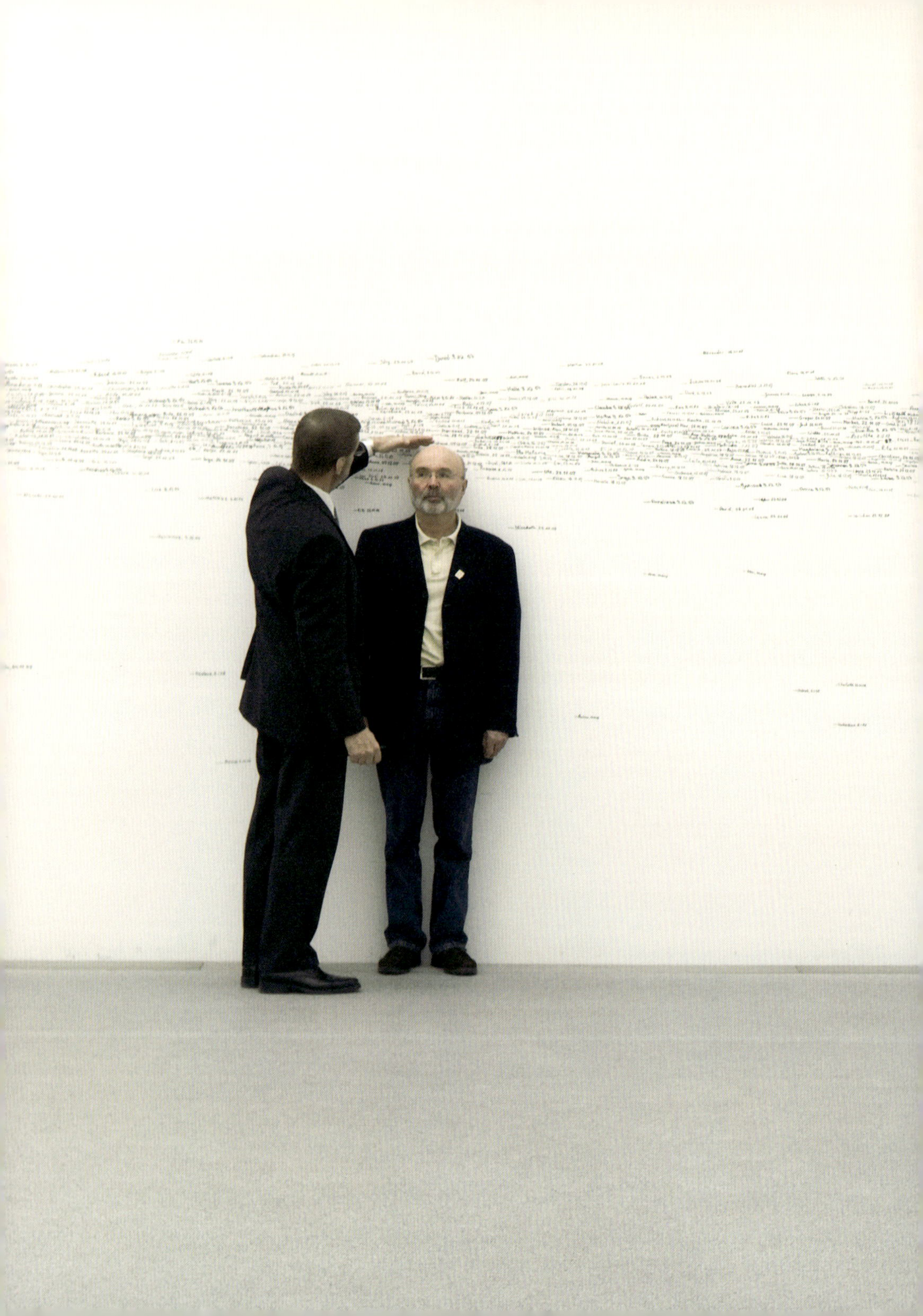

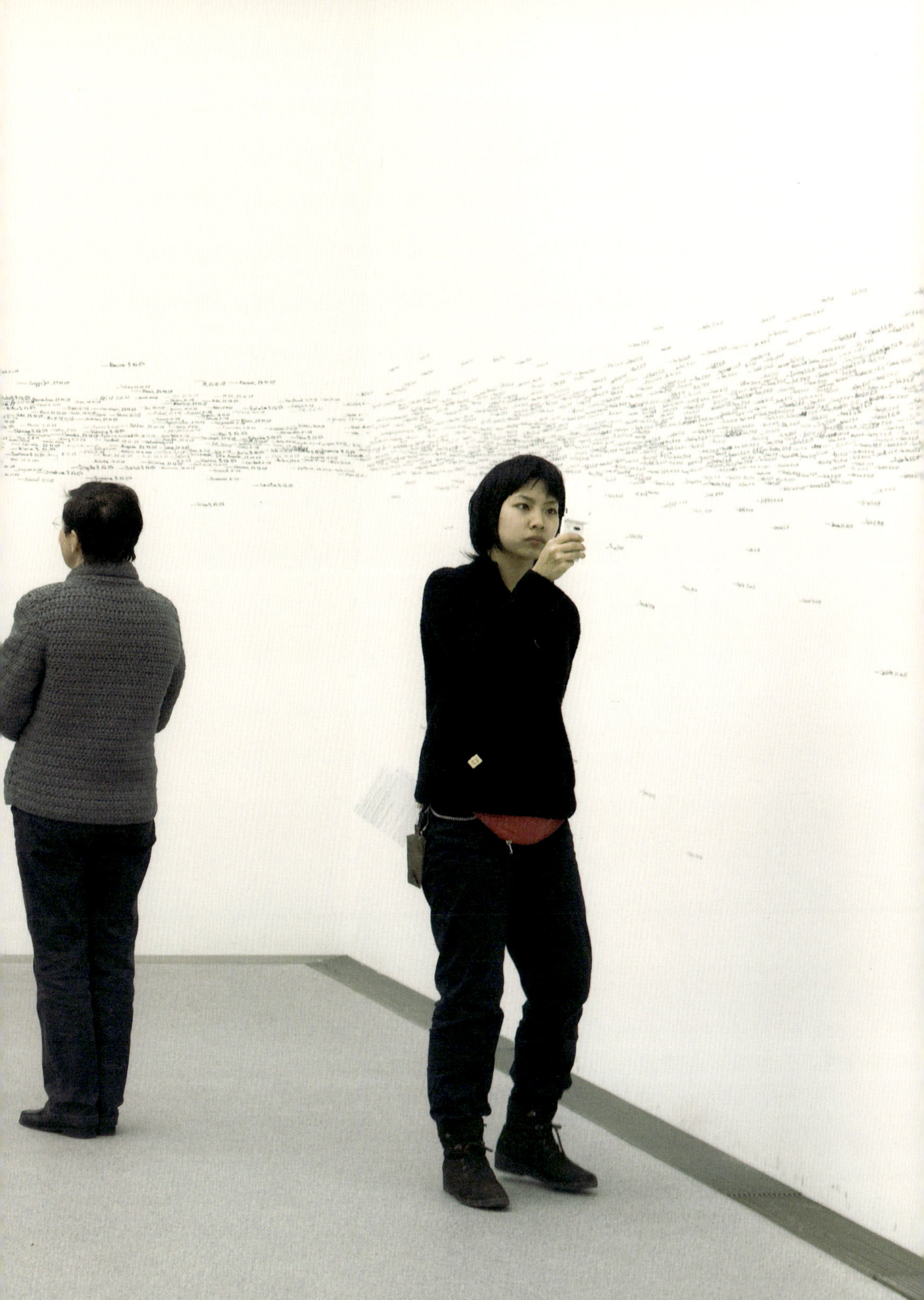

Measuring the Universe

The urge to gauge the scale of our world is age old. It is based in an uneasy regard of the intangible and, at the same time, the need to comprehend. The way in which this approximation has been sought in science and art through the millennia is as diverse as it is contradictory. There have been repeated attempts to depict the 'canonical' and 'calculable' without eliminating the 'unpredictable' and the 'mysterious'. Studies by the Roman architect and theorist Vitruvius, above all the 'man in a circle' and the 'man in the square' (taken up again, particularly by Leonardo, in the Renaissance), make this ambivalent point of view clear in exemplary fashion: depending, namely, upon man's position within a circle and square, the centre of the body shifts, demonstrating the autonomy of man and geometry. The geometric figure is, nevertheless, defined as a basic derivation of a model found in nature. In this sense, rationality is not the opposite of something which accrues organically: the circle and square are shown to be ideas which were already present in nature, to a certain degree as simplifications or 'abstractions' of the human body.

It is in this tradition of calculations rooted in nature, in 'human measurement' of the world, that Roman Ondák situates the work *Measuring the Universe* (2007), which was realized in a 400-square-metre space with a square floor plan in Munich's Pinakothek der Moderne. This first site of Ondák's piece can easily be seen as metaphoric or paradigmatic, as a readily comprehensible *pars pro toto* for the world at large and the great variety of processes occurring within it. There are tens of thousands visitors to the museum space at the Pinakothek each month – in varying frequency and intervals, of course, with different levels of foreknowledge and awareness, and with different expectations. It is precisely this disorderly flow – an unpredictable circulation of energy – the shared participation in an 'excerpt' of the world, in other words, which is measured. Before the exhibit began, the space was fixed up in order to demarcate a starting point: the hall was given a pristine coat of white paint and consciously transformed into a white cube – a canvas without a past. Once this prerequisite is met, history can occur paradigmatically, according to a specified, comprehensible procedure.

Measuring the Universe is a performance involving museum attendants and visitors who are coequal in the process through which the artwork comes into being. The attendants become the *acteurs* – in the artist's stead. The performance begins with a prologue of sorts, which is invisible to the public: the artist formally hands over the exhibition space to the attendants. Ondák sets out to attain a cordial yet frank and matter-of-fact dialogue between attendants and visitors: "We are measuring the height of the visitors. Will you join in?" Those who consent are measured with the utmost respect. The visitor stands with his or her back to the designated wall. Then the attendant ascertains his height by placing an outstretched hand on the wall above the participant's head in a manner that keeps physical contact to a minimum. As soon as the visitor steps aside, the attendant marks his or her height on the wall. This is always done with a black, felt-tip pen that the attendants carry with them, and they are the only ones allowed to make these marks.

— Richard, 28.3.08

— Steffen, 30.3.08

— Owen, 6.4.08

Ralf, 1.04.08
— Riccardo, 4.4.08

— Tim, 29.3.08.

— Fl

— Benjamin, 5.04.08 Madlen, 31.3.08 —

— Naa

— Djamila, 30.3.08

— Loes, 9.04.08

rid, 30.3.08 — Hans-Jörg, 12.4.08

— Ingelise, 30.3.08
— Celeste 2.04.08
— Michelle, 4.4.08

— Raf

— Wies, 28.03.08   — Ruth, 8.04.08

— Victoire, 5.4.08

— Sar

— Christin, 12.4.08

— Queena, 1.4.08
— Sofia, 5.4.08

— Emanuela, 4.4.08

_ Emanuele 28. 03.

_ Birgit, 4.04.08

_ Melissa, 30. 3. 08

_ Masato, 4.04.08

_ Maja, 1. 4. 08

_ Joëlle, 4.4.08
_ Ati, 5.4.08

_ Anna, 28.3.08

_ Liz, 30.3.08   _ Ryoko, 3.04.08
_ Corinna, 30.3.08

_ Fadime, 5. 4. 08

— Torsten, 2.4.08
— Saâdane, 28.3.08   — Ma

— Zhang Qing, 3.4.08
Roman, 27.03.08
Mareike, 5.4.08

—T-yong, 3.0

——Robert, 5.4.08

—— Corise, 2.4.08

Hatami, 5.4.08   — Daniel, 2.4.08
Aurélie, 28.3.08

irsten, 28.3.08   — Gerrit,
— Gabi, 6.4.08 ——— Honesty, 31.3.08

——Barbara, 2.4.0

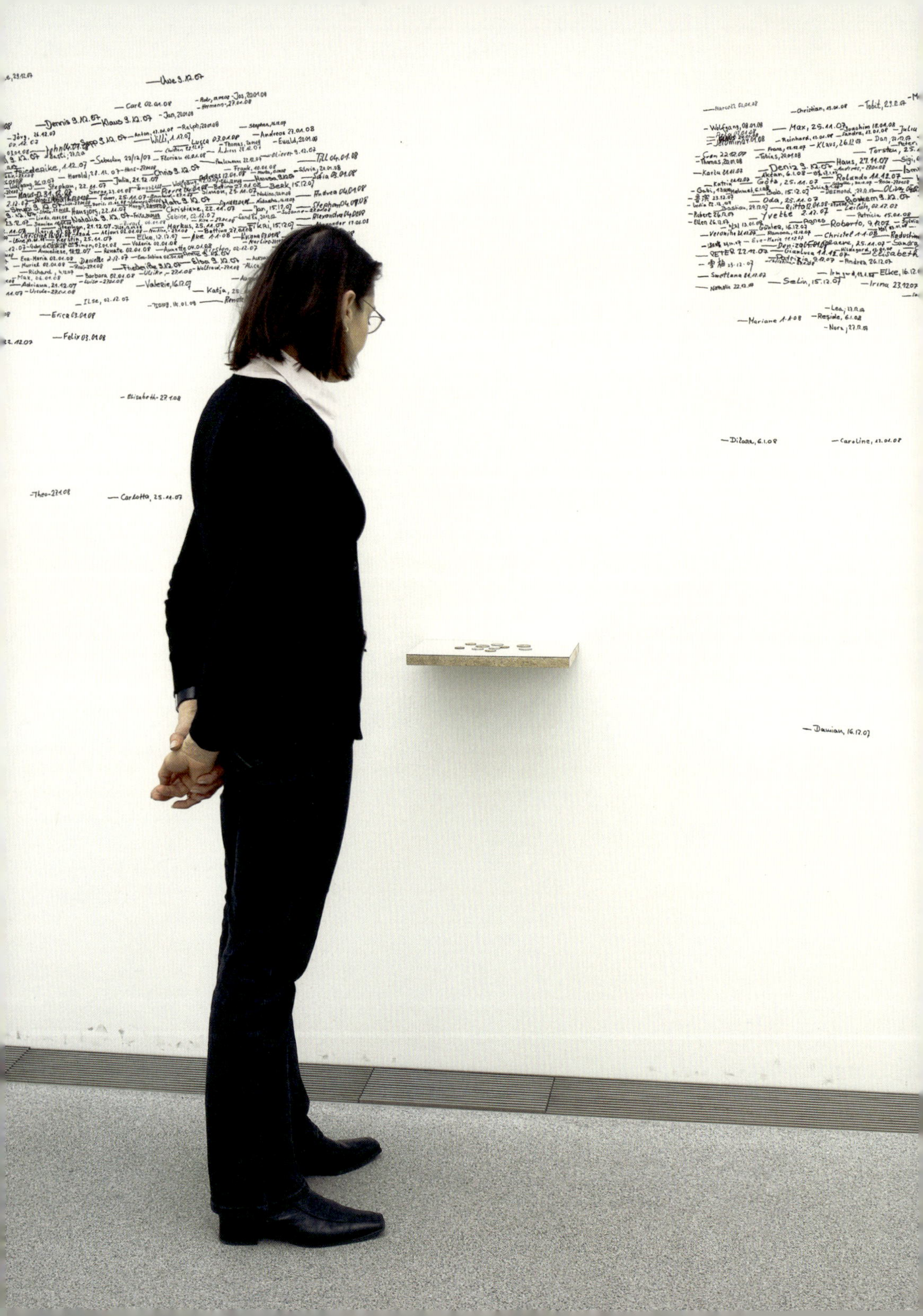

Measurement and notation occur according to a pre-defined, unvarying schema. The person's first name is written to the right of a horizontal line, about two centimetres in length, followed by a comma. Next, separated by periods, the three-part date (day.month.year) is added. The uniformity of the notations provides a basis for comparison, which becomes more complex with each additional notation. Yet the museum visitors are by no means passive: one person might express the desire to have his name appear in a significant location – in a corner, for example, or near a door. Others want to be close to family members, friends, acquaintances or – purely associatively – next to an attractive-sounding name. They come one by one, in pairs, or as part of an entire school class. Some are shy, and others are brusque – and ready to pull out a pen and start writing. Yet, as mentioned, only the attendants are allowed to make the notations, and this holds true even if a visitor's name is unusually long, or the notation must be executed beyond an attendant's normal reach.

The walls' denotation is also structured: the 'complex' and the 'unclear' are ordered and incorporated in a system. Since the notations are handwritten, there will inevitably be departures from the control system: some foreseeable, some spontaneous, and others which suggest improvisation and fantasy on the part of the participants. What happens, for example, if a person enters the space who does not understand German, or is 'uncommon' in the broadest sense? Someone who is not versed in the Roman alphabet, but knows the Devanagari, Cyrillic or Arabic alphabet, or Chinese ideographs, for example? The exception – as determined by the artist – proves the rule: in cases where the attendant has no command of the necessary characters, the visitor may write his or her name with the attendant's marker. And similarly, if a baby who cannot stand on its own is held at the base of the wall, only an approximate measurement can be made. And what happens when an attendant's pen slips? Or if she is tired and no longer guides the marker with a steady hand? The artist accepts all of these situations as natural departures from the norm, which likewise give rise to an aesthetic result and take a subordinate role to the overarching whole. Norm and anomaly, rule and deviation, system and anti-system all become intertwined and are part of the process.

When the measuring began in the Pinakothek space, the high walls were still largely bare and empty, and the individual names were infinitesimal in the expanse of the white hall. But over the course of the following weeks and months, the number of marks increased: a wall drawing encircled the space, becoming more and more dense, the black intensifying, its darkest zone in the middle of the stripe levelling out an average height. In some spots it makes odd current conditions discernible and elucidates a process that seems in equal measure tentative and dynamic. A viewer of *Measuring the Universe* – to emphasize this aspect again – is a witness *(subject)* to the artwork's origination and an integral part of its conception *(object)*, and thus is to an equal degree *acteur* and *motif*. The traditional hierarchy between artists and non-artists, or authors and readers, has been done away with; in the same vein, through their participation in the work, the viewers unify everyday reality and pictorial reality. With such frequent repetition, taking the measurements – which at first seemed theatrical – increasingly becomes routine and starts to resemble other social rituals that occur on a daily basis. The work makes reference, with extreme simplicity, to the cyclical structures of human life, which, next to numerous other processes, also consist of recurrent bodily movements. Time is henceforth perceived as a succession of endless repetition, deemed 'progress' in the bigger picture. Although *Measuring the Universe* only marks out the walls' surfaces, it deals first and foremost with the exploration of spatial dimensions. It addresses the creation of an enabling space, a space for thought, an experiential space and naturally, it addresses temporal space. Every notation, each and every measurement, arrests time, measures points in time within a lifetime, a generation, an epoch. The growing space-drawing also makes it possible to observe time, with the variety of moments contained therein: obscurity, impermanence, mutability, concentration. *Measuring the Universe*, it becomes clear, embodies time dedicated to learning, teaching, nurturing, contemplating, considering and experiencing.

Paradoxically, the existence and presence of material per se becomes perceptible – as does the impermanence of all things physical – in the absence of materiality. *Measuring the Universe* is an ephemeral venture, which exists in large part in the minds of the visitors. It uncovers that which is otherwise invisible: thousands of people, visitors to the museum, see the same space, go through the same procedure and immerse themselves in a shared world of experiences, albeit gradually. But by leaving behind these traces of their presence, they also maintain a palpable presence for subsequent visitors. Past and present relativize the meaning of the individual, without allowing it to become meaningless.

Measuring the Universe repositions a common, in many cases private, act – namely marking someone's height, something parents often do with their children to make them aware of the passage of time and of change – at the centre of attention and transforms it into a public, collective operation. A representation of meaning comes into being, yet it simultaneously implies the physical and temporal insignificance of the individual. The artist defines himself thereby as a communicator and catalyst of thought and action. As an aesthetic avowal to dispense with everything material or monumental, and anything ideological or spectacular, Roman Ondák's work testifies – unwaveringly and not seeking to cause a stir – to an art involving simultaneously ethical and astute acts. *Measuring the Universe* is an homage to the sensual qualities of cerebral space and the opulence of emptiness.

Bernhart Schwenk

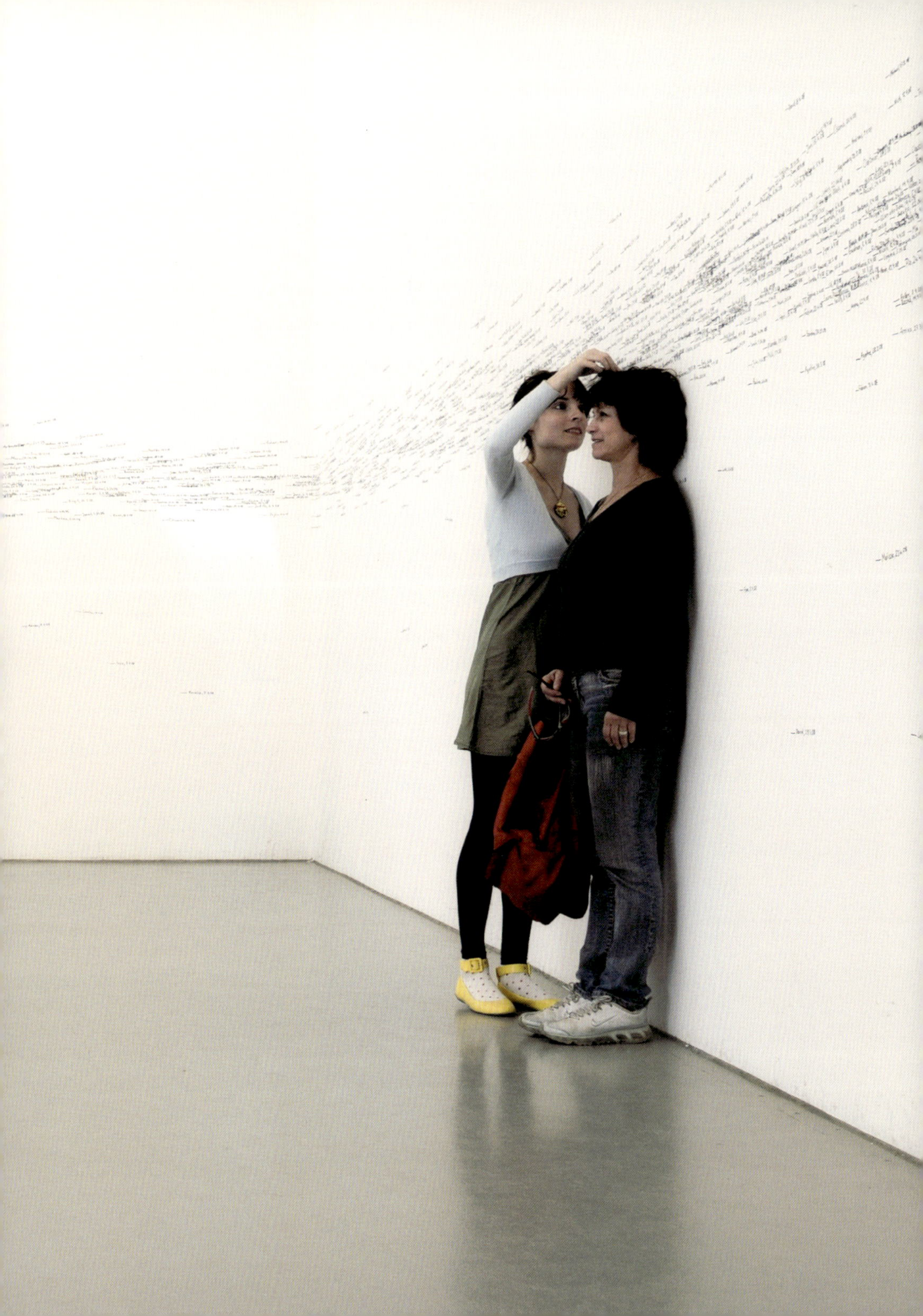

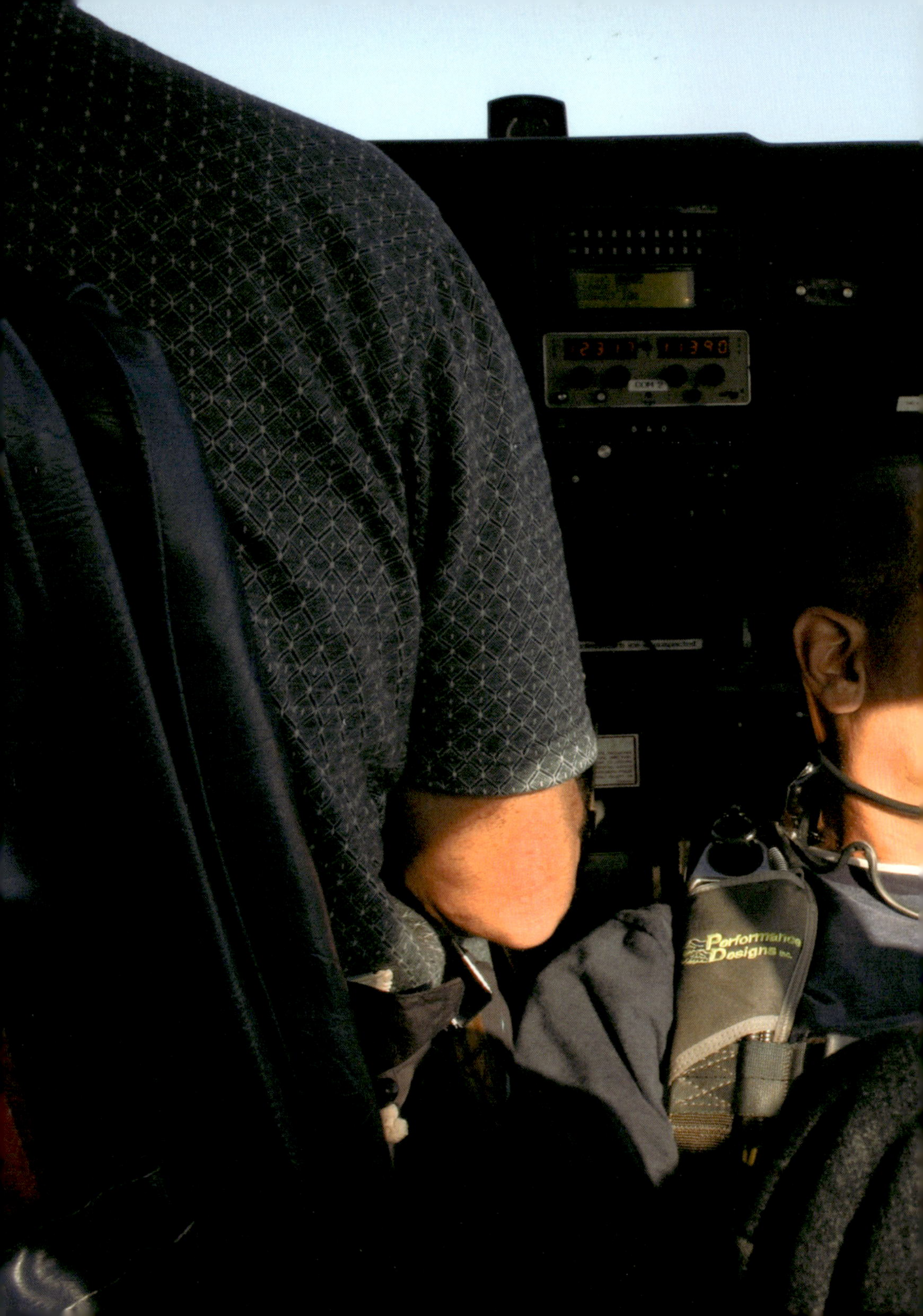

Performance
Designs Inc.

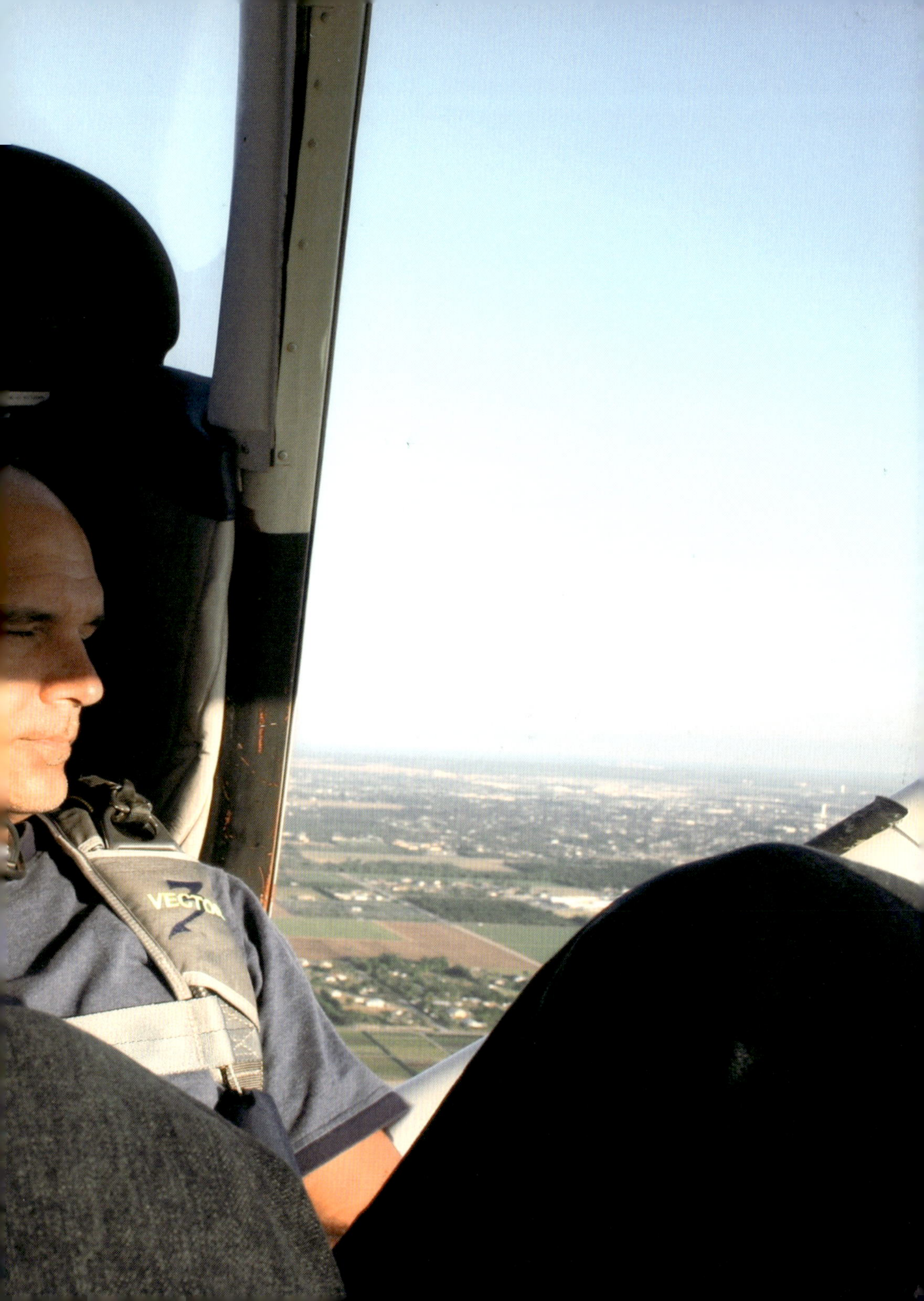

— Matthias, 16.12.07

— Armin, 16.12.07
— Thorsten, 16.12.07 — Thomas 11.12.07
— Andreas, 16.12.07 — Ditmar, 16.12.07
— Jürgen, 16.12.07
— Georg 14.12. Wolfgang 08.12.07   Michael 03.12.07   — Eike, 16.12.07
— Michael, 16.12.07   Florian, 13.12.07 — Volker, 01.12.07 — Sebastian, 16.12.07   — Hans, 23.11.
— Lasse, 16.12.07 — Patrick, 16.12.07 — Michael, 13.12.07   — Simon, 27.11.07
— Andreas, 16.12.07
竜太郎, 16.12.07 — Christina 14.12.07 — Hans, 16.12.07 — Axel, 16.12.07 Olga, 8.12.07 — Andreas, 16.12.07 — Reinhard, 8.12.07
— Niklas, 16.12.07 — Petra, 16.12.07 — Nico, 16.12.07 — Thomas, 12.12.07 — Nikt, 16.12.07 — Katharina, 16.12.07 — Dario, 22.11.07 — Christian 17.11.07
— Sigi, 12.12.07 — Chris 14.12.07 — Simon, 16.12.07 — Pedro, 16.12.07 John-Paul 8.12.07 — Roberto, 16.12.07 Dieter 01.11.07 — Franz, 5.12.07
— Tanja, 16.12.07 — Steffen, 13.12.07 — Georg, 12.12.07 — Beno, 13.12.07 — Sebastian, 6.12.07 — Frank, 16.12.07
— Markus, 16.12.07 — Michael, 16.12.07 — Gabriele, 16.12.07 — Daniel, 8.12.07 — Heike, 27.11.07
— Dieter, 16.12.07 — Brigitte, 16.12.07 — Sebastian, 12.12.07 ANA C. 08/12/07 — Elena, 16.12.07 — Sonja, 16.12.07
— Alicja, 16.12.07 — Judith, 16.12.07 — Andy, 12.12.07 — Wolfgang, 6.12.07 Sibylle, 27.11.07 — Konrad, 28.11.07
— Thomas, 16.12.07 — Robert, 12.12.07 — Petra, 16.12.07 — Joachim, 27.11.07 — Hugo, 5.12.07
— Annette, 16.12.07 8.12.07 MMFL. — Johannes, 12.12.07 — Linus, 13.12.07 — Birgit, 16.12.07 — Rudolf
— Alex, 16.12.07 — Marcela, 16.12.07 — Anna, 16.12.07 — Raouf, 16.12.07 — Tobias, 12.12.07 — Jürgen, 22.11.07
— Kai, 16.12.07 — Isabel, 16.12.07 — Ingo, 16.12.07 — Dagmara, 23.11.07 — Claudia, 8.12.07
— Sarah, 16.12.07 Pia 14.12.07 — Manuel, 16.12.07 Maija 8.12.07 — Franziska, 16.12.07 — Berthold, 6.12.07 — Monika
— Stephan, 16.12.07 — Eric, 16.12.07 — Simone, 13.12.07 Lotte 8.12.07 TORÜ 1.12.07 — Brandon, 13.12.07 — Sabine 8.12.07
— Tatjana, 16.12.07 — Ingrid, 12.12.07 — Mladen, 16.12.07 — Alexandra, 16.12.07 — Judith, 16.12.07 — Miriam, 16.12.07 Sero, 16.12.07 — Franziska, 16.12.07
— Marie-France, 13.12.07 — Astridmaria, 16.12.07 — Martina, 16.12.07 08/DIC/2007 BEGOÑA — Karin, 16.12.07 — Ortrud, 22.11.07
— Henriette, 12.12.07 — Katharina, 16.12.07 Elaine 8.12.07   Birgit, 30.11.07
— Anja, 16.12.07 — Nino, 12.12.07 — Edward, 12.12.07 — Corinna, 2.12.07 — Ursula, 16.12.07 — Laura, 6.12.07
— Regina, 13.12.07 — Angelika, 16.12.07 — Rupert, 13.12.07 — Giulia, 16.12.07 — Cornelia, 16.12.07 — Sarah, 16.12.07 — Cecilia, 16.12.07
— Charlotte, 16.12.07 — Hiromi.Japan 太太, 16.12.07 — Ulrike, 13.12.07 — 지인, 13.12.07 — Helga, 16.12.07 — Emma, 16.12.07 Pancha, 5.12.07 — Thorsten, 6.12.07 Erika, 27.
— Verena 11.12.07 — Kathrin, 16.12.07 — Christine, 16.12.07 — Stefanie, 16.12.07 Nami, 1.12.07 — Sarah, 30.11.07 — Sayd, 30.11.07
— Maryline, 16.12.07 Christine 14.12.07 — Angelika, 16.12.07 — Doris, 13.12.07
— Emy, 12.12.07 — Carmen, 12.12.07 — Biane, 16.12.07 — Jana, 16.12.07 — Natalie, 16.12.07 — Karine, 16.12.07
— Sandy, 16.12.07 — Barbara, 16.12.07 — Kacena, 13.12.07 Mirjam 14.12.07 — Brigitta, 6.12.07   华体, 16.12.07
— Simone, 16.12.07 — Paola, 12.12.07 — Felix, 13.12.07   Leslie, 12.12.07
— Marius, 16.12.07 — Elfriede, 16.12.07

— Jenny 14.12.07   — Ingrid, 13.12.07   — Tammy 11.12.07

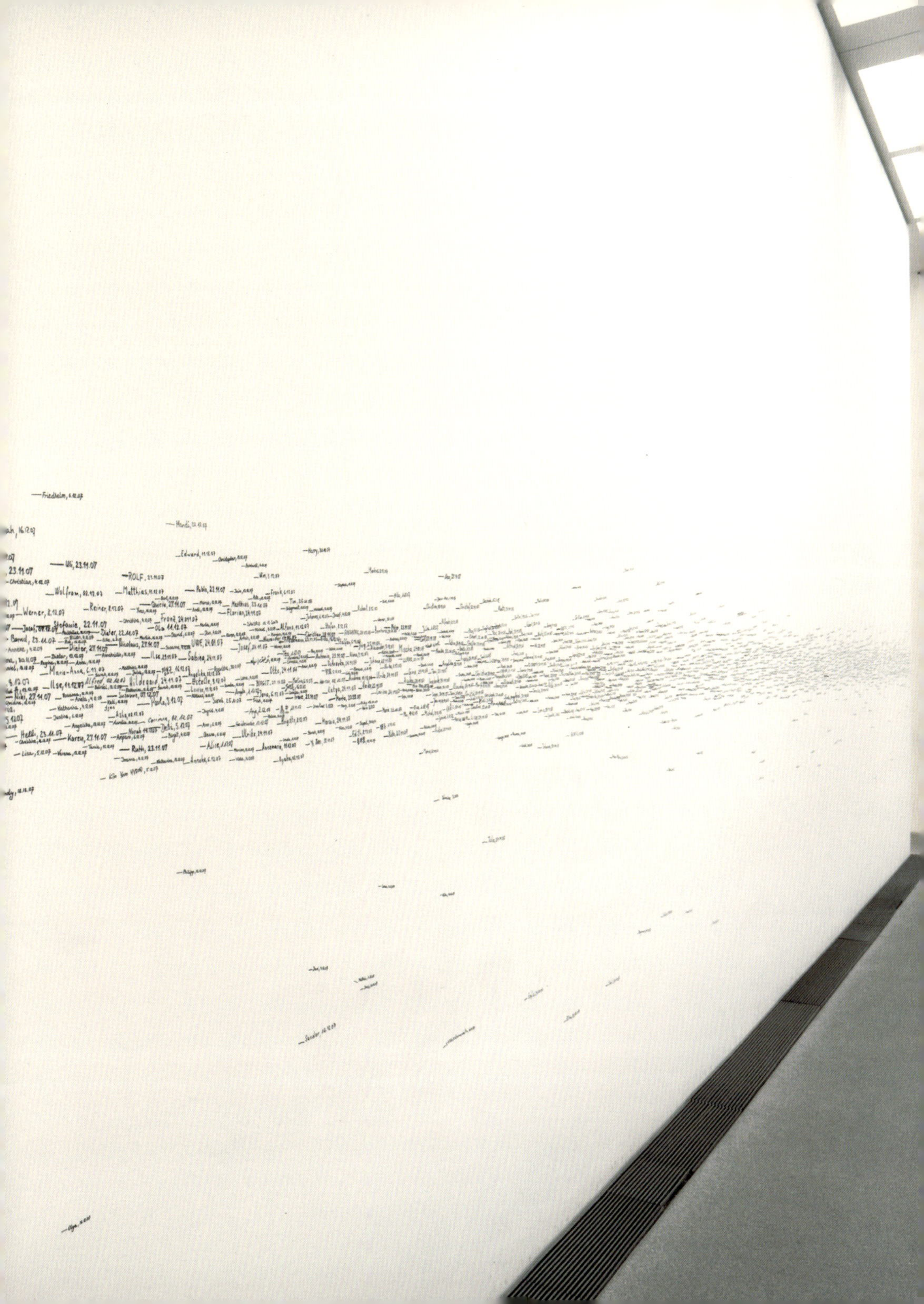

—Friedhelm, 6.12.07

ah, 16.12.07

—Mardi, 12.12.07

—Edward, 11.12.07
—Christopher, 11.12.07

—Uli, 23.11.07
23.11.07
—Christian, 4.12.07

—ROLF, 21.11.07

—Wolfram, 02.12.07   —Matthias, 11.12.07   —Pablo, 22.11.07

—Werner, 2.12.07   —Reiner, 2.12.07   —Dmitri, 27.11.07   —Matthias, 23.12.07   —Tim, 16.12.07
—Christine   —Franz, 24.11.07   —Florian, 24.11.07

—Josef,   Stefanie, 22.11.07   —Olu, 11.12.07
—Dieter, 22.11.07
—Bernd, 23.11.07   —Nicolaus, 27.11.07   —URE, 24.01.07   —Josef, 23.11.07
—Dieter, 27.11.07
—Dieter, 02.12.07   —Ilse, 23.11.07   —Sabine, 24.11.07
—Marie-Anne, 6.11.07   —1982, 16.12.07   —Otto, 24.11.07

Ilse, 11.12.07   —Alfred, 02.12.07   —Hildegard, 24.11.07   —Estelle, 3.12.07   —BIRGIT, 23.11.07
—Niki, 27.11.07   —Susanne, 07.12.07   —Paola, 3.12.07   —Sarah, 25.11.07
—Katharina, 2.12.07
—Justine, 6.12.07
—Angelika   —Corinna, 12.12.07   —Debi, 5.12.07   —Ulrike, 23.11.07
—Helli, 23.11.07   —Karen, 27.11.07   —Norah 14.11.07   —Alice, 2.12.07
—Christine,   —Tania, 11.12.07   —Ruth, 23.11.07
—Lisa, 5.12.07   —Verena
—Kim Van 11.12.07, 7.12.07

dy, 12.12.07

—Philipp, 11.12.07

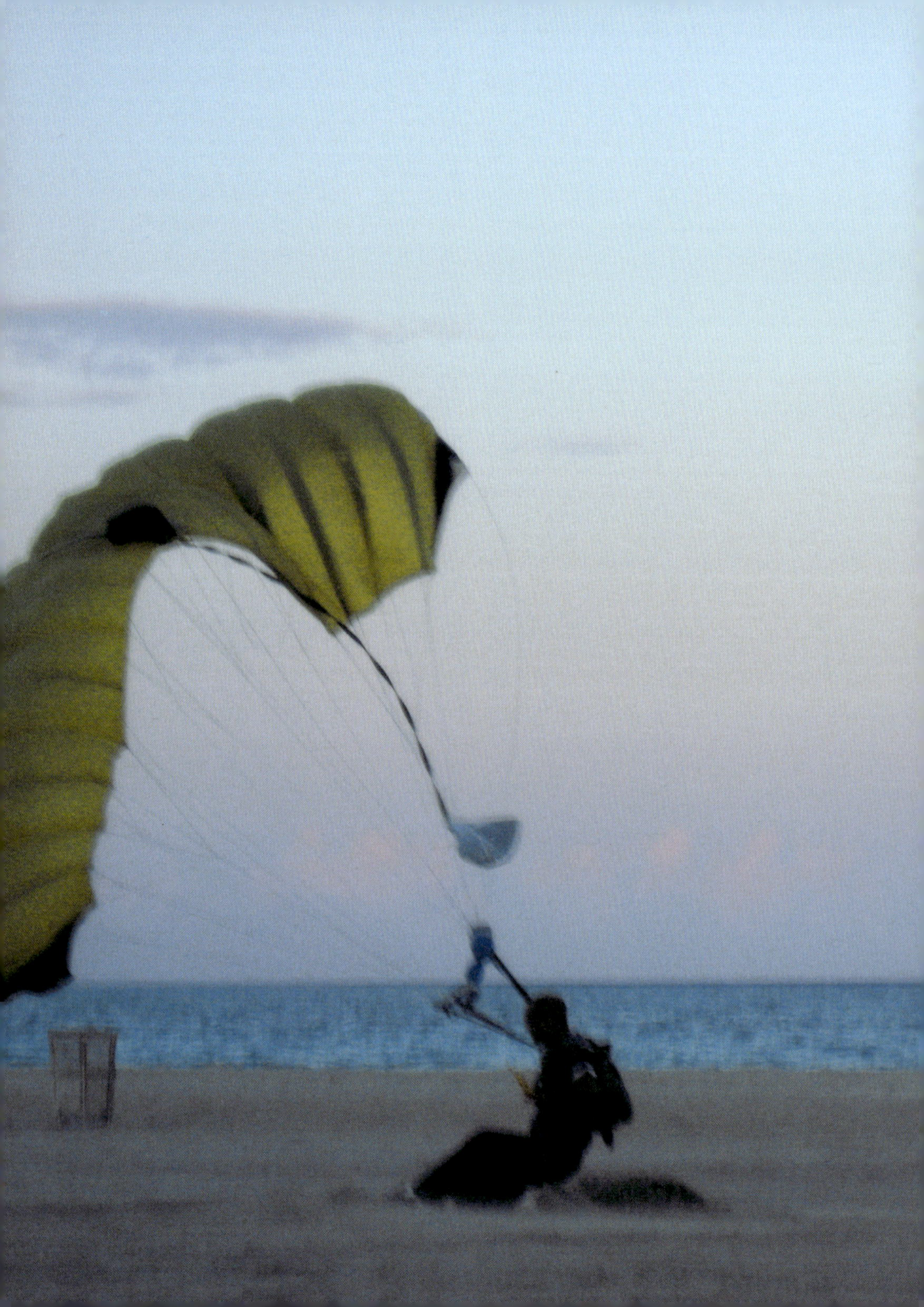

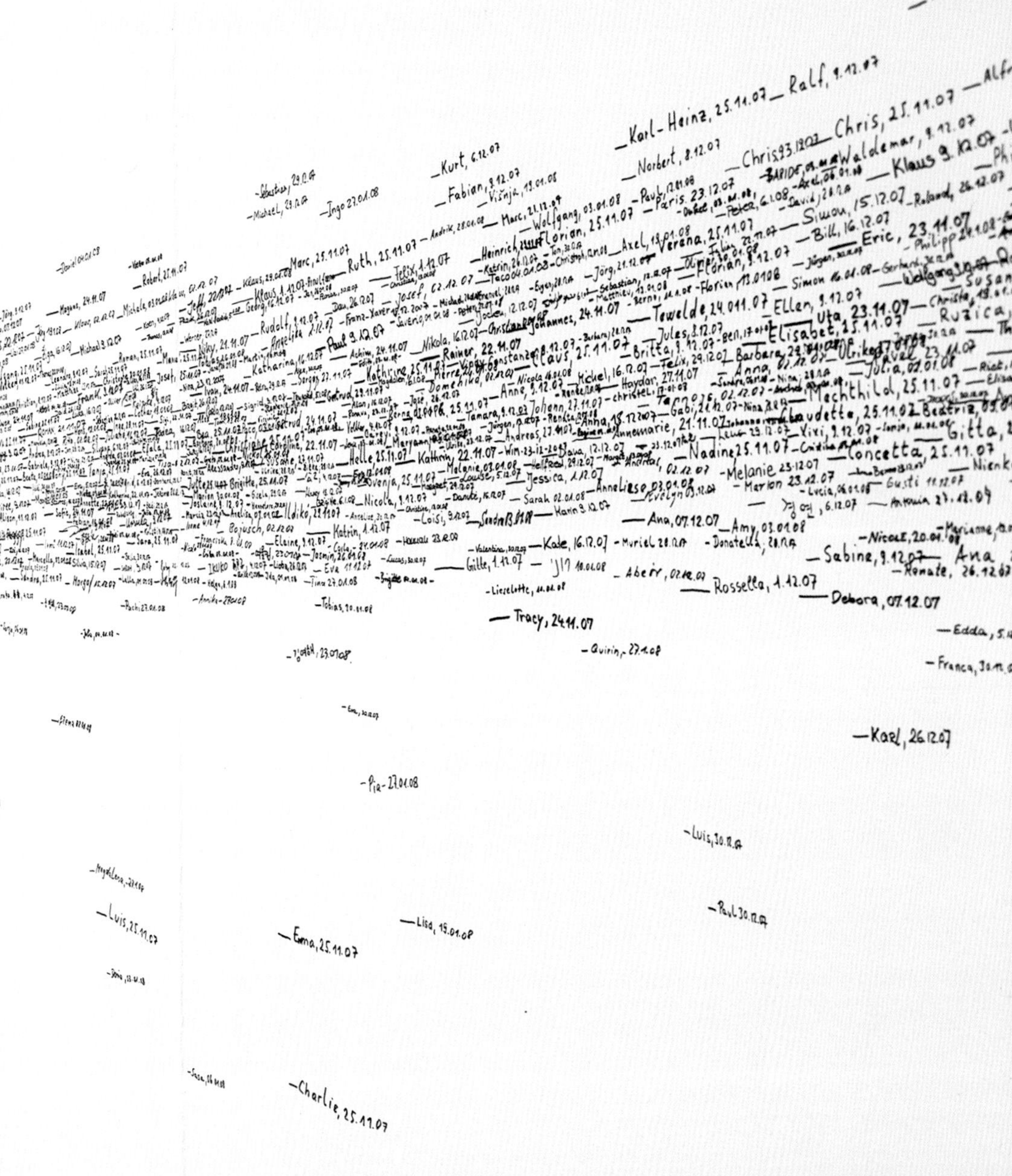

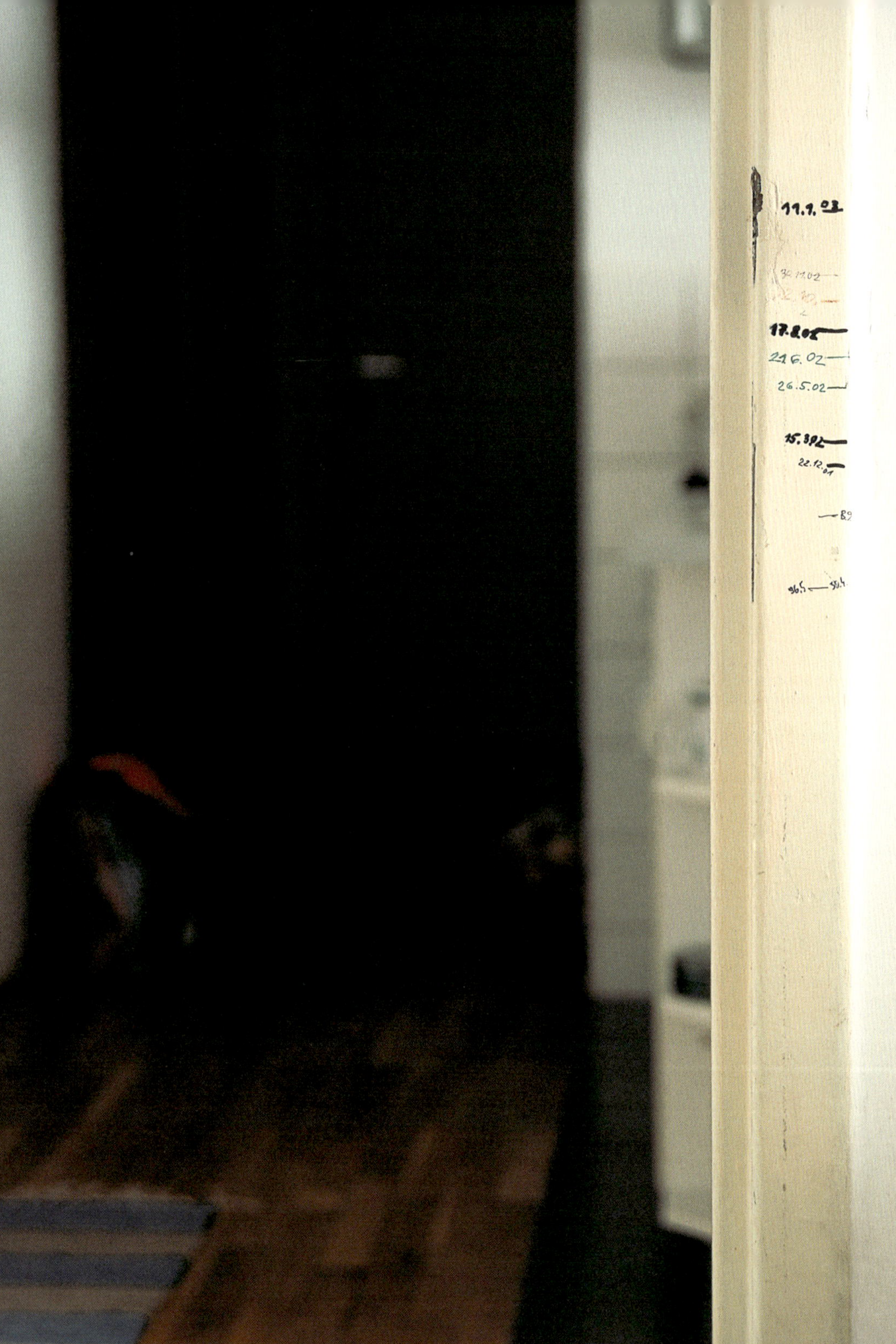

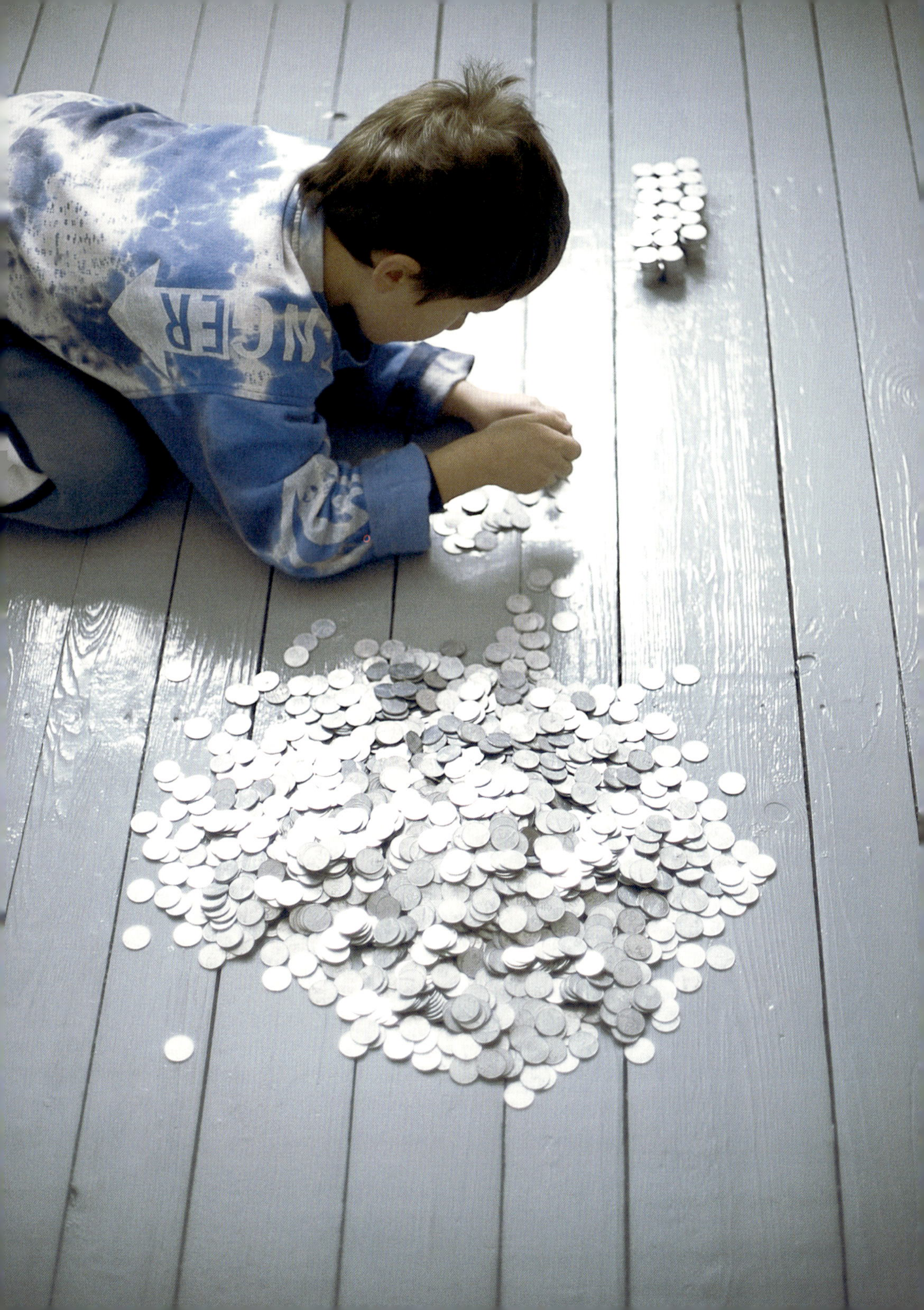

Arnd, 25.4.08
Giorgio, 17.04.08
Richard, 28.3.08
Alastair, 5.4.08 — Chris, 5.4.08
Stephan, [illegible]
Jacky, 6.4.08 — Steffen, 10.1.08
Eugen, 6.4.08 — Felix, 6.4.08
Owen, 6.4.08
Tim, [illegible]
Vytautas, 7.4.08
Sonja, 5.4.08 — Denis, [illegible] — Caterina, 5.4.08 — Ralf, 2.04.08
Evelyn, [illegible] — Peter, [illegible] — Valerio, [illegible] — Yves, 23.03.08 — Gianluca, 4.4.08 — Alexandra, [illegible] — Matthias, [illegible]
Ronald, [illegible] — Lorenzo, 17.04.08 — Bert, 8.04.08
Simone, [illegible] — Camilo, 26.4.08 — Jocelyn, [illegible] — Elisabetta, [illegible] — Teodor, 5.04.08
Massimo, [illegible] — Sonja, [illegible] — Matthias, 12.1.08
Razvan, 6.4.08 — Laura, 5.04.08 — Kevin, 4.4.08 — Tim, [illegible] — Djamila, 16.1.08
Tonja, 5.4.08 — Hans-Jörg, 17.4.08
Barbara, 12.4.08 — Nadia, [illegible]
Xenia, 5.4.08 — Georg, [illegible] — Wes, 21.03.08 — Ruth, 8.04.08
Tara, [illegible] 5.4.08 — Barbara, [illegible] — Marcia, [illegible] 5.4.08 — Verena, [illegible] — Queena, 6.4.08
Martina, 4.4.08 — Ralf, 28.03.08
Ruth, 16.4.08 — Betty, 17.04.08 — Sofia, 5.4.08
Anna-Maria, 6.4.08 — Emanuela, 4.4.08

Martyn, 8.04.08
Roland, 24.08 — Matthias, 22.4.08 — Michael Martin, [illegible]
Kim, 14.4.08 — Peter, 24.08 — Manuel, 5.4.08
Fred [illegible] — Emanuel, 4.4.08 — David, 26.4.08 — Benjamin, 16.1.08 — Ramon, 25.4.08 — Hasko, 10.4.08
David, 5.4.08 — Mladen, [illegible]
Martin, [illegible] — Florin, 14.1.08 — Antonio, [illegible] — Christopher, [illegible] — Ken, 24.4.08 — Franck, 5.4.08 — Lib, 30.3.08 — Thomas, 5.4.08 — Ante, 25.4.08 — Barbara, 5.04.08
Klaus, [illegible] — Nils, 12.15.08 — Maurizio, [illegible] — Karl-Heinz, [illegible] — Becky, 4.4.08 — Franzel, 5.4.08 — Nava, [illegible]
Loretta, [illegible] — Jutta, [illegible] — Jean-Philip, [illegible] — Martin, 24.4.08 — Anette, 5.4.08 — Fron, 25.4.08 — Daniela, 4.04.08 — Susan, 5.4.08
Mark, 6.4.08 — Josi, [illegible] — Livia, 5.4.08 — Elisabeth, [illegible] — Lesley, 5.4.08 — Susanne, 26.03.08 — Veronique, [illegible]
[illegible] — Francesca, 29.03.08 — Annie — Kosta, 12.3.08 — Andrea, 8.4.08 — Silvia, 5.4.08 — Susanne, 5.4.08 — Elfriede, [illegible]
Albina, 5.4.08 — Jenny, 5.4.08 — Eric, 4.4.08 — Saida, 5.4.08 — Daniella, 2.4.08 — Tatjana, 8.4.08 — Petra, [illegible]
[illegible]
Simon, 30.3.08

— Rico, 5.4.08

— Charlie, 15.4.08

— Felipe, 5.4.08

— Homer, 5.4.08   — Alex, 8.4.08   — Peter, 30.3.08   — Robin, 30.3.08

— Jonathan, 19.4.08   — Simone, 18.4.08   — Roberto, 5.4.08   — Alex, 20.0
                         — Nathan, 29.4.08   — Christopher, 14.04.08
                                — Alessandro, 7.4.08   — Timo, 30.3.08   — Sebastian, 24.4.08
— Frank, 5.4.08   — Antti, 23.4.08 — Roger, 5.4.08   — Jelle, 5.04.08
   — Florian, 16.3.08   — Marzia, 5.4.08   — Tommy, 19.4.08   — Rolf, 26.3.08   — Da
         — Haars, 5.4.08   — Jess, 28.3.08 — Paul-Etienne, 28.01.08   — Hernan, 5.04.08 — Valerio, 19.4.08
  — Marc, 6.4.08 Rodrigo, 5.4.08 — Michael, 28.3.08   — Katie, 13.04.08   — Paolo, 6.4.08   — Peter, 28.03.08   — Norbert, 4.4.08   — Jani, 5.4.08   — Bent, 18.4.08
       — Julien, 30.3.08   — Manele, 28.3.08   — Vibi, 28.3.08   — Kees, 30.3.08   — Esther, Eleanor, 34.08
  — Christo, 7.04.08 — Roman, 7.04.08 — Kain, 19.4.08 — Francesca, 7.4.08 Nicola, 4.4.08 — Henin, 28.3.08 — Felipe, 5.4.08   — Vero, 28.3.08   — Bert, 30.3.08   — Franco, 4.04.08   — David, 7.4.08
      — Roman, 25.4.08   — Fabian, 16.3.08 — Bradz, 8.4.08   — Danjin, 28.3.08 — Nora, 34.3.08   — Fabian, 16.4.08 — Katrin, 6.4.08 — Anna, 24.4.08   Paulo, 5.04.08   — Alex, 5.4.08
  — Ellen, 24.08   — Valentin, 5.4.08   — Jean-Hubert, 28.3.08 — Leslie, 19.4.08 Foudris, 5.04.08   — Abbe, 17.04.08   — Laura, 4.4.08 Sonja, 30.3.08 Borte, 6.4.08 — Elke, 30.3.08 — Iris, 5.4.08   — Euridice, 9.4.08
  — Teo, 24.08   — Anna, 5.4.08   Valentina, 5.4.08 Mar, 25.4.08 — Cameron, 30.3.08   — Michael, 4.4.08   — Katharina, 30.3.08   Tanja, 17.4.08   — Jan, 20.4.08   — Gizeh, 27.3.08   — Siobhan,
       — Herts, 28.3.08 Stephan, et al.   Ajey, 28.3.08   — Sansa, 4.04.08   — Tayl Christian, 6.4.08   — Cristiana, 4.4.08   Clara, ... — Daniela, 6.4.08 Marie, 30.3.08   — Marieke, 24.08   — Louise, 8.4.08
  — Francesca, 5.4.08   — Ajey, 20.4.08 Nancy, 6.4.08 — Lilian, 5.4.08 — Bic, 10.3.08   — Horre, 15.4.08 — Daniela, 7.4.08   — Minna, 23.4.08   Gulia, 30.3.08   — Konrad, 30.3
      — Brigitte, 5.4.08 Irena, 5.4.08 — Julie, 28.3.08   — Tord, 5.4.08   Mavo, 06.04.08   — Ayse, 21.03.08   — Rot, 22.04.08   — Alex, 30.3.08
     — Gaelle, 5.4.08   — Magrit, 30.3.08 — Gianna, 5.4.08 Cecilia, 5.04.08 — Katrin, 5.4.08 Gaia, 5.04.08 — Renate, 7.4.08   Yoko, 4.4.08   Sara, 5.4.08   — Sabrina, 4.04.08   — Corine, 34.08
  — Jacqueline, 7.4.08 — Nina, 5.4.08 — Melanie, 5.4.08 — Ingen, 18.4.08   — Raffaella, 6.4.08   — Ann-Marie, 8.4.08 — Henna, 23.4.08 — Kathrine, 4.4.08   — Sara, 19.4.08 — Alex, 30.3.08
                                                                                                                       — Erika, 7.4.08   — Rily, 28.3.08
                              — Jennifer, 30.3.08   — Serih, 30.3.08   — Isabel, 10.4.08

— Margreta, 18.4.08

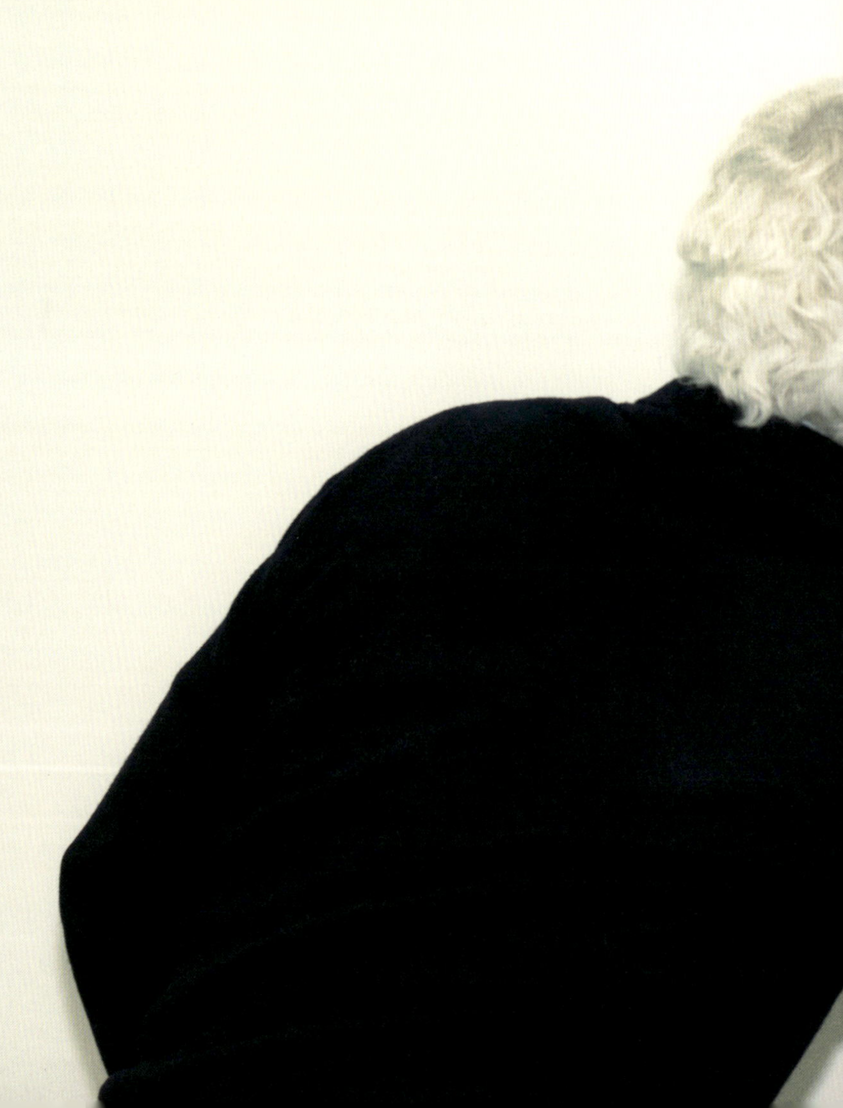

—Ina, 25.11.07 —Lydia, 25.11.07
—Eva, 24.11.07
—Leoni, 25.11.07

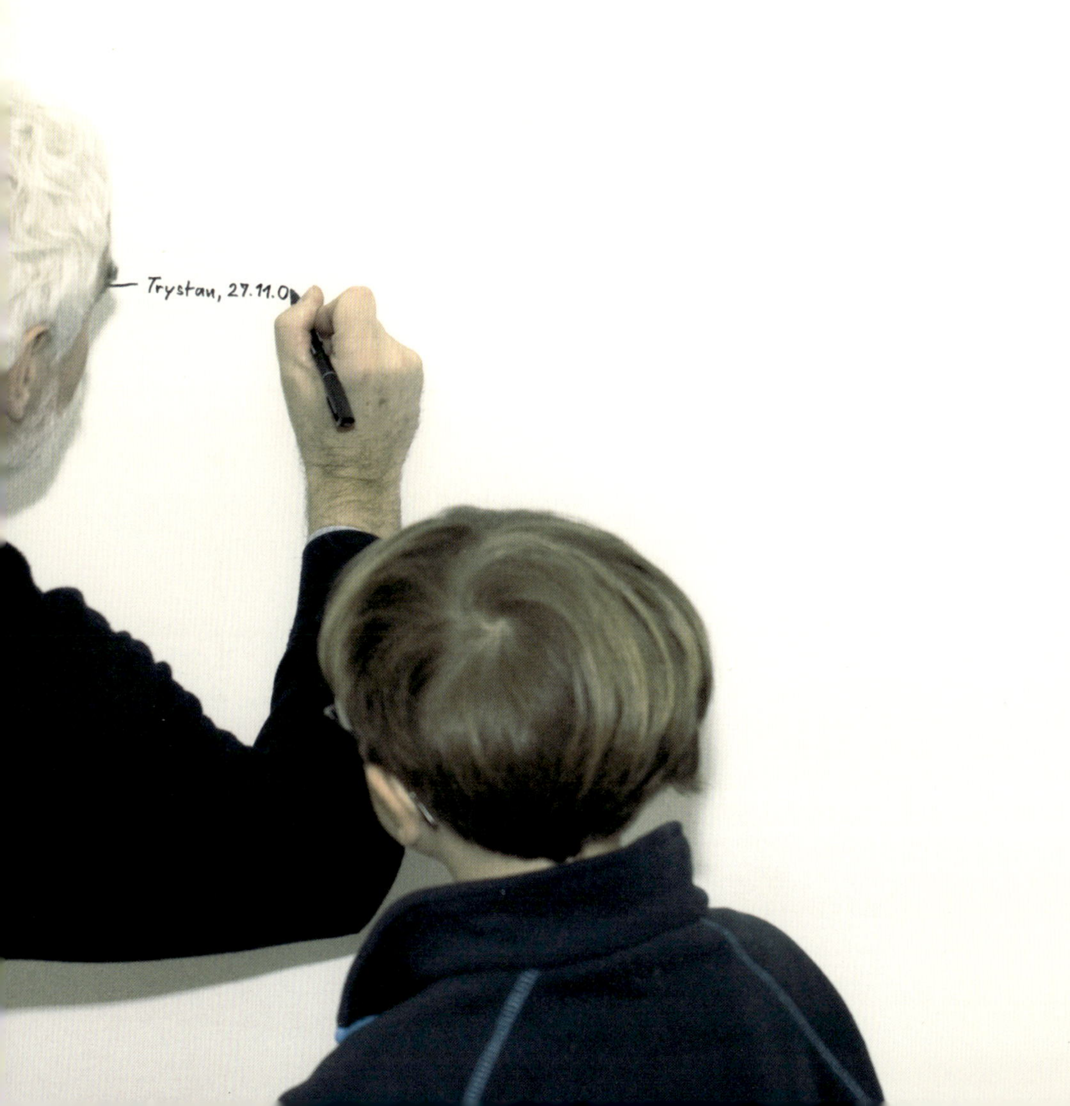
VERONICA, 24.11.07   Giovanna , 23.11.07
Trystan, 27.11.0

— Tiago, 5.4.08

— Pieter, 5.4.08

Sigrid, 5.4.08
3.08 — Stephan, 5.4.08

— Jan, 7.04.08   — Mathieu, 6.0.

— Patrick, 5.4.08   — Patri

Andreas, 5.4.08 — Volker, 28.03.08 — Lothar, 5.4.08
— Lilou, 5.4.08

— Teemothee, 4.04.08 —

-Chris, 6.4.08
— Anna, 5.4.08   — Vittorio, 5.4.08

— Carola, 28.03.08   — Marika, 30.3.0

8   — Mehtap, 5.4.08
— Rhonda, 2.4.08 — Lara, 30.3.08

1.08   — Konstanze
— Vincenzo, 5.04.08 — Cra

— Niklas, 28.03.08

— Eva, 5.04.08 — C

runa, 5.04.08   — Bärbel, 5.04.08   — J

— Yaël, 30.3.08

— Harald, 5.04.08   Andrea, 5.4.08

—Edoar

— Hannes, 5.4.08   — Emilien, 6.4.08

— Astrid, 28.03.08

3.08

— Moi, 5.4.08
, 5.04.08   —— Caroline, 4.04.08   — Christian, 6.4.08
— Sonja, 28.03.08 Welmoed, 28.03.0
Wannes, 5.4.08   —— Apostolos, 2.4.08
—— Denoae, 4.0
mke, 30.3.08   — Emilie, 5.4.08
_ Peter, 28.3.08 Sofia, 5.4.08
08
— Alicia, 5.04.08
4.08   — Jannik, 30.3.08   — Annie,
— Christine, 1.4.08 —

7.03.08   — kika, 2.4.08
line, 5.4.08

— Kim, 30.3.08

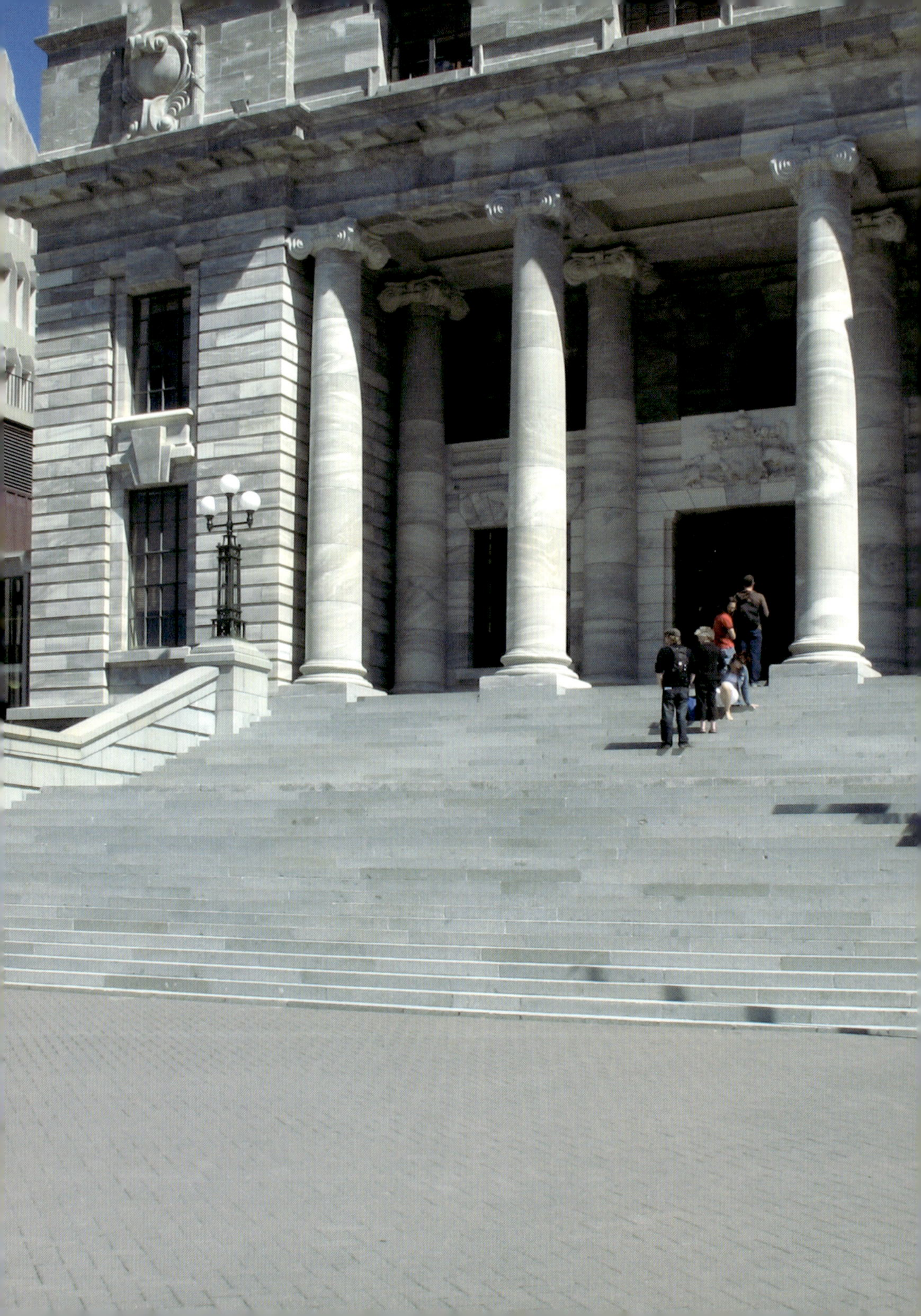

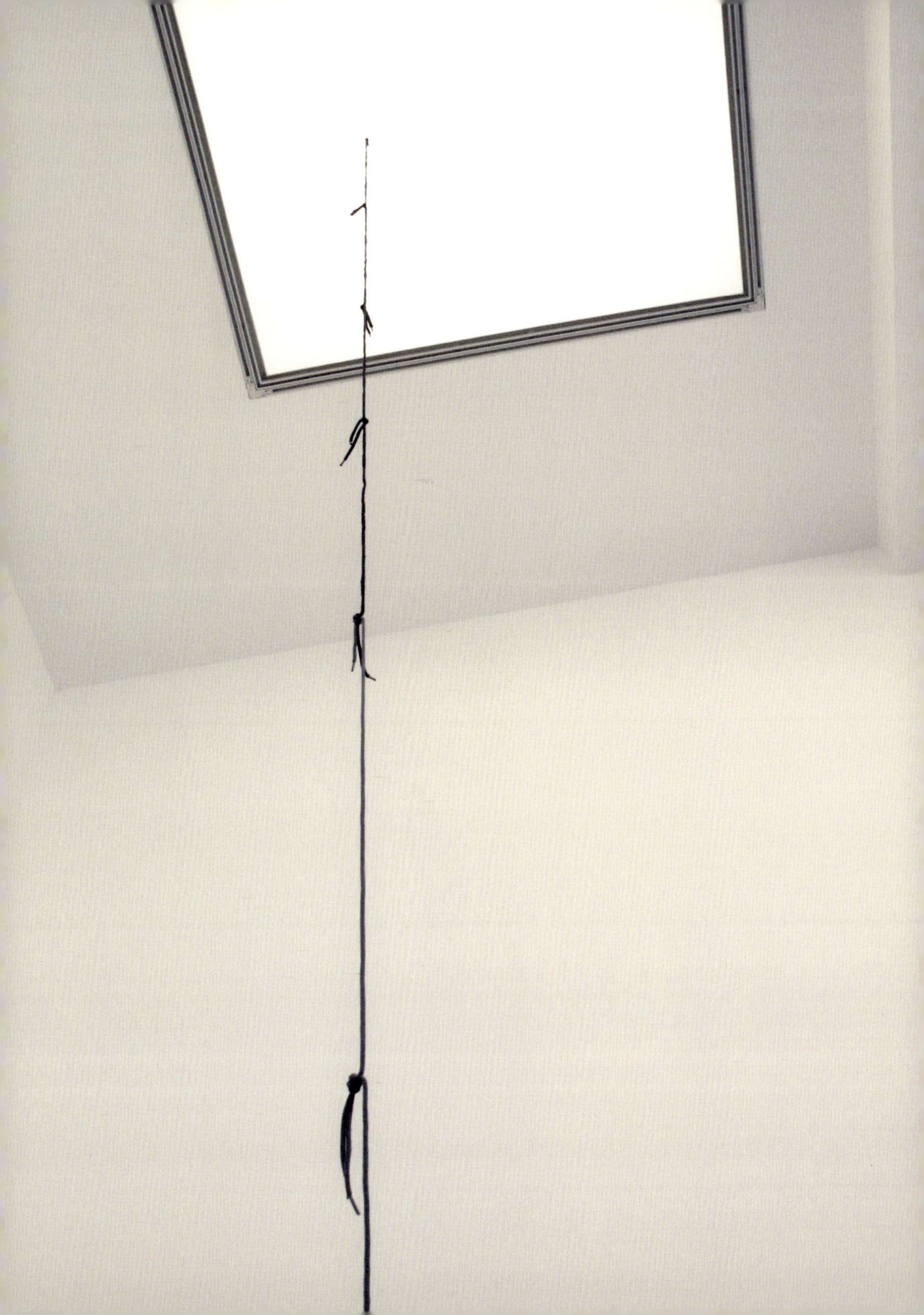

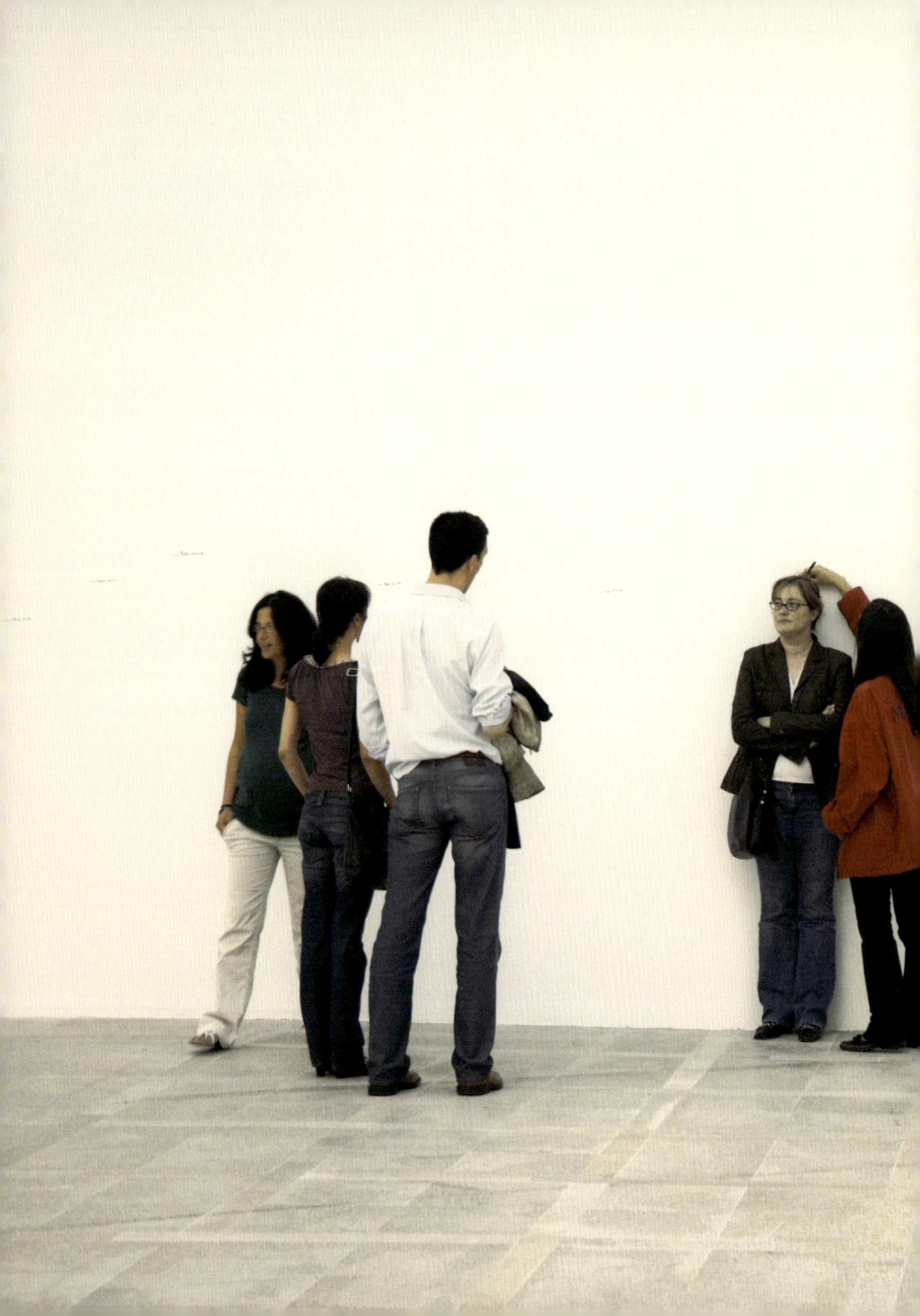

__ Bernhard, 28.3.08

__ Wolfgang, 29.3.08.   __ Marcus, 28.3.08
                          __ Linas, 1.4.08

.08
                                                    — Florent, 28.3.08
ro, 2.4.08 __ Matthias, 6.4.08
                  __ Mello, 4.4.08

                                                    — Bernhar
03.08 — Stefan, 29.3.08.   __ Hong King, 2.4.08
          — Frederic, 5.4.08
3.08.   __ Jennifer, 1.04.08   — Ali
aka, 31.3.08   — Fabio, 4.4.08   — Graham, 2
— Clare, 31.3.08   __ Werner, 29.3.08.

                                                       — Setyanto, 3
                                                       — Josh, 4.4

              __ Lara, 5.4.08
          — Grăeyci, 1.4.08 __ Bianca, 4.4.08 __ Cindy, 4.4.

— Aya, 2.4.08

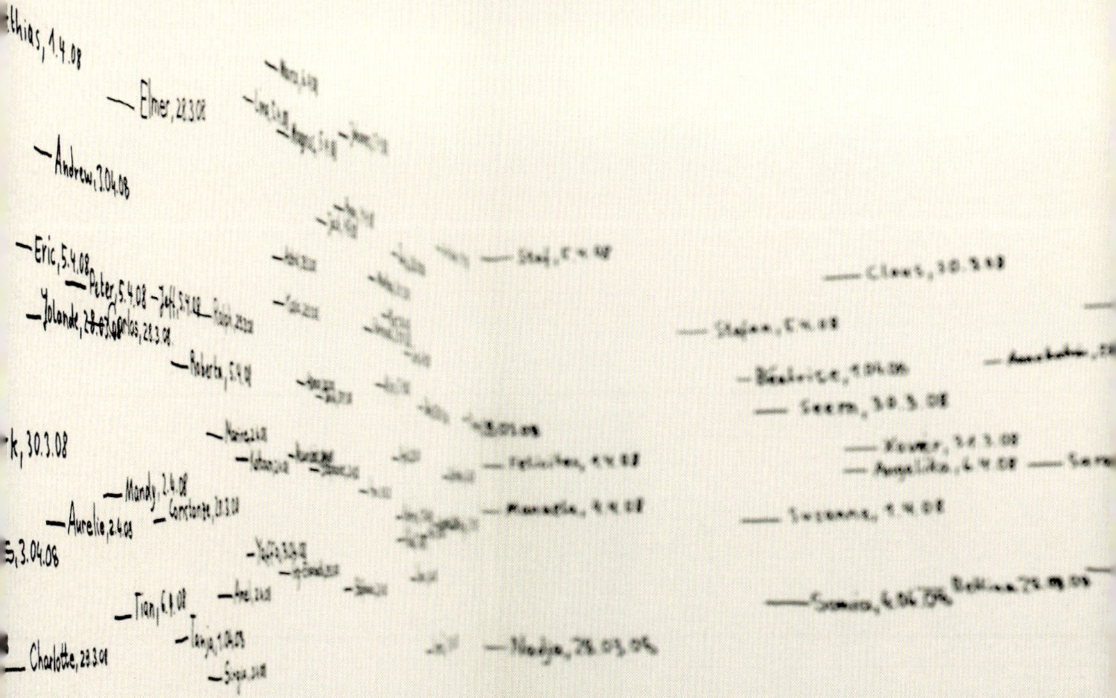

thias, 1.4.08

Elmer, 28.3.08

Andrew, 3.04.08

Eric, 5.4.08
Peter, 5.4.08 — Jeff, 5.4.08 — Ralph, 28.3.08
Jolande, 28.08 Carlos, 28.3.08

Roberta, 5.4.08

k, 30.3.08

Mandy, 2.4.08
Constanze, 28.3.08
Aurelie, 2.4.08

s, 3.04.08

Tian, 6.4.08
Tanja, 1.04.08
Sopa, 2.4.08

Charlotte, 28.3.08

Claus, 30.3.08

Stefan, 5.4.08

Béatrice, 4.04.08
Beatrice, 4.04.08

Seem, 30.3.08

Werner, 30.3.08
Angelika, 6.4.08 — Sara

Susanne, 4.4.08

Sonica, 6.04.08   Bettina, 28.03.08

Nadja, 28.03.08

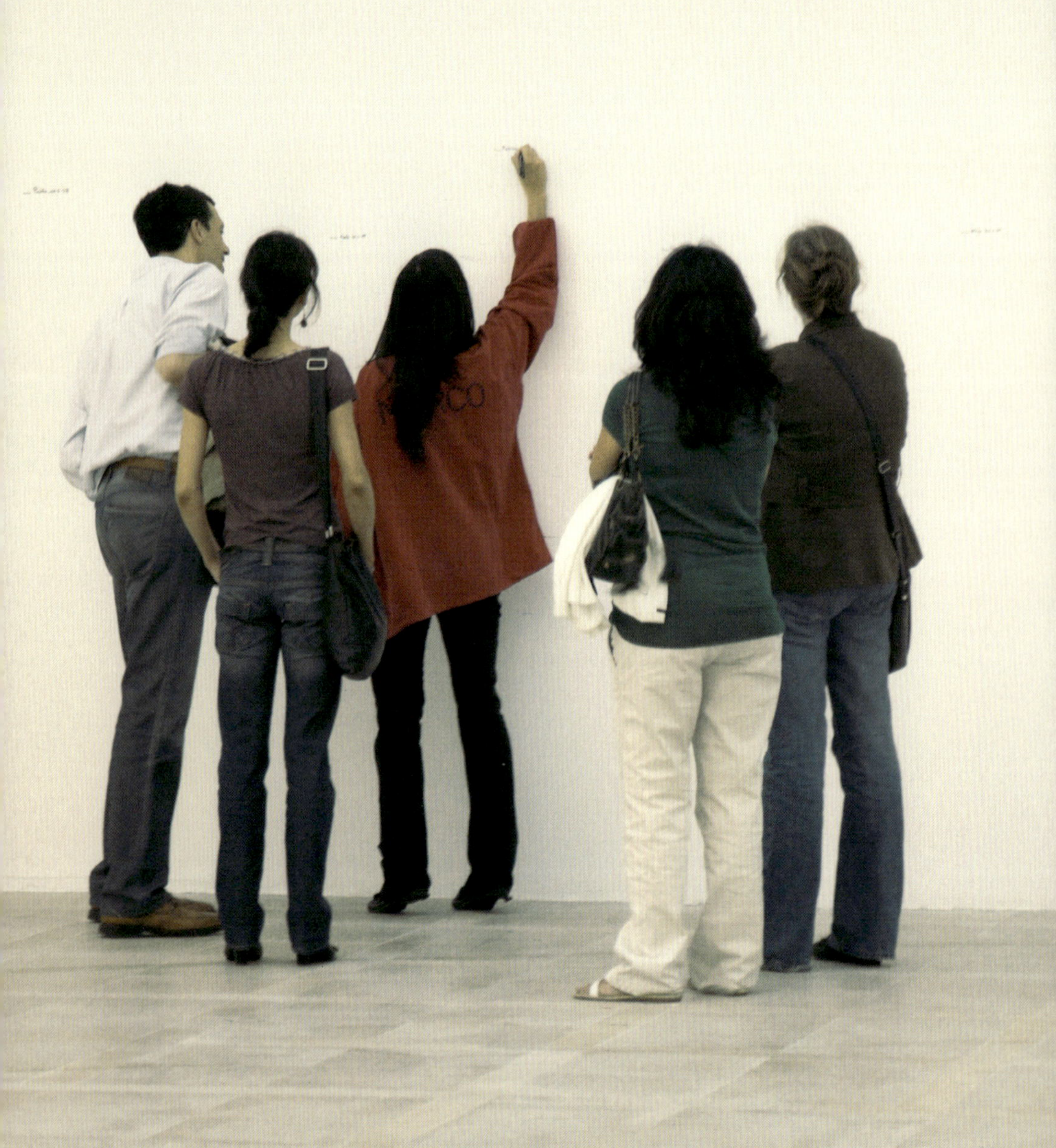

_ Germano[illegible]
_ Antoine, 25.[illegible]
_ Thomas, 3.0[illegible]
_ Masato[illegible]
_ [illegible] 31.08

_ Natalia, 5.4.08

_ Kathleen, 3.04.08
_ Judith, 4.04.08 _ Petra, 29.3.08
_ Yoko, 4.04.08 _ Joëlle, 4.4.08
_ Ati, 5.4.08
_ Kerstin, 28.03.08
_ Anna, 28.3[illegible]
_ Andrea, 28.3.08

_ Marisa, 3.04.08 _ Liz, 30.3.08 _ Ryok[illegible]
_ Corinna, 30.3.[illegible]

_ Jamellee, 1.4.08

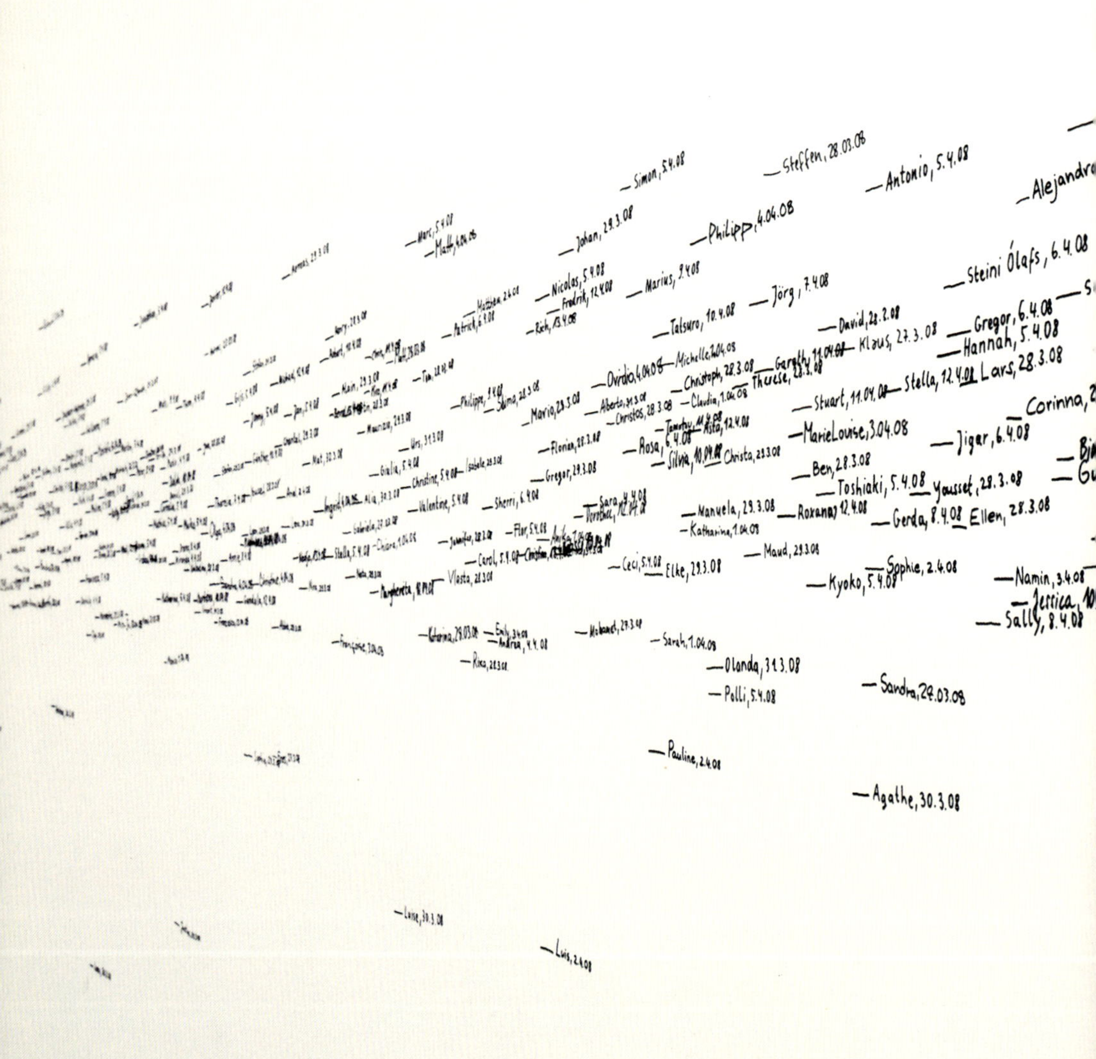

— Foeke, 2. 4. 08
— Jorge, 28.3.08 KLvnsen
— Michael, 27.3.08
— Nick, 12.4.08   — Paul, 31.3.08
                        — Peter, 11.4.08   — Kai, 12.4.08
08
        — Karason, 6.4.08   — Matthi
tmar, 28.3.08   — Burkard, 4.4.08   — Peter, 5.4.08   — Tom, 8.4.08
                        Ina, Leon 27.3.08   — Bao Cha
ie, 29.3.08 Georg, 8.4.08   — Laurent, 5.4.08   — S
                                Ghislaine, 29.3.08 — Laurent, 5.4.08   Sabine, 29.3.08.
                                        — Vito, 12.4.08   — Sabine, 29.3.08. Wilhelm, 28.3.08
5.4.08 — Manfred, 14.4.08 Volker, 2.4.08   — Faisal, 28.3.08   — Fr
  — Corinne, 2.4.08 — Vanessa, 5.4.08 — Nada, 28.3.08   Anna, 29.3.08.
Philippa 5.4.08   — Gika, 12.4.08   — Barbara-Anna, 6.4.08
Jean, 29.3.08   — Palash, 4.4.08   — Lauren, 4.04.08 — Haleh, 12.4.08
                        Pablo, 8.04.08   — Lauren, 8.0408 Pedro, 29.3.08.
  — Patricia, 4.4.08 — Mia, 12.04.08 — Margot, 30.3.08 Ami, 29.3.08.   — Melodie, 12.0
— Nicole, 12.4.08 Véronique, 28.3.08 — Ingrid, 3.4.08
4.08 — Virginie, 5.04.08
08   — Susanne, 12.4.08
1.4.08 — Mario, 13.4.08
                        — Pangyu, 9.4.08
        — Peppo, 31.3.08   — Jessica, 31.3.08

        — Hellen, 8.4.08
        — Suzka, 11.4.08   — Dede, 2.4.08

                                                        — Rosa, 8.4.08
28.3.08   — Annika, 27.3.08   — Alexander, 13.4.08

4.08

        — Noah, 31.3.08

Mars rovers named 'Spirit' and 'Opportunity'
NASA-KSC RELEASE
Posted: June 8, 2003

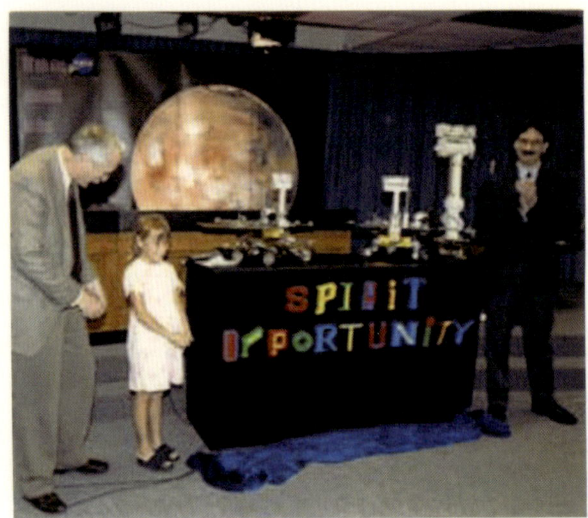

Sofi Collis unveils the Mars Exploration Rover names with NASA Administrator Sean O'Keefe and Brad Justus, LEGO senior vice president. Photo: NASA

Twin robotic geologists NASA is sending to Mars will embody in their newly chosen names -- Spirit and Opportunity -- two cherished attributes that guide humans to explore.

NASA Administrator Sean O'Keefe and 9-year-old Sofi Collis, who wrote the winning essay in a naming contest, unveiled the names this morning at NASA's Kennedy Space Center. "Now, thanks to Sofi Collis, our third grade explorer-to-be from Scottsdale, Ariz., we have names for the rovers that are extremely worthy of the bold mission they are about to undertake," O'Keefe said.

Sofi read her essay: "I used to live in an orphanage. It was dark and cold and lonely. At night, I looked up at the sparkly sky and felt better. I dreamed I could fly there. In America, I can make all my dreams come true. Thank you for the 'Spirit' and the 'Opportunity.'"

Hers was selected from nearly 10,000 entries in the contest sponsored by NASA and the LEGO Co., a Denmark-based toymaker, with collaboration from the Planetary Society, Pasadena, Calif..

Collis was born in Siberia. At age two, she was adopted by Laurie Collis and brought to the United States. "She has in her heritage and upbringing the soul of two great spacefaring countries," O'Keefe said. "One of NASA's goals is to inspire the next generation of explorers. Sofi is a wonderful example of how that next generation also inspires us."

Collis' dream of flying now takes the form of wanting to become an astronaut. Meanwhile, she enjoys playing with her older sister, swimming, reading Harry Potter stories, and her family's three dogs and one cat.

LEGO President Kjeld Kirk Kristiansen, commenting on the naming contest, said, "The early days of space exploration stimulated the creativity of an entire generation, expanded our imagination and encouraged us to push our limits, making us better and braver human beings. With this project, the LEGO Co. wants to bring part of that magic back. Everything we do is aimed at giving children that same power to create, and by involving children in the Name the Rovers Contest and other related playful learning activities, we hope to motivate and inspire the next generation of explorers."

Eleven miles from today's naming ceremony, Spirit, formerly called Mars Exploration Rover A, waited for a launch opportunity on Monday at Cape Canaveral Air Force Station. Opportunity, the second twin in what is still named the Mars Exploration Rover project, is being prepared for its first launch opportunity on June 25.

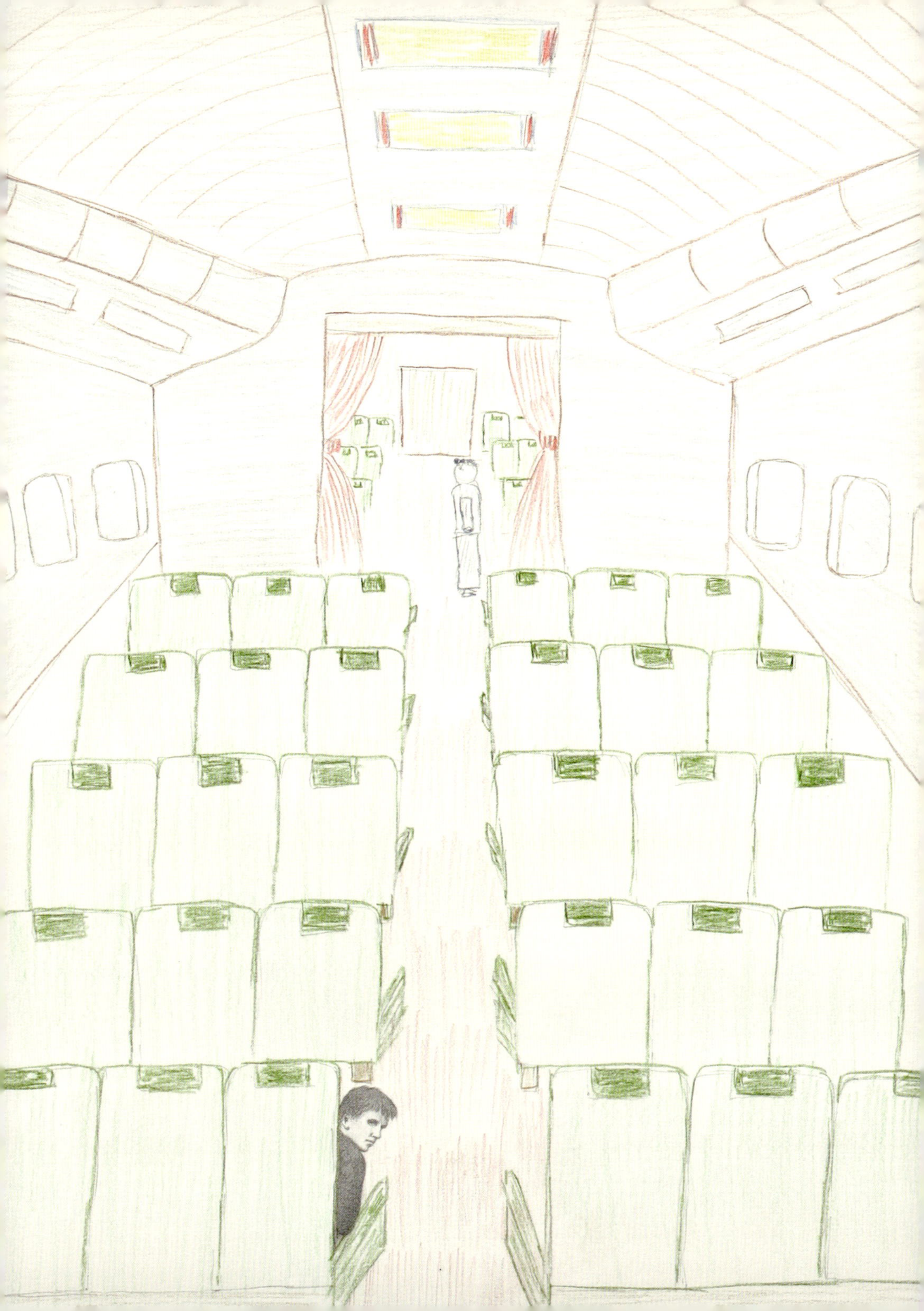

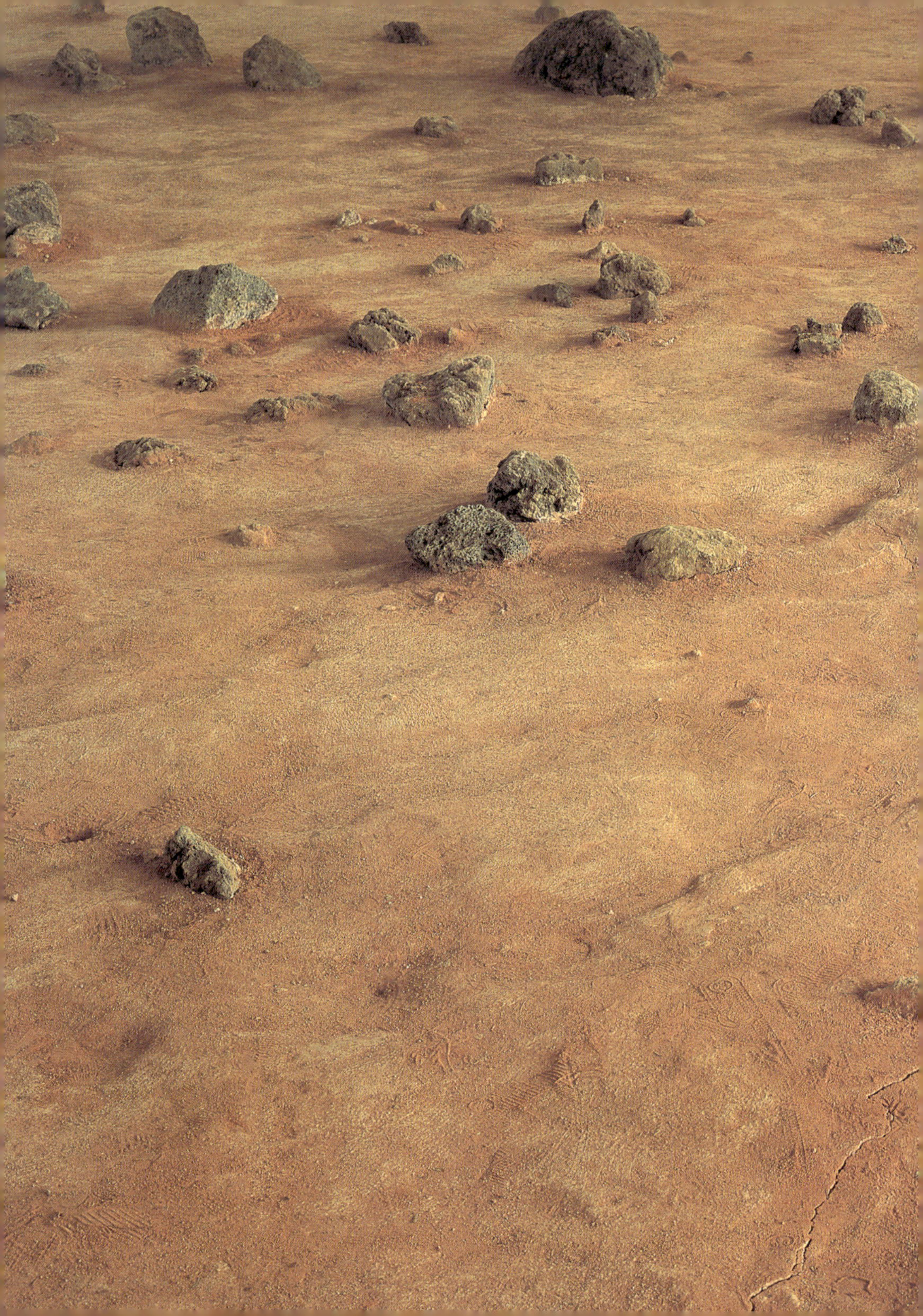

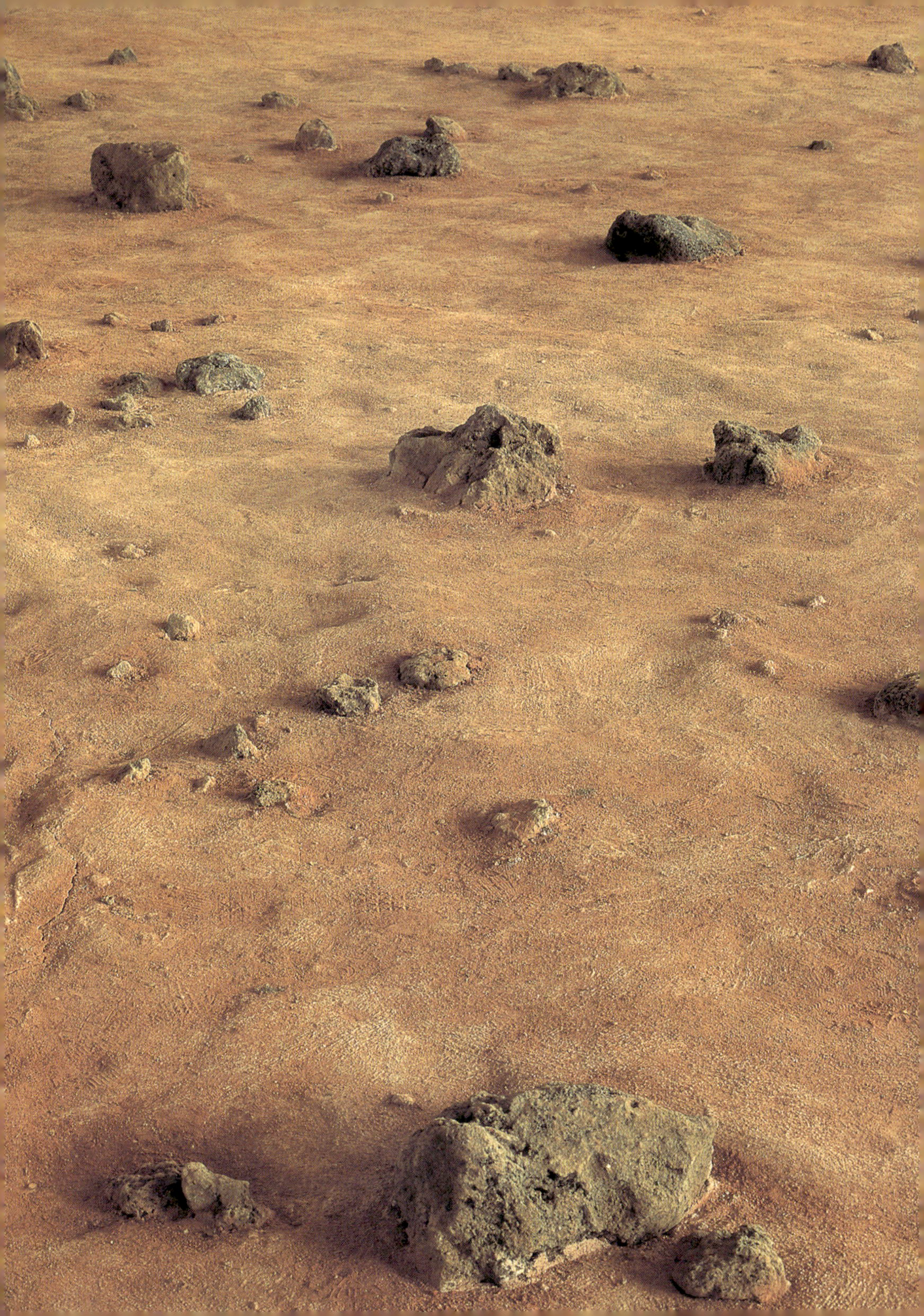

Jochen, 4.04.08
Wilfred, 5.4.08   Juliane, 1.4.08   Hans-Peter, 5.4.08   Andreas, 28.03.08   Simon, 4.4.08
Jan, 2.4.08
Sascha, 5.4.08   Marcel, 30.3.08   Toby, 4.4.08
Gerd, 28.3.08
Nicolas, 28.3.08   Guido, 3.4.08   Polly, 4.04.08   Jay, 4.04.08
Aoife, 5.4.08   Jessica, 4.04.08   David, 30.3.08   Dominic, 28.3.08   Inga, 30.3.08   Marjon, 23.3.08
Anne, 3.04.08   Claire, 5.4.08
Zenita, 5.4.08   Ernesto, 4.4.08   Brigitte, 5.04.08   Serge, 30.3.08   Chris, 4.4.08   Cecile, 3.4.08   Kathy, 4.04.08
Ilona, 30.3.08   Catherine, 30.3.08   Francesca, 31.3.08   Risa, 5.4.08   Kathrin, 2.04.08   Frauke, 2.04.08
Jeanine, 30.3.08
Bettina, 4.4.08

— Ulrich, 5.04.08

— Busso, 5.04.08

— Denis, 4.4.08

— Tim, 2?

— Erick, 5.04.08

— Tim, 3.04.08   — Bart, 29.3.08

— Neodis, 2.4.08

— Andreas, 5.04.08

— Paul, 5.04.08   — Daniel, 29.3.08   — Martin, 28.03.08   — Danica, 5.04

— Sigrid, 5.4.08   — Dimitri, 30.3.08   — Mirjam,

— Daniel, 5.4.08

— Nathaniel, 31.3.08   — Erik, 3.4.08   — Jutta, 05.04.08   — Ferdina

— Johanna, 29.3.08   — Stefana 31.3.08   Patrizia, 5.04.08

— Heinu 5.4.08   — Jos, 29.3.08   — Lisbeth, 30.3.08 Stefano, 5.4.08 Andi, 5.4.08

— Eva, 4.4.08   — Steven, 29.3.08   — Randi, 5.4.08   — Burkhard, 5.04.08 — Jeanne, 29.3.08

— Tanja, 30.3.08

— Carl, 4.4.08   — Kacha, 5.4.08   — Thierry, 5.4.08 Anna, 29.3.08

— Sihem, 30.2.08   — Elisa, 29.3.08   — Chantal, 5.4.08   — Linda, 31.3.08

— Janna, 30.3.08   — Veronica, 31.3.08   — Alex, 5.4.08

— Giulia, 5.4.08   — Gitte, 5.4.08   — Sara, 4.04.08

— Frie, 5.04.08   — Katja, 31.3.08   — Eran, 30.3.08   — Ester, 31.3.08 — Ania, 29.3.08   — Daniela, 29.3.08

— Chiara, 31.3.08   — Andrea, 5.4.08   — Akiko, 5.04.08   — Montse, 5.04.08

— Isabella, 31.3.08

— Roberta, 31.3.08

— Annabell, 28.03.08

— Taha, 30.3.08

— Tobias, 30.3.08

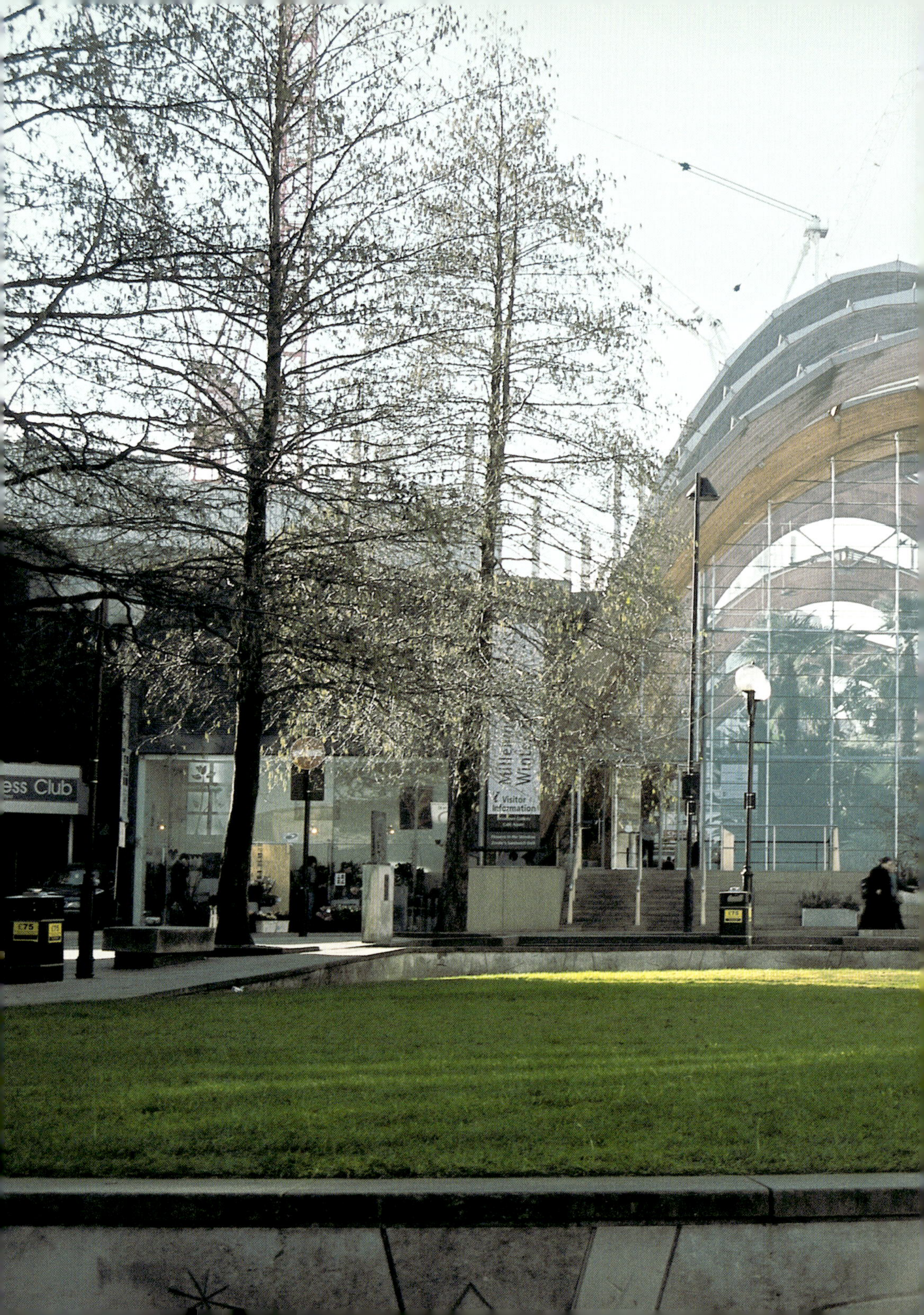

ess Club
£75
£75
Millennium
Visitor
Information
£75

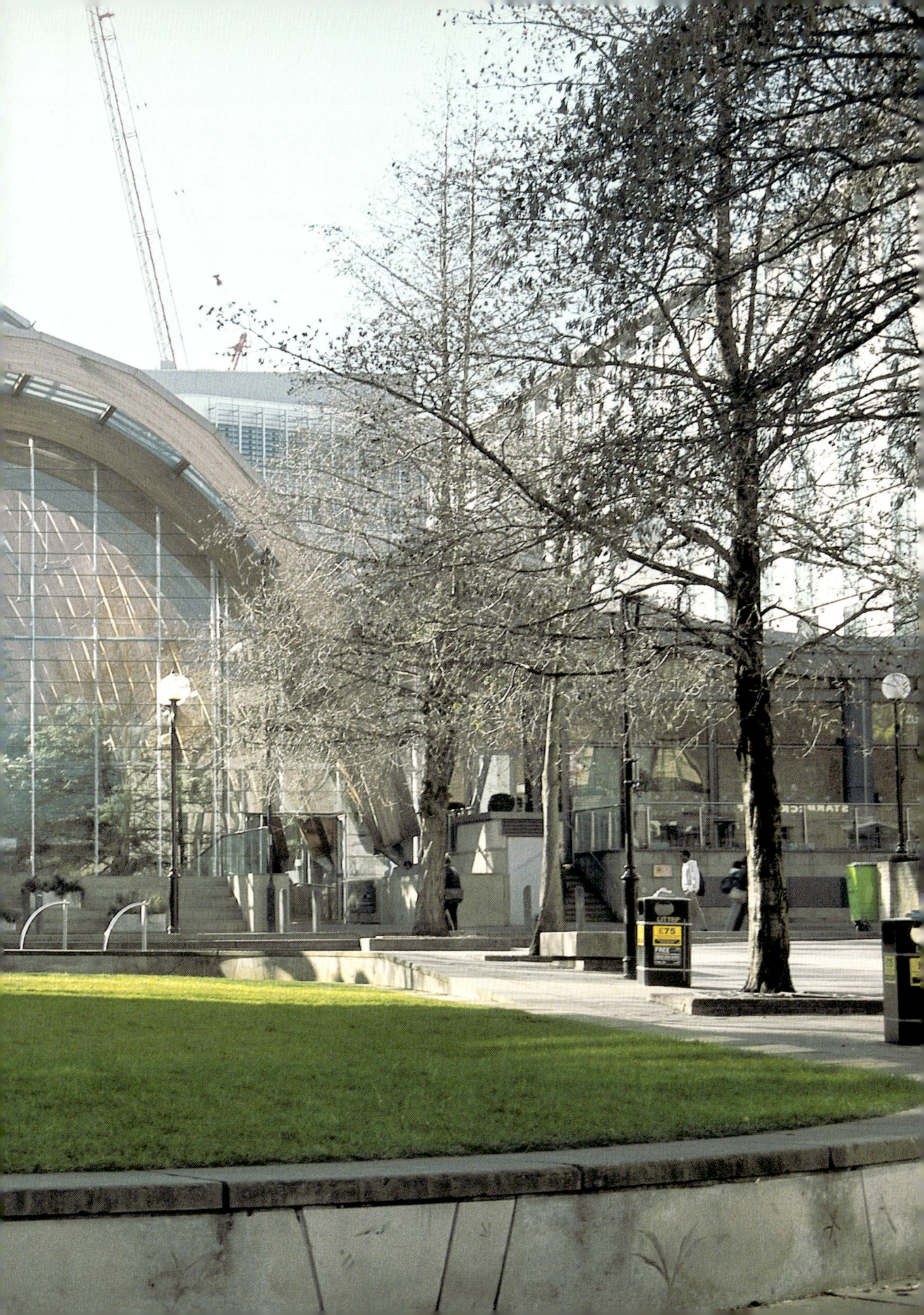

Failed Fall:
Time and Matter Out of Place

The desire, on the part of Roman Ondák, to restage and reorder the seasons by infiltrating a glasshouse garden with autumn leaves in February may seem Canute-like in its vain intention to stall and control the diurnal course of nature. However, the human manipulation of the seasons is a task already performed by the architects of a winter garden, a temperate urban oasis of evergreen plants presenting a perpetual summer. In this context the project represents a performative interruption into an already highly constructed reality.

As with many of Ondák's projects the final piece represents a 'contextual discrepancy'[1], a modest incursion into the everyday, behind which sits a rigorous conceptual alchemy of site and action, time and matter. To stop and isolate the seasons seems a quixotic task requiring, in equal part, the collaboration of local authorities, street cleaners, botanical experts and the availability of overwintering leaf depositories, but one that concluded in a subtle and strangely joyful intervention in the public realm.

During their hibernation period, when the leaves were held in a large warehouse, there was a certain sublimity in their mute and multitudinous 'there–ness', an artificiality in this purely natural medium, en masse. In contrast and also surprising was their apparent naturalness in the context of the installation. Like dazzle camouflage (a form of elaborate wartime camouflage aimed at producing confusion rather than concealment) the work, though highly visible and anomalous, also somehow displaced itself within its environment. Though entirely out of place and time, the leaves lost their previous sublimity and became more modest, almost to be expected. Yet they nonetheless worked on the viewer a slow perceptual dislocation.

Anthropologist Mary Douglas in her book *Purity and Danger* famously suggests that dirt is just 'matter out of place', implying both the existence and the contravention of a pre-ordained order governing society. She describes how every society creates divisions and classifications, which give it a sense of order and ostensibly make it civilized. There is no more 'civilized' space than a traditional winter garden; an orchestrated garden in a glasshouse, redolent of a patrician, Sunday afternoon, ambulatory conservatism. It has in common with the classic white cube an origin in bourgeois lifestyle and education and the exclusion of the messy business of life in favour of a structured, timeless aestheticism.

Despite the more radical umbrella-like architecture of the glass structure in Sheffield's Winter Garden and its enthusiastic use by all kinds of people – in this it conforms to Henri Lefebvre's denomination of 'social space', formed and used by those seeking a city-centre space to sit inside at leisure, without the necessity of buying anything – it is still essentially a hermetically-sealed, ersatz garden in which the seasons are ordered to man's desires, producing a stalled summer. *Failed Fall* (2008) generated a tiny breach in this order of civilization and in the order of nature, introducing an atemporal autumn into the strident summer, implying by its very temporary presence of just five days a suggestion of the potential transience and failure of the structures which order our existence, even the seasons.

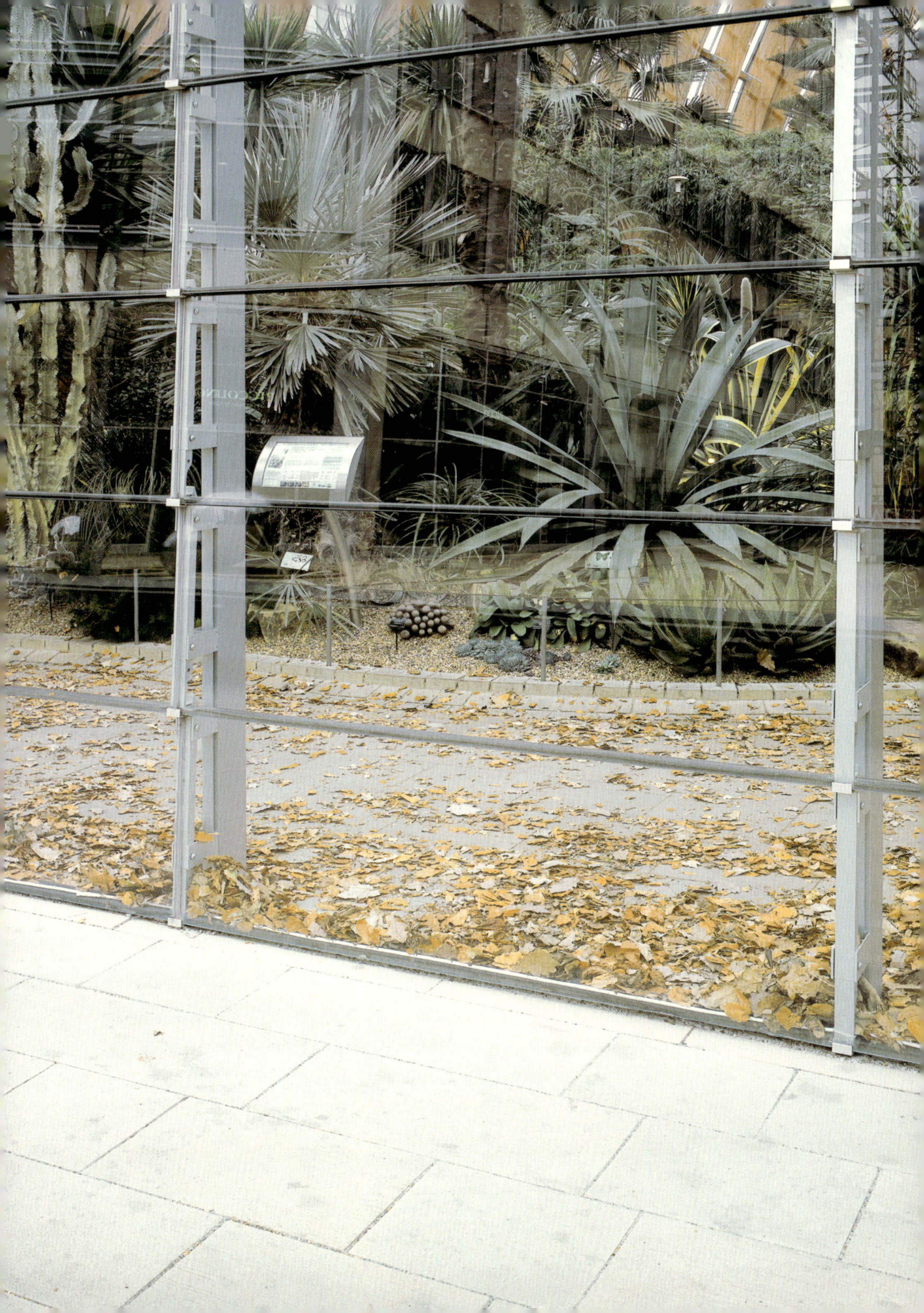

The most resonant art, particularly in the public realm, often functions as 'matter out of place', drawing us up short out of habitual patterns and creating a moment of pause in the everyday, a temporal or spatial dislocation. In doing so it opens up the potential for other orders, other patterns of behaviour, other social and political possibilities. *Failed Fall* certainly seemed to do this.

For Lefebvre town planning, which would presumably include such structures as a winter garden, prescribes a set social programme for everyday life, but one which can nonetheless be short-circuited by what he terms 'irreducible remainders' (such as desire, love, play, rest), which produce 'dysfunctional disruptions' to this predestined programme. These disruptions are defined as 'intensely experienced, limited in duration, punctuating taken-for-granted routines', all very appropriate descriptions of *Failed Fall*. Similarly he suggests that the linear time of everyday life (influenced by capital accumulation and digital technologies) cannot entirely supercede cyclical time (based on the physical processes of equinoxes and biology), which reasserts itself by means of 'discontinuous moments'[2], such as that staged by Ondák.

Reception of the work, after the initial double take or discomposure as the spatio-temporal dislocation of this 'discontinuous moment' was felt, was often joyful, a kind of carnivalesque inversion of structures, which functioned both within and without the classification of art. It was described in one review as 'holiday-spirited seasonal adjustment, aural as much as visual, and the frisking children were capable of grasping its license without delimiting it as art'[3]. But there was clearly also (perhaps inevitably in such public projects) for some of those invested in the space, the feeling of over-stepping the boundaries, overturning the natural (un-natural) order of the place – a feeling that this matter was out of place. Both responses seem to function as vital components of the work.

Failed Fall was a fleeting intervention, which even before its removal marked an absence rather than a presence. It represented a yearning for the season or situation we are not in, or perhaps a longing for such absent control of natural forces – indicated in the human desire to set up such structures as winter gardens in the first place. It also evinced a desire to suspend time, step out of everyday routines and 'smell the flowers' or in this case play in the leaves, to extract ourselves from the tyranny of time and mortality, merged at the same time with the rational knowledge of the impossibility of sidestepping such forces. Nonetheless in that moment of out-of time perceptual imbalance, there is a transformative possibility of introducing hitherto unimagined shifts in the structures that surround us. If the time is out of joint and matter is out of place, why should we not also try to shift our position within things, even if that attempt may fail?

1 Jessica Morgan, 'Insite and Outsite' in *Roman Ondák*, eds. Silvia Eiblmayr, Galerie im Taxispalais, Innsbruck and Maria Hlavajova, BAK, basis voor actuele kunst, Utrecht (Cologne: Verlag der Buchhandlung Walther König, 2007), 20.

2 As noted in Alex Law's 'The Critique of Everyday Life and Cultural Democracy', online at: http://www.variant.randomstate.org/29texts/law29.html.

3 Ian Hunt, in a review of Art Sheffield 08, the biennial citywide contemporary art event, of which *Failed Fall* was a part, published in *Art Monthly* (April 2008).

Jeanine Griffin

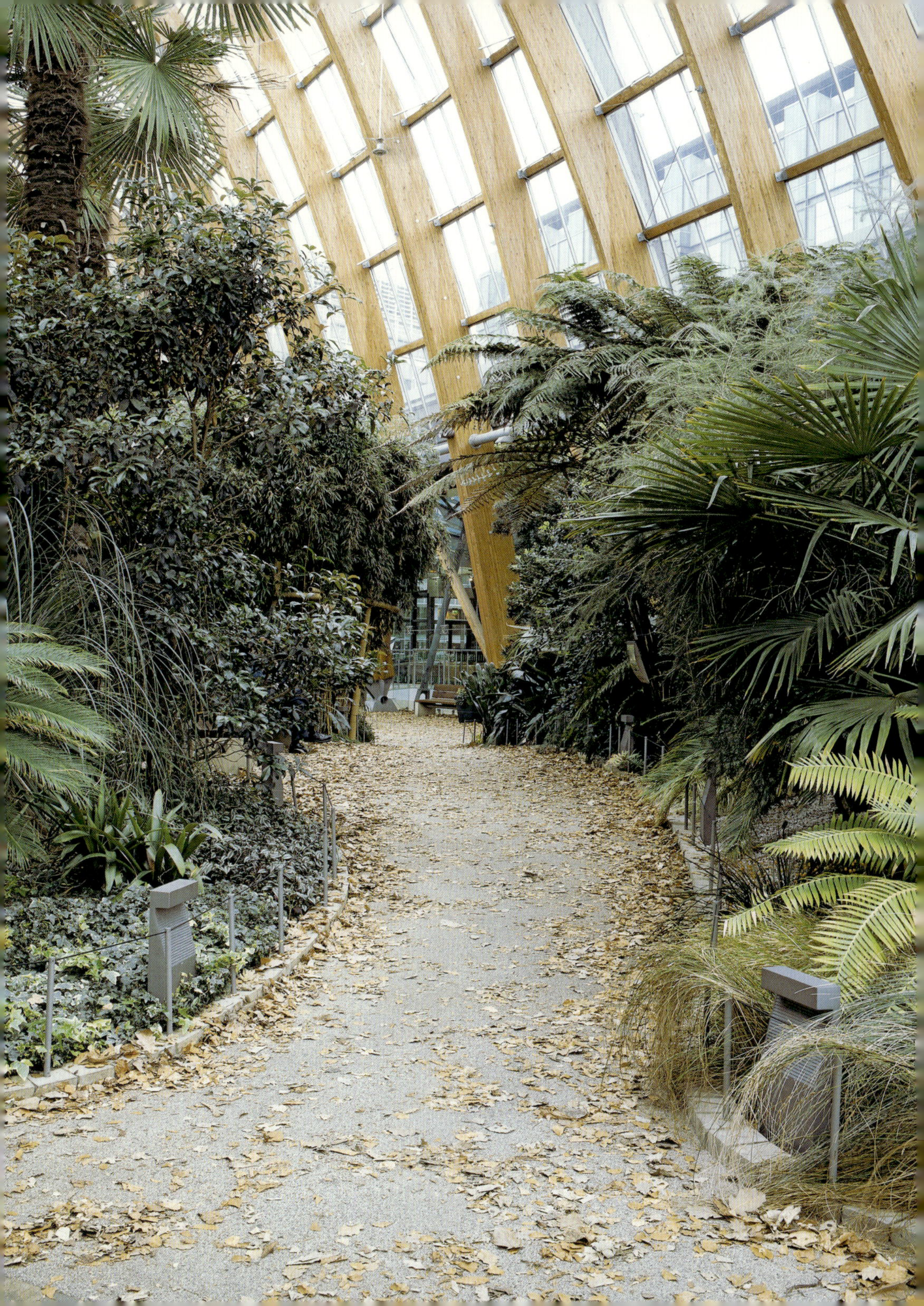

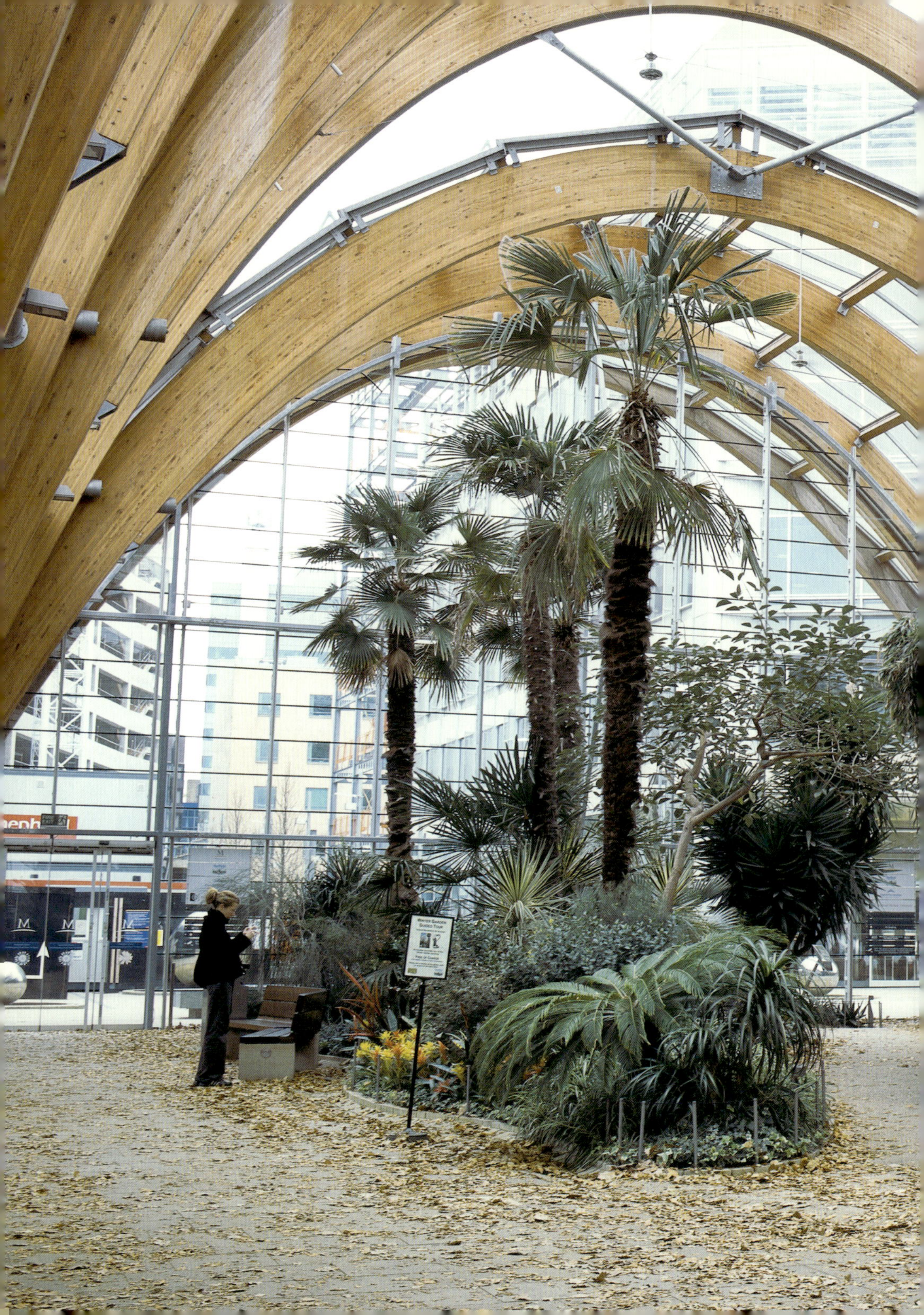

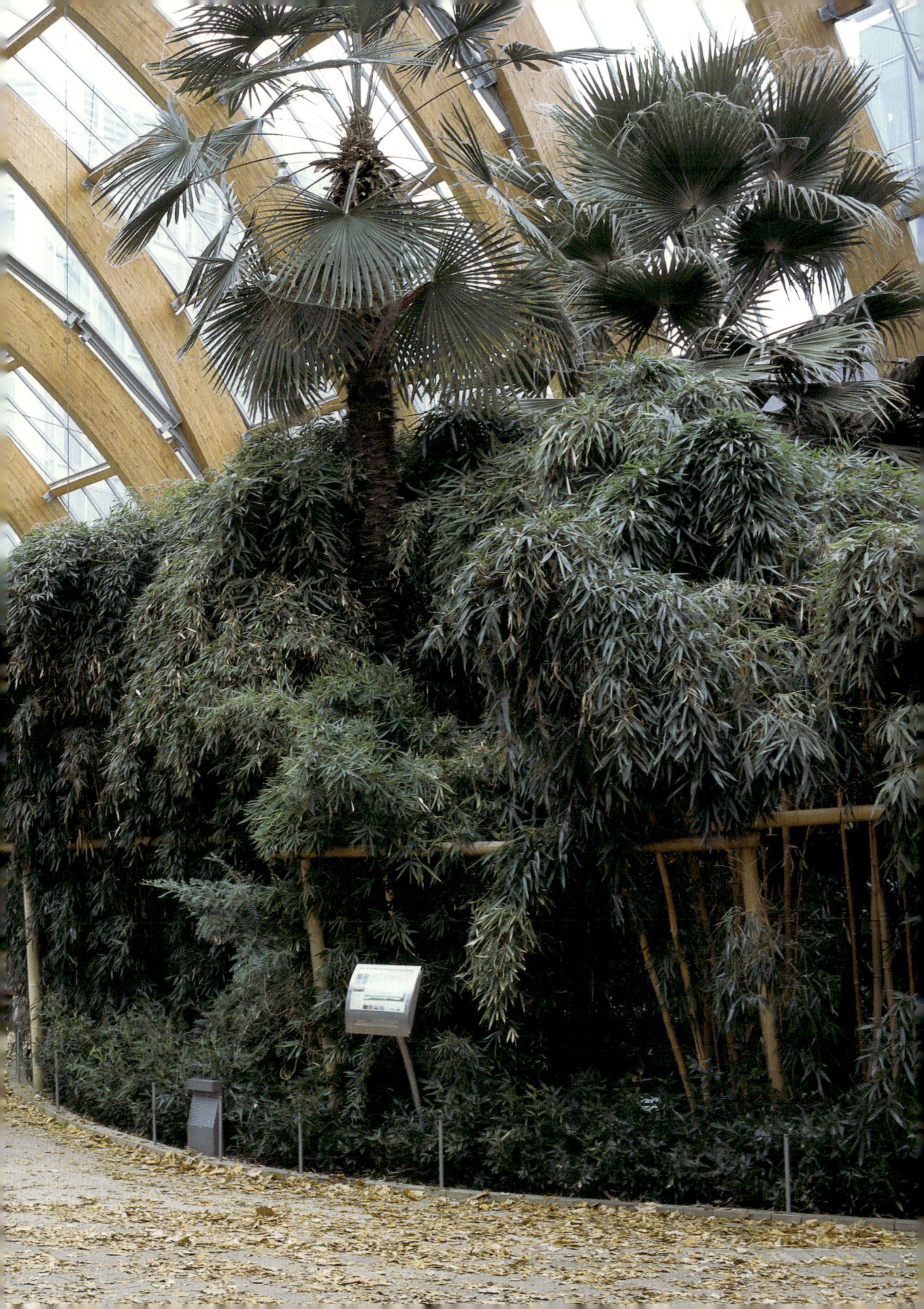

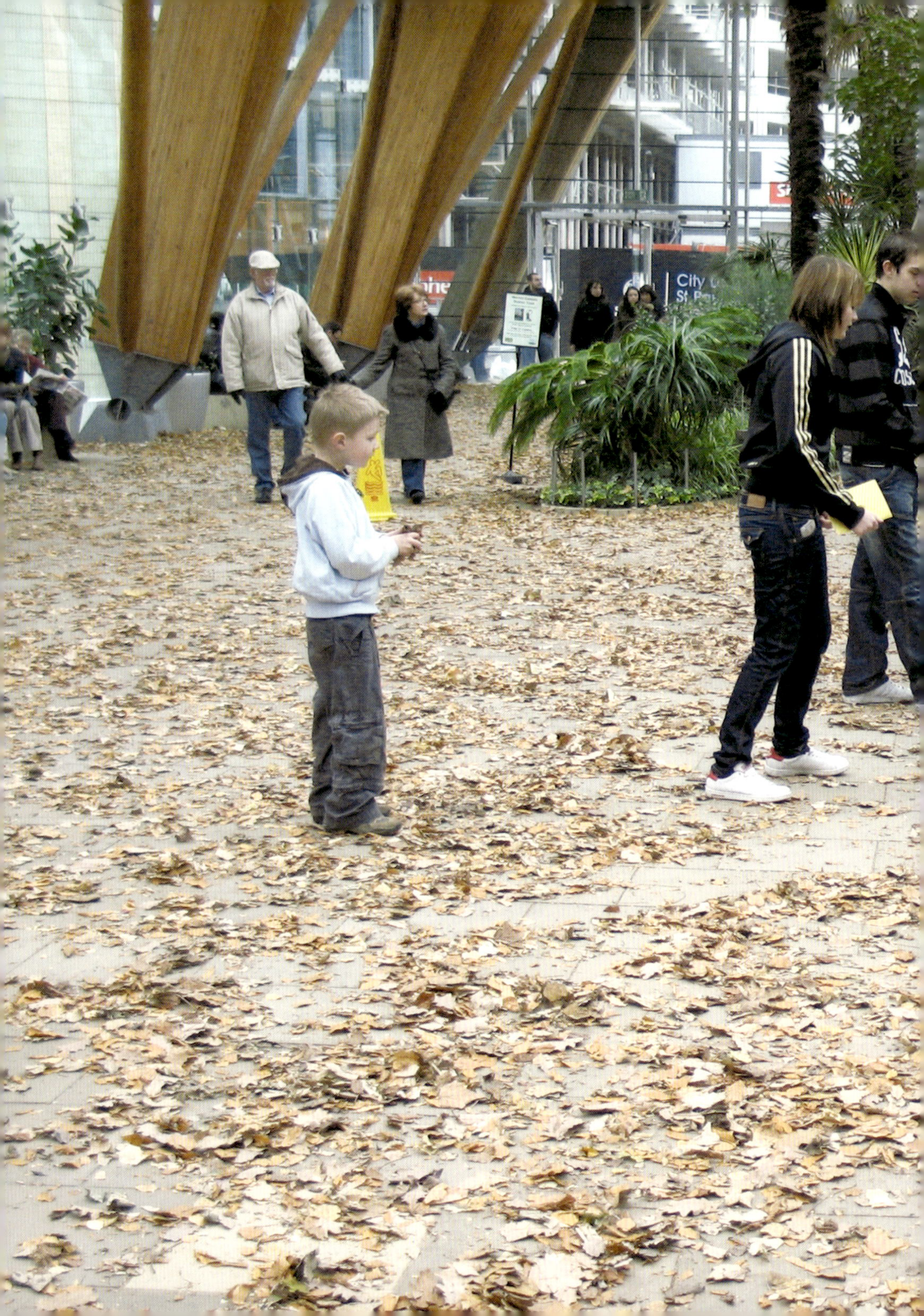

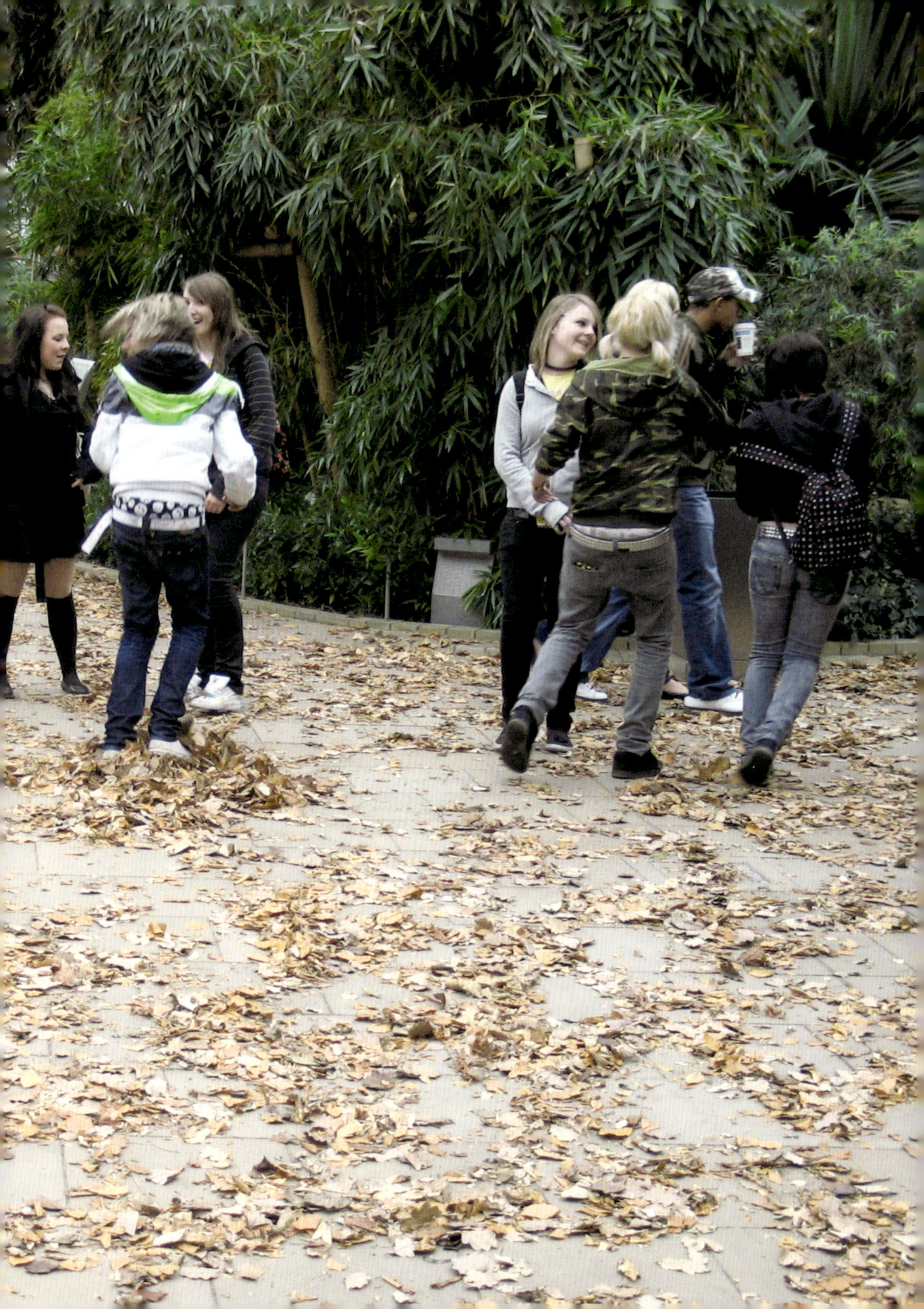

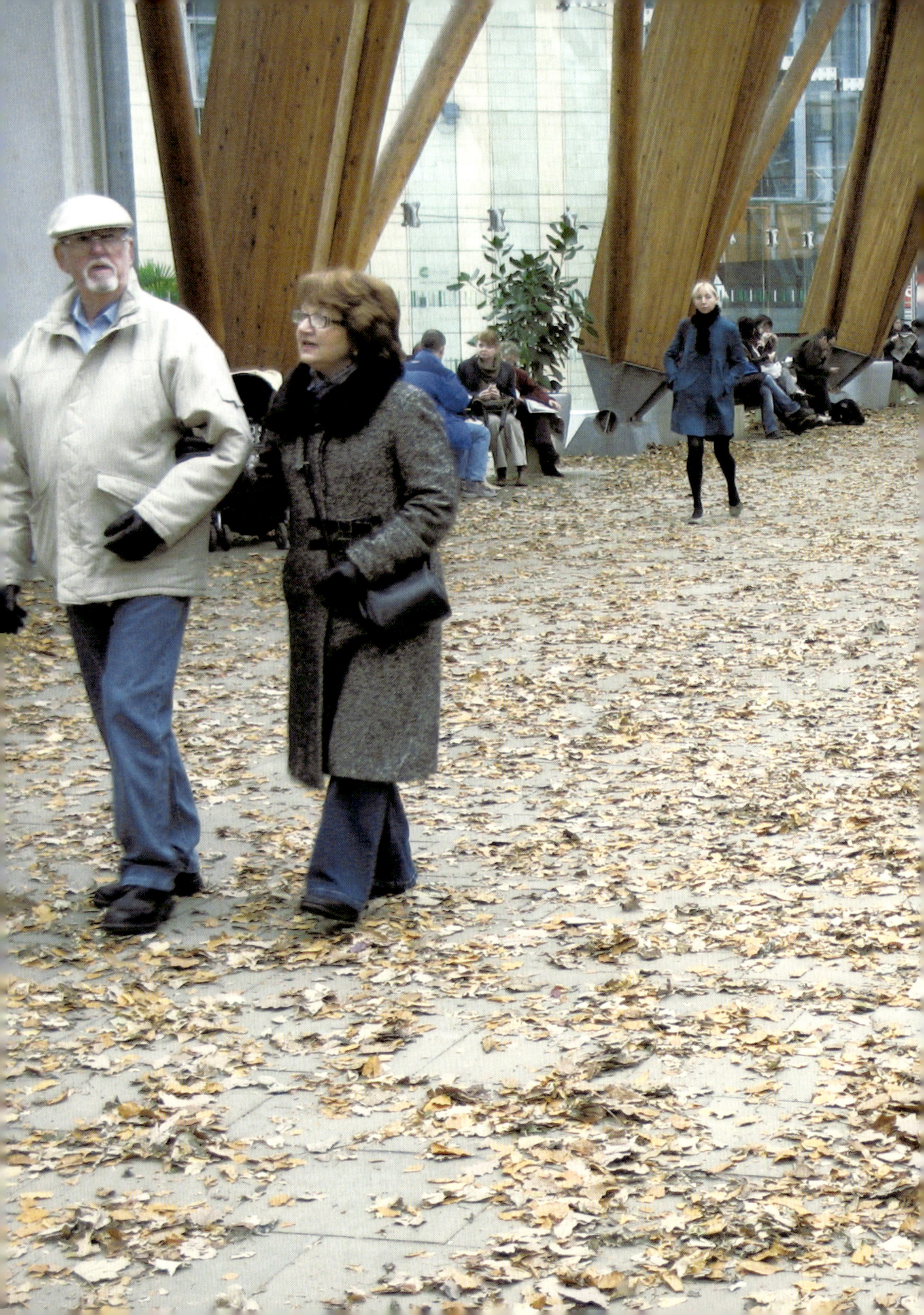

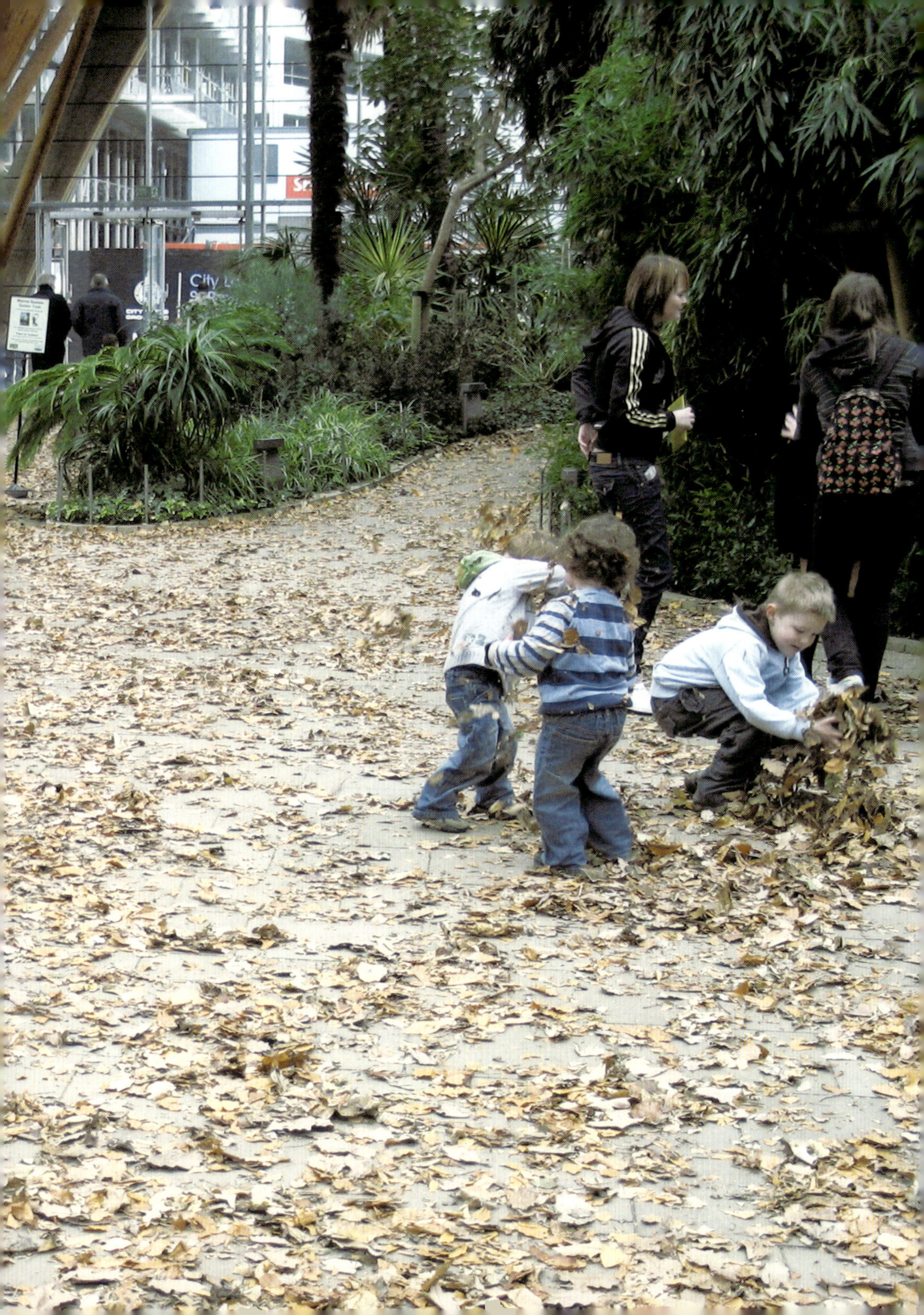

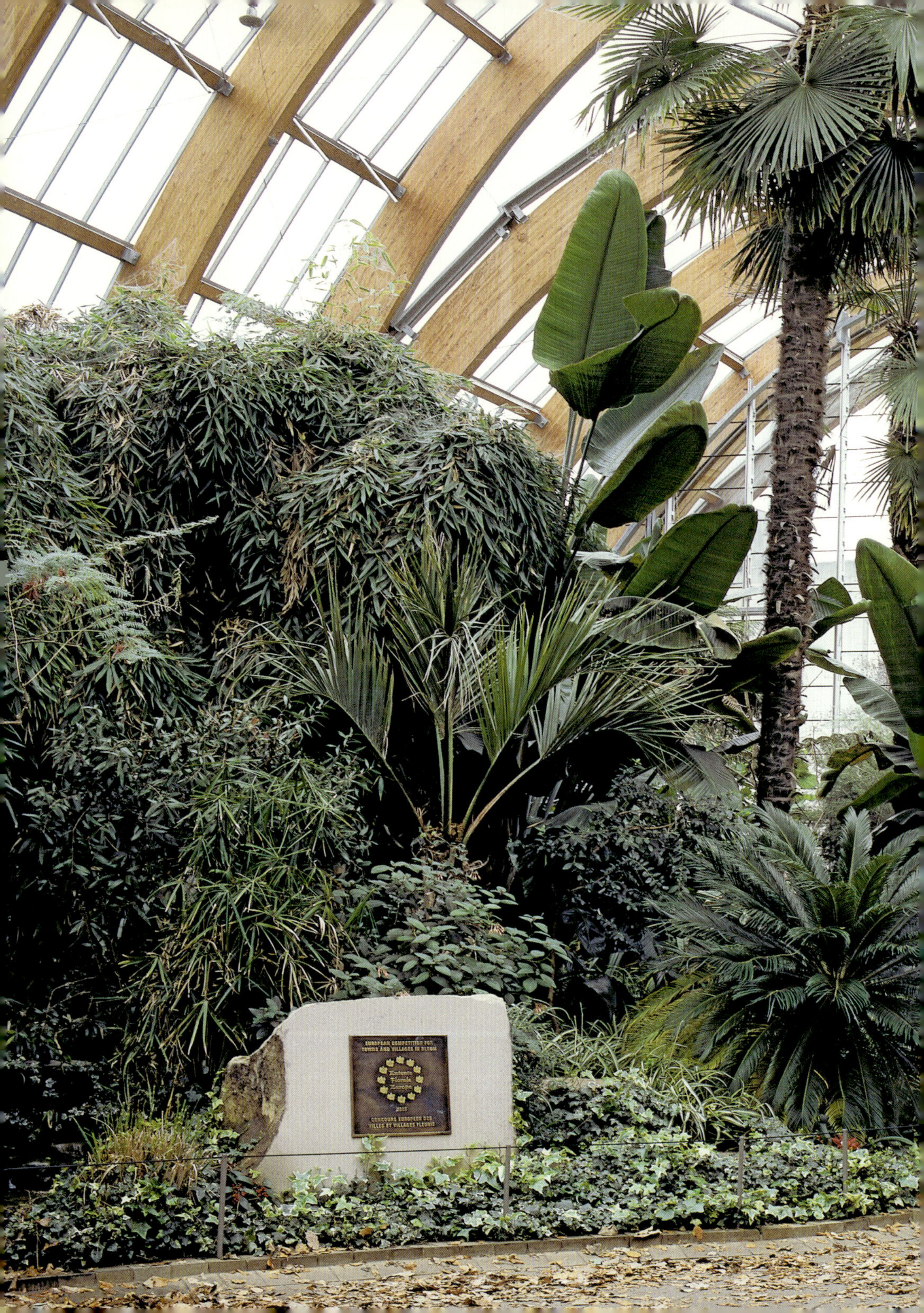

EUROPEAN COMPETITION FOR
TOWNS AND VILLAGES IN BLOOM
Entente
Florale
Europe
CONCOURS EUROPÉEN DES
VILLES ET VILLAGES FLEURIS

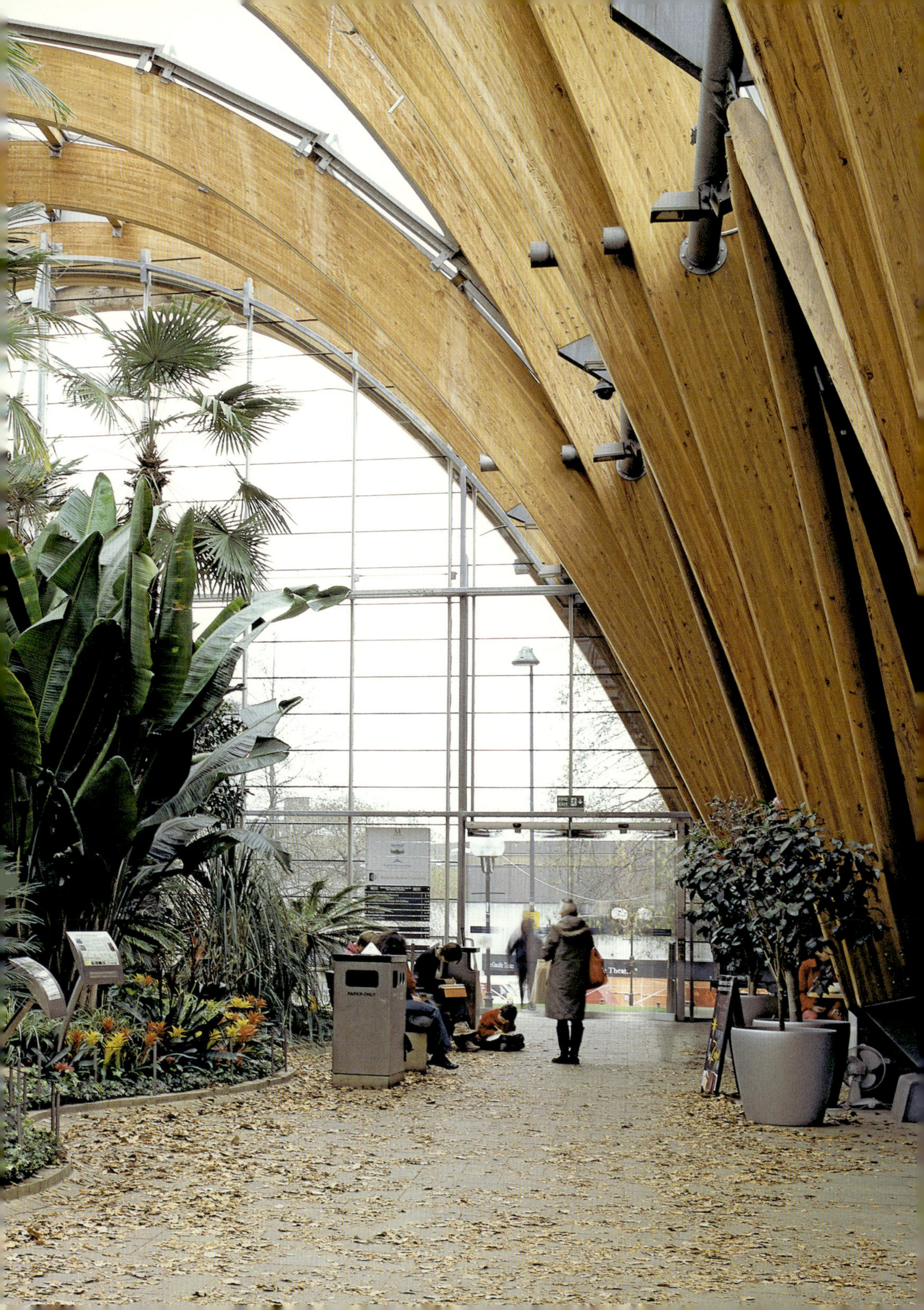

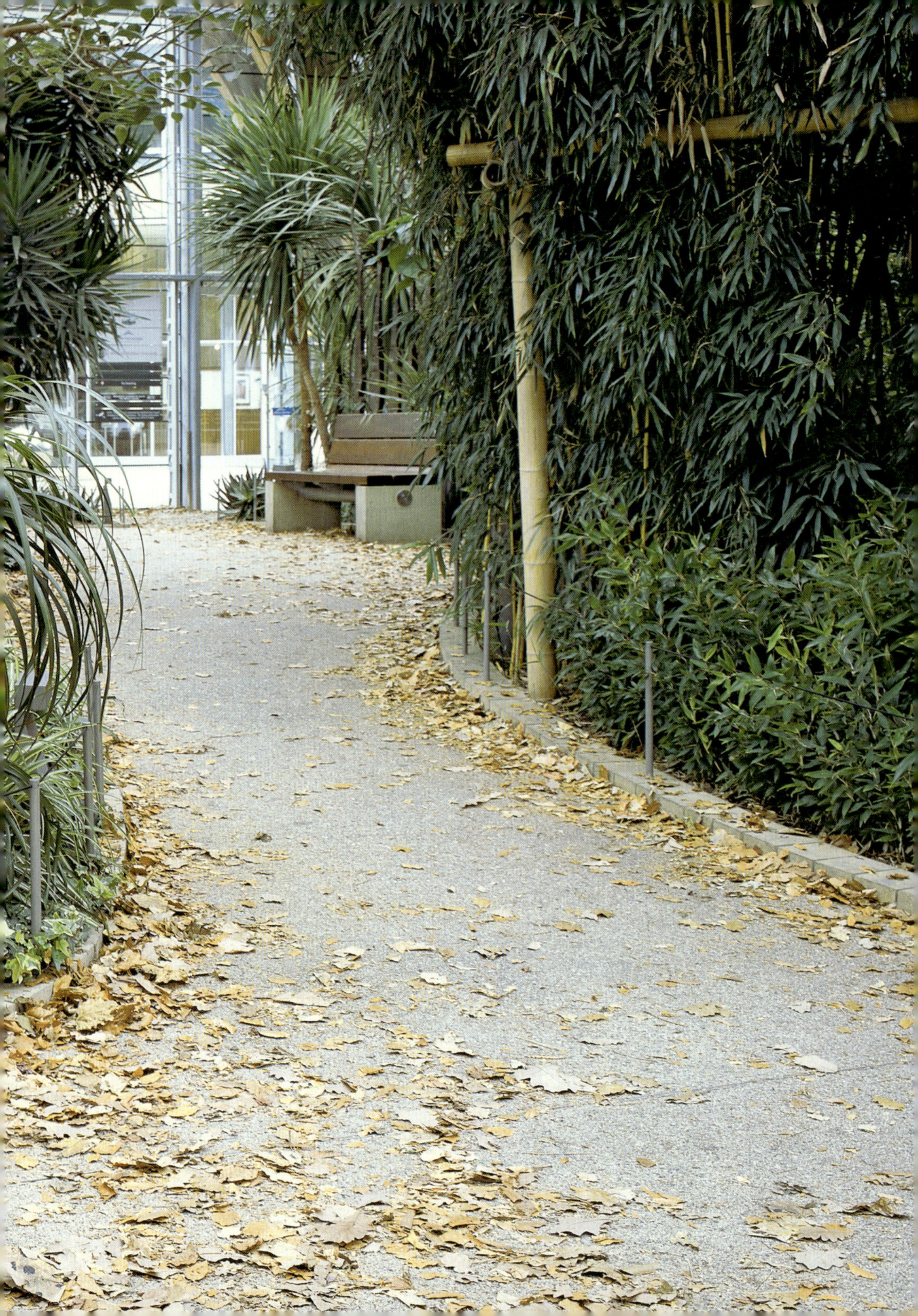

Roman Ondák covered the floor of the city's Winter Garden with autumn leaves – confusing first by virtue of switching the seasons and second because the Winter Garden is filled with evergreen trees. The first thing that hit me walking through the space yesterday was the smell. Something deep, earthy, walking-in-the-woods… in any case a far cry from anything you'd expect in there. At the opening lots of people venture stories about reactions to the leaves. Adults don't notice them so much one person says, it's more the kids that engage with them, as if the adults don't have time. It's true that during the opening event speeches there are a few kids scooping handfuls of the leaves and chasing each other. Someone else describes how one particular shop/coffee stand owner in the Garden was sweeping away the leaves in a neat circle around her space. *It's good I think*, says Roman, *she becomes my performer.*

Tim Etchells

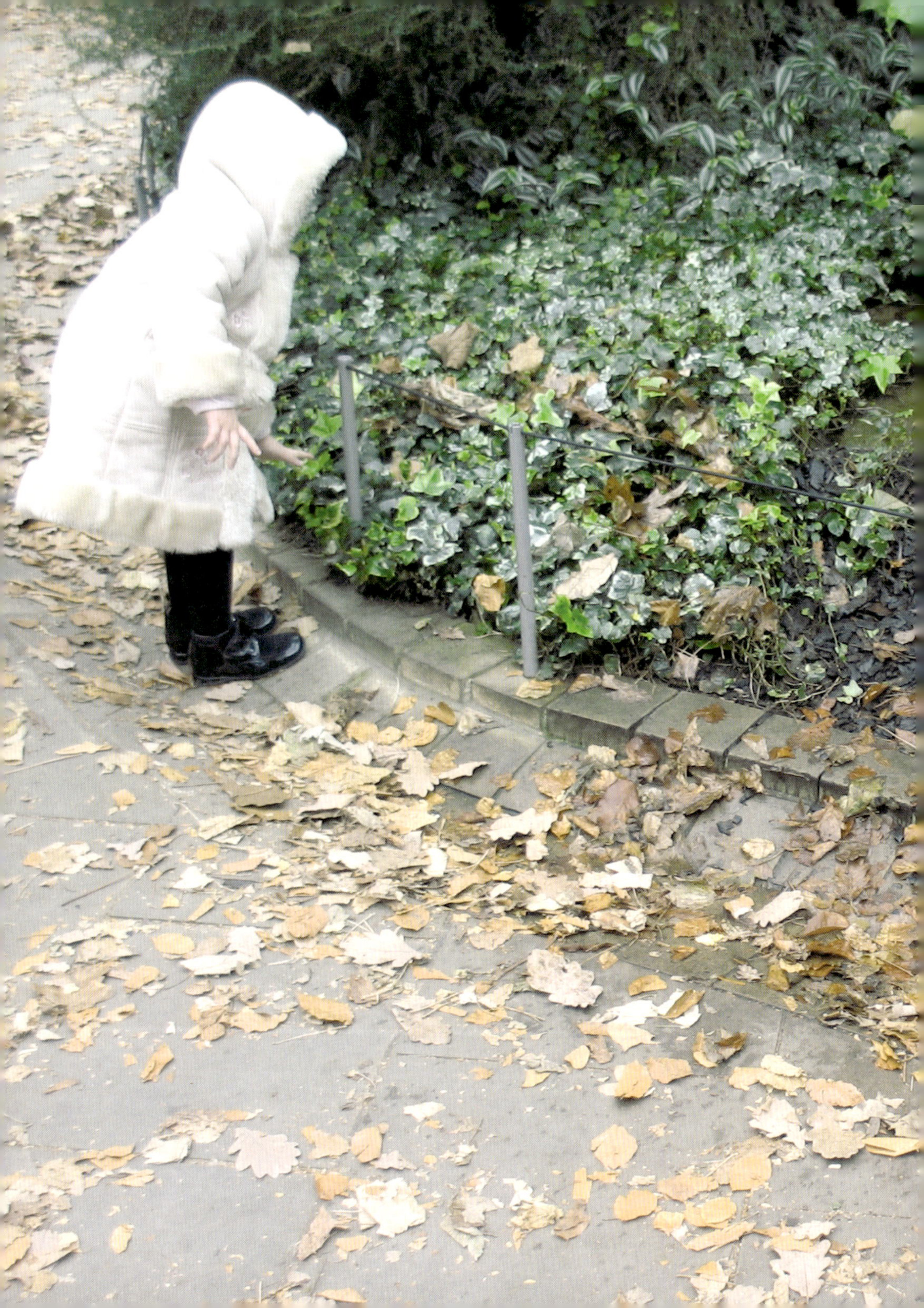

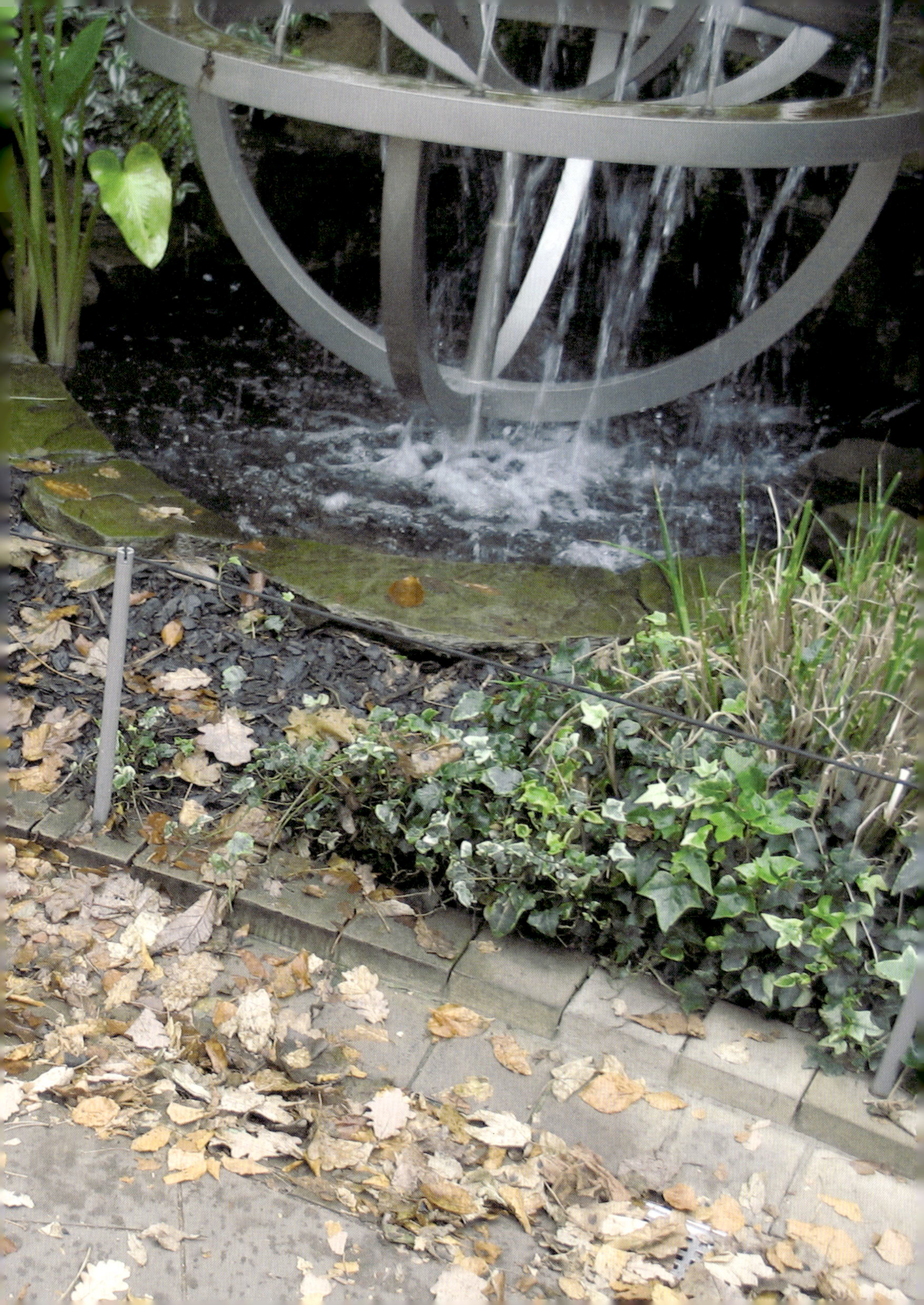

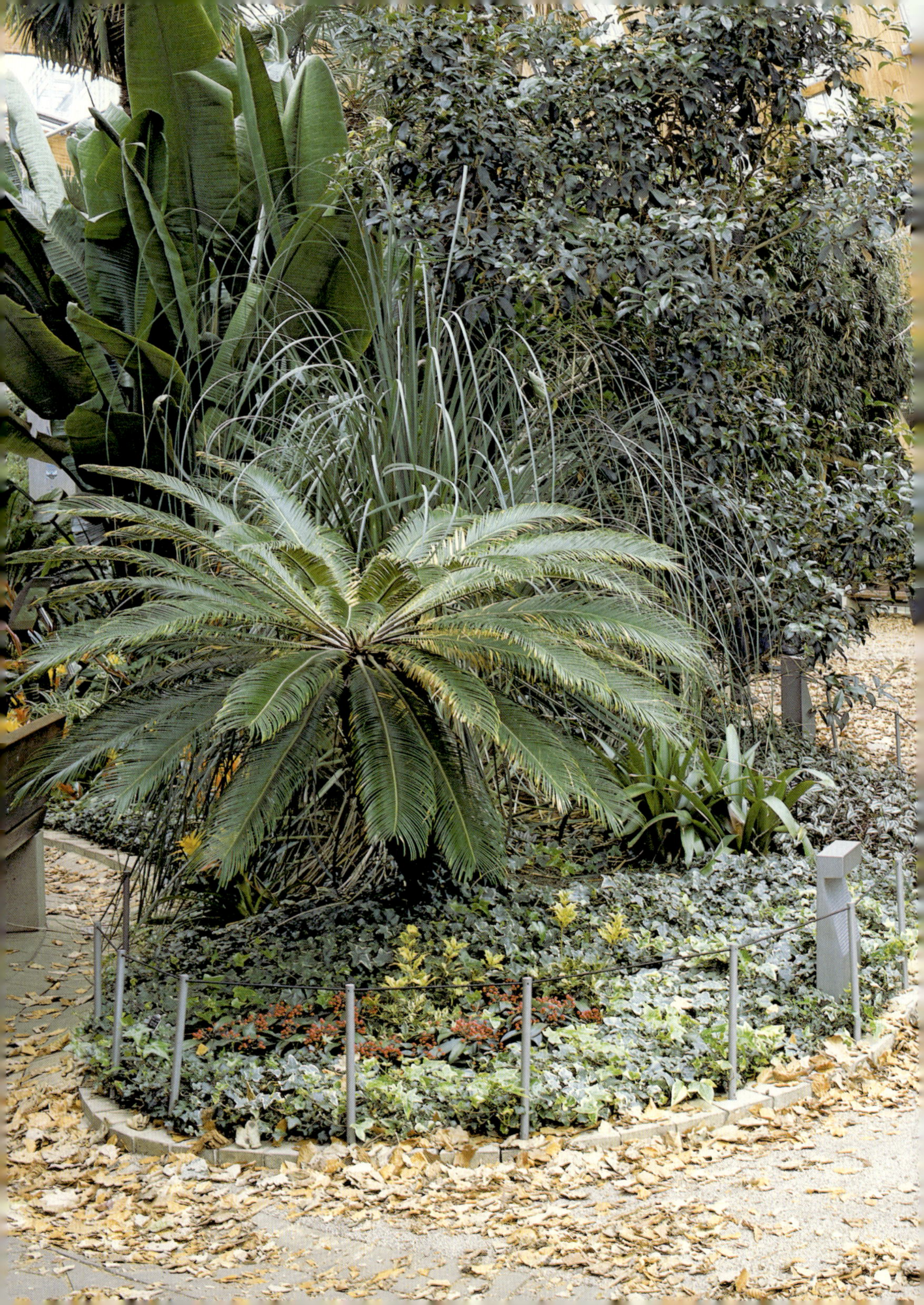

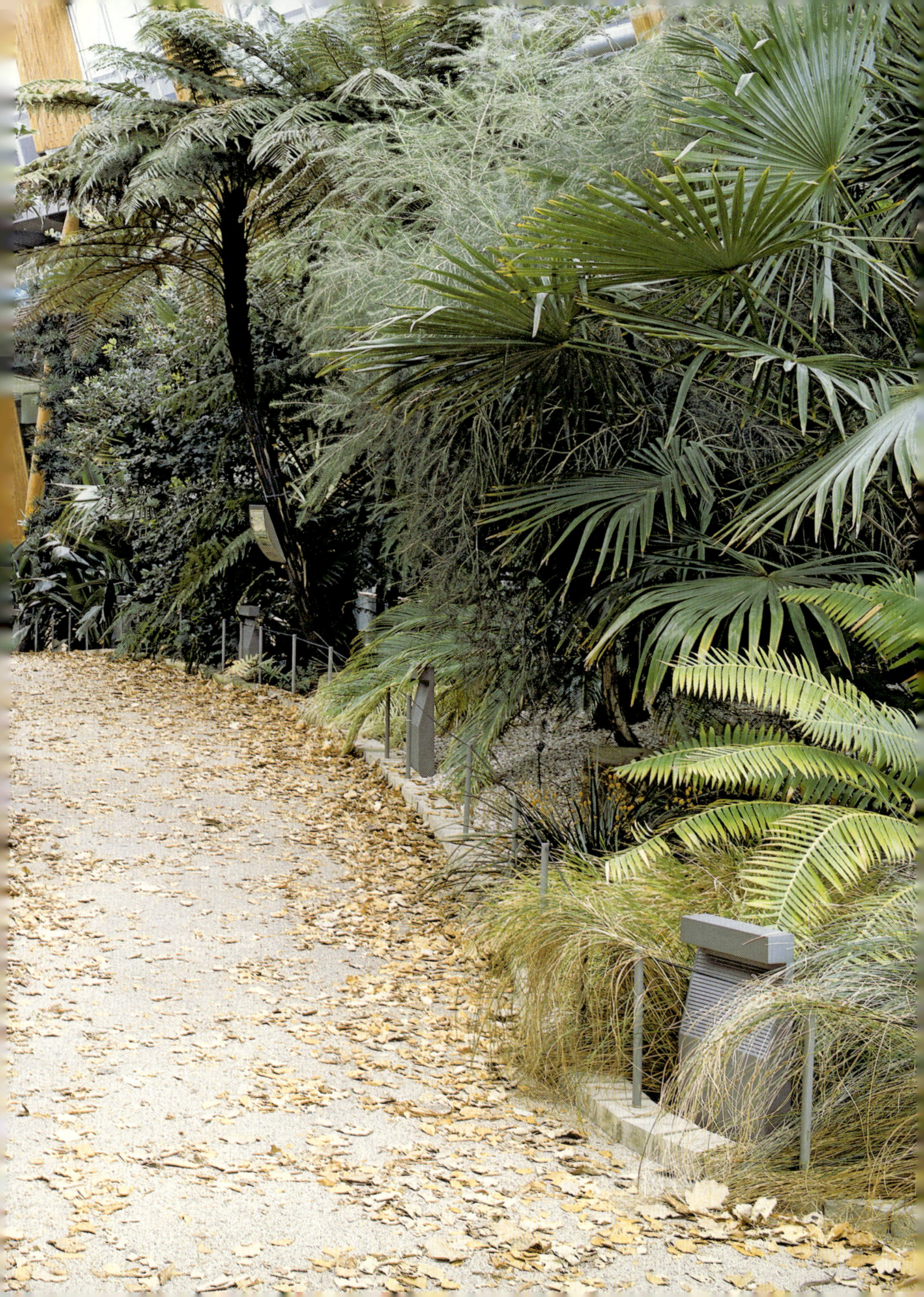

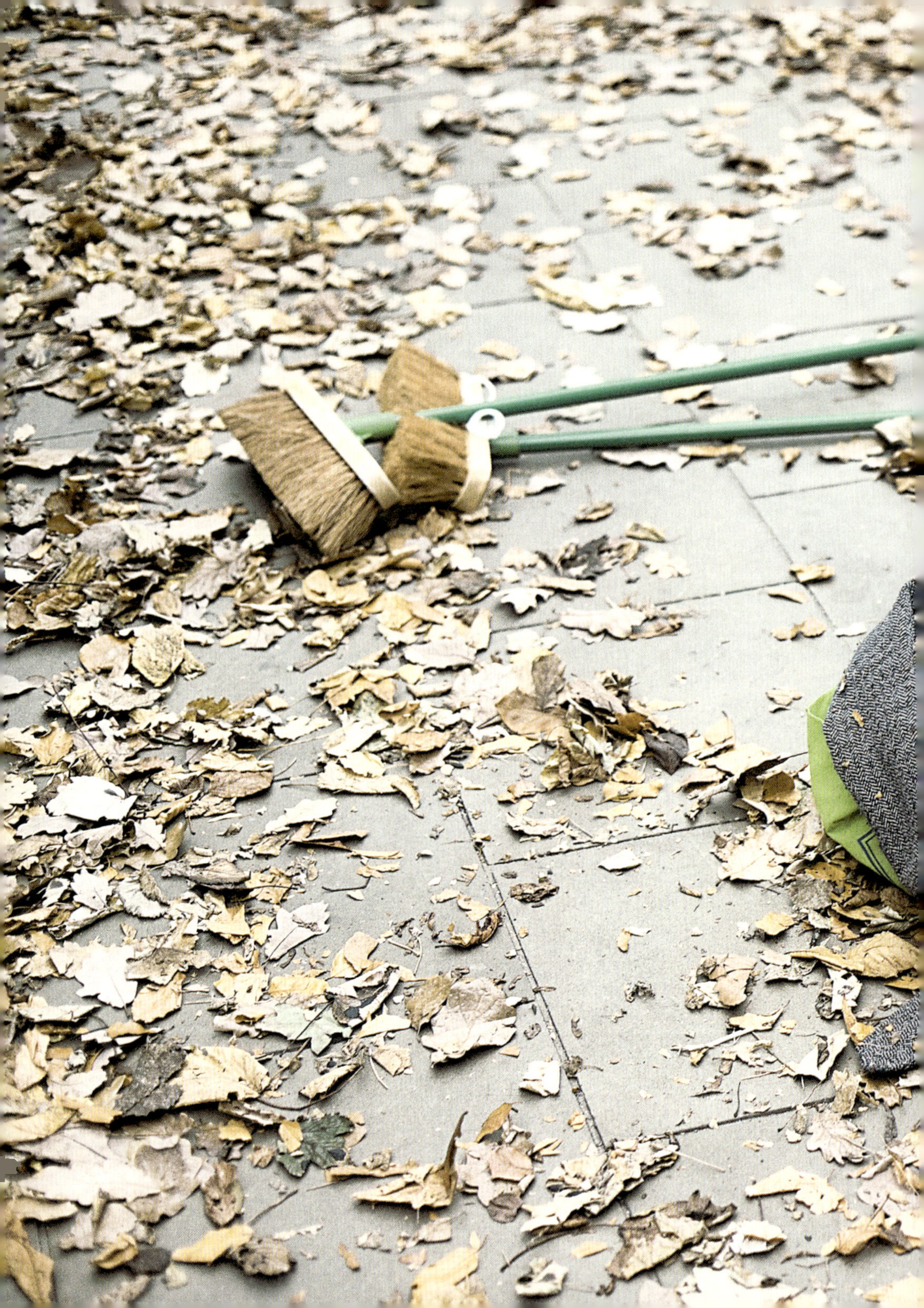

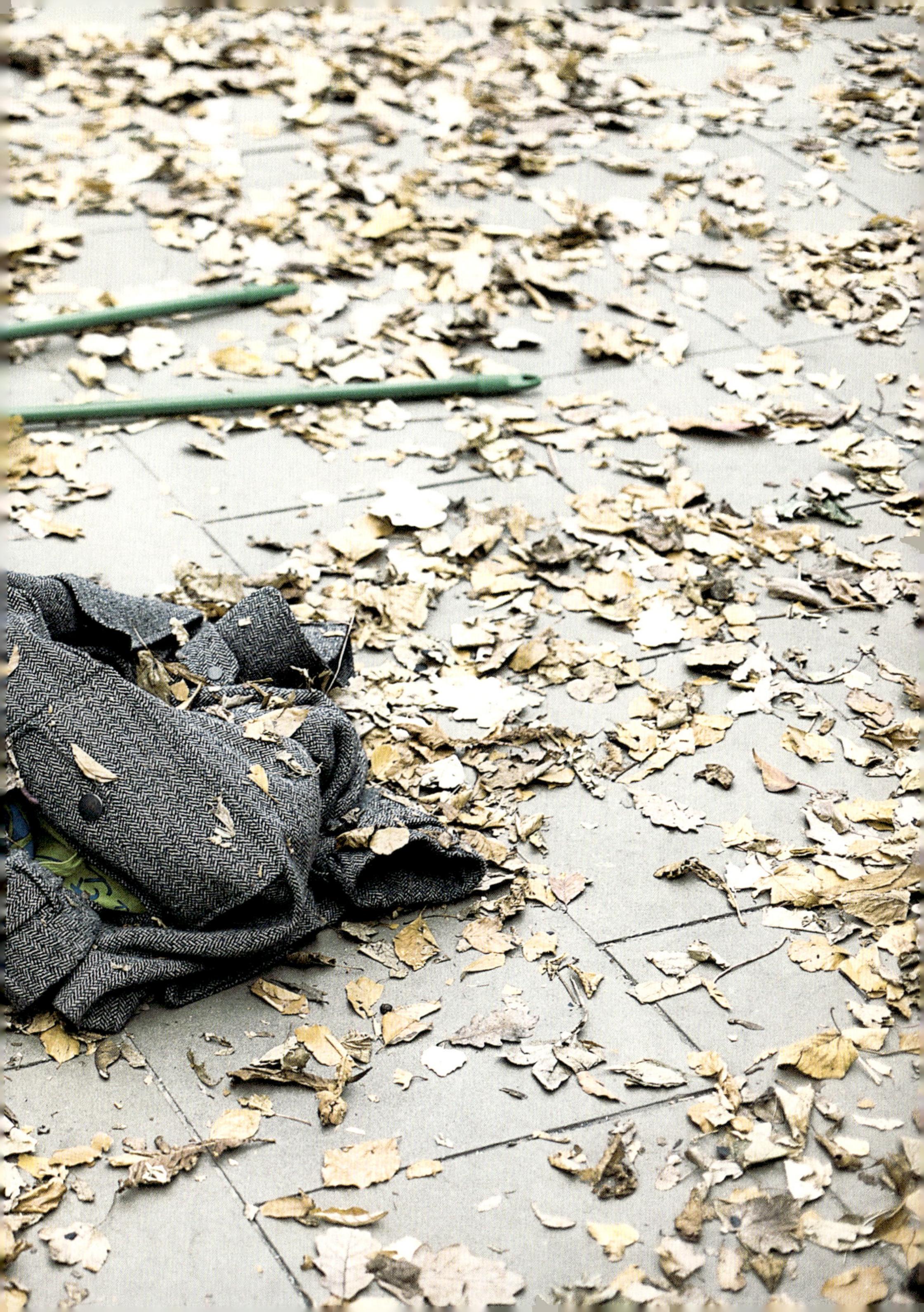

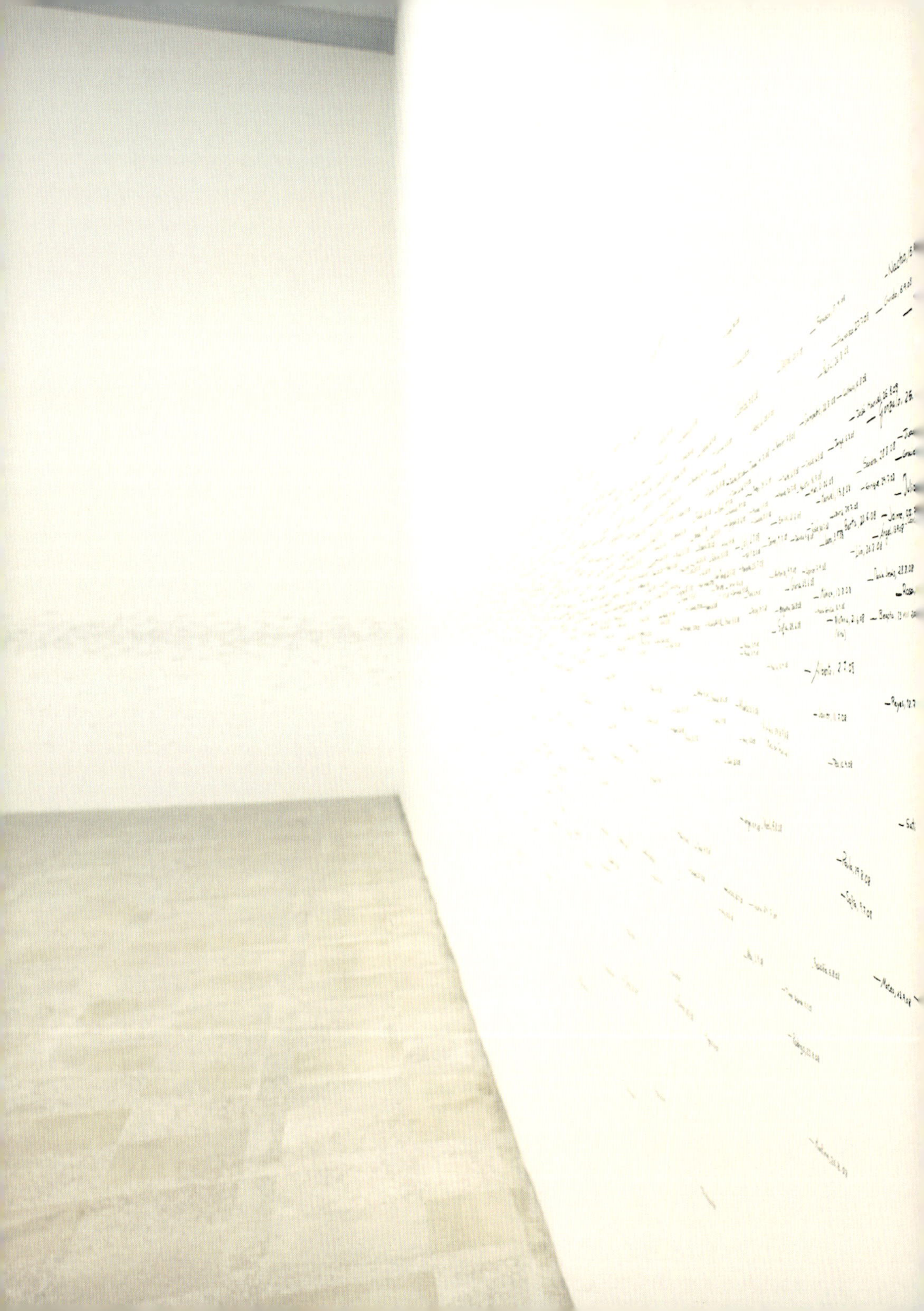

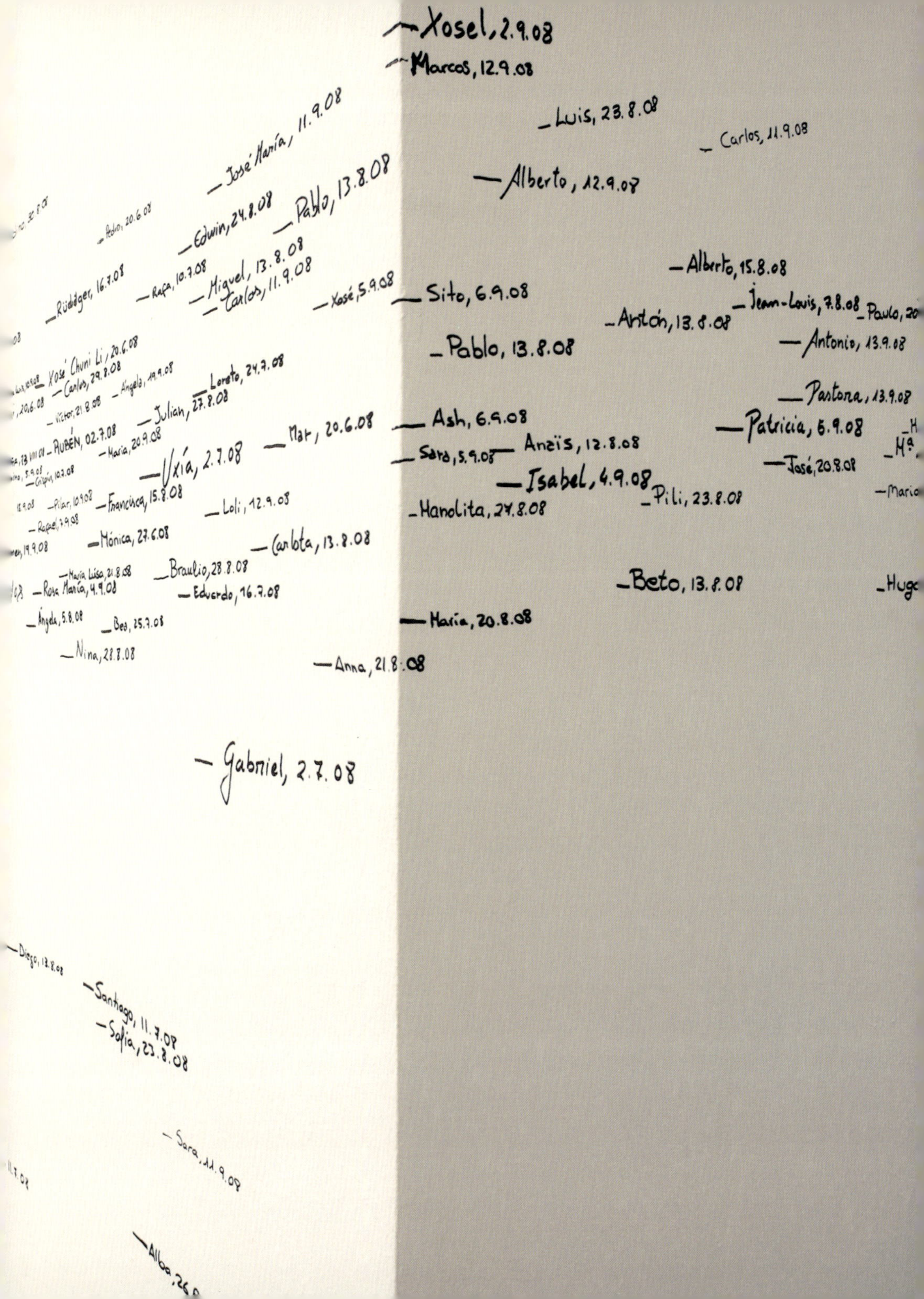

— Xosel, 2.9.08
— Marcos, 12.9.08
_ Luis, 23.8.08
_ Carlos, 11.9.08
— Alberto, 12.9.08
— José María, 11.9.08
_ Pedro, 20.6.02
_ Edwin, 24.8.08
_ Pablo, 13.8.08
_ Rüdiger, 16.7.08
_ Rafa, 10.7.08
_ Miguel, 13.8.08
_ Carlos, 11.9.08
_ Xosé, 5.9.08
_ Sito, 6.9.08
— Alberto, 15.8.08
_ Jean-Louis, 7.8.08
_ Paulo, 20
_ Antón, 13.8.08
— Antonio, 13.9.08
_ Pablo, 13.8.08
Xosé Chuni Li, 20.6.08
_ Carlos, 29.8.08
_ Ángela, 19.9.08
_ Loreto, 24.7.08
_ Victor, 21.8.08
_ Julian, 27.8.08
_ RUBEN, 02.7.08
_ Maria, 20.9.08
— Pastora, 13.9.08
_ Ash, 6.9.08
_ Mar, 20.6.08
_ Uxía, 2.7.08
— Patricia, 5.9.08
_ Sara, 5.9.08
_ Anaïs, 12.8.08
_ Isabel, 4.9.08
_ José, 20.8.08
_ Pilar, 10.9.08
_ Francisca, 15.8.08
_ Loli, 12.9.08
_ Pili, 23.8.08
_ Rafael, 7.9.08
_ Manolita, 27.8.08
_ Mónica, 27.6.08
_ Carlota, 13.8.08
_ Maria Luisa, 21.8.08
_ Braulio, 28.8.08
_ Beto, 13.8.08
_ Rosa Maria, 4.9.08
_ Eduardo, 16.7.08
_ Ángela, 5.8.08
_ Bea, 25.7.08
_ Maria, 20.8.08
_ Nina, 28.8.08
— Anna, 21.8.08
— Gabriel, 2.7.08
— Diego, 12.8.08
— Santiago, 11.7.08
_ Sofía, 23.8.08
_ Sara, 11.9.08
_ Alba, 26

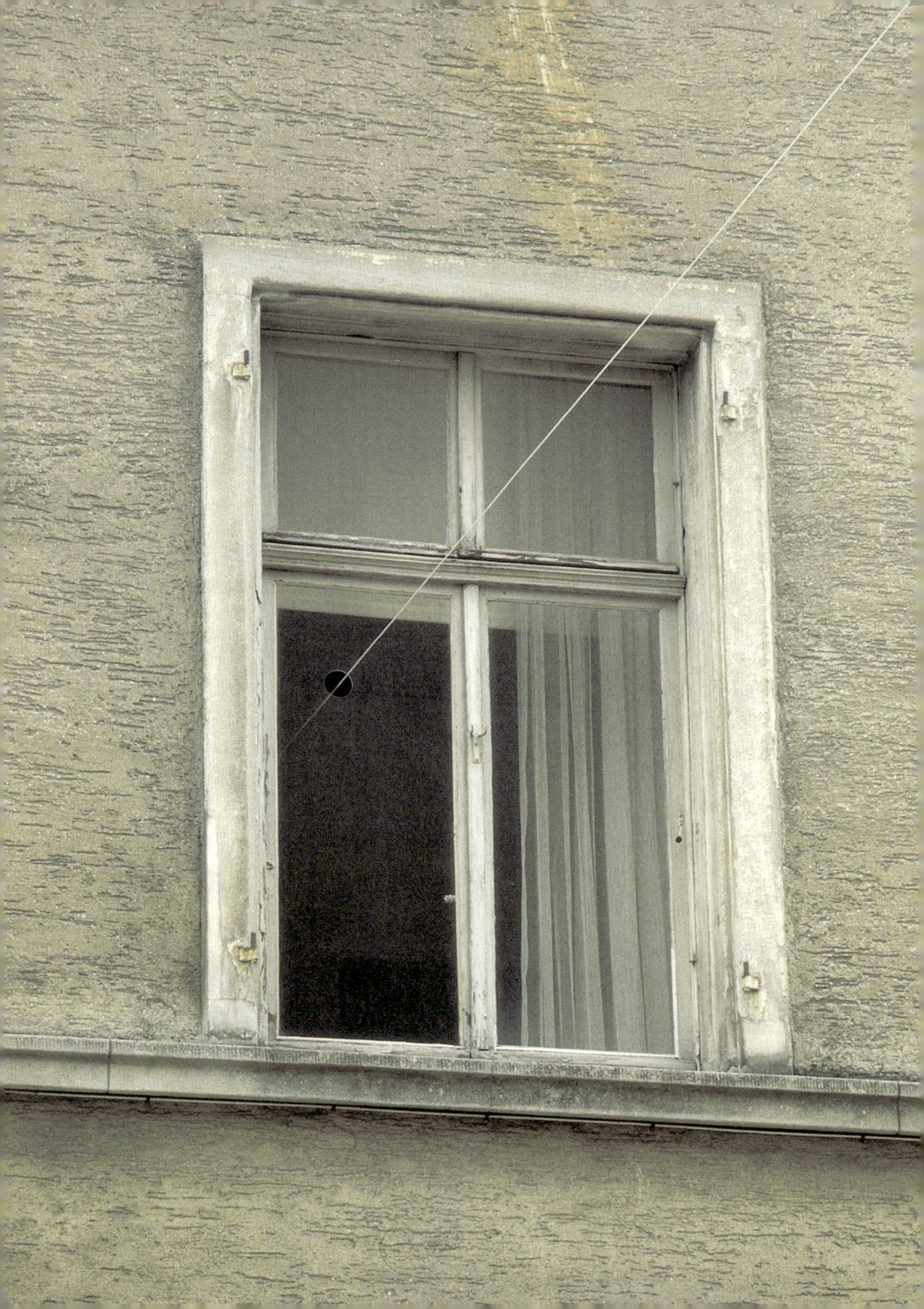

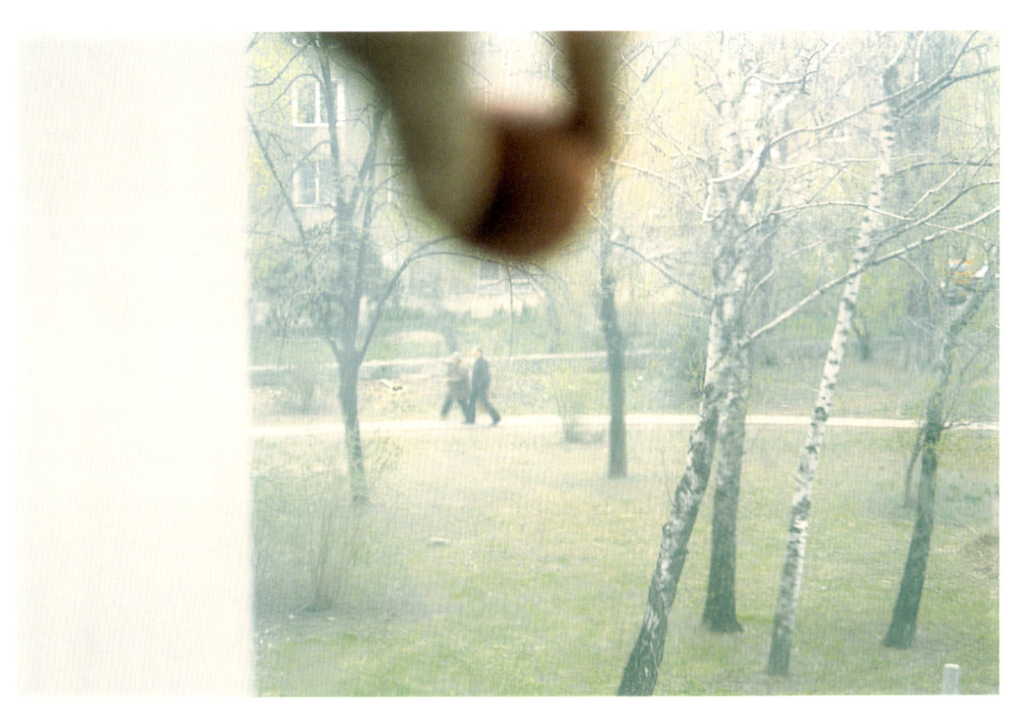

—Adrian, 8.4.08

ofie, 8. 4. 08

—— Rosalie, 5. 4. 08

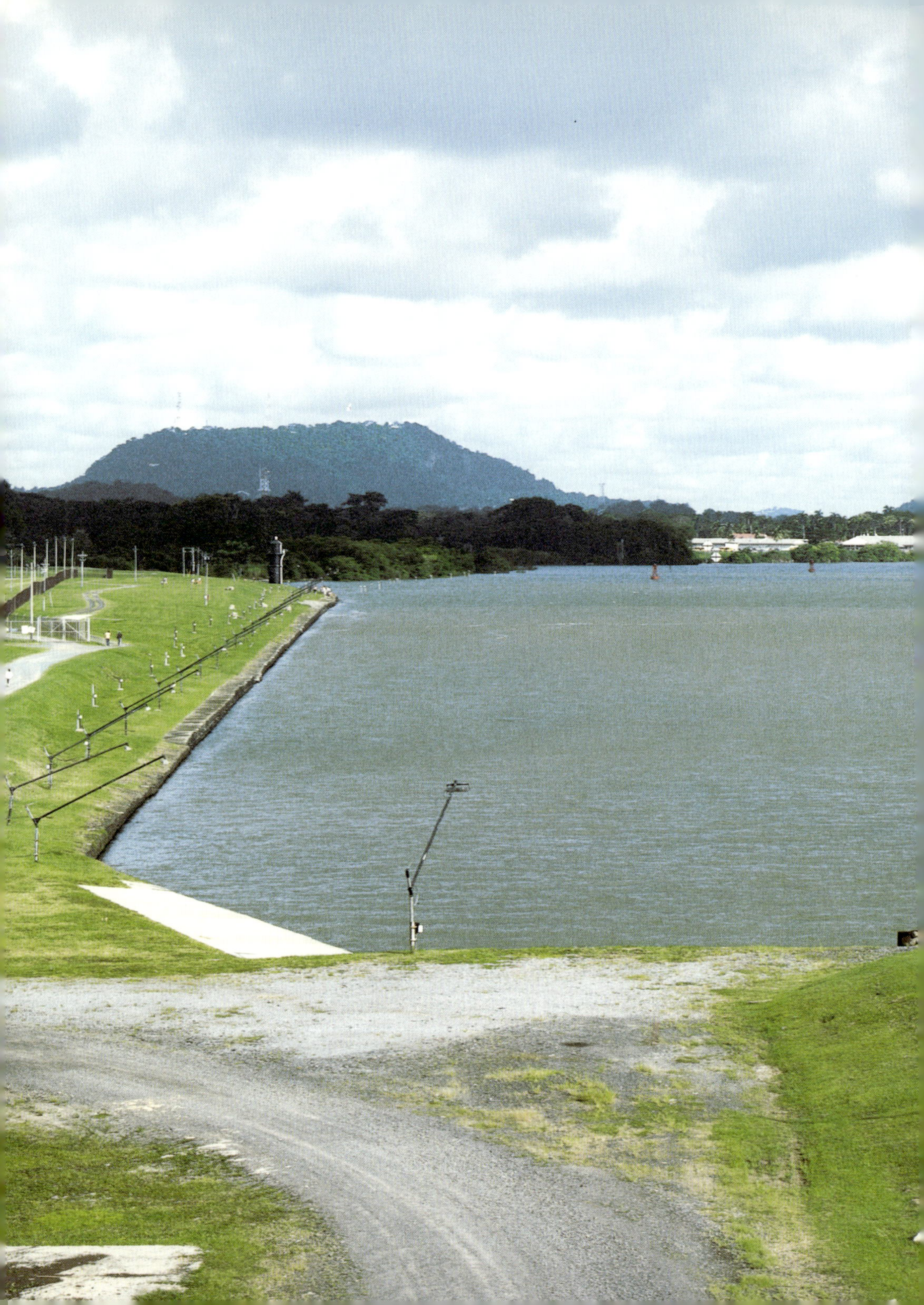

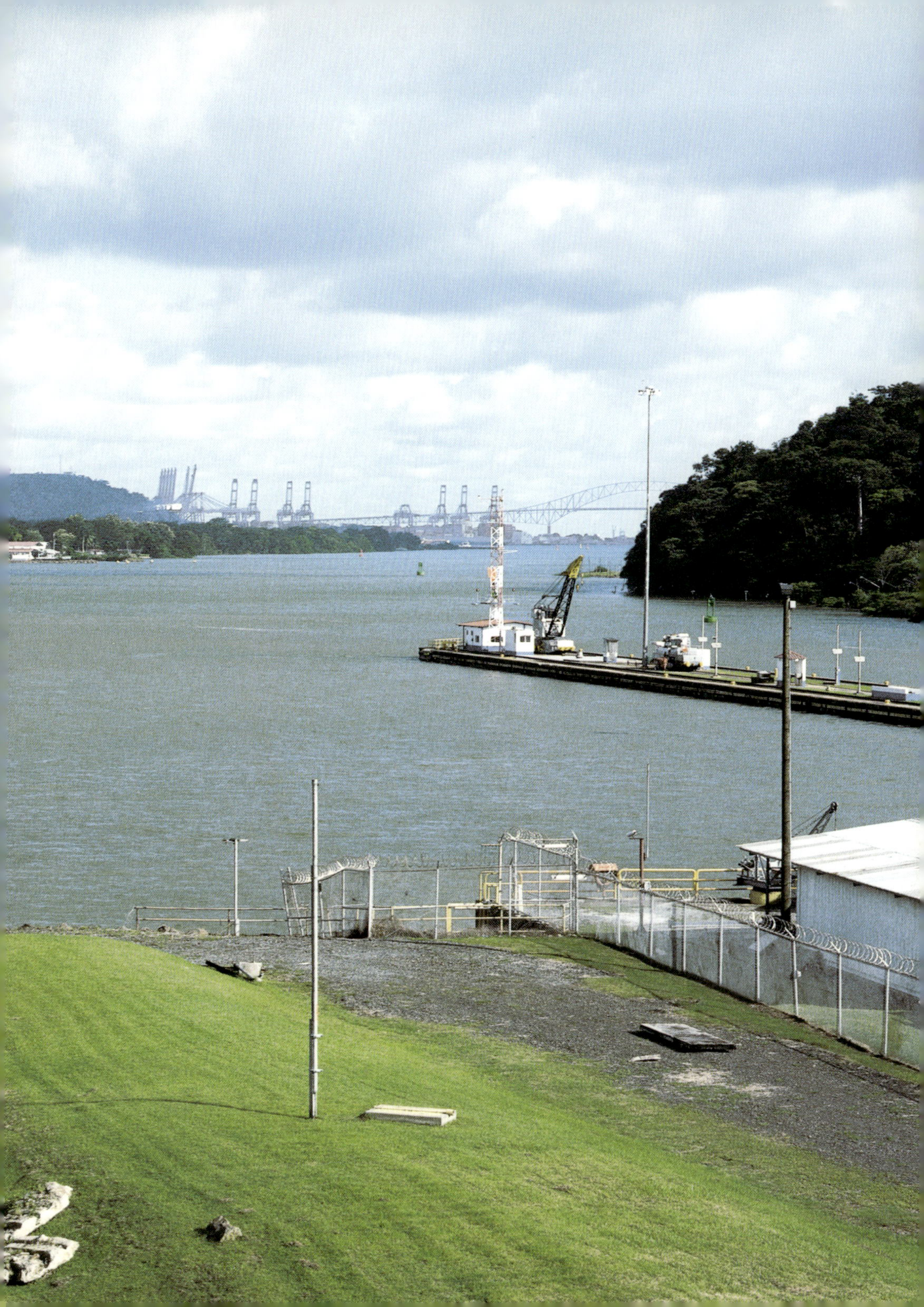

English:

Play ducks and drakes
Stone skipping
Stone skimming

Español:

Cabrillas (aparece en DRAE)
Hacer cabrillas (España)
Hacer patitos (México y cono sur)
Hacer patito (Argentina)
La Rana
Sapito
Hacer sapito (Argentina)
Hacer la rana (España)
Pan y quesito (Colombia)
Jugar a las tagüitas (Argentina)
Hacer chipichapas (o txipitxapas)
Hacer hondas
Hacer locitas (Honduras)
Hacer sopas
Hacer aguadinas
Capar el agua
Cortar el agua
Hacer tabletas
La Chata
Passanelles (Catalán)
Jugar la chata (Guatemala)
Pijotas
Epostracismo

EPOSTRACISMO (Etim. – Del gr. epostrakismos, deriv. de epostrakizeim, arrojar la concha á la superficie del agua, de epí, sobre, y óstrakon, concha.) m. Dep. ant. Juego ó deporte de la edad clásica, que consistía en lanzar una concha, un palo ó una piedra, haciéndole resbalar y rebotar sobre la superficie del agua en un lago ó estanque. Se le declaraba vencedor, según los escritores griegos y latinos que describen este juego, á aquel que lanzaba el proyectil más lejos el mayor número de veces.

Los jugadores son "epostracistas."

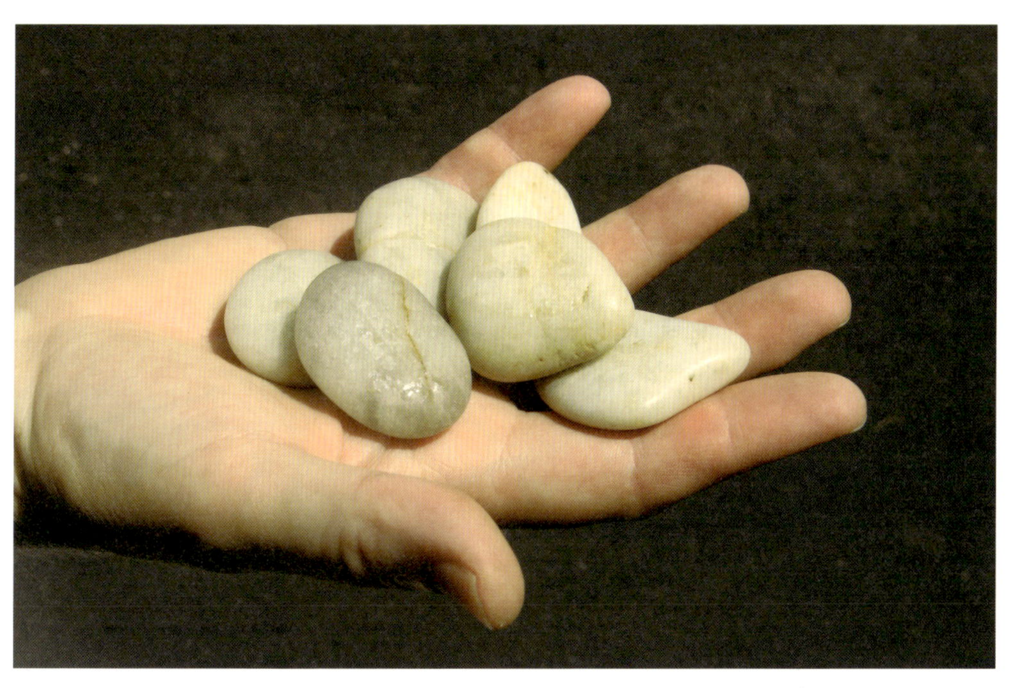

Quivers of an Unproductive Gesture

When Roman Ondák first mentioned stone skimming as an event to be orchestrated on the shores of the Panama Canal, the image that came to mind was that of a Friedrich–like solitary wanderer confronting a vast and tropical setting. Stone skimming is a humble action that is usually practiced by someone who has time, who is wasting time or is trying to kill time. One wonders how such a candid and idle activity can be read when performed by a collectivity against the backdrop of one of the busiest and most productive places on earth? Ondák's seemingly purposeless event not only confronted the obvious economic and bureaucratic machinery of the canal with a self-defeating innocence. It also intended to modestly cope with the waterway's complex historical context, a peculiar saga involving politics, treachery, national prides, displacement of borders and the loss of thousands of human lives.

Although the idea of building a canal joining the Pacific and Atlantic Oceans dates back to the sixteenth century, it wasn't until 1881 that Ferdinand de Lesseps, who had triumphantly built the Suez Canal, tried his fortunes again in Central America. But he had none. Many factors added to the Frenchman's spectacular failure in building a sea level canal, among them the weather, landslides, yellow fever and malaria (22,000 men are estimated to have died), faulty design and ultimately a double bankruptcy, which ruined not only himself but also hundreds of thousands of French rentiers who had acquired public shares of the *Compagnie Universelle du Canal Interocéanique*. In 1903 Philippe Bunau-Varilla, a French citizen and Panama's self-appointed ambassador to United States, signed the Hay-Bunau-Varilla Treaty granting the US the right to build and indefinitely administer the Panama Canal, as well as to seize and control an area extending five miles on each side of the waterway – an agreement that was reached in exchange for military support provided to Panamanians to achieve their separation from Colombia, but that also ended up dividing the new country in two. Having purchased whatever remained of Lesseps's second company, the *Compagnie Nouvelle du Canal de Panama*, and after a great deal of excavating and sanitizing of the region (a total of 75 million cubic metres of earth is estimated to have been removed), a lock canal was finally inaugurated in 1914 in the occupied territory that came to be known as the Canal Zone, under the motto 'The land divided/The world united'. Simultaneously a military reservation, a company town and a colony, the Canal Zone remained under North American control until the 1977 Torrijos-Carter Treaties were signed, stipulating that the territories of the Zone would revert on 1 October 1979 and that Panama would gain control over its canal at midnight on 31 December 1999. Today the water and the politics in the Panama Canal flow in a rather smooth way although, when standing on its shores, one is constantly reminded of the amount of human effort that was required to split a continent in two, and to later bring a country back together.

Ondák's intervention consisted of a Sunday open call for an amateur stone skimming gathering on the bank of the Canal. In keeping with the nature of the game, Ondák's initiative wasn't as

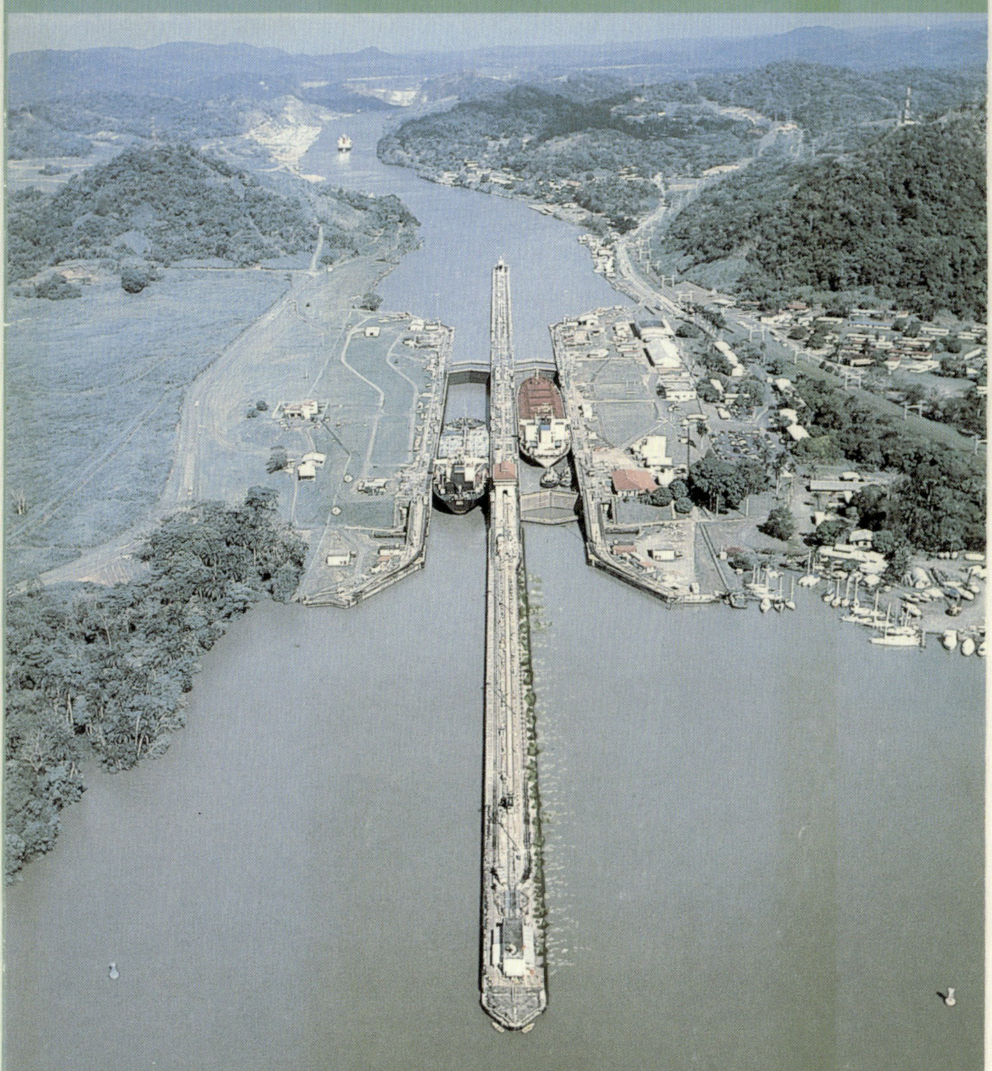

Guide
Canal de Panama
EDICIONES
BALBOA

much about winning as about participating in an event for which the main conceptual motif and motive was distance. Whereas the Canal was first conceived as a shortcut from east to west (read, mainly from New York to San Francisco), *Across that Place* (2008) focused on bridging the distance (some would say the *divide*) between north and south. It was also meant to restore the possibility of gesturing, at least momentarily, towards the reunification of a divided – and formerly occupied – territory, at a time when the Canal is going through a whole set of modifications aimed at increasing its width as well as its capacity. From that perspective, the event was perceived less as a competition or spectacle than as the silent and shared experience of a collectivity participating in a symbolic action. It reflected on the vanity of both the unrestrained pride that the US originally took in halving a continent and boasting its colonial presence in this small Latin American country, as well as on the apparent futility of the artist's own undertaking in confronting expectations and scale. As it happens in many of Ondák's works, this harmless initiative became transgressive as it unsettled the social codes one usually associates with the innocence of early age by transferring them into a politically significant context: by bringing together a group of adults to play a children's game, Ondák orchestrated an everyday action which, striving against a larger-than-human and politically engineered situation, reads as a celebration of its own unproductive logic.

Magali Arriola

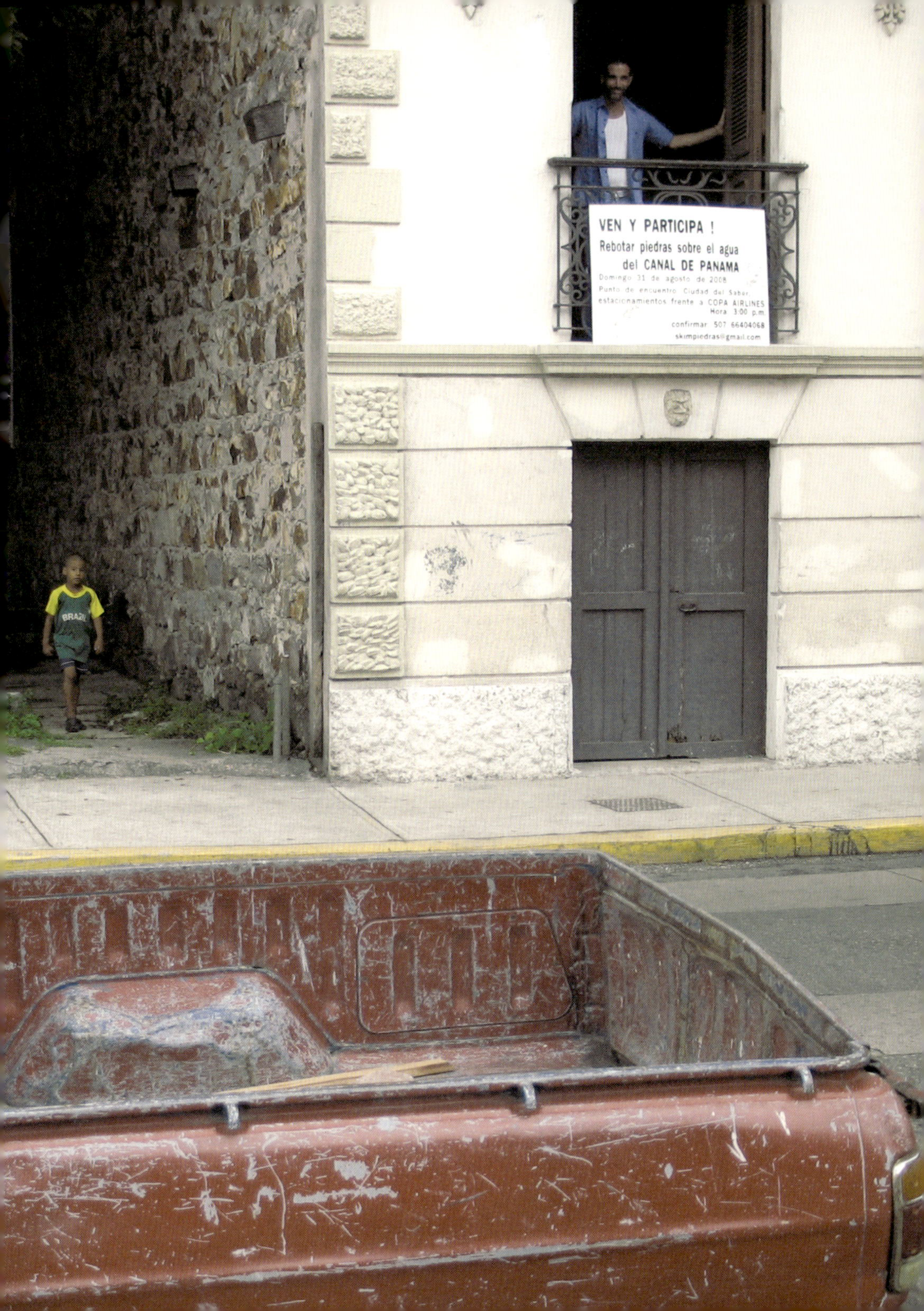

VEN Y PARTICIPA !
Rebotar piedras sobre el agua
del CANAL DE PANAMA
Domingo 31 de agosto de 2008
Punto de encuentro Ciudad del Saber,
estacionamientos frente a COPA AIRLINES
Hora 3:00 p.m.
confirmar 507 66404068
skimpiedras@gmail.com

BRAZIL

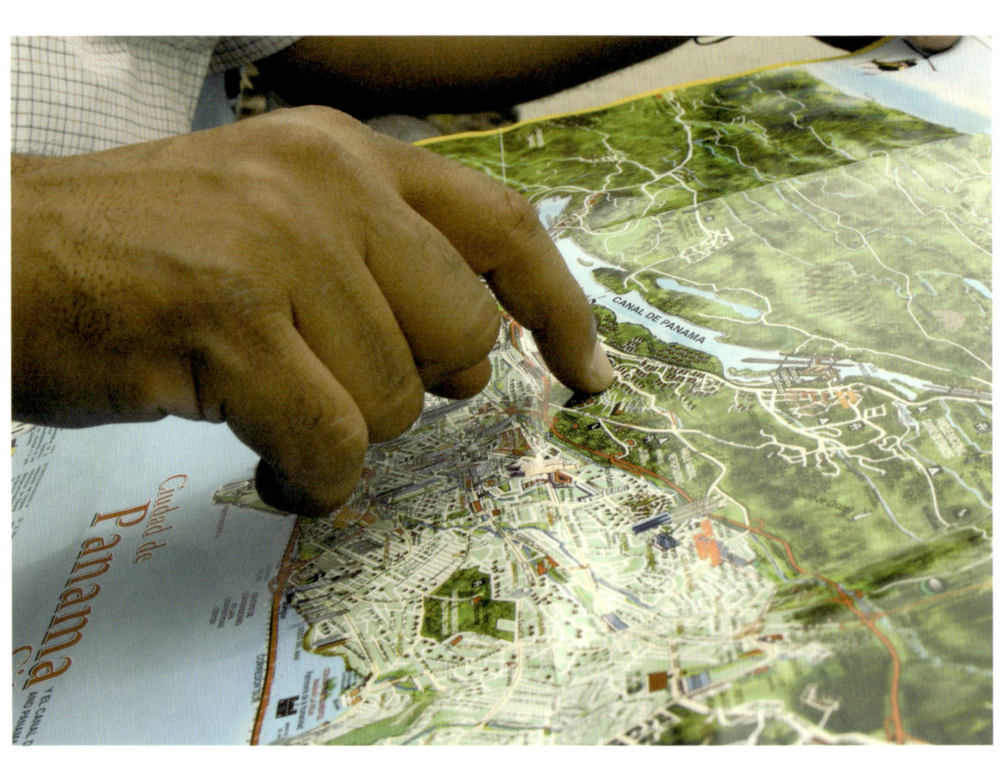

CANAL DE PANAMA
Ciudad de
Panama
Y EL CANAL D
AND PANAM

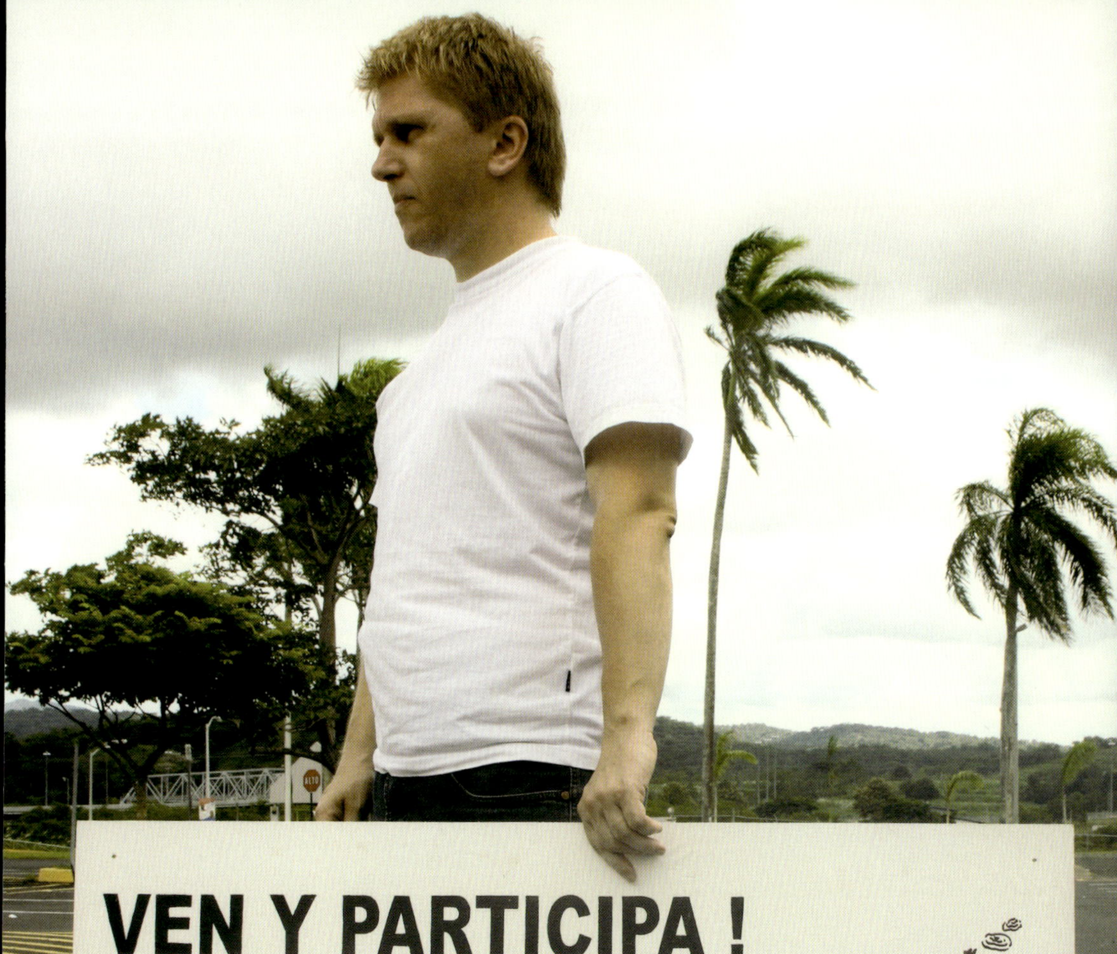

VEN Y PARTICIPA !
Rebotar piedras sobre el agua
del CANAL DE PANAMA
Domingo 31 de agosto de 2008
Punto de encuentro: Ciudad del Saber,
estacionamientos frente a COPA AIRLINES
Hora: 3:00 p.m.
confirmar: 507 66404068
skimpiedras@gmail.com
PANAMA CANAL

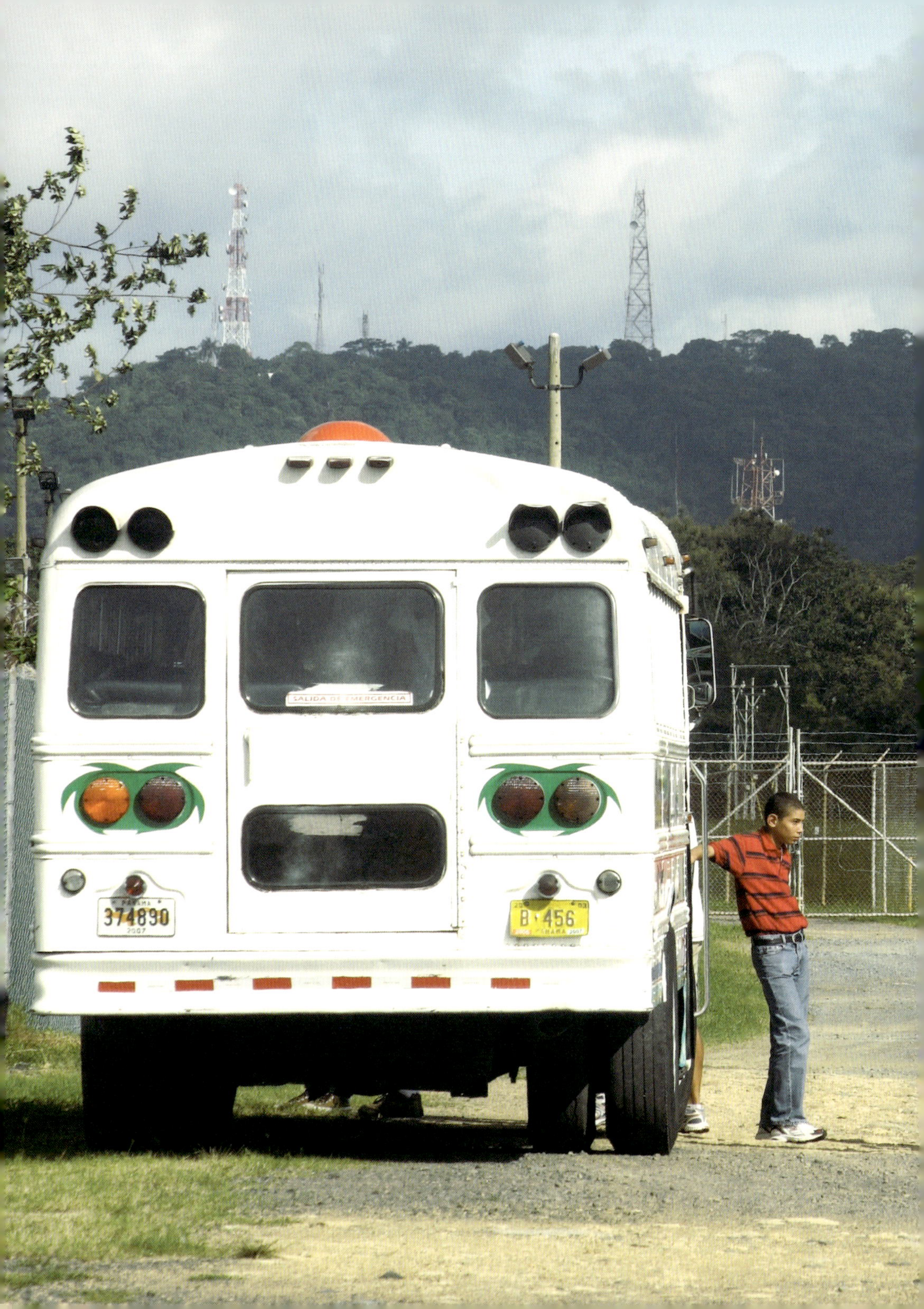

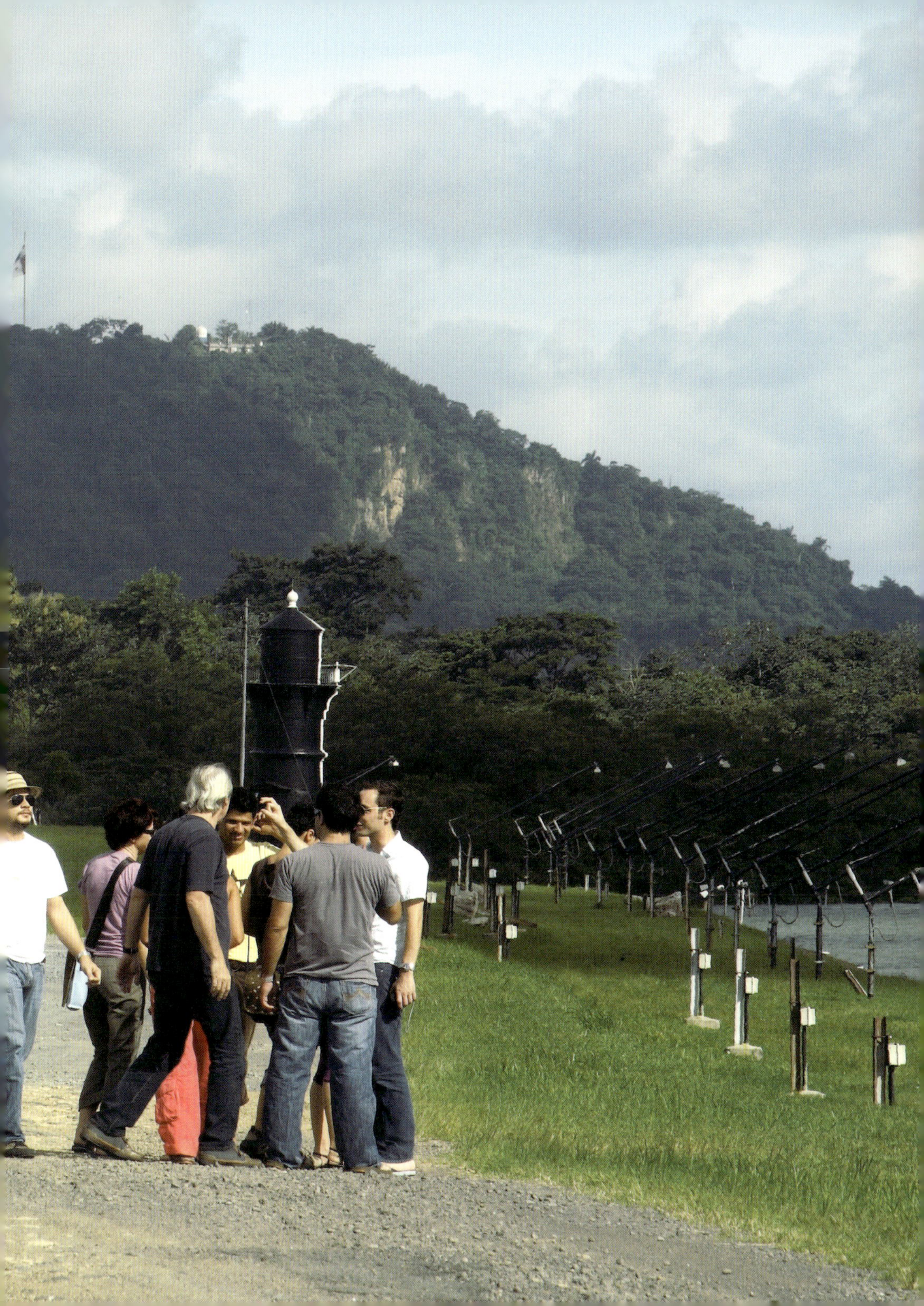

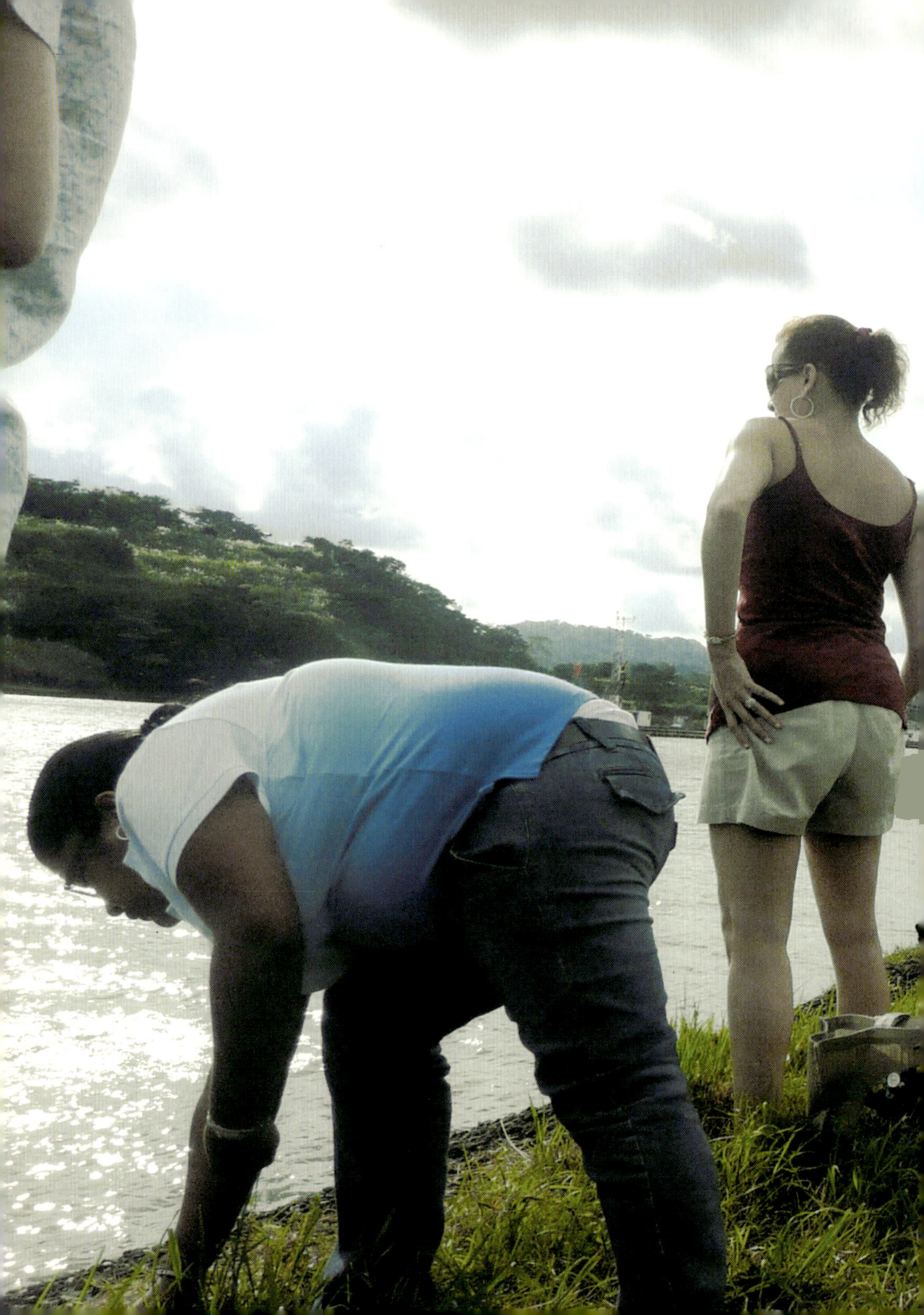

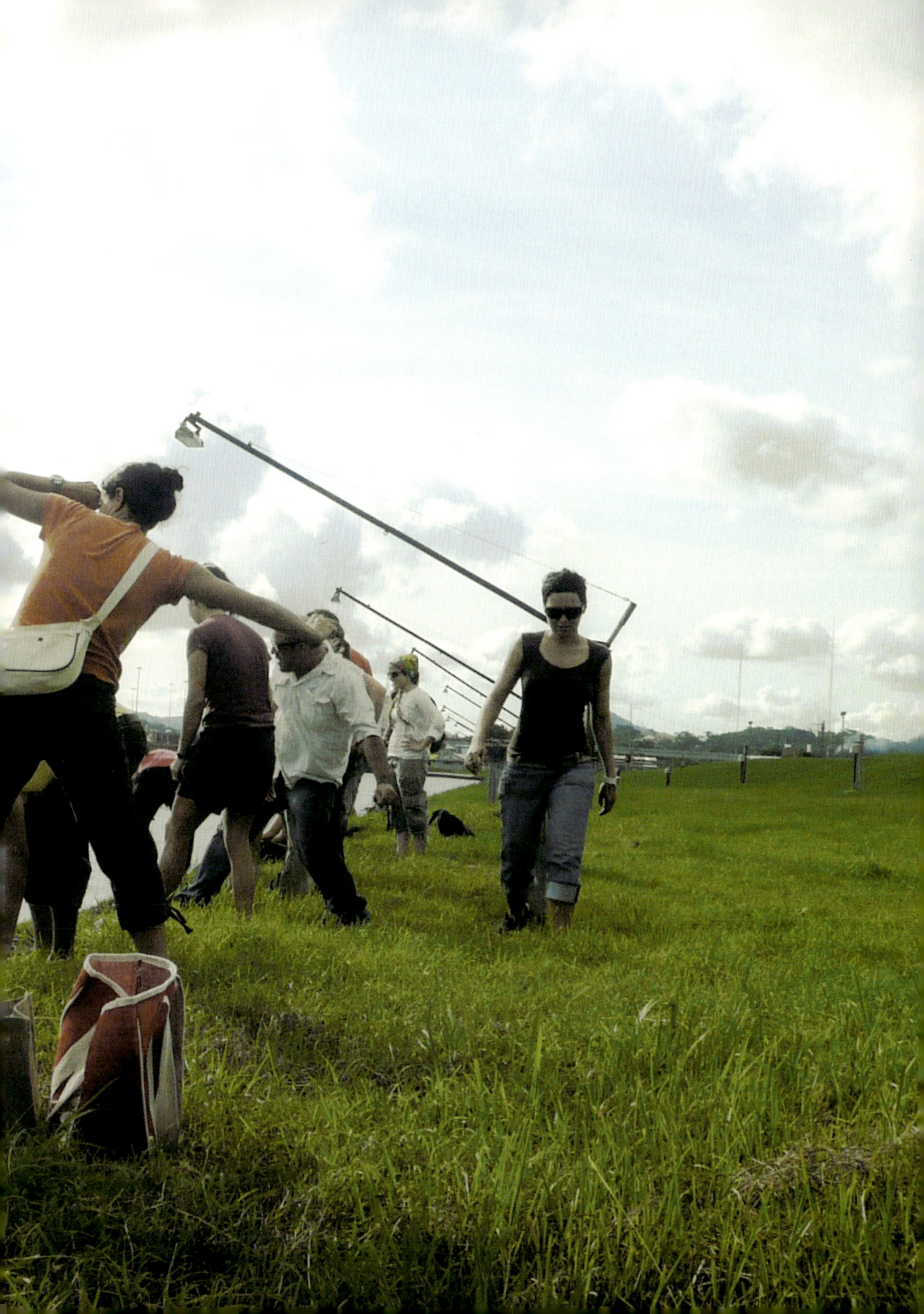

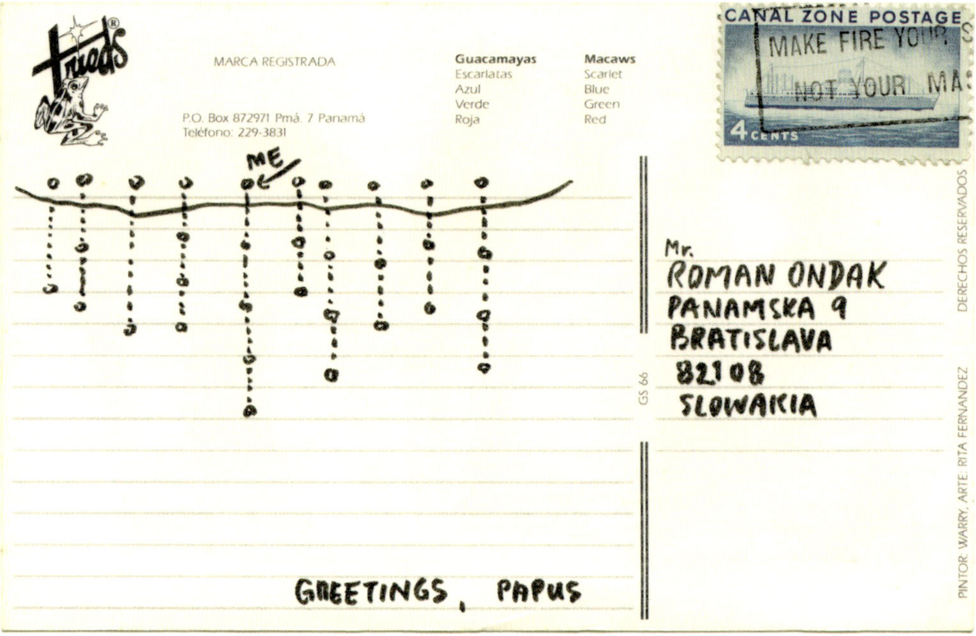

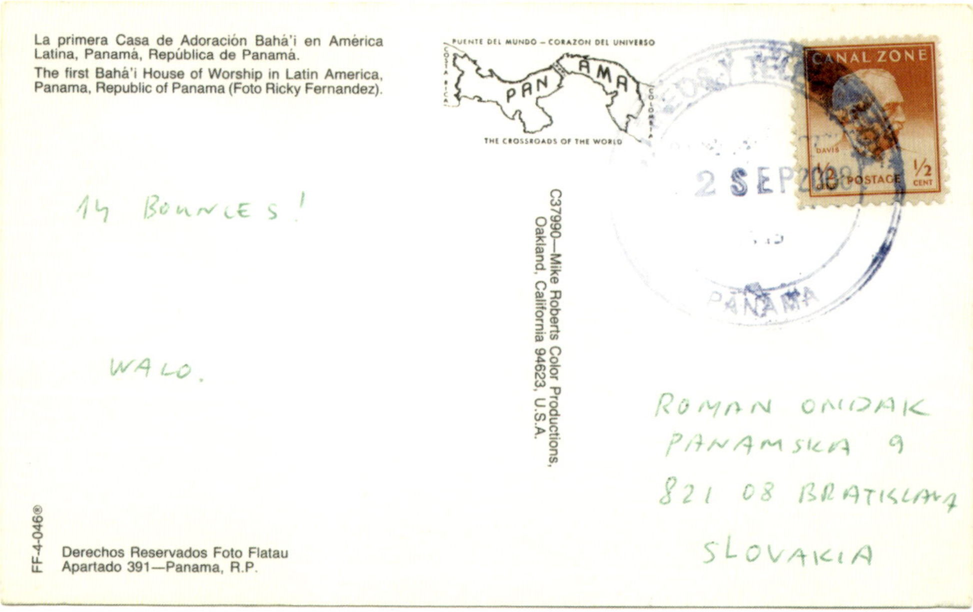

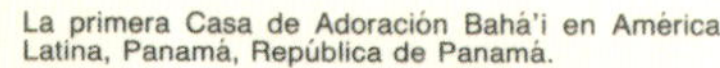

La primera Casa de Adoración Bahá'i en América Latina, Panamá, República de Panamá.
The first Bahá'i House of Worship in Latin America, Panama, Republic of Panama (Foto Ricky Fernandez).

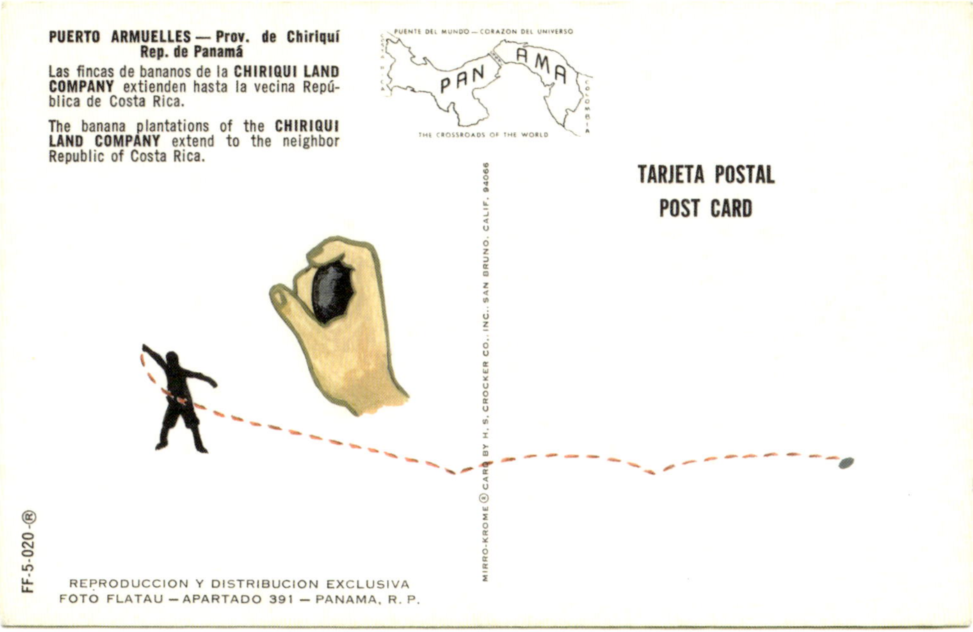

PUERTO ARMUELLES — Prov. de Chiriquí
Rep. de Panamá
Las fincas de bananos de la CHIRIQUI LAND COMPANY extienden hasta la vecina República de Costa Rica.
The banana plantations of the CHIRIQUI LAND COMPANY extend to the neighbor Republic of Costa Rica.
PUENTE DEL MUNDO — CORAZON DEL UNIVERSO
PANAMA
THE CROSSROADS OF THE WORLD
TARJETA POSTAL
POST CARD
MIRRO-KROME® CARD BY H. S. CROCKER CO., INC., SAN BRUNO, CALIF. 94066
FF-5-020-®
REPRODUCCION Y DISTRIBUCION EXCLUSIVA
FOTO FLATAU — APARTADO 391 — PANAMA, R. P.

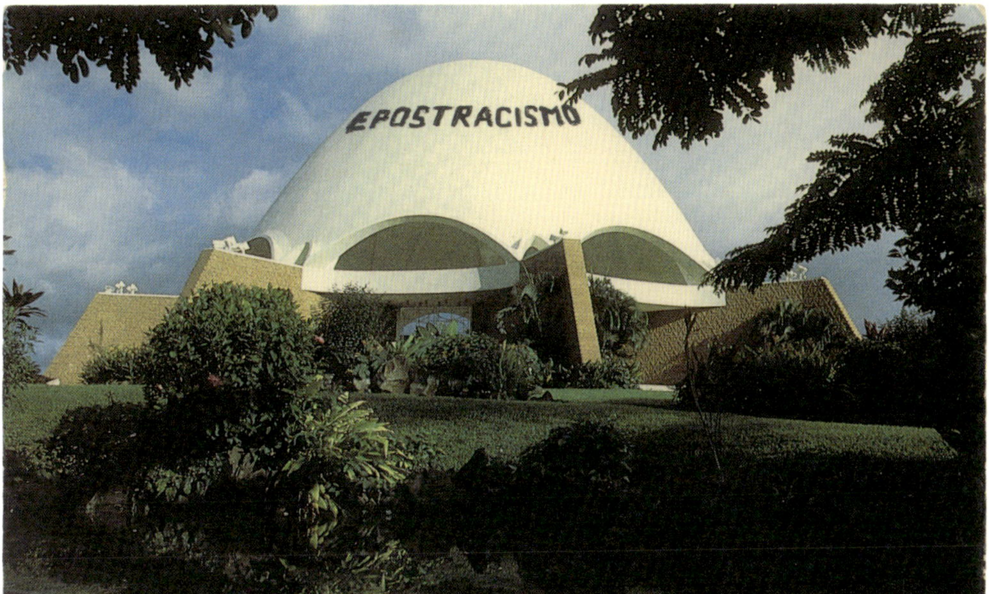

EPOSTRACISMO

Roman Ondak
Zilina / Slowakei 1966

Measuring the Universe, 2007

Performance
Eigentum des Künstlers | Courtesy Galerie Martin Janda, Wien |
gb agency, Paris

My Summer Shoes Rest in Winter, 2007

Schnürsenkel | Shoe laces
Eigentum des Künstlers | Courtesy Galerie Martin Janda, Wien |
gb agency, Paris

Passage, 2004

500 japanische Stahlarbeiter erhielten jeweils eine Tafel Schokolade
und wurden gebeten, aus der Aluminiumfolie der Verpackung
Skulpturen zu formen, nachdem sie die Schokolade gegessen hatten. |

500 Japanese steel workers were each given a bar of chocolate
and asked to mould sculptures from the aluminium foil wrappings after
eating the chocolate.

Installation: Aluminiumfolie, Tisch | Aluminium foil, table
2006 Schenkung des Outset Contemporary Art Fund an die Pinakothek der Moderne

Pocket Money of My Son, 2007

Münzen, Regal aus dem Teil eines Tisches | Coins, shelf made
from a section of a table
Eigentum des Künstlers | Courtesy Galerie Martin Janda, Wien |
gb agency, Paris

30.01.08

Friedhelm, 6.12.07 — Romuald 23.12.07

Mandi, 07.12.07

Tjard 10.02.08 — Antonia, 13.01.08 — Micah, 16.12.07 — Erik 19.01.08 — Michael 09.01.08 — Karsten, 13.01.08

Paul — 10.2.08 — Sorin, 13.01.08 — Michael, 13.02.08 — Klaus, 30.12.07 — Edward, 11.12.07 — Christopher, 13.12.07

e, 16.12.07 — Sebastian, 16.01.07 — Kirim, 06.01.08 — Fabian 10.02.08 Thomas, 30.01.08 — Michael, Carlo, 06.01.08 — Cornelius, 11.01.08 — Matthias 02.02.08

Volker, 01.12.07 — Peter, 11.01.08 — Hans, 23.11.07 — Michael, 06.01.08 Michael, 1.12.07 Uli, 23.11.07

Michael, 13.12.07 — Simon, 27.11.07 — Frank, 8.01.08 — Marco, 1.12.07 — Michael, 23.11.07 — Jürger, 11.01.08 — Christa, 01.02.08 — ROLF, 21.11.07 — Pablo, 23.11.07 — Jain, 11.01.08

Max, 29.12.07 — Thomas 10.01.08 — Reinhard, 8.12.07 — Christoph, 13.12.07 — Michael, 23.11.07 Christian, 4.12.07 — Matthias, 11.12.07 — Marco, 12.12.07 — Christopher

Andreas, 16.12.07 — Otto, 13.02.08 — Randolf 23.12.07 — Peter, 11.01.08 — Felix, 16.12.07 Sebastian 05.01.08 — Gregor 19.01.08 — Wolfram, 02.12.07 — Simon, 22.12.07 — Quirin 27.11.07 — Andi, 12.12.07 — Florian

Christian, 13.11.07 — Clemens — Franz, 5.12.07 — ANDINOS — TANG 5.12.07 — Hussein 24.01.08 Georg, 18.01.08 — Reiner, 8.12.07 — Yves, 16.12.07 — Franz, 24.01.07 — AXEL

Martin, 01.01.08 — Dieter 04.01.08 — Raphael, 11.01.08 — HANS, 13.01.08 — Andrea 11.01.08 Werner, 8.12.07 — Roland, 5.1.08 — Christian, 11.01.08 — Christina, 4.01.07 — Martin, 16.01.08 — Ole

Gerrit 29.01.08 — Frank, 16.12.07 — Leena 24.01.08 — Max, 16.12.07 — Jason, 11.01.08 Victoria — Stefanie, 22.11.07 — Christopher, 11.01.08 — Ola 11.12.07 — David, 12.12.07 — Karen

Daniel, 2.12.07 — Heike 27.11.07 — Anneros, 6.12.07 — Josef, 09.12.07 Hans 14.01.07 — Matthias, 11.01.07 — Dieter, 22.11.07 — Elke, 11.01.08 — UWE, 24.01.07 — Jose

Sibylle, 27.11.07 — Heike 2.2.08 — Sonja, 16.12.07 — Erwin 6.12.07 — Roxanne, 29.12.07 Bernd, 23.11.07 — Rob, 16.12.07 — Ellen, 4.01.07 — Nicolaus, 27.11.07 — Susanne — Hartmut, 24.1

Dagmara, 25.11.07 — Joachim, 27.11.07 — Hugo, 5.12.07 — Ursula, 13.12.07 — Luka, 30.01.08 Dieter, 3.12.07 — Anna, 6.12.07 — Roberto 1.1.08 — Ilse 23.11.07 — Sabine, 24.11.07 — Petra, 11.01.08

mariella 23.12.07 — Birgit, 16.12.07 — Simon 11.01.08 — Raudolf, 12.12.07 Hanns-Jorg, 24.01.07 — Annkristin, 16.12.07 — Amanda 16.01.08 — Roswitha, 30.11.07

Claudia, 8.12.07 — Kathrin, 16.12.07 — Laurie 11.01.08 — Daniel, 13.12.07 — Sarah 11.01.08 — Anna, 6.12.07 — Hildegard 24.11.07 — Estelle — Louise, 11.11.08

Victoria, 30.01.08 — Monika, 16.12.07 — Gudi, 16.12.07 — Kristina 11.01.08 — Niki 27.11.07 — Alfred 02.12.07 — Susanne, 07.12.07 — Niklas, 11.01.08 — Sarah 25.11.07

Ingrid, 11.01.08 Brandon, 13.12.07 — Anna, 4.11.07 — Julia, 11.12.07 — Claudia, 11.01.08 — Ursula 16.12.07 — Antje — Guido, 4.12.07 — Iris

Birgit, 30.11.07 — Bertram, 6.12.07 — Ulli, 11.01.08 Paula, 5.12.07 Aurelia, 11.01.07

Luisa, 29.12.07 — Diana, 11.01.08 — Angelina 17.12.07 — Viktoria, 5.12.07 Flavia, 11.12.07 — Stephen, 11.01.08 — Sofie, 11.01.08 — Morita, 11.12.07

Sarah, 16.12.07 — Hanelore 02.02.08 — Armelie, 11.12.07 — Valentina, 30.12.07 — Steffi, 06.01.08 — Angelika, 13.12.07 — Girina, 02.12.07

Bianca, 5.12.07 — Cecilia, 16.01.07 — Christine, 22.11.07 — Courtney, 11.01.08 — Regina, 11.12.07 — Helli, 23.11.07 — Maya, 06.01.08 — Natalie, 11.01.08 — Norah 14.11.07 — Debi, 5.12.07 — Ann, 11.01.08 — Eva

Sarah, 30.11.07 — Thorsten, 6.12.07 — Erika, 27.11.07 — Elfride, 11.01.08 — Christina 18.01.07 — Karen, 27.11.07 — Amparo, 6.12.07

Sayd, 30.11.07 — Renate, 11.01.08 — Georgia, 30.11.07 — Gertinde, 11.01.08 — Tania, 12.12.07 — Inga, 11.01.08 — Ruth, 23.11.07 — Heide

Brigitta, 6.12.07 — Nathalie 6.02.07 — Anika 11.01.07 — Andreas 11.01.08 — Irene, 12.12.07 — Christa, 11.01.08 — Lisa, 5.12.07 — Verena, 13.12.07 — Mirko 05.01.08 — Hannah, 11.02.07

16.12.07 — MARGRET, 17.01.08 — Christa, 13.12.07 — Monika, 11.02.08 — Regina, 23.12.07 — Joanna, 4.12.07 — Ruth, 23.01.08 — Eva 07.01.08 — ice, 11.12.07 — Diana

Gila, 03.02.08 — Luzie 24.12.07 — Ayu, 12.12.07 — Katharina, 13.12.07 — Anneke, 6.12.07 — Marian

Ingrid, 13.12.07 — Pia, 23.12.07 — Liesa, 13.12.07 — Sandy, 12.12.07 — Thomas, 09.02.08 — Leyla, 13.01.08 — Kim Youn HYEON, 5.12.07 — Gisela, 13.01.08 — Viola, 11.01.08

Tammy 12.12.07 — 志敬 — 19.01.08 — Dorothea, 06.01.08 — Maike, 11.01.08 — Barbara 22.01.08

23.01.08 — Pippa, 13.01.08 — Aunaleanor, 11.01.08 — Claudia, 13.01.08

Louisa, 13.01.08 — Domingo, 13.01.08

nrad 27.12.07 — Luisa, 13.01.08 — Paula, 13.01.08 — Jara 05.01.08

06.01.08 — Zoa, 30.12.07 — Viktoria, 13.01.08

Victoria 03.02.08 — Philipp, 16.12.07

Sophie 19.01.08. — Niklas, 17.01.08 — Sophie 19.01.08 — Sebastian, 09.02.08

Emma, 13.01.08

Elsa, 13.01.08 — Verena, 13.01.08 — Hannah 02

Emanuel — 10.2.08

Zeno, 25.1.08

Amelie, 13.01.08 — René, 07.02.08

Odile, 22.12.07

Mira Levana, — 10.2.08

Miriam, 27.12.07

Olga, 16.12.07

Veronika, 16.12.07

Leonidas, 27.11.07

Nelson, 9.01.08

— Harry, 30.11.07   — Jörg, 18.12.07   Alex, 27.11.07

Christopher, 13.12.07   — Jürgen, 5.1.08   — Volkier, 30.12.07   Markus, 8.12.07   Jürgen, 11.01.08

— Matthias, 02.02.08   — Wim, 9.12.07   Wolfgang 19.12.07   Stephan, 16.12.07   Milo, 1.12.07   Piergiorgio, 02.01.08   — Jean-Marc, 4.12.07

Pablo, 23.11.09   — Iain, 12.12.07   Frank, 6.12.07   Frederik Treugut 28.12.07   Thomas   Andreas, 02.02.08   Christian, 02.12.07

Pete, 12.12.07   Tim, 25.11.07   Klaus, 30.12.07   Josef   Brigitte 18.12.07   Robert, 8.12.07   Niklas   Inge, 02.02.08   Christian, 02.12.07

Florian, 24.11.07   Fabian, 21.12.07   Johanes 6.12.07   Josef, 4.12.07   Victor   Alfredo, 8.12.07

Eugene, 29.12.07   Isabel, 04.02.08   Franz 28.12.07   Peter, 23.11.07   Julie, 1.12.07   Bodo, 30.12.07

Alfons, 11.12.03   ANDREAS, 21.11.07   Bernhard, 24.11.07   Heike, 4.12.07   Michael   Carl, 27.11.07

NE 24.01.07   Josef, 24.11.07   Alexander, 17.11.07   Christian 28.11.07   Steffen, 6.12.07   Jörg, 25.11.07   Alice, 18.12.07   Katrin, 24.11.07

Hartmut, 24.12.07   Julia   Jonatan   Erika, 16.12.07   Alexander, 9.12.07   Mischa, 24.01.07   Monika, 22.11.07

Roswitha, 30.11.07   Dubravka 24.11.07   Johana, 28.11.07   ULRIKE, 21.11.07   Ella   David, 12.12.07   Angelika 25.11.07

Otto, 24.11.07   Andrea 11.12.07   Ulrike, 24.11.07   Gina, 24.11.07   Jani, 27.11.07

BIRGIT, 21.11.07   Martina, 6.12.07   Marcus   Heike, 25.11.03   Asuka, 24.11.07   Ingbert, 24.11.07

Irene, 23.11.07   Doris 1.1.08   Katya, 24.11.07   Corina 24.11.07   Hin Kee 11.07   Klaudia

Sarah, 25.11.07   Marta, 23.12.07   Adrian, 30.11.07   Sept 24.11.07   Camp

Anna 2.12.07   27.11.07   Maria, 22.11.07   Eva, 1.12.07

Ulrike, 24.11.07   Marzia 24.11.07   Edith, 8.12.07   Yiota, 25.11.07   Giulia, 28.11.07   Giulia 1.1.08

Alice, 1.12.07   Conny 02   Annemarie 11.12.07   Nina, 4.12.07   Sayed, 30.11.07   Maria, 28.11.07

Ayaka, 02.12.07   Charlotte, 5.1.08   Johanna, 07.02.08

Kate 20/1/98   Michael, 08.02.08   — Johannes 22.12.07   Marina 24.1.08

— Hagen 02.01.07

— Emilia, 13.01.08   — Leon, 03.01.08   — Johanna 8.12.07

— Nick, 20.01.08   — Irena, 07.02.08

— David, -10.2.08

— Emma, 13.01.08   — David, 07.02.08

— Hannab 02.01.08   — Lena, 4.12.07

— Libby, -10.2.08

— Frederik, 25.1.08   — Béla, 16.12.07

— René, 07.02.08   — Miriam, 08.01.08   — Laura 27.01.08

— Jari, 4.12.07   — Leonie, 13.01.08   — Greta, -10.02.08

— Antonia, 13.01.08   Mathis, 4.12.07

— Ines, 16.12.07

— Sander, 16.12.07

— Tabea, 08.01.08

— Liam, 13.01.08   — Undine, 30.12.07

— Nelson, 9.01.08   — Clara, 13.01.08

Ferdinand 1.1.08

— Björn,- 10.02.08   — Franz, 20.12.07   — Adrian, 16.12.07

ric, 21.12.07   — Markus, 11.01.08   Maxime, 11.01.08   — Rainhold, 6.12.07
— Andreas, 23.11.07   Toksadumola, 18.12.07.   — Jacques, 11.01.08   — Matthias, 30.12.07
Christoph, 15.12.07   Martin, 02.12.07   W.F.K. 20.12.07
Martin, 11.01.08   Moritz, 24.11.07   Julien, 13.01.08   Marko, 11.01.08 Markus, 26.01.08 Glen, 15.12.07 — Enrico, 23.11.07
ANDRIES, 11.01.08   — Simon 09.02.08 Dieter, 7.12.07 — Jan, 11.12.07   Roland,- 10.2.08 — Lüs, 06.01.08   Michael, 03.01.08 Christian, 24.11.07 Peter, 09.02.08 — Hanna, 8.12.07
— Rudolf 09.02.08   Peter, 11.01.08   Christian, 18.01.08 — Philip, 18.12.07   Andrew, 19.12.07 Philippe 01.01.07 Ahmed, 11.12.07   — Sigsi, 17.1.08
Siegfried, 16.12.07   Paul 24.11.07   Karl, 24.11.07   Robert, 24.11.07 Josef, 21.12.07 Georg, 9.12.07   MARTIN, 21.11.07   Ursel 02.02.08   Franz, 30.11.07   — Sergey, 14.12.07
11.07   Alfred 8.12.07   Klaus, 30.11.07   Niels, 25.11.07   Wolfgang, 13.12.07 Rolf, 9.12.07   Francesca, 5.12.07 Ralf 26.01.08   Andreas, 24.11.07   Dirk, 30.11.07
1.07 — Harald, 11.01.08   Oskar, 13.01.08   Mike, 8.12.07 Nick, 26.12.07   Deniz, 30.11.07   Freja, 9.12.07   Stefan, 6.12.07 — Sandi, 8.12.07   MEGAN, 22.12.07
— Antonia, 30.11.07   Hiltrud 24.11.07 HONAM, 19.01.08 Uli, 22.11.07 Martin 23.12.2007   Antonio, 18.11.07   Bruno, 15.12.07   Christian, 25.11.07
Suzanne, 24.11.07   Claudia 02.02.08 Bernard, 24.11.07   Anja, 02.02.08   Simone, 02.02.08   Ingo 24.11.07   Anike, 16.12.07   Corinna, 24.11.07
 bel AMY, 17.01.08   Ndeni, 11.01.08 Jasmin, 13.12.07 Danielo 24.11.08 CO.NGOANH Giorgia, 11.12.07   Karin, 11.01.08   Bärbel, 16.12.07   FELICITAS, 21.11.07
stine 24.11.07 HANN, 21.11.07   Summer, 9.12.07   Anni, 23.11.07   Christin, 9.12.07   Michael, 8.12.07   Franziska 6.12.07 Sebastian, 30.11.07   Herbert 23.11.07   Christina, 7
Heike, 17.01.08 Margarethe, 6.12.07 Lisabeth, 29.11.07   Sara, 4.12.07   Rachel 23.11.07   Mila, 28.11.07 Melani 24.11.07   Filiz 23.11.07   Tina 24.11.07
— Hanne, 8.12.07 Daniela, 29.12.07 Alexandra, 23.11.07   Bibbi 24.11.07   Gudrun, 24.11.07   Ingeborg, 18.12.2007   Elisabeth, 4.12.07   Helga, 15.12.07
Christoph, 23.11.07   Blanka, 11.11.07 Heidi, 24.11.07   Brenda, 24.11.07   Yvonne, 21.12.07 Erika, 26.01.08   Sam, 22.01.08   Halle 8.12.07
Florin Nana 8.12.07   Beatrice, 9.12.07   Irene, 30.11.07 Mariella Francesca, 30.11.07 Maria, 23.11.07 Katia, 23.11.07   Frederike, 8.12.07   AnnaMaria, 6.12.07
— Katja, 11.01.07   Timo, 30.11.07 — Doris, 19.02.07 — Evangelia 27.12.07 Sabine 27.01.08   NEVENA, 11.01.08   Sabine, 11.01.07   Miriam, 11.12.07   Alexandra, 11.11.07
Stephanie, 20.12.07   Andie   Lara, 30.11.07 Conie, 24.11.07 HATEA 15.12.07   Anne 04.01.08   Nina, 1.12.07
na, 1.01.08   Anika, - 10.02.08 Martina, 04.02.08   — Dal, 11.1.08 Inneke, 12.07   Christel, 11.07 — Anja, 28.11.07   — Anja, 23.11.07
— Daria 6.02.07   — Pranvera, 30.11.07 — Nina 6.02.08   Eli 27.01.08   Aldrina 02.12.07   — Elko 26.12.07 Brigitte 23.12.07   Olga 27.1
— Gyöngyi, 30.11.07   — Shino, 10.02.08   — Ingeborg,- 08.02.08   Naira, 29.11.07   — Aline,- 31.01.08
— Karli,- 10.02.08   Kurdi, 30.11.07 — Johanes, 24.11.07   — — HERRA, 9.12.07   — Martha, 30.12.07   — 平田祥, 15.01.08
— Emil, 22.12.07

                                                                                — Marie, 07.02.08

— Caroline, 07.01.08,   — Sophie, 11.01.08   — Severin,- 10.2.08   — Anna- M

— Manuel 08.01.08   — Jan 27.01.08   — Mina, 25.1.08   — Fanny, 02.01.08   — Aleksander 02.01.08

— Hannes, 13.01.08   — Esther,- 10.02.08

— Julia, 24.11.07   — Solina 22.12.2007

              — Max 27.01.08   — Thomas, 20.01.08 Paula, 30.12.07
                                                                                                  — Vinnie 23.12.2007

— Γιάννης, 27.12.07   — Denis 03.01.08   — LIVIA 22.12.2007

                                                                                              — Lenny 23.12.07

                                          — Florian, 11.01.08
                                                                                              — Raphaeli 10.2.08

                      — Sofia, 24.11.07
— Finn, 29.11.07

                                                                                                        — Emili, 24.

                        — Eline, 25.11.07

_ Steven, 8.12.07

_ Basti, 24.11.07   _ Nils, 05.01.08

_ Michael, 11.01.08

d, 6.12.07   _ Gerd, 4.12.07   _ Dominik, 09.02.08
_ Matthias, 30.12.07   Brian, -10.2.08 Avne, 24.11.07   _ Manuel, 03.01.08,
_, 15.12.07 _ Enrico, 23.11.07   _ Mario, 30.12.07   _ Jon, 15.12.07   _ István, 24.11.07   _ Walter, 29.12.07   _ Nie
_, 29.12.07   _ Hanna, 8.12.07   _ Tobias, 30.12.07 _ Andi, 28.12.4   _ Peter, 30.12.07   John, 06.01.08   _ Dietmar, 16.12.07 _ Simon, 3.12.07
_, SIGGI, 17.1.08   _ Paul, 23.12.07   _ David,-10.2.08   _ Daniel, 02.02.07 _ Pleasance, 02.02   Gustav, 11.01.08
_ Sergey, 14.12.07   _ GERARD, 19.12.07   _ Dan 03.01.08 _ Samuel, 02.02.07   _ Philipp, 02.01.08   _ Thomas 25.11.07 _ Boris, 16.11.08 Bernd, 24.11.07   _ Cesare, 07.12.07   _ Martin 22.12.07
_ Dirk, 30.11.07 _ Philipp, 03.02.08   _ Boris, 24.11.07 _ Dominik, 23.11.07   _ Klaus, 15.12.07 Sebastian, 11.04.08   _ Helmut, 01.01.08   _ Klaus, 17.01.08 _ Alina, 21.12.07   _ Jochen, 22.11.07   _ Klau
_, 30.12.07 _ Johannes, 04.02.08 KABa, 14.11.07   _ Anatoli, 03.08.08   _ Rico, 30.11.07 _ Stefan 30.01.07   _ Danilo, 11.12.07   _ Gerhard, 8.12.07   _ Heitor 04.01.08   _ STEFAN 23.12.07 _ Cliff, 03.01.08 _ Mordisei, 26.1
_ Hansdieter, 9.01.08   _ Kathrin, 8.12.07 _ Joachim, 23.11.07   _ Digiu, 28.11.07 _ Jonas, 8.12.07   _ Gerhard, 8.12.07
MEGAN 22.12.07   _ Udo, 23.11.07   _ Josef, 23.11.07 _ Kristin, 8.12.07   _ Mirko, 11.12.03   _ Hardi, 22.01.08   Stephanie, 6.12.07   Ronja, 26.01.08   Anita, 21.12.07   Nico, 28.
_ Katrin, 8.12.07   _ Pavel, 6.12.07   _ Philipp, 30.12.07 _ Frouke   _ Katerina, 30.12.07   _ Jakyb 6.12.07   _ Friedhelm, 02.02.08   RESSA, 21.11.07   Benjamin, 04.02.08 JeníČek, 23.11.07   _ Wolfgang, 20.
_, 5.11.07 Fernanda 04.04.08   16.01.08   _ Sandra, 24.11.03   Sonja, 22.11.07   _ Jan, 15.01.08   _ Sylvia, 03.02.08 Mozor 02   _ Mary, 21.11.07 _ Deborah, 8.12.07   Andr
_ Hrafnhildur, 16.2.07 _ Alexander, 11.12.07   _ Roger, 26.12.03 _ Astrid, 08.01.08 _ Morris, 21.12.07 _ Christian, 26.01.08 _ Mari, 03.12.07   _ Sabrina 19.12.07 _ Gerhard, 28.11.07
rinna, 24.11.07   _ Horst, 18.12.2007 _ Nils, 18.12.07 _ Bruno, 06.01.08 _ Eberhard 2009   _ Karla 30.01.08   _ Hannah, 23.11.07   _ Giovanni, 5.12.07
_ FELICITAS, 21.11.07 Leopold-Otten Dominik, 30.11.07 _ Elisej, 12.01.07   _ Klaus, 18.12.09 _ NABI, 24.11.07   _ Mario, 24.11.07   _ 101   _ Lena, 22.01.08 _ Marion, 5.12.07 29.12.07
_, 23.11.07 Birgit Stern Carolin, 5.12.07   _ Niklas, 11.9   Erika, 05.01 _ Maria, 11.10.4 Johanna, 4.12.07   _ Silvia, 24.11.07 Rosetta, 11.08   _ Sandra, 6.12.07 Sachiko, 03.01.08   Brett,
_ Christine, 25.11.07   _ Regina, 18.01.08   _ Kiona, 31.01.08   _ Marie-Odile, 25.11.03   _ Melina, 25.11.03 Ludmila, 24.01.08   _ Frans, 19.01.08   _ Thomas, 22.11.07   Isabelle, 28.11.
_ Tina, 24.11.07   _ Arabella, 9.12.07 _ Lukas, 29.11.0 _ Dolphine, 3.12.07   _ Hana, 6.12.07   _ Eva, 24.11.07   _ Svitlana, 02.12.07 Ariane, 24.11.07 _ Thomas, 27.11.07
_ Helga, 15.12.07   _ Heike, 11.12.07 _ Sophie, 04.02.08 _ Lydia, 13.1 Antero, 2.12.07 _ Roswila, 06.02.08   _ Hanna, 23.11.07 _ Eva, 8.12.07 _ Ingrid, 15.12.07 _ Philip, 8.02.07 _ Oksana, 02.12.07 Pauline
_ Toni, 04.02.08 _ Reza, 23.11.07   _ Heii 18.2.07   _ Renate, 4.12.07   _ Maria, 8.12.07   _ Vladimir, 24.11.07   _ Jovanni, 24.11.07 _ Christina, 01.12.07   _ Mann, 23.12.07   _ Eva, 04.11.07 Eli
_ Anna, 8.12.07   _ AnnaMaria, 6.12.07 Inci, 6.12.07 _ Maria, 30.12.07 _ Kristine, 24.11.07   _ Ulli, 8.12.07 _ Elisabetta, 30.11.07 _ Petra, 30.11.07 _ Gabriele, 26.01.08 _ Eva, 04.01.08 Eth
_ Alexandra, 25.11.07 _ Myriam, 22.12.07 _ Kagal, 13.12.07   _ Julia, 30.12.07 _ Sim 27.01.08 _ Dorit, 24.11.07 _ Kaffia, 13.02.07   _ Marina, 26.01.2001   jenny, 17.01.07 Waltraud
_ Miriam, 11.12.07 _ Angela 8.12.07 _ Sergei 3.12.07 _ Jovita, 6.12.07   _ Maja, 30.12.07   _ Letizia, 3.02.07 _ Ulrike, 30.12.07 Ondine, 31.12.07 _ Renate, 02.12.07 _ Kim, 11.12.07   _ Sophia, 01.12.07 Eleon
_ Nina, 1.12.07 UH 21 26.12.07   Johanna, 26.12.07   _ Henry 15.12.07   _ Susanne, 51.08   Erika, 19.01.08   _ Lucia, 24.11.07 Lara 20.01.08   Andr
itte 23.12.07   _ Gabriele, 17.01.07   _ Josy, 3.01.08   _ Julia 27.12.07   _ Ismirin, 30.12.2007   Ophelie, 23.12.07 Lambri, 01.02.07 Caroline, 01.01.08   _ Ingrid,
_ KARiN- 17/11/08 Olga 27.12.09 _ Jula, 6.12.07   BANTE, 22.12.07   _ Antonella, 24.11.07   _ Andrea, 24.11.07 _ Sima 09.02.08   _ Muriel, 23.12.07
_, 15.01.08   _ Chantal, 17.01.08   _ Johanna 31.01.01 Renate 02.01.08   _ João 04.01.08 Antonia, 04.01.08 Mayte, 8.12.07   _ Maria, 01.08   _ Katharina
_ Aline, -31.01.08   _ 21307 WALTER THAILAND 10.2.08   _ Karin, 01.02.08
_ Stephanie 1.02.04   _ Aline, -02.02.08   _ Elisabeth, 12.12.07   _ Olga, 6.12.07
_ Judit, 29.11.07

_ Anna-Maria, 24.11.07 _ Frederick, -10.2.08   _ Johann 04.01.08   _ Jasp
verin, -10.2.08   _ Hilda 20.01.08
_ Jonathan 05.01.08
_ Carla, 16.12.07
_ Loan 05.01.08
_ Tερψιχόρη, 30.2.07
_ Juanna, 07.02.02   _ Jesús, 07.02.08
_ Fran, 07.02.08
_ Maria 04.01.08
_ David, 07.02.08   _ Liv, 25.1.08
_ Vinnie 23.12.2007
_ Tamara, 12.01.08
_ Diego, 07.02.08
_ Emma 04.01.08

jenny 23.12.07

_ Nelio, 26.01.08

_ Raphaeli, 10.2.08   _ Floyd, 13.01.08

_ Benjamin, 11.12.07   _ Franziska, 51.08   _ Felicia, 11.12.07
_ Emma, 8.12

_ Emili, 24.11.07   _ Friday, 20.12.07   _ Kolja 08.01.08

—Wolfgang, 29.12.07

Christian, 8.12.07   —Richard, 13/01/08

—Jose, 07.02.08   —Alexander 27.11.07, 24.11.07   —David, 11.12.07

Alex, 03.02.08   —Stephan, 12.01.08   —Marcus, 20.12.07   —Thomas, 09.02.08

Dirk, 8.12.07   MAGNUS, 21.11.07   —Philip 25.12.07   —Erik,   —Johanetta,   —Ralf, 12.12.07

—Gerhard 08.01.08   —Jan, 23.11.07   Brad, 21.12.07   Stefan, 28.11.07 Kolja, 02.12.07

Sebastian, 15.12.07   Flo Bernd 04.01.08   —Irun, 19.12.07   Harald 27.01.08   Tobias,   Stefan, 28.11.07 Martin, 23.11.07

Johann, 22.11.07   Matthias 18.12.2007   Stefan, 23.11.07   Snake, 12.12.07   Chris, Martin, 23.11.07

Thomas, 24.11.07 William, 23.11.07   Johanes, 28.11.07   Sigmund, 26.12.07 Holly, 22.01.08

Antonio, 07.02.08   Ofer, 03.02.08 Werner, 17.01.07   Regine, 19.01.07   Michael, 28.11.07 Heidi, Davorin, Bettina, 02.12.07

Raphael, 23.11.07—Kevin 23.12.07   Graziello, 29.11.07 Florent 2.2.08 Waldemar, 6.12.07   Christiane, 9.12.07

Christoph, 02.12.07   Adrienne 02.02.08   Andreas 24.12.07   David 23.11.07   Jürgen, 6.12.07   Mark, 23.11.07 Claire, 21.11.07

Etienne, 28.11.07   Johen, 25.11.07   John, 24.11.07   Christian, 21.11.07   Sandra 9.12.07 Margit, 9.12.07 Samuel,

Macarena,   Robert 27.12.07   Monika 02.12.07   Elisabeth, 18.12.2007   Enrico, 24.11.07 Ingulf, 11.12.07

Brigit 24.12.07 5.12.07   Isabel 21.01.07   Hilly, 9.12.07   David, 28.11.07 Gisela, 01.02.07   RKa, 23.11.07   Elenore 22.12.07

Martin 02.12.07   Beate 11.12.07   BENGT 24.11.07

Gabi, 11.12.07   Dirk 24.11.07   Lidija 26.01.07   Lars, 24.11.07   Alfons,   Hermann, 07.12.07 Sara,

Roger, 26.12.07   Meg, 24.11.07   INGRID, 29.11.07   Ingrid, 28.11.03   Gerhard, 28.11.07   Hanka, 6.12.07   Daniela 28.11.07

Barbara, 24.11.07 Aline, 22.11.07   Jenny, 16.12.07   Rose, 10.12.07   Hubert 03.12.07 Sabrina   Lenry 26.12.07   Myriam, 07.12.07 Anita,

Sanni, 9.12.07   Miriam, 26.12.07   Christina, 02   Victoria, 23.11.07   Lucia 16.12.07   Silvia, 8.12.03   Kate, 23.11.07   Tris, 02.12.07

Sophia, 24.11.07   Franceska, 02.01.08   Melina 08.01.08   Elena, 22.01.08   Julia, 07.12.07   Kiki, 02.12.07

Audrey 5/12/07   Aghese 22.01.08   Ai Phuong, 7.12.07   Manuela, 16.12.07   Ricky, 11.12.07

Claudia, 02.01.08 BRAGANA 02.12.07   Leonie, 13.01.08   Erin, 23.12.07   Angelika 16.01.08   Lisa, 28.11.07   Maria, 28.12.07 Jakob 05.0

Stefania, 28.11.07   Anne-Laure 3.01.08   LiLia, 07.12.07   Miyuki 13/12/02   Julia, 29.07.08

Irene, 28.12.07   Andreu, 09.02.08   SORO 13.12.07   Pepa, 24.11.07   Alexandra, 16.12.07   Karla, 07.02.08

Tiphaine 13.12.07   —Roselys 04.01.08   —Noa, 03.02.08   —Julia 20.12.07

—Jusi, 02.01.08

—Anita, 29.01.08 —Rebekka, 13.01.08

—Maximilien 22

—David, 03.02.08   —Zoe, 26.12.07   —Anna, 26.12.07

—Lea, 13.01.08   —Barbara 29.12.07   —Charlotte, 03.02.08

—Patrick 03.02.08   —Kajetan, 03.02.08   —Kevin, 03.02.08 —Leon, 16.12.07

—Isabel, 6.1.08

—Ole, 03.02.08   —Filip 25.01.08   —Javi, 07.02.08

—Frederik 20.01.08   —Enzo, 13.01.08   —Anna, 07.02.08   —Davi, 09.02.08

—Romi, 10.02.08

—Valentin 20.01.08

—Maiwenn, 03.02.08

—Sarah 20.01.08

—Thorvald, 21.12.07

—Olivia, 24.11.07

— Simon, 23.12.07

— Gereon, 11.12.07

— Horbert 05.01.08

— Jens, 27.11.07

11.12.07   — Frank, 03.02.08   — Matthias, 03.02.08

— Nicolas, 24.11.07   — Christian, 9.12.07   — Peter, 27.12.07

olf, 12.12.07   — Antoine 27.01.08   — Hans-Peter, 13.01.08   — Markus 04.01.08   Peter, 28.11.07   Christoph, 03.02.08   Brian, 9.12.07   — Nicolas 05.01.08

— Philipp, 11.01.08   — Todd, 02.12.07   — Lukas- 08.02.08-   Sylvia, 28.11.07   Martin 27.01.08   Stefan, 9.12.07   — Daniel, 02.12.07

3.11.07   Friedrich 04.01.08   — Steffan, 22.01.08   Alessandro, 16.12.07   Thierry, 22.12.07   Andy, 03.01.08   — Artur, 27.11.07   Eva, 03.02.08   Jochen, 29.12.07   Max, 31.12.08

Zsolt, 21.11.07   — Frank, 08.02.08   Peter, 28.11.07   Frank, 6.12.07   — Melanie, 13.04.08   — Christoph, 25.1.08   Harald, 02.01.08   Felix, 9.12

— Dieter, 09.02.08   — Cyrille, 29.12.07   — Christian, 28.11.07   — Heinz, 17.01.08   — Marco 1.1.08   Gunnar, 26.12.07   IVAN   Raimund, 06.01.08

Tina, 02.12.07   — Massimo, 02.12.07   — Maxime 05.01.08   — Jerome, 03.02.08   Martin, 23.11.07   Kristina, 22.01.08   Lothar   Siegfried, 23.11.07   Anil, 22.01.08   Ludi, 30.11.07

Werner, 22.01.08   — Monika, 29.11.07   Hous, 22.11.07   Berud, 15.12.07   Heino, 11.12.07   Hanns, 02.01.08   Emma 02.01.08   Kevin, 23.11.07   Silvio, 2.1

git, 9.12.07   — Daniel, 02.12.07   Reinhard, 10.01   Tomas, 24.11.07   Frank, 23.11.07   — Jürgen, 16.12.07   Korbinian, 28.11.07   Carmin, 16.12.07   Katja, 21.11.07

gulf, 11.12.07   — Roland 26.01.08   — Franziska, 20.12.2007   Dylan, 29.11.07   — John, 18.01.08   Björn, 28.11.07   MATTEO, 24.11.07   Stefan, 26.12.07   Eric, 10.01.08   Tabea, 9.12.07

Diane, 22.12.07   — Constantin   6.12.07   Genevieve, 24.11.07   katharina   Corinna, 23.11.07   Maviah 29.11.07   Alexander, 23.11.07   József, 29.11.07

MICHAELA   — Riddick, 17.01.07   Franzi   Valentin   Jürgen   Ute, 23.11.07   Elke, 23.11.07   Carlotta   Corina, 23.11

— Lilith   — Agathe, 23.11.07   Bärbel, 23.11.07   Haike, 02.01.07   Marion, 2.11.07   Yvonne, 30.11.07   Constanza   Moira, 23.11.07   Katja, 02.12.07   Loren

— Tanja   — Christina, 23.11.07   — Claudia, 23.11.07   Diane, 9.12.07   Steffi, 23.12.07   Elke   Gabi, 11.12.07   Louisa, 16.12.07   Sarah, 5.1.08

Iris, 02.12.07   — Christiane 9.12.07   — Catu, 5.12.07   — Inge 02.01.07   Maria, 23.11.07   — Inge, 11.12.07   Mia   Nieves, 6.12.07   Christine 23.12.07   Barbara, 24.11.07   Leila, 9.1

— Anna, 24.11.07   Charlotte, 27.11.07   Valentina, 02.01.07   Ursula, 02.01.08   Michael   Isabella 9.12.07   Madeline 27.11.07   Undine, 6.12.07   Felix 29.11

— Maria, 24.11.07   Andrea, 15.12.07   Ann Kathrin 20.12   Molly   Ashley, 5.1.08   Charlotte, 02.12.07   MIHHA 29.12.07   SINAEJWON 9.12.07

— Jakob 05.01.08   — Rena 30.01.08   Ulla, 12.12.07   Nora 9.12.07   Franziska, 26.12.07   MAYKO, 17.01.08   Majka 9.12.07

— Fabiola 29.12.07   Kelsey, 5.1.08   Milena, 02.01.08   Dorotea, 27.11.07   Hannah, 24.11.07   Michiko 26.12.07   Sicia, 03.01.08

Karla, 03.02.08   — Franca, 02.12.07   — Christa 04.01.08   — Felix, 29.12.07   Alex, 02.02.08

— Sandra 01.02.08   — Linus, 03.02.08   — larah, 13.01.08   — Nils, 06.01.08

— Tim, 13.01.08   — René, 07.02.08

— Sergey, 07.02.08   — Benjamin 04.01.08   — Florian, 25.01.08

— Natalia, 07.02.08

Maximilian 22.12.07   — Jakob, 03.02.08   — Claudia, 24.11.07

— Catharina, 08.02.08

Charlotte, 03.02.08   — Daniel, 07.02.08   — Eduard, 13.01.08

16.12.07   Tobias 20.01.08

— Malin, 03.02.08   — Justin, 8.02.2008

07.02.08   — Sara, 02.12.07   — Jonas, 03.02.08

02.08   — Copete, 09.00.08

— Justin, 02.12.07   — Lea 25.01.08   — Louise 25.01.08   — Tobia

— Vincent, 6.1.08

— 유비 30.12.07   — Marisi, 08.02.08

— Lilia, 03.02.08   — Kara, 26.12.07   — Eva 23.12.07

— Ada, 06.01.08

— Johanna, 06.01.08

— Casimir, 13.1.08

— Robert, 20.12.07

— Robert, 07.12.07 — Arne, 03.02.08 — Martin, 22.11.07

— Willy, 29.12.07 — Claas, 17.01.08 — Sebastian, 6.12.07 — Stefan 20.01.08

— Jan, 23.11.07 — Hanswerner, 9.12.07 — Matthias, 20.12.07

Alessandro, 6.12.07 — Benjamin, 02.12.07 — Franz 26.12.07 — Christian, 18.12.07 — Nils, 16.12.07 — Bernhard, 23.02.07

hael, 24.11.07 — Andrian, 6.12.07 — Fran, 6.12.07 Andreas 03.02.08 — Emmering, 29.01.08 — Roberto 10.01.08

Niklas, 24.11.07 — Peter, 19.12.07 — Evelyn, 02.04.08 — Sam, 21.12.07 — Adrian 20.12.07 — Marc, 30.12.07

Esra, 6.12.07 — Stefan, 30.12.07 — Kai, 1.12.07 — Gord, 02.02.08

Tobias, 9.12.07 Wolfgang, 6.12.07 — Andreas 9.12.07 — ALTER Michael, 9.12.07 Massimiliano 28.12.07 Raphael, 24.11.07 Tyler, 9.12.07

Markus 26.12.07 — Richard 9.12.07 Timo, 22.12.07 Alexander 24.11.07 — Claudy 20.01.08 Hu, 02.12.03 Johanes, 28.11.07 Beata, 03.02.08

Albert 9.12.07 — Karl, 26.12.07 — Klaus, 06.01.08 Fabian 08.04.08 Herbert, 02.04.08 Ferro 23.11.07 Amalia, 02.01.08 Andreas 9.12.07

Martina, 11.12.03 Jürgen, 24.11.07 — Andreas 9.12.07 Robi 19.12.07 Daniel, 1.12.07 Darrin 23.11.07

Nicola, 24.01.07 — Robin, — 31.01.08 Helena, 23.11.07 Hans, 24.11.07

WALTRAUT 23.11.07 Helene 6.12.07 — Melissa 30.12.07 Dominik 03.02.08

Odilia, 24.11.07 — Eva 9.12.07 — Shannon 4.4 TOYS! 24.11.07 Carolina, 25.11.07 Rosa 9.12.07 Johanes 02.01.08 Rowena, 4.2.07 Hermann — W. 27.12.07

Marie, 21.12.07 Hans-Peter, 6.12.07 Kai, 12.12.07 Rainer, 24.11.07 Claudia Andrea 24.11.07 Carola 9.12.07

Elisabeth, 28.11.07 Maria, 23.11.07 Ingrid 24.11.07 Deike Christiane 21.11.07 Evelyne 23.11.07 NERINA 24.11.07

Edith Marion 24.11.07 — Caroline Gaby 27.12.07 Christiane 21.11.07 Ursula, 28.11.07

Stella, 3.12.07 Natalia Silvia, 24.11.07 — Esther Vera 24.11.07 Heidrun, 24.11.07 Altamira, 6.12.07 — Gabi, 8.12.07 Leonie, 4.12.07 Brigitta

Korinna — Christel — Maria, 30.11.07 Eva, 22.01.08 Vera 24.11.07 Rocio, 6.12.07 Anna-Maria, 24.11.07 Lisel, 24.11.07 Marianne

— Kathrin 27.01.08 Jana, 23.11.07 — Melinda, 23.12.09 Daniela, — Merce, 6.12.07 Weni, 28.12.07 Nina, 30.12.07 Tina, 11.12.07 Ulrike, 24.11.07

5.12.07 — Carla, 3.01.07 Barbara 02.01.08 Elisabeth 04.01.08 Simon, 6.1.08 — Andrea 26.12.07

— Jana, 6.12.07 — Alena, 24.11.07 — Corinna, 20.12.2007 Isabelle, 27.11.07 — Veronika, 2082 Silvia, 4.12.07 — Jennifer, 22-12-07 — Max, 29.12.07

— Butet, 11.01.08 — Janett 04.01.08 Marie 23.12.07 — Paul 20.01.08

— Laurin, — 08.02.08 — Helge, 07.02.08

— Elisabeth, 9.12.07

Jessica 27.01.08

— Julius 08.02.08 — Valerie 03.04.08

— Hanah, 13.01.08

Lynne 29.12.07 — Sophie, 30.12.07 — Valentin, 13.01.08 Lothar, 24.11.07

— Milon 30.12.007 — Julius 20.12.08

— Carolin, 08.02.08

— Elena, 29.11.07

— Anttae 29.12.07 — Maja, 30.12.07

— Amélie, 9.12.07 — Anna 02.01.08

— Sabrina, 13.01.08

— Amelie, 02.01.08

— Justin, — 10.2.08

— Thomas, 5.1.08

_ Stefan 03.02.08 _ Guido, 23.11.07   _ Jan, 03.01.08,   _ Folker, 9.12.07   _ Alexander, 24.11.07
tin, 22.11.07   _ Franz, 02.01.08
_ Top, 12.02.08   _ Markus, 13.1.08   _ Frank, 02.12.07   _ Jan 04.01.08   Mattias, 24.011.07   _ Thomas 19.02.08   _ Zach, 13.01.08
_ Tobi 02.12.07   Koustautin, 25.1.08 _ Sébastian, -31.01.08   Dieter, 02.12.07   _ Berthold 21.11.07
_ Sebastian, 9.12.07   _ Bertold, 11.01.08   Stefan, 9.12.07 Philip Thomas, 27.12.07   Frieder, 24.11.07   _ Gunter, 02.12.07   _ Hafeld 27.12.7   _ Eliza, 8.12.07 Veronika,
_ Carsten, 23.12.07   _ Claudia, 6.12.07   _ Christoph, 9.12.07   Michael, 9.12.07   _ Jörg, 24.11.07   Klaus
_ Franziska 20.12.07   _ Jean, 24.11.07 _ Aleksandra, 22.12.07 _ Dmitri, 24.11.07   Myriam, 9.12.07   Roland, 8.12.07   _ Matthias
Eljko 28.11.07   Peter, 15.12.07   _ Katharina, 16.12.07 _ Deborah, 29.11.07 _ Claudia, 24.11.07   _ Maike, 02.12.07   Guido, 9.12.07   SEBASTIAN
MILENA, 28.11.07   Hans-Jörg, 9.12.07   Stefan, 28.12.07   _ Paul, 07.12.07   Pierre, 23.11.07   Gerhard, 8.12
_ Anita   _ Birgit, 23.11.07   _ Evert, 24.11.07   _ Katharina, 11.06.06   Horst, 24.11.07   _ Julie, 07.12.07   _ Christoph
Claudia, 9.12.07   Maria Luisa, 24.11.07   Uta, 24.11.07   _ Corinne, 29.11.07 _ Tobi   Anna, 16.02.07   _ Magdalena, 02.12.07
Robert, 24.11.07   _ Amélie 15.12.07   Horst Peter, 23.11.07
Jamie, 1.12.07   Iris-Maria, 02.12.07   _ Susan, 21.12.07   Beau, 23.11.07   _ Charlotte, 24.11.07   Julie
Matina, 24.11.07   _ Rose-Marie, 29.11.07   _ Katharina, 9.12.07 _ LISA   Nora, 9.12.07   _ Marlies, 02.12.07
Brigitte, 24.11.07   _ Eva-Maria, 22   _ Martina, 18.12.07   _ Christina, 26.   _ Kathleen, 28.11.07   _ Isabelle, 9.12.
Martina, 9.12.07   _ Tanja, 28.01.08   _ Katja, 07.12.07   _ Katja, 9.12.07   _ Elvira, 02.01.08   Elena, 26.01.08
Marianne, 5.11.07   _ Constantin, 28.11.07   _ Susie, 02.12.07   _ Heidrun, 29.11.07   Evamaria, 23.11.07   _ Franziska, 18.12.07
_ Celine, 02.12.07   MELANIE 26.07.08   _ Anneliese 8.12.07   _ Elisabeth 05.02.08   _ Elisabeth 20.01.08   Veronika, 26.12.07

                                                                                                                        _ Doris Jo. 9.12.07

_ Carolina, 5.12.07   _ 山本典子 1.1.08   Elsa, 6.1.08   _ Diana, 05.01.08

                                        _ Christa, 15.12.07
                                            _ Paul, 08.02.08

_ Hannes, 17.01.08

            _ Paulina, 17.01.08

                                                                          _ Theresa, 02.02.08   _ Mattias, 24.11.07

            _ Tessa, 02.02.08
            _ Ronja, 29.12.07   _ Elena, 23.12.07

                                        _ Caleb, 02.02.08   _ Philipp, 02.02.08

_ Philip 9.12.07   _ Horst, 24.11.07 _ Meghan, 02.02.08

                                                                                  _ Will, 30.12.07
_ Maja, 30.12.07   _ Jannik, 02.01.08

                    _ Carla, 28.01.08   _ Samantha, 02.02.08   _ Maya,
                        _ Ethan, 02.02.08   _ Thao Holly, 03.02.08

                                                                                              _ Karch, 02.02.08

                                                                                                    _ Chia Leo, 08.0

                                        _ Fabian, 26.01.08

as, 5.1.08

                                        _ Katharina, 27.12.07

Beppi, 24.11.07
Sebastian, 8.12.07
Hermann, 07.02.08
Leif 9.12.07
Horst 20.01.08
Andy, 22.12.07
Michael, 02.12.07
Jan, 6.12.07
Detlef, 16.12.07
Yannick 02.01.08
Friedl 20.12.07
Tierry, 28.12.07
Harry 20.01.08
Gerhard, 01.02
Elaine, 24.11.07
Kristian, 26.12.07
PAPA 24.11.07
Nick, 20.01.08
Waldemar, 26.12.07
Lazar, 02.01.08
Maarten, 7.12.07
Augusto 15.01.08
Steve, 22.11.07
Oly, 24.11.07
MARC 29.12.07
David, 11.12.07
Richard 04.01.08
Jim 16.01.08
Leo, 5.01.07
Cern 6.01.07
Klaus, 16.12.07
Karee Kieran, 27.11.07
Simon 21.11.07
Jean, 02.01.08
Frank, 8.12.07
David, 28.11.07
Hagen
PETER 28.12.07
Hanry, 03.01.08
Nicolas, 28.12.07
Sven, 02.12.07
Rainer, 02.12.07
Ulrike 6.11.07
Fried 24.11.07
Johannes
Fabiano, 02.01.08
Brita, 4.12.07
Robert, 8.12.07
WINKAR, 30.11.07
Walter, 12.12.07
Olga
Diana 02.12.07
Fried 29.11.07
Hildegund, 23.11.07
Daniel, 5.12.07
Ulrike, 16.12.07
Christof 16.12.07
Rosalinde, 9.12.07
Tessa, 19.12.07
Jaak 23.11.07
Andreas, 23.11.07
Vanessa, 23.11.07
LAURA 28.11.07
HELENE 24.11.07
Marie-Denise, 28.11.07
Nina 29.12.07
Mandy
Barbara, 8.12.07
Pietro, 23.11.07
Antonia, 28.11.07
Louisa, 6.12.07
Sandra, 02.12.07
Alex 24.12.07
Angelika, 02.12.07
Nina, 29.11.07
Sandra 24.11.07
Michele, 24.11.07
Marion, 24.11.07
Anita 02.12
Sonia 20.12.07
Elke, 8.12.07
Jess, C. 12.12.07
Sophie, 9.12.07
Anna 01.02.08
Gennaro 24.11.07
Natalia
Erica, 28.11.07
Yann 24.11.07
Beate, 02.12.07
Keiko 30.11.07
Ralph, 28.11.07
CHIARA
Elica, 8.12.07
Josefine 24.11.07
Sarita, 02.01.08
Suncica 02.03.08
Paola, 16.12.07
Maryellen, 21.12.07
Irina, 02.12.07
Odile
Marielvise
Elena
Zissi, 24.12.07
JARNA, 24.011.07
Johana 9.12.07
Christian, 02.01.08
Lisa 01.02.08
Maša, 02.01.08
Moniko, 24.11.07
Elena D. Ka.
MARTINA 28.11.07
Veronika 26.12.07
Jennifer, 23.11.07
Jean-Philippe, 8.12.07
Dagmar, 24.11.07
Katharina 27.01.08
Zahra, 15.12.07
Gisela, 16.12.07
Maggie, 28.12.2007
Bruna 9.12.07
Clara, 23.12.07
Johana, 24.11.07
Brooke, 30.12.07
Kyung-Ja, 3.01.08
Coline 6.12.08
Edith, 10.02.08
Pauline, 20.01.08
Sophie, 1.01.08
Simona, 02.12.07

Eva 06.02.08
Viktoria, 24.11.07
Maxine, 20.01.08
Lion, 02.12.07
Matthias, 09.02.08
BiBri 30.12.07
VERENA, 24.11.07
Giulia, 03.02.08
Antonia, 31.12.07
Eva-Margaux, - 08.02.08
Lukas, 6.1.08

Jakob, 3.01.08
Alice, 02.12.07
Christoph 27.01.08
Sebastian 27.01.08

Paul 05.01.08
Helena 06.02.08
Georgia 30.12.07
Feline, 9.01.08
Jonna, 02.01.08
Paul, 07.02.08
Pauline, 6.12.07
Clara, 03.02.08
Clemens 29.12.07

07.02.08

—Leif 9.12.07   — Dieter, 26.01.08   — Jörg, 02.12.07 — Dominik, 31.01.08   — Ralf, 1.01.08   — Robert, 20.12.0   — Matthew 03.0

— Roland, 29.12.07   — Markus 1.02.08

— Harry 20.01.08   — Gerhard, 07.02.08   — Maximilian, 30.11.07   — Pablo, 16.12.07   — Christoph, 30.11.07 — Frederico 03.01.08   — André,- 08.02.08   — Markus, 23.11.07

— Andreas, 30.11.07   — Gerold, 30.11.07

— Nick, 20.01.08 — Flo,- 02.02.08   Burkhard, 23.11.07   Andreas, 07.02.08   Michael, 24.11.07   Alexis, 8.12.07 — Johannes 04 Adrian, 02.12.07   Rober[..]p. Walter, 16.12.07   — Roland

Stefan, 02.12.07   Gigiotto 1.1.08   — Günter, 07.02.08   Sebastian

Oly, 24.11.07 — MARC 29.12.07 Philippa 02.01.08   — Pablo, 01.01.08   Flo, 13.12.07   Daniel, 13.12.07   — Sabine, 27.07.08   Matteo, 02.01.08 — Simonetta, 16.12.07   Uli, 6.1

Roger, 28.11.07 Floris, 28.11.07   Hagen, 02.12. Helga 16.01.08   — Kevin, 22.01.08 Bastian 5.1.08   — Jørgen, 26.1.08   — Mathias, 30.11.07   — Jens-Peter, 1.12.07   Anne, 02.12.07   Mark, 07.02.08 Matthias, 1.12.07

Sebastian, 6.1.08   Gottfried, 16.12.07 — Aleksandra 03.01.08   Martin, 22.11.07   Jürgen   — Jenny, 28.11.07   Daniel, 1.12.07 — Steffi 15.01.08   Kerstin, 30.11.07

Fried 24.11.07   Ulrike 11.12.07   ARIF, 22.01.08   — Nils, 12.12.07   Patrick 03.01.08 — Tanja,   Alexander, 8.12.07   Otmar, 29.12.07   Nele, 1.12.07

— Alexander 1.1.08   Alexander, 16.12.07   Gabrielle 26.12.07   Jakub   Martin, 02.12.07 Fred 27.11.07 Kur   Oliver, 11.12.07

— Tessa, 29.12.07 — Fried 29.11.07   Angelo 02.12.07   Petra, 02.12.07   Susanne, 23.11.07   Martin, 02.12.07   Karl, 24.11.07

Diana, 02.12.07   Moritz, 21.12.07   Felix, 21.12.07   Oleg, 16.12.07   Kathrin, 07.02.08   Albert, 22.11.07   Linda,   John, 21.12.07   Ingeborg, 02.12.07

Mandy, 02.12.07   ALEXANDER, 17.01.08   Brigitte, 23.11.07   Uwe, 19.12.07   Fritz, 8.12.07   Andreas   Dimitri, 21.12.07

— Alex 21.12.07   MANUELA, 21.11.07   Nina, 26.12.07   Anna 24.11.07   Catherine, 16.12.07   ANNA 17.12.07   Andrea 24.11.07   Susanne

Ana, 9.12.07   Iris 11.12.07   EVA 24.11.07   Felip, 8.12.07   MICHAEL, 18.12.07   Maricel, 02.12.07   Inge, 6.12.07 — Nina 16.12.07   Lydia 24.11.

Erica, 24.11.07   Anita, 24.11.07   Mina 6.12.07 — Katja, 24.11.07   Silke 03.03.08   Michael, 18.12.07   Maria, 8.12.07

Elisa, 6.12.07   Katharina 16.12.07   Anja 06.02.08   Doris, 29.12.07   Ingrid 24.11.07   Francine 23.11.07   18.12.07 — Daniela, 16

— Marieluise, 11.12.07   Nadja 16.12.07   Renate, 15.12.07   Daniel 24.12.07   Natalie   Carolin   Renata 24.11

Ilona, 24.11.07   Regine, 29.12.07   CHIARA 26.11.07   Beatrix, 02.01.08   Brigitte, 30.11.07   Frederic,

— Mariko, 24.11.07   JANINA 28.12.07   — Mireia, 6.12.07   K: ELIN, 22.01.08 HARGHERITA 25.11.07   Maria, 24.11.07   Kathrin, 19.11.07

— Frederica, 23.12.2007   Francis, 11.12.07 — Katharina, 08.01.08   Jasna 9.12.07 — Melanie 27.02.08   Jutta, 02.12.07

— Margret, 15.12.07   Imangulare, 8.12.07   — Koustantinos, 22.12.07   — Opietns, 10.01.08

— Simona, 02.12.07   — Maria Tresa, 30.12.1007

— Nils, 02.12.07

— Géulia, 03.02.08   — Alessandra, 23.12.07

— Charlotte 05.01.08

— Sonosyke, 16.12.07   — Linus 6.02.08

— Theo 27.01.08

— Paul 05.01.08

— Lena 06.02.08   — Linus, 03.02.08

— Eloise,- 02.02.08

— Ganesha, 23.12.2007

— Karl 27.01.08

— Juno, 16.12.07

— Ricarda, 30.11.07

—Michel,- 02.02.08

— Samuel,- 08.02.08

— Lorenz, 29.12.07

_ Markus 15.1.08   _ Oliver, 16.12.07   _ Jörg, 27.11.07

_ Kyle, 5.1.08   _ Thomas, 09.02.08   _ Stephan, 29.12.07

_ Stephanie 2.1.08   _ Peter, 26.12.07   _ Benjamin, 29.11.07
_ Jonas 03.01.08 _ Carlo, 6.12.07
Dimitris, 16.12.07   _ Saša 22.12.07 _ Ryan 04.01.08 Michael, 02.12.07   _ Ian, 07.02.08   _ Michael, 19.12.07   _ Marc 04.01.08
...1.01.08 _ John, 07.02.08 _ Karl-Heinz, 2.11.08 _ Thomas, 8.12.07   _ Federico 28.12.07   _ Hanu 15.01.08   _ Bernd 26.01.08 _ 02.12.07 Gerald 27.01.08
...der 1.02.08   _ Helmut 6.01.08 Mirko, 02.12.07 _ Rico 10.01.08 _ Matthias, 7.1.08   _ Walter 8.12.07 _ Jan, 07.12.07 _ Jens 07.02.08 Sebastian, 02.12.07 _ Patrick 05.01.08
...and, 24.11.07 _ Michael, 9.01.08 _ Sabine, 27.11.07 _ Destino 1.1.08   Mattia, 11.12.07 Sebastian 09.02.07 Alexander, 13.12.07   _ Jürgen 27.01.08 _ Thomas, 4.12.07
...07 _ Christoph, 04.01.08 _ Caspar 03.01.08 _ Markus 07.02.08 Fabio 03.01.08   _ WOLFGANG 28.12.07 Gotthard 09.02.08 _ Jan-Carlo 02.08 _ Thomas, 13.12.07 _ UDO   _ Peter, 22.11.07   Pablo, 02.12.07
_ Tom, 9.12.07 _ Gottfried 11.12.07 _ Dieter 11.12.07   Mario 9.12.07 Philipp, 6.11.07 MARIAN 23.11.07   _ Phil 21.12.07   Christine, 24.11.07   _ Leo, 16.12.07
_ Francesco, 16.12.07 _ Klaus 06.02.07 Karl, 27.11.07   Danilo, 29.12.07 Martin, 02.12.07   Jessica 02.08 Barbara, 16.12.07   _ Antonio 1.1.08   _ Michael 13.12.07
...enna _ Jochen 22.11.07 _ Jens, 6.12.07 Luca 04.01.08 Angela, 02.12.07 Julian 11.12.07 Daniel, 13.12.07   Lorenzo 24.11.07 _ Vei, 16.12.07
_ Iris, 16.12.07 _ Anne, 16.12.07 Heiko 12.07 Susanne 11.12.07 Dagmar, 6.12.07   _ Ursula, 29.11.07   _ Christoph 16.12.07
Vivienne 26.11.07 _ Katja, 30.12.07 Claudia 21.09.08 _ Geli, 22.11.07 Tsila, 18.12.07 _ Aljaz   _ Gaby 23.12.07   Christine 24.11.07   _ Viney 02.01.08
_ Katharina, 27.11.07   Emilie 28.12.07 _ Shirly, 1.01.08   Nicola 15.04.08   Gudrun, 16.12.07   Joyce 10.01.08
_ Claudia, 6.12.07 _ Ivonne, 19.12.07 Anita, 24.11.07 Marga, 11.12.07 Sigrid, 22.11.07 Dana, 06.01.08 Rosi, 8.12.07   Eva, 16.12.07
24.11.07 _ Maya, 02.12.07 _ Barbara, 07.12.07 Liane, 02.12.07 Barbara, 27.11.07 Marina, 24.11.07 Sibylle 16.12.07   Olympia 16.12.07
9.12.07 _ Beatrice 23.09.07 _ 24.11.07 Selke, 24.11.07 Kiki 28.12.07   Helmuth 03.02.08   Sara 28.11.07 KRISTIN, 28.12.07
...gie, 16.12.07 _ Elena, 16.12.07 Christina, 6.12.07 Tuba 21.12.07 Silvia 15.12.07 Steffi, 6.12.07   Alison 16.12.07   Helga 13.12.07   _ Eva-Maria, 4.12.07   Denise 04.01.08
Felipe 15.01.08 _ Yasmin 09.02.08 _ Vivian 01.08 Anna, 1.01.08 Jennifer 26.01.08   _ Marta, 08.02.08 _ Carina, 17.2.08 _ Monica 1.1.08 _ Felix 20.01.08
_ Halina, 13.12.07 _ Uncle 12.12.07   _ Marie, 13.12.07   _ Ursula, 30.01.08   _ Stefania 1.1.08

Bärbel, 22.11.07 _ Verena, 02.02.08   Marzia 03.01.08   _ Jan, 16.12.07
9.12.07   _ Anna 19.12.07   _ Niniamon 9.12.07 Jingjing 3.12.07   Ursula, 28.11.07 _ 12.07   _ Ruth, 4.12.07   _ Gabriella, 15.12.07
.12.07   _ Holly, 11.01.08
           _ Justus 06.02.08

        _ Felix, _ 02.02.08   _ Jakob 30.12.07

              _ Johnston   _ Nina 02.11.08
                    06.02.08   _ Paulina, 24.11.07

     _ Antonia 9.12.07

                           _ Adelheid, 12.12.07

              _ Leo 6.02.08

_ Joris, 1.01.08

              _ Lelli 05.01.08   _ Finn, 30.12.07

_ Gilbert, _ 02.02.08

              _ Len, 07.02.08

—— Eckhard 30.12.07

— Kevin, –10.2.08
—— Marc 04.01.08

—— Jan, 26.01.08

— Jan, 4.12.07   — Michael, 22.11.07   — Hans, 01.02.08
    — Fredi 02.01.08   — Rolf, –10.02.08   — Claudio, 21.12.07 — Robert, 09.02.08 — Mathias, 02
                                                              — Timo, 1.12.07
— Nils, 22.11.07   — Claus, 6.1.08   — Chris, 16.12.07   — Stefan, –08.02.08 — Arnd, 09.02.08   — Armin,
    — Ulli, 8.12.07 — Fabio, 15.12.07   — Dide, 15.01.08   — Rainer, 28.12.07
        — Roman, 23.01.08   — Martin, 09.12.08 — Volker, 30.12.07   — Sven, 8.12.07
                      — Thomas 20.01.08   — Lars 10.01.08
— Erinna, 22.11.07 — Rainer 27.01.08   — Philip, 16.12.07 — Mathias, 27.01.08 — Simon 02.01.08 — Jan, 09.02.08 — Markus 10.01.08
    — Enrico, 18.12.07   — Felix, 08.12.07 — Marion 04.01.08 — Kathrin, 11.01.08   — Miltos, 26.01.08 — Cesário, 30.12.07
— Julia 05.01.08 — Reinhard, 13.12.07 — Tom, 18.12.07 — Ben, 30.12.07 — Matthias, 10.2.08 — Alberto, 29.11.07 — Jack, 29.11.07 — Bryan, 16.12.07 — Franz, 07.02.08 — Simone, 8.12
    — Sabine, 13.01.08 — Peter 02.12.07 — Pierre 12.08 — Margie, 502 — Alex, 11.12.03 — Magena 04.01.08 — Dominik, 09.02.08 — Ralf, 01.01.08 — Aimegan, 10.2.08   — Berti, 8.12.07
        — Sofia 05.01.08   — Ludovico, 29.11.07   — Jürgen, 28.11.07   — Claus, 20.01.08 — David, 6.12.07 — Eva, 31.1.08 — Else, 01.02.08 — Claire, 21.12.07
— Katharina, 16.12.07   — Wernfried, 3.1.08 — Oliver, 04.01.08   — Christine 17.01.08 — Benedikt, 13.01.08   — Hanieh, 8.12.07
— Oliver, 13.01.08 — Tania 04.01.08 — Dieter 4.12.07   — Barbara 27.01.08 — Katharina, 29.11.07 — Robert, 12.08 — Oscar, 04.01.08   — Delaine, 29.11.07 — Lisa, 11.12.07   — Andreas,
— Alexandra, 23.12.07   — Paul, 6.12.07   — Hary, 1.01.07 — Maria 06.02.07 — Marc, 28.11.07 — Katha, 6.12.07 — Johannes, 07.02.08 — Max, 07.01.08
— Noelia, 12.12.07 — Marie 08.02.08 — Maea, 6.1.08 — Stefan 09.02.08 — Raphaela, 30.01.07 — Caren, 17.01.07 — Clementina, 15.12.07 — Heide, 09.02.08   — Nicol
— Petra, 19.01.08 — Sylvia, 30.08 — Eleonora, 29.11.07 — Philipp, 21.12.07 — Christian 11.12.07 — Ingrid 12.2.07 — Dr. 31.12.07 — Günther, 24.11.07
— Hanriette 16.12.07 — Elena, 29.11.07 — Katja, 09.02.07 — Petra, 24.11.07 — Margot, 18.12.2007 — Kenilde, 17.12.07 — Stuart, 07.12.08 — Nicol
— Henrike, 6.1.08 — Hanna, 29.01.08 — Siginde, 28.11.07 — Barbara 12.08 — Ingrid 06.01.08 — Giancarlo, 6.12.07 — Christ 22.11.07 — Monika 12.08 — Anselm 09.02.
— Arnica-Verena, 6.12.07 — Katja, 23.01.07 — Carlo, 22.11.07 — Marco, 29.11.07 — Lisa, 23.11.07 — Harald, 11.12.07   — Usa, 6.1.08 — Adelina, 02.01.08 — Franziska, 29.11
— Esther 05.01.08 — Maritta, 11.12.07 — ILKA 14.12.07   — Bärbel, 24.11.07   — Heidi, 27.11.07 — Ulrike 20.01.08 — Lothar, 25.11.07   — Elina, 6.12.07
— Claude 25.11.07 — Judy, 09.02.08 — Alberto, — Melanie 17.01.08   — Werner 28.11.07   — Waldborg 30.12.07 — Mono, 30.12.07 — Mercedes, 29.12.4 — Roswitha 09.02.07 — Guggy, 25.11.07
— NogahIme, 08.02.08 — Ulrike 04.01.08 — Rike 04.01.08 — Ingrid 01.06 — Roberta, 28.12.07 — Ute, 11.12.07 — Janine, 11.4.08 — Carmen, 12.07 — Sieyle 23.12.07
— Nale, 29.11.07 — Federica, 28.11.07 — Marianne, 25.11.07 — Brigitte, 13.12.07 — Julia, 01.02.08 — Chikako, 27.11.07 — Lydia 04.01.08 — Julie
— Cory, 30.12.07 — Ferdinand 28.01.08 — Sylvia, 25.11.07 — Angelika, 16.12.07 — Steff, 16.12.07 — Shigeru, 27.11.07 — Deposita, 26.01.08 — Saskia 23.12.07 — Olga, 5.12.07 — Uvja
— Cecilia, 29.12.07 — Conny, 18.01.07 — Cecilia, 29.11.07 — Edith, 22.01.08 — Nadli, 10.02.08 — Heidi, 6.12.07 — Maya 04.01.08 — Elke 30.12.07 — Eva
— ELFI, 07.02.08 — Mary.T 31.01.08 — Carlotta, 08.02.08 — Coretta, 29.11.07 — Anja, 10.02.08 — Renate, 01.02.08 — Joshua, 07.02.08 — Gillian 29.12.07 — Theresia 05.01.08 — Ana, 25.
                   — Carlotta, 21.12 — Johanna, 20.XII.07 — Birge 6.02.08 — Bettina, 22.01.08   — Katja 12.01.08 — Erika, 12.12.07
            — Toni 20.01.08   — Christoph 30.12.07   Ria, 24.01.08

— Marilene 06.01.08 — Rosmarie 1.1.08   — Sabine, 09.02.08   — Nadja, 03.02.08
        —— Marcus 30.12.2007   —— Sabine, 28.11.07   — Olivia 20.01.08   — Lucia 6.02.08
                                                                      — Max, –08.02.08

            — Arianne, 2.2.2008

                — Florian 00.01.08   — Lois, 6.1.08
                            —— Kerst 05.01.08   — Henry, 27.01.08

    —— Leonard 05.01.08   — Sophia 20.01.08
        — Elena 20.01.08   —— Sabine 30.12.07
            —— Virginio 05.01.08   — Stephan, 30.12.07

        — Nadia 20.01.08   — Elena 26.12.07   — Nikl, 25.11.07   — Sara, 16.12.07

                        —— David, 2.2.2008

                                — Alena 20.01.08

— Paul, 07.02.08

— Andreas H. 20.01.08
— Karl Heinz 04.01.08   — Christian, 13.01.08   — Anton, 07.12.07   — Felix, 8.12.07   — Jacobus 30.12.07   Антон, 07.12.07
— Claus, 21.12.07   — Kai, 16.12.07   — Diego, 26.12.07   — Stefan, 10.2.08   — Clemens, 16.12.07
— Ralf, 06.01.08   — Helmut, 31.1.08   — Matthias, 19.12.07   — Peter, 29.01.08
— Peter, 26.12.07   — Bryan, 31.1.08   — Gregor, 30.01.08   — Jürgen, 26.12.07   — Andrej 1.1.08   — Mauro 1.1.08   — Josef 6.02.08   — Matti, 07.12.07   — Rafael
— Christian, 31.01.08   Alexander, 25.11.07   — Jonas, 29.12.07   — Thomas, 03.02.08   — Markus, 30.12.07   — Felix, 07.02.08   — Andreas, 28.11.07   — Helga 17.01.08   — Stefano, 1.1.08
Axel 16.01.08   — Felix, 13.01.08   — Vincent, 06.01.08   — Thomas, 6.1.08   ПОЛИНА, 02.01.08   — Martin 04.01.08   — Matthias, 6.12.07   — André, 29.01.08   Heidrun
Markus, 25.11.07   Ulf, 8.12.07   Kennan, 07.12.07   Hans 1.1.08   Chisco, 25.11.07   — Silvio, 03.01.08   — Nico, 28.11.07   Kiki 16.12.07   — Emilian 1.1.08   — Manuel, 16.12.07   — Gerhard, 12.01.08
Patricia, 16.12.07   Günther 17.01.08   Ferdinand, 19.01.08   Joachim 22.01.08   Anna 1.12.07   Tiina, 07.12.07   Alexander, 22.11.07   Cristina 1.1.08
Jens, 17.01.08   Othmar, 16.12.07   Gard 02.01.08   Jürgen, 29.11.07   Rufus, 07.02.08   Heimo, 27.11.07   Dena, 07.12.07   Inka, 27.1
Franco, 07.12.07   Stephane, 22.01.08   Mario, 15.12.07   Sabine, 24.11.07   Willi, 29.12.07   Linda, 07.12.07   Silvio, 1.1.08   Ralf
Laura, 21.12.07   Daina, 6.12.07   Antonis 18.12   Christine 22.12.07   Eckhard, 4.11.08   Helena, 8.12.07   Richard 07.12.08   Lena, 07.12.07   Christiana, 26.12.07
Andreas, 13.01.08   Elke, 24.11.07   Conny 02.01.08   Rüdiger, 4.12.07   Hans 12.09.07   Reinhold,   Andre 02.01.08   Valeria, Flo.12.07   Dorothee, 27.11.07   Lucia, 07.12
Fred, 25.11.07   Leandro, 5.12.07   Ruth, 01.02.08   Mary, 02.01.08   Luigi, 3.12.07   24.11.07   Ingrid, 8.12.07   Silke, 01.02.08   Edith, Heidi, 6.12.07   Katrin, 8.12.07
Lesley, 16.12.07   Aawa, 23.11.07   Sigrid, 29.11.07   Judith, 25.11.07   Annette 1.1.08   Tereza, 23.11.07   Julia, 09.02.08
Filrina, 22.01.08   Nikola 22.11.08   Marja, 27.11.07   Katarina, 02.01.08   Elisabeth, 07.02.08   Irene, 1.1.08   Georg, 07.12.07
Josef, 06.01.08   Katrin R.   Ayfer, 6.12.07   Nicoletta, 6.12.07   СВЕТА, Lavissa, 06.01.08   Olivia, Giovi 04.01.08   Berit, 01.01.08   Walbraut
Silke, 25.11.07   Melanie, 07.12.07   Barbara, 29.12.07   Anne-Marie   Louise, 07.12.07   Renate, 02.02.08   Lily, 1.1.08   Maria, 27.11.07   Karola
Tatjana, 20.01.08   Janine 27.01.08   28.11.07   Johanna, 22.11.07   Maria, 16.12.07   Sylwia, 29.11.07   Carolin, 1.1.08   Inka 23.12.07   Daniel, 1.1.08
Doina, 02.12.07   July, 06.01.08   Samantha, 24.12.07   Reitta, 4.12.07   Maria, 1.1.08   Eva, 25.11.07   Ute, 02.01.08   28.11.07   Otto Okt 20.XII.2007   Gertrud, 14.12.07
28.12.07   Augenlik, 8.01.08   Laura, 07.12.07   Bilar 04.01.08   Elisa 1.1.08   Vte, 02.01.08   Christl, 1.01.08   Mira, 12.01.08   Elke, 29.11.07   Gartie, 27.11.07   Micaela, 06.01.08
Elisabeth, 16.12.07   28.11.07   Carolaine, 03.01.08   Ketty, 29.11.07   Jacqueline 22.12.07
emanuela, 04.12.07   Milchram 12.01.08   — Henry 04.01.08   — Anna, 29.11.07   Jussi

— Hariann 20.01.08   Léon, 06.01.08   Nils 02.02.08   Judith, 03.02.08   — Claudia, 25.11.07   — Naomi 6.02.08   — Francesca, 1.1.08   — 倫子, 21.12.07
— Jonathan, 03.02.08
— Emily, 28.12.07   — David 6.02.08
— Ruven 1.1.08
— Aiko, 08.02.08

— Anima, 25.11.07   — Nils, 16.12.07   — Max, 02.12.07
— Paul, 16.12.07   — Jacqueline, 16.12.07   — Karl, 16.12.07
— Andreas, 02.12.07
— Max, 16.12.07
— Franz, 16.12.07   — Leo, 10.2.08
— Vincent, 16.12.07

— Julian, 30.12.07

— Zacharias, 2.2.08

— Frank, 25.11.07   — Mark, 19.1.08

— Felix, 8.12.07   — Jacobus 30.12.07   Антон, 07.12.07
Sau. 13.01.08   — Anton, 07.12.07
— Diego, 26.12.07   — Stefan, 10.2.08   — Clemens, 16.12.07
2.07   — Matthias, 19.12.07   — Peter, 29.01.08
— Andrej 1.1.08   — Mauro 1.1.08   — Josef 6.02.08   Matti, 07.12.07   — Michaele 1.1.08   — Hans Peter, 07.02.08   — Robert, 07.02.08
us, 30.11.07   — Felix, 07.02.08   Andreas, 28.11.07   Helga 17.01.08   — Stefano, 1.1.08   Rafael, 8.12.07   Piercarlo   Lorenzo 30.12.07   Olaf, 27.11.07   — Petros, 27.11.07
— Martin 04.01.08   — Matthias, 6.12.07   André, 29.01.08   Heidrun, 25.11.07   Ali, 07.12.07   Konrad,–   Lukas, 12.01.08   Rui, 07.12.
25.11.08   — Silvio 03.01.08   Nico, 28.11.07   Michl 16.12.07   Emilian 1.1.08   Christhna, 22.01.08   Frank, 4.12.07   10.02.08   Gustav
Joachim   29.11.07   Josef 12.01.08   Maria Sylvie, 01-01-08   Alexander, 22.11.07   Gerhard, 12.01.08   Anne 12.01.08   Alfred, 02.12.07   Alfi 08.02.08   Theo, 02.01.08   Max 12.01.08   Pe.
— Rufus, 07.02.07   Tiina, 07.12.07   RUTA 22.01.08   Cristina, 1.1.08   Inka, 27.11.07   Marzia 1.1.08   Wolfgang, 06.01.08   Kai, 16.12.07   Marie, 23.11.07   Ste
— Sabine, 24.11.07   Willi, 29.12.07   Heimo, 27.11.07   Silvio, 1.1.08   Ralf 25.11.07   Karl-Heinz 28.11.07   Martin, 23.11.0   Margareta 11.0   28.11.07
Erhard, 1.08.08   Hartmut, 01.02.08   Linda, 07.12.07   Christiana, 26.12.07   Carmen, 01.02.08   Stefanie 26.01.08   Michael, 07.12.07   Fran
Reinhold,   Helena 8.12.07   Richard   Eva, 16.12.07   Lena, 07.12.07   Mark, 02.02.08   Lucia 07.12.07   Jens, 29.11.07   Ros   Anne Sophie 15.12.07   Aurelia 23.11.0
Eckhard, 1.08.08   Andre 02.01.08   Irmgard 08.08.08   Beate 01.01.08   Leo 10.12.07   Gerrit   Franz 02.12.07   Heidelies 6.12.07
y, 02.01.1887   Luigi, 9.12.07   5.A., 24.11.07   Ingrid, 8.12.07   Thekla, 16.12.07   Edith, 16.12.07   Heioli, 6.12.07   Katrin, 8.12.07   Elli, 9.12.07   Brigitte, 17.01.07   Awe 25.11.07   Hanna, 30.01.08   Stefa
Judith, 25.11.07   Annette 1.1.08   Adso, 06.01.08   Tereza, 23.11.07   Julia, 09.02.08   Jessica 18.01.08   Sylvia, 6.12.07   Jorgen, 02.12.07   Elisabeth 20.02.02   Ischo, 08.08.09   Nina, 25.11.07   Catherine   Catherine   Lindi, 02.01.
Elisabeth 07.02.08   Franz 24.01.08   Irene, 1.1.08   Miriam, 20.12.07   Georg, 07.12.07   Marjolijn, 17.01.08   Ursula, 22.11.07   Isabella, 8.12.07   Ursula, 28.11.07   Sabrina,   Natalia, 8.12.07   Jerne   Christine, 6.12.07
Ra, 29.12.07   Anne-Marie   Louise, 07.12.07   Maria 11.12.07   Nina, 07.12.07   Olivia, 25.11.07   Berit, 11.12.07   Ute Zedroa   Michael, 16.12.07   Meredith 11.12.07   Iris, 02.12.07   Maaike, 12.01.08   Nino, 30.01.08   Maria, 18.12.07
na, 22.11.07   Katharina 10.01.08   Sylvia, 29.11.07   Carolin, 12.01.08   Inka 23.12.07   Daniel,   Maria 27.11.07   Simona 1.1.08   Nora 23.12.07   Antje, 06.01.08   Claudia, 12.01.08   Anna, 12.01.07   Gert
— Maria, 1.1.08   Jana, 16.12.07   Ute, 02.01.08   J.J., 28.11.07   8 Pina, 30.01.08   Karola 03.02.08   Anna-Lisa 6.01.08   Stefanie, 02.12.07   Moni Ko, 10.02.08   Pizda, 22.11.07   Kristina 02.01.08   Lisa   Astr
sa 1.1.08   Eva, 25.11.07   XII 2007   Gertrud, 14.12.07   Maria, 03.01.08   Giovanna, 03.01.08   Asma, 1.01.08   Isabella 15.01.08   Elena,
Christl, 1.01.08   Mira, 12.01.08   Arnold 20. XII 2017   Sarjimi, 08.02.08   Na young Lhee, 30.12.07   Pachi, 1.1.08   Ewa, 07.12.07   Heinz 1.1.08   Toko 09.01.08   Sandra, 07.12.07   A
07.08 Ketty, 29.11.07   Honnelare 31.08   Elke, 29.11.07   Gertie, 27.11.07   Micaela, 06.01.08   Margot, 15.12.07   Chiara, 02.01.08   Juli
— Jacqueline 22.12.07   — Anna, 29.11.07   Jussi, 07.12.07
— Henry 04.01.08
—Naomi 6.02.08   — Francesca, 1.1.08   — Moritz, 15.12.07
25.11.07
— 倫子, 21.12.07   — Maria – Teresa, 8.12.07

— David 6.02.07

— Ruven 1.1.08

— Aiko, – 08.02.08
—Em

— Gabriel, 30.12.07

— Fabien 6.02.08

, 02.12.07

— Karl, 16.12.07
acqueline, 16.12.07

—Andreas, 02.12.07   — Daniel, 30.12.07

—Max, 16.12.07

—Franz, 16.12.07   — Leo, – 10.2.08

—Carolina 6.02.08

— Phil, 25.11.07

— Lutta, 25.11.07

— Louis, 25.11.07

Florian 20.0... Flamen, 30.12.07 — Axel 28.12.07 — Christoph, 29.01.08 — Andi, 30.12.07 — Volker, 09.02.08 — Joseph, 06.01.08
24.11.07 — Massimiliano, 11.02.08 — Cris, 07.02.08 — Yannik, 07.12.07 — Antonio, 15.01.08 Ramsey, 29.12.07 — Jordi, 26.01.08 — Jens
— Markus 10.01.08 — Noa 29.12.07 — Christopher, 25.11.07 — Ernst 14.01.08
— Tilman, 29.11.07 Stephan 13.01.08 — Ina, 09.
...rd, 07.02.08 — Manfred 6.02.08 — Carlus 20.01.08 Luca Frassen Daniel, 07.12.07 — Hermann, 16.12.07 — Anja, 30.12.07
Valerio 20.01.08 — Ricardo, 22.01.08 — 28.11.07 — Selcuk, 16.12.07 — Walter, 13.12.07 Nick, 12.12.07 — Jens, 20.01.08 Florian, 22.12.07
...a 04.01.08 Sven, 26.01.08 Simone Philipp, 14.12.07 Timo 04.01.08 — Bengt, 26.12.07 Martin, 6.12.07 — Simon,
— Diana 13.01.08 — Thorsten, 07.12.07 — Andreas, 25.11.07 — Eva, 30.12.07 — Mel, 22.01.08 — Corina, 31.01.08 — Hans Peter 6.02.08
16.12.07 — Irene, 6.1.08 — Larissa, 02.02.08 — Niki, 29.11.07 — Fulvio, 28.12.07 — Jensen, 25.11.07 — Viviane, 22.12.07 Jordan, 16.12.07 Jeanni, 08.02.08 Paulo, 20.12.
— Veronika, 16.12.07 — Fabiola, 16.12.07 — Ursula, 13.01.08 — Renate, 07.02.08 — Vinicius, 06.01.08 — Christoph, 12.1.07 — Ewald, 02.02.08 — Noel, 19.01.08 — Seli
02.12.07 — Karl-Heinz, 5.1.08 — Julia, 30.01.08 — Anne 10.01.08 — Alexandre, 07.12.07 — Alberto, 07.12.07 — Bea 25.11.07 Silke, 09.02.08 Ewald, 16.12.07 — Karlene, 25.1.08 JOHANNES, 4.12.07 — Ilona, 09.02.08 Alex
— Egbert, 17.01.08 — Claudia, 6.02.08 — Reus 28.11.07 — Sarah, 21.12.07 — Hanna, 01.02.08 — Kate, 09.02.08 — Berndhart, 27.11.07 Eva, 2.08 Gisela 09.02.08 MARI 8.12.07 — Heiner, 29.12.07 — Sa
01.08 Hayato 07.12.07 Theresa Regina, 02.12.07 — Barbara, 17.01.08 — Bärbel, 17.01.08 Rainer, 17.01.08 Marlene, 17.01.08 — Tobias, 30.12.07
lke, 16.12.07 — Nadeshda, 30.12.07 — Raluca, 8.12.07 — Claudia, 26.12.07 — Karim, 6.12.07 Georg, 07.02.08 Nadine, 6.1.08 — Mima, 11.12.07 Susanne Janet, 4.1
— Victoria, 21.12.07 — Ruth, 8.12.07 — Martyn, 03.01.08 — Felicitas, 6.02.08 — Veronika, 07.12.07 — Jutta, 30.01.08 — Maria, 07.12.07 Hannah, 22.01.08 Annalisa, 13.12.07 — Natasha, 30.1.08 — Enrica, 06.1.0
— Erika 23.12.07 — Elena, 07.12.07 — Bernadette, 30.01.08 — Armelle, 07.12.07 — Erika 04.01.08 — Anne, 25.11.07 — Elisabeth 07.02.08 — Ricardo, 07.12.07 — Natalia 22.01.08 Friederike 19.01.08 — Tanja, 22.1.07 — Angela, 22.01.08 Shaf
— Zu, 23.11.07 — Selene, 30.12.07 — Sabine, 16.12.07 — Guido 01.02.08 — Julia, 07.12.07 — Kalima, 21.12.07 Nataša, 16.1.07 YaYa 5.02.08 — Sofia, 30.1.07
arina, 23.11.07 — Hendrik, 4.12.07 — Cindy, 16.12.07 — Eugenia, 8.12.07 — Magdalena, 16.12.07 — Jvon, 2
02.08 — Maria 04.02.08 — Camilla 05.02.08 — Pina 01.02.08 — Elke 22.11.07 — Sarah, 07.02.08 — Anna, 14.12.07 — Julia, 30.12.07 — Annika 18.01.08 — Shan
07.12.07 — Simone, 01.02.08 — Rosalia, 07.12.07 — Romi, 29.12.07 — Melanie, 19.01.08
06.01.08 — Maggy, 24.01.08 — Patrizia, 07.12.07
— Nurdan, 01.02.08 — Lilly 03.01.08 —

Celia, 8.12.07

— Alexander, 19.01.08

— Felipe 04.01.08

— Monja, 29.12.07

— Tobias, 29.12.07

Bernd 20.12.07

Hanuel 02.01.08

Claus, 09.02.08   Patrick, 02.12.07

, 22.11.07   Jörg 10.01.08   Christoph, 30.12.07   Max, 09.02.08   Bob, 09.02.08

Harold 04.01.08   Jens, 30.12.07   Wern 20.12.07   Alexander, 22.11.07

Theo 02.01.08   Frank, 14.12.07   Floh 19.12.07   Walter-Mario, 25.11.07   Fabian 30.12.07   Александр, 21.12.07   Nikolai 12.01.08   Matthi

01 16.01.08   Andreas, 09.02.08   20.01.08   Torsten   Ulf, 12.12.07   Eann 02.01.08   Ruhser, 16.12.07   Alex, 6.1.08   Harry, 8.02.08   Adam,

02.08   Nikolas, 15.12.07   John, 25.11.07   Francesc 07.02.08   Jngo 23.12.07   Klaus, 31.1.08   Christophe, 28.12.07   Joost 18.01.08   Matthieu, 06.12.07   Stephan

Christian, 15 2.07   Ivan, 11.12.07   Franz, 22.01.08   Allison, 07.12.07   Alessio 24.11.07   Ulrike 08.02.08   Oswin, 30.12.07   Dominik, 22.01.08   Bernhard, 29.01.08   Stephan

Roger 02.01.08   Martin, 09.02.08   Dieter, 04.02.08   Carlo 04.01.08   Salvatore, 4.12.07   Christian 18.01.08   Tilla, 22.11.07   Hermut   Dieter 15.12.07   Oliver 29.01

30.11.07   Stefan, 07.12.07   Sandra, 02.12.07   Melanie, 25.11.07   Martin   Matteo, 29.12.07   Dina   Branka   Pia 1.08   Tobias, 12.

Diethard 03.04.08   Isabel, 06.01.08   Andrei 02.01.08   Ronald, 22.01.08   Wildelm, 07.02.08   Desiree 17.12.07   Carina   Jürg, 23.11.07   Buffo, 3.01.07   An

Sophia, 21.12.07   Julia,   Sandra, 25.11.07   Frank, 19.01.08   Ursel, 18.01.08   Anna 6.02.08   Daniel, 29

Gontje, 26.01.08   Stefano,   Georg, 02.12.07   Edmund 16.12.07   Anton Heinrich, 07.12.07   Chris, 22.01.08   Bina, 11.12.07   Werner, 22.

ander, 16.12.07   Franco, 15.01.07   Calo, 02.12.07   Christian   Debbie, 28.11.07   Titus, 09.12.07   Carina, 15.12.07   Maghan, 07.12.07   J樣   Jürgen, 15.12

Alexander, 15.12.07   Berndl,   Anton, 6.12.07   Daniel   Irene, 28.12.07   Berta, 17.01.08   Quentin, 22.01.08   Jomita, 18.12.07   Julia

bine, 25.11.07   Birgit, 26.12   Edith,   La, 02.12.07   Annette 21.12.07   Viola,   Lena 22.12.08   Isabelle 25.12.07   Kathi, 13.12.07   Carina, 11.12.07   Karin

18.01.07   Sonja,   Katrin,   Julia, 21.12.07   Lara, 30.12.07   Katrina 09.08   Ulrike 07.12.07   Sibylle 23.12.07   Jasmin, 08.01.09

Silued 6.1.08   Aurelia, 5.12.07   Elena 02.01.08   Françoise, 15.12.07   Joanna, 07.12.07   Vanessa   Anja, 25.11.07   Mirka, 12.   Gabi, 30.11.07   Petra, 07.12.07

Anne 25.12.07   Pauline 20.01.08   Anna, 30.12.07   Susanne 05.01.08   Frederike, 16.12.07   Nicole, 17.01.08   AnniKa, 6.1.08   Astrid,

Doris, 07.12.07   Javiera, 5.12.07   Jelena, 21.12.07   Philippe, 02.12.07   Tiago, 09.02.08   Elena, 21.12.07   Veronika, 25.11.07

iga, 29.11.07   Christina 02.04.08   Martine, 21.12.07   Katia, 09.02.08   Dorl, 12.01.08   Sylvia, 5.12.07   Nicole, 23.11.07   Marina, 12.01.08   Anna, 09.02.08   Ursula, 18.12.07

Lena, 31.01.08   Monika, 05.11.07   Heike, 22.11.07   Katharina, 16.12.07   Margot, 07.12.07   Viktoria 13.01.08   Ant je, 30 0A   Fernanda, 09.02.08   Judith,

511.07   Anja, 07.02.08   Menni, 20.12.07   Conceição 09.02.08   Anola, 12.01.08   Katharina, 4.12.07

non, 12.12.07   Regula   Birgit, 15.12.07   Charlotte, 22.12.07   Christelle, 26.12.07   Eva, 30.12.07   Anna, 30.12.07   Lisi 13.12.07   Mihoko, 16.12.07   Karin, 23.

Dorian 19.1.08   Fabiola, 10.2.08   Dorothea, 03.01.08   Regina, 01.02.08   Ana, 09.02.08

16.01.08   Melike 24.01.08   Kevin Weber 12.11.07   Günter, 6.1.08

Paul, 22.12.07

Orlando, 30.12.07   Sarah, 07.01.08

Qui

Vincent, 19.01.08

Kikei 09.02.08

Josetomas, 30.12.07

Jan, 09.02.08

Yella, 22.11.07

Leander, 22

— Harald, 30.12.07

— Jan-Philipp, 07.02.08   — Thomas, 02.02.08

David, 07.12.07

— Fabian, 14.12.07   — Mo 12.01.08   — Richard, 07.02.08   — Terry 22-12-07
— Thomas, 27.11.07   Benedikt, 12.12.07 — Reinhard, 10.12.08   Johannes, 13.12.07 — Iwan, 1.1.08   — Wolfgang, 06.01.08   — Andreas, 25.11.07
                                                                     Joachim. 27.11.07   — Stephan, 14.12.07   — Volker, 30.12.07

— Philipp, 14.12.07   Hadrian, 16.12.07   Luis, 25.11.07   — Robert, 08.01.08 — Josef, 27.11.07 — Christian, 21.12.07 — Thomas, 08.02.08   — Werner, 30.12.07
Christel, 07.12.07   — Marcel 27.01.08   JanLucas, 07.02.08 Michael, 6.12.07   — Benedikt, 25.11.07   — Johannes, 29.12.07 Andreas, 22.01.08 Felix, 25.11.07 Bob, 12.01.08   Alex,
                      Florian, 25.11.07 — Jean-François, 29.11.07 — Angelo, 30.12.07   — Isabell, 11.12.07 Josef 16.01.08 — Georg, 11.12.07 — Robert 27.01.08
Volker, 6.1.08 Sabine, — Helmut, 06.01.08 — Hans Dieter, 31.12.07 Thomas, 30... Paula, 30.12.07 — Norbert, 08.01.08 Elmar, 31.08 — Marco 17.12.07   Heimo, 25.11.07 — Norbert, 13.01.08 Josef, 02.12.07
— Angelika, 29.12.07 — Markus 30.12.07 Klaus, 29.12.07 — Ulrike, 8.12.07 — Maximilian, 02.12.07   — Birgit 27.01.08   — Antonia, 28.11
— Johann, 25.11.07 — Wolfgang 02.12.07 Dagmar, 25.11.07 — Karl, 9.12.07   — Pat, 02.12.07   — Günter, 18.12.07 Fernando,   — Reinhold, 6.12.07
David 11.12.07 Klaus 03.01.07 — Georg 12.12.07 Petra, 16.12.07 Peter, 13... — Katrin, 11.06.07   Peter, 22.11.07 — Moritz, 22.12.07 Eberhard,
— Ann-Kathrin, 30.11.07 Christine Werner, 8.12.07 Sophie, 24.01.08 Alex 1.1.08 — Michael — Rebekka, 27.01.07 — AELIN 11.12.07 Andreas,
Shojo, 27.11.07 — Anna, 02.01.08 Maureen, Lisa, 15.01.08 Sabine, 4.12.07 20.12.07 Marliese, 8.12.07 Jennis, 7.12.07 — Kirek,   Nils, 16.12.07 Michaela, 06.01.07 — Inge 02.12.07   Helmut, 11.12.07
— Stefan 5.12.07 Margot 02.12.07 Maximiliano Heike, Lena, 3.01.07 Corinna Julie 22.11.07   Gitt 02.12.07 — Renate, 6.1.08   Jenny 6.12.07 Anna, 22.12.07
25.11.07 Daniela 11.12.07 Irmgard, 1.01.08 Erhardt, 4.12.07 Barbara, 9.12.07   Reinhard 08.02.08 29 12.07 Gerhard 09.02.08 Daniele Marion, 02.11
Petra, Ingrid, 12.12.07 Adriana, 15.12.07 Gudrun, 18.12.07 Svonne, Viktoria, 02.12.07 Maria, 06.01.08 Irma, Martine, 30...
— Editha, 18.12.07 Ilse 09.02.08 Katrin, 25.11.07 Bianca Teresa 23.11.07 Tanja, 25.11.07 Viktoria, Julia 11.12.07 Milan, 07.02.07 Sara, Michele, 16.12.07
Sara 02.01.08 Jazz 15.12.07 — Christine, 15.12.07 — Elena, 28.11 Thanos, 9.12.07 Ibra 18.12.07 Hara Margeta, 25.11.07 Lina, 17.01.08 Natalie, 19
EKCAHDPA, 27.11.07 — DONNA, 17.01.08 Goby 20.01.08 — Christa, 30.12.07 Mariana, Emanuelle, 11. Marlene, Paola, 1.1.08 Kathrin, 30.12.07 Luis Lina, 27.11.
Johanne 12.01.08 — Christine, 20.12.07 Janine, 26.01.08   Spiela, 16.12.07 Vera, 25.11.07 — Dagmar 23.12.07 — Beate, 09.02.08 — Anna, 30.12.07 — Sophia, 5.12.07
— Max, 30.12.07   Althea   — Emy, 13.01.08   — Yoshiko, 16.12.07   23.12.07 Sabrina, 26.12.
                                  23.12.07.
                        — AALOHA, 02.01.08 Paolo 1.1.08

— Miriam, 30.12.07   — Katia 1.1.08   — Sonja, 22.11.07
                                — Trisha 1.1.08 — Vincent, 30.11.07

— Nina, 30.11.07

— Leone 1.1.08

— Francis 6.02.08   — Sarah 6.02.08   — Marko, 30.12.07

— Mara, 51.08

6.12.07

Ramona, — 24.01.08

—Ralf,

—Martin, — 02.02.08

—Werner, 30.12.07   —Christian, —10.02.08   —Valerio, 30.12.07   —Roman, 02.01.08
S, 25.11.07   —Ausias, 25.01.08   —Frank, 30.12.07   Gero, 02.12.07
—Lewis 02.01.08   —Christoph, 8.11.07   RUDOLF 24.11.07   —Hervé, 06.01.08   —Angelika 02.01.08   —Moritz 27.01.08
07, 30.12.07   —Barrin—10.2.08 —Peter 20.01.08   —Thomas, 22.12.07   Ralph, 07.02.08   Horst, 13.01.08   —Jens, 30.12.07   GIAMMARINO, 30.   —Claus, 25.11.07   —Dirk

—Andreas, 23.12.07   Valentin, 27.11.07   Jana, —Helmut, 10.2.08   —Etienne, 30.08   —Philipp, 30.11.07
Alex, 6.12.07   —Miguel, 20.11.08   Jürgen, 29.12.07   Roland 07.01.08 —Günther, 14.01.08   —Jens, 07.02.08   Werner, 02.12.07   Stefan, 27.11.07   —Christoph, Jann   —Hartmut, 11.12.07
iner, 28.01.08   Stefan, 11.12.07   —Reinhard, 30.12.07   Dani, 27.11.07   Philip, 8.12.07   Carlos, 19.01.07   Ilse, 6.12.07   Carola, 8.12.07   Sebastian, 22.11.07   —Jan 23.11.07   —Raj
Morten, 13.01.08   —Joel 21.12.07   —Kerstin, 30.11.07   Amir, 03.02.07   —Vadim,   Wolfgang, 25.11.07   Beke, 30.12.07 —Bianca, 30.12.07   Antonio, 30.12.07   —Mikael 9.12.07 —F
Ferdi, —   Edwin 23.11.07   Axel, 6.12.07   Markus, 09.02.08 Thomas, 6.12.07   Thomas, 25.11.07   DANIEL, 28.12.07   Ernst, 20.01.08   Felix, 15.12.07   —Susanne, 080207   Alexandra, 17.01.08
—   Enno 02, —Alfred 24.   Paul, Jan, 6.12.07   Claudia, 11.01.08   Arnaud, 30.01.08   Marco, 07.12.07   Dagmar, 8.12.07   —Flavie, 30.11.07   Jonas, 12.01.08 —Stefan, 13.12.07   Günter
hard, 2.12.07   —Christal, 30.11.08 Uli, 1.1.08 Rachal 02.02.08   Christiane, 03.02.08   CHRIS, 24.11.07   Lydia, 07.02.07   —Annika, 11.01.08   Harst 27.11.07   Johanna 5.1.08   Damian 29.11.07
Gerda, 13.01.08 — Conni, 4.12.07   Bruno 03.12.08   Kati, 6.1.08   Bong, 27.11.07   Kerstin, 02.12.07   Wolf-Peter 02.12.07   Katharina, 07.02.08 —Stefan, 18.12.07   Papouch 23.11.07
—Max, 27.12.07   —Peter 15.01.08   Maryse, 1.1.08   Maria, 20.01.08   —Jen, 30.08   Gabriel, 16.12.07   Ferdinand 24.12.07   Emanuel 22.12.07   Birma, 07.12.07   Agnes 27.11.07   Isabelle, 27.11.08
—   Sabine, 21.12.07   Norbert, 15.12.07   Jo, 24.11.07   LISA 16.12.07   Erwin 4.12.07   Dieter 13.01.07   Birgit 27.01.08   Artaur, 13.12.07   Eva, 4.12.07   —Timmo, 15.12.07   Grete, 27.11.08
12.07   Thomas, 6.1.08 —Ica —02.07 Ariane, 02.08   Martin, 02.02.08   Nadine, 25.11.07 —Mathias, 6.11.08   Sarah, 22.11.07   Liz, 22.01.08   Verena, 16.12.07   Kathryn,
—Bea 25.11.07   Bente, 26.01.08   Rosaria, 15.12.07 —Marc, 23.12.07   Josefine, 25.11.07 —Mathias, 6.11.08   Petra 16.12.07   Jeremy, 30.01.08   Sylvie 25.12.07   Josef, 30.01.08   Annett, 16.12.07
ion 08.02.08   Simone 6.12.07   Maria, 27.11.03   Ricarda 27.01.08   Isolde, 30.11.07   Yosuke, 06.11.08   Nadine, 6.1.08   Ivy 07.01.08   Benno, 22.11.07   Dorothea, 02.12.07   Franziska, 28.11.07
Comp   Margit, 21.12.07 —Giulia 14.02.08 Ricarda, 28.12.07   Cristina, 27.01.08   Regina, 25.11.07   Hedy, 30.11.07   Ella 03.01.08 Helga, 29.11.07   Hortense 01.01.08   Astrid 6.1.08   Verena 10.01.08   —Alina
Michaela, 9.12.07   ALINE 8.12.07   —Heide 07.12.07 —Ana 30.01.08 Cristina, 27.01.08   Petra, 30.12.07   DANIEL 8.12.07   Evaline 02.12.07   Muxo, 02.01.08 Lisa, 30.01.08   Martina, 8.12.07   Sara, 01.01.08   Jamina 23.11.07
Natalie, 19.01.08   —Gitta, 02.02.08 Gisela, 25.11.07   Nicole, 02.12.07   Barbara, 01.02.08   Inge, 5.12.07   Sasa 02.01.08   Karin, 30.01.08   Lucia, 25.11.07   —Juliana
—   Birgit, 22.11.07 —Karin 26.12.07   Silvia 30.12.07   Brigitte 02.01.08   —Martina, Jan 6   Barbel, 27.11.07   Paula, 30.01.08   Colette, 16.12.07   Lena, 27.11.07
ing, 27.11.07   —Noelia, 02.01.08   Marina, 5.12.07   ANDREW, 17.01.08   Angelas, 24.12.07   MARIA, 9.12.07   Miriam 12.01.08   Karola, 30.01.08 —Diana, 30.01.08   —Johanna, 5.12.07   Barbara, 02.12.07
—Christine, 10.2.08   Claudia, 20.01.08   Jana, 07.02.08 Giana, 30.01.08   —   Wilhelm, 22.11.07   Bettina, 11.12.07   Alica, 27.11.07   Stephanie 8.12.07 Heike, 8.12.07 —Annemarie 06.01.08
Carina, 27.11.07   —   —Bianca, 30.12.07   Gisela, 27.11.07   Agnes, 09.02.07   Maika, 4.12.07   —Caroline 03.01.08   —Alica, 31
vina, 26.12.07   Elfi, 6.12.07 —Christel, 12.01.08   —Angelika, 30.11.07   Bettina, 27.11.07   —Alexandra 6.02.08   Rita, 22.11.07   —Emyly, 30.12.07   —Andrea 6.02.08   —A
Xonad   —10.2.08   Johanna, 5.12.07   —   —Davinna, 13.12.07
Theresa, 29.01.08   —Erinna 03.01.08

—Carmen, 16.12.07   —Yesenia 23.12.07

—Therese, 20.01.08   智子 —10.2.08
Tomoko

—Lisa, 29.12.07

—Luisa 26.12.07

—Luis, 23.12.07   —Charlotte, 16.12.07

—Adrian, 19.01.08

—Ella, 02.12.07   —Clemens 20.01.08

—Tom, 28.12.07

—Felix, 25.11.07

—Lena, 25.11.07   —Ella 10.2.08

—— Andy, 23.11.07

—— Andreas, 28.11.07   —— Andreas, 02.12.07

—— Albert, 25.11.07   —— Dieter, 16.12.07   Dirk, 12.04.08 Stefan, 6.12.07   —— Ralf, 03.02.08

—— Matthias, 02.12.07 —Gerhard, 23.12.07   Christoph, 23.12.07 —Amir, 29.01.08 —Ferdinand, 14.02.08   —— Winfried, 07.02.08   Martin, 15.12.07

—Christoph, 16.12.07 —Karsten, 02.12.07 —Stefanos, 9.12.07 —Josef, 22.01.08 Gerd, 2.12.07 — Karl, 16.12.07 —Christoph, 29.12.07 —Lukas 16.12.07 —Raina 21.12.07 —Richard — Johannes, 29

—Peter, 8.12.07   —Bernd, 24.11.07 —Justin, 18.01.08 —Robert, 25.11.07   Maurizio, 15.12.07   Vera, 30.12.07

—Antje, 17.12.07   —Martin, 17.01.08   —Marcel, 01.02.08   Michal, 23.11.07   —Matthias 23.12.07   Johannes 12.01.08

—Andreas, 30.12.07   Alfons, 12.12.07   —Karl   —Georg, 30.12.07   Rainhold, 8.12.07   Norbert, 28.11.07   Enrico, 3.1.08

—Tina 10.01.08   —Penn, 30.11.07   Ramona 3.1.2008 Lukas, 27.11.07   —Martin, 27.11.07   —Claus, 02.12.07   —Andrea, 15.12.07

—Paul, 18.12.07 —Heiner, 6.1.08 —Tatjana 22.12.07   —Klaus 23.12.07   —Petra, 30.12.07   —Brigitte, 15.01.08

—Charlott 26.12.07   —Adela, 02.12.07   —David, 02.12.07   —Britta 22.01.08   —Verena, 02.12.07   —Stefan, 02.12.07   —Ruben, 25.11.07

—Christina 12.01.08   —Dom, 18.12.07   —Michael, 28.11.07   —Pernilla, 26.12.07   —Wenny, 02.12.07   —Nikola, 02.12

—Gabriele, 25.11.07   —Gabriela, 23.11.07   —Wolfgang, 9.12.07 —Katrin, 25.11.07   —Markus, 16.12.07   —Andrea, 8.12.07   —Anna, 16.12.07

—Manfred, 8.12.07   —Tom, 8.1.08   —Tamara, 02.12.07   —Chiara, 16.12.07   —Maria, 13.12.07   —Mirko, 03.01.08   —Nora, 25.11.07   —Dasha

—Stefan, 18.12.07   —Cecilia, 26.12.07   —Andrea, 16.12.07   —Alessandro, 3.1.08   —Outi 26.12.07   —Beate 04.01.08   —Monika, 29.12.07

—Marianne, 18.12.07   —Susanne, 07.12.07   —Anna   —Heinz, 8.12.07   —Susanne 16.01.08

—Lucka, 02.12.07   —Oso, 23.12.07   —Beate 22.11.07 —Vicky, 9.12.07   —Beata, 22.11.07   —Gunther 17.01.08   —Annette —Manfred   —Anja, 25.11.07

—Dagmar 22.01.08 —Elke, 23.11.07   —Verena, 27.11.07   —Elke 26.12.07 —Gerrit, 6.1.08   —Birgit 02.01.08   —Sina 16.12.07   —Marianne 02.12.07   —Ubla, 27.11.07

—Lea-Kristin, 27.11.07   —Katarina, 9.12.07   —Marian, 16.12.07   —Johanna, 27.11.07   —Franziska 27.11.07 —Katarina, 27.11.07   —Clara, 30.12.07   —Maria 9.12.07

—Elisabeth, 27.11.07   —Yasmin, 30.12.07   —Nalin, 13.12.07   —Annemarie, 20.01.08   —Adriana, 9.12.07   —Viola, 8.12.07   —Anne, 30.12.07   —Annegret, 06.01.08   —Maria, 22.11.07

—Francesca, 29.12.07   —Houika, 16.12.07   —Pauline, 24.11.07   —Birgitta 22.01.08   —Kathi 27.01.08   —Giselle 11.12.07 Uta, 03.01.08   —Tamara 04.01.08

—Anja, 09.01.08   —Conny 27.12.07   —Zübeyda, 8.12.07   —Silvia 30.12.07   SIMONE, 04.12.2007   —Claudia 04.01.08   —Anja 20.01.08   —Irene 20.01.08   Sophia, 21.12.07

—Christl, 6.1.08   —Ruby, 02.12.07   —Katrin, 10.02.08   —Monique —Monka, 12.12.07   —Ingrid, 11.01.08   —Karren, 20.01.08

—Isabell 26.12.07   —Gabriela 08.01.08   —Laura, 20.02.08   —Felix, 30.12.07

—— Hugo, 02.12.07   —Malu, 070208   —Lisa, 25.11.07

—Christopher, 8.12.07   —Lea, 8.12.07   —Sebastian, 30.12.07

—Julia, 07.02.08

—Sonja 30.12.07

—Stella, 2.2.08

—Benjamin, 16.12.07

—Luisa, 27.11.07

—Lara, 07.01.08

—Camille, 07.02.08

—Emile, 16.12.07

—Amélie 20.01.08

—Nelly 28.12.07

—Fabian, 30.12.07

Martin, 23.11.07
...m, 16.12.07
...ia, - 10.02.08
6.01.08
Stephan 12.01.08
А н т о н, 27.11.07
Stefan 03.01.08
Felix 05.01.08
Niels, 22.01.08
Rüdiger 02.01.08
Roman, 4.12.07
Scotty 11.12.07
Henrik, - 10.2.08
Ulrike, 02.01.08
Roland. 07.12.07
Simon, 22.01.08
Claudio, 25.01.08
Günter, 02.01.08
Tobias 9.12.07
Jens, 02.01.08
Frank, - 10.2.08
VOJT...
02.08
Bernhard, 30.12.07
Marius, 1.12.07
Tom, 23.11.07
Michael, 03.01.08
Christer 27.01.08
Halmut, 19.01.08
Florian, 05.01.08
Mark 18.01.08
Stefan, 02.12.07
Marius 18.0...
Patricia 2...
2.07
Jürgen 23.12.07
Heinz, 03...
Ernst, 8.12.07
Christoph, 30.12.07
Jörg, 8.12.07
Jens, 16.12.07
Mateo, 16.12.07
Enrico, 6.12.07
Rowland, 16.12.07
Stefan, 13.01.08
Torsten, 1.01.08
Hans, 30.01.08
Max, 27.11.07
Clovis, 15.01.08
Eduard. 17.01.08
Thomas 31.1.08
Stefan 18.01.08
Raimund 18.0...
Urs, 8.12.07
Zdravko, 9.12.07
Tommy, 03.01.08
Andreas, 12.01.08
Meinrad 10.0...
Antonino, 30.12.07
Denis, 15.01.08
Carolin, 11.01.08
Timo, 16.12.07
Claus, 8.12.07
Anne 27.01.08
Etienne, 22.11.07
Ryan, 22.01.08
Alexandra, 9.12.07
Tobi 27...
Gius...
22.12.07
Heinz, 22.01.08
Antonia, 30.11.07
Matti, 02.12.07
Richard, 29.12.07
Ludwig, 27.11.07
Bruno, 03.02.08
Stefano, 30.12.07
Sarhiy, 02.01.08
Anke, 8.12.07
Dženi, 9.12.07
Jonas, 4.12.07
Hans 04.04.08
Thomas, 1.12.07
Margit, 16.12.07
Vicente, 25.11.07
Winfried, 02.12.07
Oskar, 8.12.07
Christine, 22...
Chris, 4.12.07
Janika 08.02.08
Stefi, 02.01.08
Francisco 23.12.07
Serzan 22.01.08
Simone, 22.12.07
Gaëlle, 02.12.07
Michael, 16.12.07
Werner 22.0...
Enrico, 3.1.08
Lui, 25.11.07
Anna 02.01.08
Birgy, -10.2.08
Suzannah, 30.11.07
Andreas, 26.01.08
Andreas, 02.12.07
Slava, 23.12.07
Sibylle 2...
Claudia, 12.07
Ursula 03.02.08
Loreen, 30.01.08
Stephen, 18.12.07
Alex, 22.11.07
Udo, 9.11.07
Michael, 15.12.07
Roberta, 28.12.07
Marko, 02.12.07
Werner...
Barbara 16.12.07
Александра 23.12.07
Jasmin, 27.11.07
Andrea, 29.12.07
Piep. 02.12.07
Anja, 01.02.08
Thomas, 27.11...
Monika, 8.12.07
Koca, 3.2.08
Kathrin, 07.12.07
Helena, 28.11.07
Carla 18.07
Byron, 07.12.07
Ruth, 19.01.08
Jessica, 30.12.07
Mieke, 31.1.08
Rude, 29.12.07
EDIT, 24.11.07
Pavel, 22.11.07
Gabriela, 02.12.07
Claudio, 30.12.07
Nadine, 30.01.08
Christina, 18.12.07
Florian, 13.01.08
Veronika, 8.12.07
Katya, 6.12.07
Halil, 22.01.08
Julia, 30.12.07
Carolyn, 16.12.07
Claudia 9.12.07
Patrizia, 02.12.07
Christine, 27.11.07
Roberto, 9.12.07
Simone, 30.11.07
Petra, 16.12.07
Helena, 22.11.07
Anne-Marie, 9.12.07
Magdalena, 18.12.07
Ina, 8.12.07
Sarah, 13.01.08
KATЯ, 23.12.07
Marta 30.12.07
Klaus 9.12.07
Sabine, 02.02.08
Brigitta, 03.01.08
LI, 23.11.07
Marlen 09.02.08
Monika, 03.01.08
Stephanie, 30.11.07
Walter, 22.11.07
Christine, 31.1.08
Janes, 23.11.07
Carola, 8.12.07
Susan, 18.12.07
Katharina, 9.12.07
Helma, 30.01.08
Eoin, 15.12.07
Jenny, 26.12.07
Ute 27.01.08
Birgit, 29.12.07
Gabi, 29.11.07
Brigitte, 30.01.08
Lotte, 25.11.07
Bea, 30.11.07
Ina, 9.12.07
Blanca 25.11.07
Christiane, 28.11.07
Noria, 30.12.07
Sabine 17.01.08
Thomas, 30.12.07
Nel, 30.01.08
Nicole 16.01.08
Angel...
Barbara 08.12.07
Pia, 9.12.07
Nadine 16.12.07
Heather 16.01.08
Sabina, 22.11.07
Claudia, 16.12.07
Ursula, 02.12.07
Uschi 29.11.07
Olympia, 07.12.07
Lisa, 6.12.07
Margarita 22.04.08
Sabine, 30.12.07
Theresa, 27.11.07
Joana, 12.12.07
Anni, 03.01.08
Viktoria 11.12.07
Anna 18.01.08
Inge, 16.12.07
Afra 30.12.07
Uschi, 51.08
Editha, 17.01.08
Almerinda, 30.12.07
Heidi 04.04.08
Hanna, 12.12.07
Flavie 11.12.07
TWB, 24.12.07
Davia, 21.12.07
Bedriye, 22.01.08
Gabriella, 25.11.07
Dorothée, 02.12.07
Almuth, 8.12.07
София, 21.12.07
Pasquale, 30.12.07
Chiara, 25.11.07
Bruno 02.01.08
Itala. 07.12.07
Eun, 30.12.07
Tugce, 22.01.08
Anna, 30.12.07
Lucia, 30.12.07
Jessica, 30.1.08
Katarina, 19.01.08
Ingrid...
Florenc 29.12.07
Letizia, 25.11.07
Friederike, 30.12.07
Mönn, 30.12.07
Sophie 20.01.08
Johan, 02.02.08
David, 30.12.07
Jakob, 30.12.07
Florian, 27.11.07
Alexandra 30.12.07
Finja, 23.12.07
Maria 23.12.07
Charlotte, 30.12.07
Ac...
Valentin, 27.11.07
Lisa. 27.11.07
Julia 24.11...
Claudio, 30.12.07
Oskar, 30.12.07
Juliane, 30.12.07
Lizzi, 03.01.08.

_ Sana 18.01.08

__ Simeon, 8.12.07

— Günter, 07.02.08

_ DETLEF. 8.12.07

_ Detlef. 02.12.07

_ Marc, 16.12.07

— Maxie 05.04.08

Patrick, 9.12.07

Cristiano, 12.01.08

Franz, 15.12.07

Wolfgang, 22.01.08

Robert, 12.12.07

Matthias, 9.12.07

20.12.07 — Wolfgang Darko, 30.12.07 — Jens, 0802.08

ERIK 29.1207

Šimon, 23.11.07

Roland, 02.12.07 — Matthias 12.01.08 Bertil, 03.02.08

— Nabel 03.01.08

— Bruno, 27.12.07 — Florian, 15.12.07

Arnoldt 02.01.08

Filippo

02.01.08 — Alexander, 02.08 Roger. 02.12.07 — Marc, 5.1.08

— Thierry 02.12.07

Wolfgang, 22.11.07

05. 9.12.07 Felix, 27.11.07 David, 21.12.07

Otto 16.01.08 — Toni 02.12.07

Elisa, 03.02.08 Christoph, 02.12.07 — Stefan, 22.12.07

Arthur 18.01.08

Michael, 16.12.07

Halmut 18.02.08 Teodoro, 15.01.08

Colleen, 17.01.08 Patricia, 02.12.07 — Till, 31.1.08 — Lucas, 31.1.08

Magarete Iris 02.12.07 — Ruben, 26.12.07 — Collin Berg, 27.11.07 Jutta 03.02.08 Daniela, 23.11.07 Patrick, 16.12.07

Ulrik, 21.12.07

Jens, 9.12.07 Michael, 22.01.08 — Gerda, 23.11.07 — Michaele, 02.12.07 Graham, 27.11.07

25.12.07 — Tobias 02.04.08

Elke, 29.11.07 Felix Martin, 25.11.07

Salvat

Laura, 30.07 22.12.07 Daniel — Kent 11.12.07 Ricardo, 6.1.08 Josmyn, 27.11.07 Tatjana, 8.12.07

Heinz, 8.12.07 Michael 16.12.07 Michael

Nathalie, 02.12.07 — Werner, 16.01.08

Natali Wladek, 02.12.07

Marve, 8.12

Jürke, 22.11.07 — Clemens, 02.12.07 Stella 02.01.08

Maximilian 26.12.07 Catriona, 27.11.07 Volker 22.11.07

Birgit, 22.12.07 Kerstin Maria, 23.11.07

Lina, 02.12.07

Winfried, 24.11.07 Karlheinz, 16.12.07 Eckhart, 02.02.08 Brigitte, 27.11.07 Wayang Black, 13.01.08 Wolfgang, 25.11.07

Verena, 30.12.07

27.11.07 Ute Eva, 25.11.07

Jutta, 02.01.08 — Eduardo 01.02.08 Ingrid 08.12.07 27.11.07 Steffi, 03.01.08 — Roberta, 21.12.07 Anne, 6.1.08

Sonja, 25.01.08 — Catrine

Rebecca, 27.11.07 Christine, 24.11.07 Markus, 24.11.07 — Jan 18.01.08 Cordelia Tabian, 23.11.07

Hedda, 29.12.07 Natali 03.01.08

Emely, 30.01.08 Lusinda, 16.12.07 Stini 02.01.08 Julia 30.01.08 Ingrid, 23.12.07 Giovanna, 28.11.07 Tina Lilly, 16.12.07 Mirjam, 26.12.07

Regina, 8.12.07 Rosmarie

Diggi, 24.11.07 Klaus, 03.02.08 Gaby Melanie, 27.11.07 Andrea, 3.1.08 Freia, 22.11.07 6.12.07 Stephanie

26.01.08 — Zuleica Lena, 12.08 Katrin

Renate 27.01.08 Francesca, 28.04 — James 13.11.07 Gesine 06.01.08 Jolena 31.1.08 BARBARA 23.12.07 Susanne, 03.01.08

Valeria, 03.01.08 Julia, 16.12.07 — Silvia, 31.1.08 Norma, 02.12.07

Hilde, 29.11.07 Dtah 05.02.08 Kim 27.11.07 HATAWA, 12.01.08 Christine, 07.12.07 — EVA 10.01.08 Eva, 29.11.07 Ignacio, 9.12.07

Christine, 29.11.07

Johanna, 22.11.0

Christina, 02.12.07 Rachel, 17.01.08 Andrea, 02.12.07 Jasmine, 28.01.08 Sydney 05.01.08 Magdalen 30.07

Maria, 12.12.07

Ulrike 29.12.07

Shaye 27.01.08 Ulrike, 24.11.07 Jan 03.01.08 Amelie, 08.01.08 Malgorzata, 02.12.07 Julia, 23.11.07 Shergl, 27.11.07 Corinna Agnes 04.01.08 — Heidi, 28.12.07 Rita, 03.02.08 — Claire

Liliana, 9.12.07 — Heike-Marianne, 22.11.07 Irmgard 04.01.08 Sibylle, 16.01.08 — Anja, 15.12.07 — Barbara, 16.12

— Usu, 27.12.07 Marina, 23.11.07 — Tomoé 13.12.07 — Svenja, 5.1.08

Steffi, 22.01.08

— Corine, 03.02.08

— Felix 3.02.08

— Sara, 25.11.07

— Leon, 13.

— Wanda 02.01.08

— Lukas, 30.12.07

— Laura, 07.02.08

— Jakob, 30.12.07

Pablo, 02.12.07

——— Nastasia, 19.01.08

— Noah, 07.02.08

— Pandora 03.01.08

— Enrico, 13.01.08

— Hann

— Elias, 07.02.08

— Serafina, 19.01.08

— Josephine 23.12.07

— Alina, 30.12.07

— Jonatan, 13.12.07

— Luise 23.12.07

— Louis 20.01.08

— Anna-Bluma 15.12.07

__Mathias, 02.12.07

__Rainer, 02.12.07   __Stephan, 8.12.07 __Sven 1.1.08

__Mike, 16.12.07

__Daniel, 22.01.08

__Nikhil, -10.2.08

__Robin, 21.12.07   __Kilian, -08.02.08   __Meinhardt, 02.12.07   __Daniel 02.01.08   __Florian, 03.02.08   __Markus, 9.12.07
__Detlef 22.12.07   __Johannes, 8.12.07   __Florian, 03.02.08   __Christian, 24.11.07   __Anian, 07.12.07   __Sebastian, 27.11.07 __Marco, 9.12.
02.01.08   __Jan-willem, 28.12.07 __Jutta, 10.2.08   __Klaus, 02.12.07   __Markus, 02.01.08 __Sylvain, 13.01.08
__Michael, 12.12.07   __Geneit, 5.1.08   __Heinz-Peter, 03.01.08   __Jens, 16.12.07 __Sebastian, 28.12.07   __Stefan, 25.11.07
__Holger, 6.12.07   __Phaelix, 22.11.07 __Beate, 02.12.07 __Hans-Jürgen, 29.0.0   __Uwe, 20.01.08   __Max 08.02.08 __Jens 02.12.07   __Benedikt, 12.12.08   __Mathis, 6.1.08
__Steffen, 26.12.07 __Cameron, 22.01.08 __Stevan, __Lucas, 12.12.07 __Ralf, 22.01.08   __Johann, 9.12.07   __Eva, __Herbert, 25.11.07 __Marina, 8.1
__Kathrin 15.01.08   __Geliard 27.11 __Hans, 02.12.07   __Suzi 05.0...08 16.12.07 __Dhiya, 02.01.08   __Maria, __Helmut, 07.12.07 __Lynne, 22.   __Warwick, 28.11.07   __Reinhard,
__Christian, 27.11.07 __Volker, 25.11.07 __Karsten 9.12.07 __Klaus, 12.01.08 __Karin, 02.12.07   __Paul, 9.12.07   __Gih, 22.12.07 __Bernd 30.0   __Benedikt, __Eva, 22.1 __Lutz II 10.0
07' __Anka, 9.01.08 __Lukas, 12.12.07 __Nina, 13.0.08 __Britta, 9.12.07 __Justyna 0.02.08 __steffen, 02.12.07 __Katarina   __Urielle 29.12.07 __Marte, 28.   __Carina, 23.11.07 __Peter
__Johannes, 27.11.07 __Ulrich 02.01.08 __Leon 01.02.08 __Bryce, 8.12.07 __Klous 29.12.07 __Dieter, 16.12.07 __Elena, 22.11.07 __Sonja, 02.12.07 __Renaud 27.11.0   __Susanne, 05.02.08 __Franz   __Rebekka, 02.12.07 __Karin, 11.04.08
__Gabi, 24.11.07   __Ramón, 07.12.07   __Francesca __Inge, 28.11.07 __Ursula,   __Sam, 02.01.08   __Birgit   __Nina, 02.12.07 __Franz 01.01.08   __Franz, 15.12.07 __Anna, 03
24.11.07 __Tanja, 28.11.07 __HALILOVIC __Heinz, 27.11.07 __Mar   __Patrick __Dana, 9.12.07 __Rose 02.12.07 __Ulli   __AR __Paulina, 16.12.07 __Cara, 22.11.07 __Keem 22.12.
__Christina, 02.01.08 __Britta, 5.1.08 __Eliska, 23.11.07 __Maria   __Claudia, 16.12.07 __Thea, 16.12.07 __Solo   __Valentina   __Anna, 16.12.0
__Emanuel 26.1 __Sybill, 27.11.07 __Theresa, 22.01.08 __Benita, 02.12.07 __Sylvia, 06.01.08 __Galina 6.1.08 __Margarethe, 24.11.0   __Kristin 12.01   __Kathrin   __Upuna, 12.01.08
12.07 __Elfriede 29.12.07 __Maria, 25.11.07 __Judith 27.12.07 __Angela 03.01.08 __Eva-Maria, 24.11.07 __Sonhiete, 02.12.07 __Marina, 9.12.07 __Isabella, 9.12.07 __IBAHKA   __Carolin
__Laura, 1.12.07   __Argyro, 02.12.07 __Handy, 6.1.08 __Franziska 0.2   __Heidi, 26.01.08 __Travoll, 29.11.07 __Bura, 03.01.08   __Martha, 24.11.07
__Lorena, 8.12.07 __Petra, 02.12.07 __Dany, 07.12.07 __Anika 06.   __Theresa 22.12.07 __Ulrike, 12.01.08 __Olga, 8.12.07   __Theresia   __Renate, 6.12.07 __Gabi, 24.01.08
__Isabelle, 01.02.08 __Katharina 08.01.08 __Lynne 20.01.08 __Monika, 27.11.07 __Kate   __Paula, 29.11.07 __Edith 02.12.07   __Angela   __Christian
__Duraid 02.01.08   __Noelle, 25.11.07 __Romy-Lin, 28.12.07 __Sarah 26.12.07 __Marion 02.01.08 __Lorie 11.12.07 __Bernadette, 29.12.07 __Mary, 22.11.07 __Heike 03.01   __Leonora, 11.12.07 __Rachelle, 03.01.08
02.08   __Vanessa, 03.02.08 __Marlena 12.01.08 __Emma 11.12.07 __Simone 27.12.07   __Juliane, 02.01.08 __Jannis, 12.01.08 __Bethany, 22.01
__Maja, 22.11.07 __Elisabeth, 26.12.07 __Mario, -31.01.08 __Heathir, -27.01.08 __Erika, 02.12.07 __Sarah, 02.12.07 __Lena-
07 __Anna-Margrete, 21.12.07 __Daniel, 02.12.07   __Lvei, -31.01.08   __ん, 03.02.08   25.11.07 __Teo,
__Uli, 29.11.07   __Reira, 23.12.2007 __Nikola, 23.11.07   __Benedikt,
effi, 12.12.07   __Elsbeth, 03.02.08   Japan

01.08

__Tejal, 22.01.08

__Ferdinand, 9.12.07

__Pauline, 26.01.08 __Anne, 26.12.07

__Henriette 8.12.07

ah, 03.02.08

__Corina, 03.02.08

__Lorenz, 03.02.08
__Paul, 13.01.08

__Linus, 03.01.08 -

__Evie, 16.12.07

— Max, 5.1.08

— Stefan, 27.12.07

— Christian 20.01.08

— Simon, 07.12.07   — Jan, 02.12.07

— Christian, 22.11.07

alf. 02.12.07   — Johannes, 07.12.07   Sebastian 20.01.08   — Lorenzo, 8.12.07   — John, 8.12.07   — Benjamin, 30.12.07   — Nikolai 23.12.07   Potu, 02.12.07

1.08   — Matthew, 20.01.08   — Wenzel, 22.01.08   — Hermann, 26.01.08   Paul, 02.01.08   — Harald 02.12.07   — Hermann, 9.12.07   George

— Maximilian 08.01.08   — Frank, 22.01.08   — Andreas, 12.12.08   Nikolai, 28.11.07

— Heribert, 28.11.07   — Michael 18.01.08   — Viv, 12.12.07   Antje 20.01.08   Beau, 12.12.07   Ado 23.11.07 — Dominik 27.01.08   Dom

Johannes 28.12.08   — Miro 22.11.07   — Fabian, 02.12.07   — David, 25.11.07   Thomas 07.02.08   Yana, 21.12.07   Thorsten, 03.02.08   Bill, 8.12.07

07 — Randolph 07.02.08   — Sergey 23.11.09   — Jon, 9.12.07   — Philo 28.12.07   — 23.12.07 — Jürgen 6.1.08 Bernadine 27.12.07   Erich, 25.11.07   Thomas, 8.12.07

Stephanie 27.12.07   Michael 04.01.08   — Marianne 04.01.08   Paul 02.02.08   — Jörg 2001.08   Katrin 22.11.07   Dominic 20.01.08   Carlo, 30.12.07   Mathias, 24.11.07   Inga, 02.12.07

07 Wildemann 2008   Korbinian, 24.11.07   — John 14.12.07   Christian, 05.02.08   Norbert, 22.11.07   Werner, 16.12.07   Jt, 2001.08   Matthias, 28.11.07   Katja, 9.12.07   Jörg 04.01.08

Heidi 02.01.08   Tra, 26.1.08   Ali 18.01.08   Lucy, 02.12.07   Leila, 9.12.07 — Max, Jc 11.07   Gisbert 15.12.07   Toto, 16.12.07   Nina, 22.01.08   Hortensia, 24.11.07   VTA, 11.07

Patrick, 07.12.07 Jürgen 07.01.08   Vuokko, 26.12.07   Helga, 22.01.08 Ambra, 27.11.07   Stefan 2014   Edeltraud, 4.12.07   Sanne, 02.12.07   Ingrid, 27.11.07   Stephane, 8.12.07   Emilia

abara 02.01.08   Martjin 09.02.08   Nl 9, 8.12.07   Silke, 9.12.07   Charlotte, 9.12.07   Julia, 24.01.08   Susanne, 5.1.08   Uli 01.04.08

Hedi, 15.12.07   Patrick, 27.11.07   Eva, 22.11.07   Sarah 09.12.07   Juliana 13.12.07   Ale 21.12.07 — Volker 2008   Christian, 22.11.07   Ergül 30.12.07   Lisa 24.01.08   Beate

Jeannette 09.02.08   Freya, 25.11.07 — Nicola, 2008   Toni, 02.12.07   Jil, 23.01.08   esley, 02.12.07   Kirsten, 22.11.07   Eva 24.12.07   Theresa 28.11.07   Christoph, 29.11.07   Katharin

Barbara 26.11.07 — Sylvia, 02.12.07   — Julia, 5.01.07   Georgia 2008   Michael, 30.01.07 Lena, 27.12.07 Kerstin, 25.01.08   Elke, 23.11.07   Heike 25.12.07   Nora, 03.02.08   Freike, 02.12

— Gregor 28.12. Steph 03.01.08 Mona, 9.12.07   Manfred, 23.11.07   Clarissa 30.01.08   Stefanie, 25.11.07   Brigitte, 02.12.07   Isabella, 4.12.07   Nicole 21.01.08   Geraldine, 10

— Jesus, 07.12.07   — Maca 8.12.07   Hans am 2008   — Anja, 5.1.08   Sosie, 22.01.08   Meldem, Jc 11.07   CHTDLJ, 07.12.07   Robayo 8.12.07   — Angie, 28.11.07   Max, 27.11.07

9.12.07 — Kira, 13.01.08   Christina 26.12.07   Katharina   Beverley, 13.12.07   Zlo, 07.12.07   — Deborah, 2008   Helga, 13.12.07   Brigitte, 09.02.08   Mo ₁ 14.12.07   Lena, 4.12.07   Franziska, 26.12.07

orh M 12.07 Victoria, 27.11.07   — Olga, 9.12.07   — Justine 22.11.07 — Susanne, 28.12.07   — Hannelore d 11.07   — Brigitte, 03.02.08   Franzi(ka 11.07   Wall, 22.01.08 Gil 14.12.07   Lena, 4.12.07   Franziska, 26.12.07

Melanie 27.12.08   Tra, 26.12.07   Julia, 23.11.07   Elizabeth, 28.11.07   Velia, 16.12.07   Anja 20.01.08   Gitta, 6.1.08   Elisa, + Libuse 12.01.08   — Katharina, 15.12

Mbina 27.12.07 Christa, 07.12.07   Judith, 22.01.08   — Natascha 28.01.08   Charlotte 26.12.13   — Levenik St. 12.01.08   — Robert, 28.11.07   Nikki 28.01.08   Elena, 25.11.07   Steffi 05.01.08   Ashna 27.01.08   Dasho

Anna 10.01.08   Annerose, 24.11.07   — Kristin, 5.01.07   Agneta, 02.12.07   — EVANGELIA lrm 30.12.07   Ulricke, 03.01.08   Ruth, 28.11.07   Julia 10.01.08   Beate 2

01.08 — Narmin, 22.01.08   Irina 10.01.08   — Momike 29.12.07   Artemis, 23.11.07   Ot Ami, 07.12.07   Valenta, 13.01

5.1.08 — Regina 08.01.08 — Karin, 25.11.07   — Andrea, 14.12.07   — Olga 10.01.08   it 2 1, 06.01.08   Paola, 8.12.07 — Lynn, 05.02.08   — Satu, 11.12.07   Cli

Isolde, 30.01.08   Laurita, 8.12.07   Daria 23.12.07

— Elisabeth, 01.01.08   — Angela, 27.01.08 Živa, 25.11.07   Yu-Ling shiu (Judith) 10.2.08   — Laura, 15.01.08   — Lydia 15.01.08   — Waltraud, 5.1.08

A, 25.11.07

— Johanna, 26.12.07   — Kenyika, — 10.2.08   — Gianna, 25.11.07

— Mathis, 12.01.08   — Frederieke 23.12.07

— Chiara, 02.12.07

— Julian, 30.12.07

— Philip, — 10.2.08

— Theodora, 30.01.08   — Isabella, 5.1.08

— Cosima, 5.1.08

— Angelo — Gabriel, 02.0

7   — Ciaran 7.11.07   — Floria

— Julio, — 20.08

— Julia Maria, 30.12.07

_Tristan, 03.01.08

_Ivo, 02.12.07

_Christoph, 02.12.07

_18.01.08 _John, 9.12.07 _Armin, 25.11.07 _Андрей, 12.01.08 _Markus, 03.02.08 _Sebastian, 03.02
_Andreas, 5.1.08 _Kristina, 26.01.08 _Martin, 15.12.07 _Thomas, 27.1.08 _Bernd, 01.01.08 _Udo, 02.12
_Ulrich 26.12.07 _Heinrich, 28.12.07 _Daniel, 23.11.07 _Sylvain, 16.12.07 _Toni, 8.12.07 _Matteo
_Eeif, 1.12.07 _Martin, 03.01.08 _Tino, 02.01.08 _Cabildo, 30.11.07 _Christoph, 25.11.07 _Coruel, 15.12.07 _Dennis, 15.12.07 _Greg
_Jan, 8.12.07 _Marlies, 15.12.07 _Hartmut, 03.01.08
_Udo 10.01.08 _Annika, 03.01.08 _Stefan 08.01.98 _Timo, 18.12.07 _Nina, 28.12 _Thomas _Joaghim, 15.12.07 _Steffan, 02.01.08 _Babak, 15.12.07
_John, 15.12.07 _Elke, 22.11.07 _Jose Luis, 8.12.07 _Stephan, 19.12.07 _Nel, 03.01.08 _Zan _Frederike, 9.11.07 _Filippo, 28.11.08 _Michael
_Benno, 22.11.07 _Lucj, 03.02.08 _Hans 07.02.08 _Viktor 26.12.07 _Christian, 07.12.07 _Harald, 28.11.07 _Maximilian 26.12.07 _Marein, 24.11.07
_Achim, 1.12.07 _Kai, 02.01.08 _Helmut, 5.12.07 _Stefan, 22.11.07 _Elke, 25.1.08 _Florian, 21.11.07 _Anne, 02.01.08 _Shai, 07.12.07
_Florian, 22.12.07 _Michael, 22.11.07 _Franciska, 9.12.07 _Moritz, 03.01.08 _Konrad, 27.11.07 _Anna-Theresa 08.01.08 _Jean-Michel, 25.11.07 _Felix, 25.11.07 _Magnu
_Jochen, 30.12.07 _Andreas, 20.01.08 _Astried, 02.12.07 _Arne 01.01.08 _Markus, 16.12.07 _Wieland, 26.12.07 _Roland, 9.12.07 _Eva, 16.12.07
_Katarzyna, 25.11.07 _Annik, 08.02.08 _Christiane 9.12.07 _Linos, 15.12.07 _Michael, 08.02.08 _Jasmine, 03.02.08 _Ulrike, 23.11.07 _Andreas _Noemi, 02.12.07 _Britta, 07.12.07
_Ruth, 22.11.07 _Bernd 20.01.08 _Janny 25.11.07 _Stefan, 22.11.07 _Harald 28.12 _Ramona, 1.12.07 _Stanislaus, 20.01.08 _Andreas 29.12.07 _Rola 9.12.07
_Neckermann, 23.12.07 _Martina, 29.11.07 _Helga, 9.12.07 _Christa, 13.01.08 _Wolf, 24.11.07 _Domenique _Francois, 02.12 _Susanne 28.12.07
_Peter 8.12.07 _Lybov, 03.01.08 _Andrej, 22.11.07 _Veikko, 11.12.07 _Ingeborg, 5.12.07 _Petra 23.12.07 _Johanna, 17.01.08 _Anna _Johnny, 9.12.07 _Raingard
_Christina 28.11.07 _Erika _Martina, 9.12.07 _Kerstin, 1.12.07 _Najib, 29.11.07 _Agnes 25.11.07 _Gita, 5.12.07 _Susanne _Floria
_Shanelle, 22.01.08 _Eggert, 07.12.07 _Mascha, 1.12.07 _Felizian, 11.07 _Monika, 8.12.07 _Regine, 02.12.07 _Alex 11.12 _Guduka, 22.11.07 _Lieve, 28.11 _Buket
_Andre, 29.12.07 _Linda, 03.02.08 _Steffi, 02.12.07 _Leonardo 11.12.07 _Marta, 02.12.07 _Christine _Barbara, 9.12.07 _Lilli 28.12.07 _Anja, 30.01.07 _Michelle, 02.12.07 _Steffi, 30.11.07 _Lisalotte, 9.12.07 _Gillien _Christina _Hasa, 16.12.07
_Christine, 07.12.07 _Karina, 25.11.07 _Nicole, 6.1.08 _Helga, 24.11.07 _Huna, 28.12.07 _Ada, 03.01.08 _Marie, 22.01.08 _Itamar
_Renate, 27.11.07 _Maria Jesus, 8.12.07 _Irmgard, 5.1.08 _Hanna, 28.12 _Giuseppe, 30.12.07 _Lorenz, 02.01.08 _BEPA 23.12.07 _Marie, 25.11.07 _Rony, 18.12.07
_Nicole 29.11.07 _Annika, 25.11.07 _Laurine, 24.01.08 _Marion, 25.11.07 _Alida 17.12.07 _Stefanie, 13.01.08 _Elfriede, 03.01.08
_Janet 27.01.08 _Francisca 20.01.08 _Gisela, 08.01.08 _Anna, 26.01.08 _Christel, 27.01.08 _Ciro, 02.01.08 _Lena, 28.11.07 _Katrin, 5.1.08 _Julia
_Anne, 28.12.07 _Hendrik, 28.12.07 _Christine, 31.01.08 _Angela 26.12.07 _Einat, 15.12.07 _02.01.08 _Maria, 07.02.08 _Elisabeth, 06.01.08 _Reyo, 26.12
_Angelika, 03.02.08 _Myriam, 15.01.08 _Deborah 11.12.07 _Isabel, 5.1.08 _Yuva
_22.11.07 _黑子 23.12.07
_Natacia 20.01.08 _Patrizia, 30.12.07 _Valentina, 02.01.08 _齐, 20.01.08 _Pranukorn, 8.12.07 _Anna-Sophia
_Darian, 13.01.08 _Carla 11.12.07 _Maria, 3.01.07
_Elfriede, 07.02.08
_Larissa, 31.01.08 _Silvia 25.12.07

_Sinan, 03.02.08

_Anna, 01.01.08

_Yana, 20.01.08 _Seraphine 06.01.08

_Stephanie, 27.11.07

_Dannis, 03.02.08

_07 _Natalie, 22.11.07

_Leon, 27.01.08 _Luisa
_Franziska, 2

_Charlie, 16.12.07

_Matteo, 16.12.07

_Emily, 12.01.08 _Yunus, 20.01.08

— JÖRGi, 17.01.08

__ Oliver, 03.01.08

—Michel, 24.01.08   __ Leo, 8.12.07   — André, 24.11.07

— Luke 26.12.07   Rainer, 27.01.08   — Axel, 27.01.08   Emerich 27.01.08   — Gregor, 24.11.07

.12.07   ___ Stefan, 25.11.07   — Martin, 31.01.08   Patrick, 03.01.08   — Hendrik, 22.01.08

2, 02.01.08   Immanuel, 07.02.08   — Björn, 03.02.08   Tommo 05.01.08   Stefan 02.01.08

.12.07   — Andreas, 02.12.07   Roman 11.12.07 Mathias, 02.12.07 Marcel, 12.01.08 Daniel, 28.11.07   Robin 04.01.08

And: 03.01.08   — Matteo, 30.11.07   Fabian, 9.12.07   Hans, 02.12.07   Ulrich, 28.11.07 — Alexander 05.01.08 Christian — Franz 28.11.07

— Andreas, 15.12.07   August, 02.01.08   — Roff, 08.02.08 — Thomas, 9.12.07   Marcelo, 02.12.07 — Thomas 26.01.08 Fatih, 8.12.07   Georg, 07.12.07 Martin, 22.01.08

.12.07 — Michael 22.11.07 — Norbert, 24.11.07 Berthold, 26.12.07 — Bernhard 05.01.08 — Markus 26.12.07 — Arthur 10.01.08 Michael, 26.01.08 Arnold, 8.12.07 — Alan 04.01.08 Jim, 8.12.07 Till,

8 Panos, 15.12.07 Malte, 16.12.07 — Harald, 07.02.08 Max, 24.11.07 — Martin, 8.12.07 Lars, 21.12.07 Maria, 02.12.07 — Nancy, 24.01.08 Annika, 05.02.08 Beniamin, 30.11.07 — Iva, 8.12.07 — Romy,

02.02.08 — Gerlind, 1.12.07 — Julia, 02.12.07 — Peter, 02.12.07 Wolfgang, 9.12.07 Klaus, 03.01.08 — Andreas 23.12.07 — Wilhelm 20.01.08 Danilo, 8.12.07

Dietmar 06.12.07 Brigitte, 03.01.08 — Nati, 02.01.08 — Horst — Klaus, 19.01.08 — Cyril Peter, 6.1.08 Barnd, 11.12.07 Simon, 8.12.07

Federico, 8.12.07 — Felix 31.01.08 Costanca, 5.12.07 Irina, 23.12.07 Guillaume, 22.01.08 — Davide, 5.1.08 — Otto, 26.12.07 Anna — Rebecca,

— Tobias 16.01.08 Luca 02.01.08 Annette Detmar, 1.12.07 — Erich, 13.01.08 — Jörgen, 02.01.08 Nora, 12.01.08

Anna, 22.11.07 ЛЮБА, 02.12.07 Helmut, 27.11.07 Richard, 5.1.08 Matthias, 07.12.07 СВЕТЛАНА 30.11.07 Elena, 02.12.07 Reiner, 24.11.07 Sassi,

Fabiola, 25.11.07 David 6.12.07 Maika, 22.11.07 — Ritz, 28.12.07 Dorothee 26.12.07 Sabine, 15.12.07 Liberato 5.1.08 Claudia, 9.12.07 Nicol

— Norma, 22.01.08 Linda 20.01.08 Katrin, 8.12.07 — Nina, 16.12.07 Cristiane, 27.11.07 Elisabeth, 07.12.07 Courtney, 02.12.07

Yavet, 29.12.07 — Renate, 07.12.07 Yesim, 9.12.07 Walter 02.01.08 Rebecca, 27.11.07 — Gaby, 9.12.07 Tina, 27.01.08 Tetsuki, 27.11.07 Simone 11.12.07 Ute,

.12.07 Juli, 9.12.07 — Anne 20.01.08 Marianne 28.12.07 Iris 02.01.08 — Gina 02.12.07 Patricia, 02.12.07 Tatjana

Draga, 29.12.07 Franciska, 02.01.08 Monika, 27.11.07 Andrea 28.11.07 Katja 16.01.08 Margrit 19.01.08 Katharina, 15.12.07 Sabine 98.12.07

— Simone 27.12.07 fr. 22.01.08 Estrella, 8.12.07 Claudia, 23.01.08 Maria 16.12.07 Kristina, 03.02.08

Rosa, 28.01.08 Verena, 01.12.07 — Brigitte, 05.02.08 Nataly, 23.11.07 Sabine, 02.01.08 Birgit, 25.11.07 Karin, 23.11.07 Ursula, 25.11.

Johanna, 24.11.07 Angelika, 22.01.08 Evgenia, 07.12.07 Elisabeth, 07.12.07 Veronika, 28.12.07 — Renate, 30.01.08

Kristian 5.12.07 Christel 27.11.07 Heidi, 30.01.08 Idalene 11.12.07 Iris, 07.02.08 Silvja 9.12.07 Tesso 04.01.08 — Ruth

Cecilia Anna, 27.11.07 Margitta, 05.02.08 Regina, 28.12.07 Shohrzad, 10.12.07 Elisabeth 10.12.08 Anni, 16.12.07

Elfi, 25.1.08 Cindy, 9.12.07 — Ursula 20.01.08 Nikolle 20.01.08 Verena, 13.01.08

— Elle, 9.12.07 Sabrina, 24.11.07 — Annette, 31.01.08 Maria, 20.01.08 雅紀, 27.11.07

— Hiromi, 13.01.08 — Ruth, 01.02.08 Patrizia, 21.12.07 — Anna, 13.01.08

02.01.08 — — Donato, 12.01.08 Katalin, 11.12.07

— Lauren, 13.01.08   Serena 11.12.07

— Sonja, 01.01.08

— Paula 03.01.08   — Fabian, 24.11.07

— Stefan 28.12.07

__ Natasha, 8.12.07

__ Tizian 03.01.08   __ Leonardo, 8.12.07

— Johannes, 20.01.08

— Valerie, 28.01.08   — Franka 02.01.08

— Lyomel, 15.12.07

— Valentine 10.2.0

— Amy, 06.01.08

— Malte 02.01.08

— Fidi, 27.11.08

— Yara, 02.12.07

— Pia, 06.01.08

— Loredan, 03.02.08

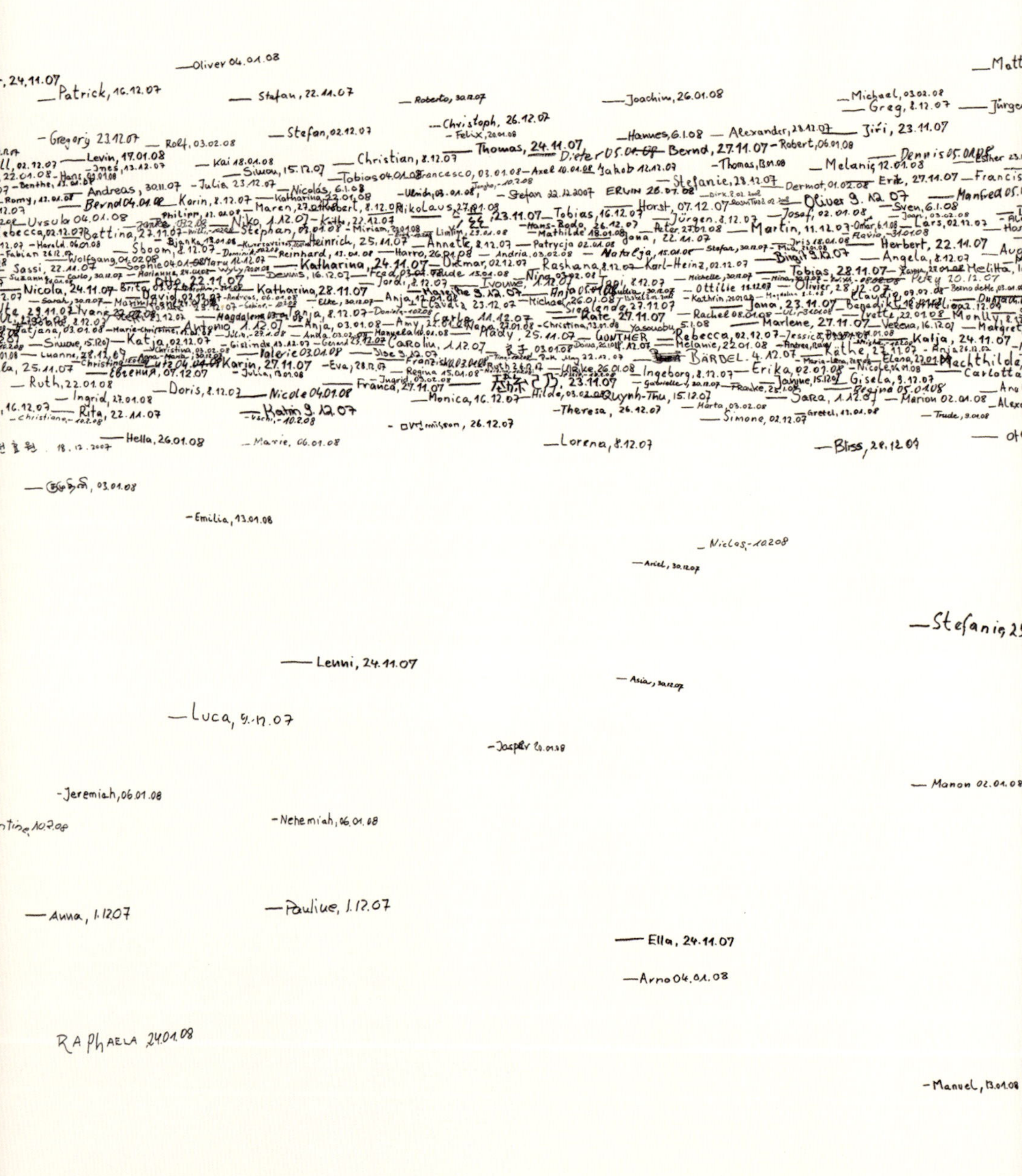

—Emilia, 13.01.08
_Niclas, 1.02.08
—Ariel, 30.12.07
—Stefania 25
— Lenni, 24.11.07
— Asia, 30.12.07
—Luca, 4.11.07
—Jasper 20.01.08
— Manon 02.01.08
-Jeremiah, 06.01.08
-Nehemiah, 06.01.08
—Anna, 1.12.07
—Pauline, 1.12.07
— Ella, 24.11.07
—Arno 04.01.08
RAPhAELA 24.01.08
—Manuel, 13.01.08

—Philip, 6.1.08

—Andreas, 13.01.08

_Robert, 27.01.08

_Stefan 18.01.08

—Thorsten, 24.11.07   Jochen, 27.01.08   — Wolfgang 18.01.08

_Stefan. 12.01.08   —Christian, 26.01.08   _Michael,— 10.02.08   _ Frank 2.12.07 _Johanns, 22.01.08

—Thierry-27.01.08   —Robert, 13.01.08   Frank, 30.12.07   —Alexander 9.12.07   _ Herbert, 20.01.08   _Stefan, 26.01.08 Alberto -02.08 —Dieter 9.12.07   —Markus

—Florian, 27.11.07   Florian, 27.01.08   Robert, 07.12.07   —Wolfram 18.01.08   Tomas, 02.01.08   Yann, 03.01.08 Ben, 27.01.08 Johan, 9.12.07   Michael, 22.11.07   Claudia

Clemens, 07.12.07   —Torsten -27.01.08   Josef, 21.11.07   Hermann, 18.12.07   —Philip, 17.01.08   HENRIK, 8.12.07   — Bernard 02.01.08   Susanne

Patrik, 02.12.07   Enrica, 02.01.08   —Christian,   —Tobi, 03.02.08   —Harald, 9.12.07   —Stefan, 06.01.08   —Mattia 11.12.07   Edward, 28.12.07   Franck

Frank, 28.11.8   Jackie 2.12.07   Oliver, 02.02.08   Bert 9.12.07 Sarah 01.08   Milan, 23.11.07   Carolin, 03.01.08 Marion, 28.11.07   Silvana 26.12.07

Georg, 24.11.07   Franco, 16.12.07   Alex   Cole 27.01.08   —Vivian 02.01.08   Wolfgang 9.12.07   Hirjam   15.12.07   Nicola 26.12.07

Lisa, 2.12.07   Markus 23.12.07   Joseph 28.12.07   Jan, 15.12.07   Cecile, 02.01.08   Julia, 22.01.08   Serge 8.01.

Lena, 03.01.08   Veronika, 05.01.08   Roland, 27.01.08   Enrico, 17.12.07   27.11.07   Ruth, 8.12.07

Bea, 07.12.07   Stephan, 25.11.07   —Benjamin 18.02.08   Ulrike, 24.11.07   Kathrin 18.12.07   Gabor, 18.01.08 Anne-Marie, 28.11

Claudia, 28.11.8   Souen 18.01.08   —Christopher, 13.01.08   Marline 03.08   Jana, 9.12.07   Ruth, 03.01.08   Kornelia 15.01.08   Jessica, 24.11.07

Heidi, 24.11.07   Marion, 03.01.08   Maria, 27.11.07   Anja   Angelika 9.12.07   Diana, 25.11.07   Claudia 28.11.07 Michaela 03.01.08   Christina 27.01.08 Silvia

Gisela, 24.11.07   Cindy, 07.12.07   Maria, 21.12.07   Ntozo 26.12.07 Christina, 08.01.08   Filippo 4.12.07   Heidi, 9.12.07   Anette, 25.11.07   03.01.08 Susann

Eve, 9.12.07   Victoria 25.11.07   Pirkko, 07.12.07   Verena   Katharina 10.01.08   Mona, 15.12.07   Irene 02.01.08   Barbel   Astrid 9.12.07   Jean-Noel, 02.12.07   Ute

Anja 02.01.08   Katharina 18.01.08   Beatrice 02.12.07   Annamaria 27.02.08   —Corbin Xiaw   FREYA, 8.12.07   Pat, 28.12.07   Burkhardin, 9.12.07

Daniela, 15.12.07   Angelika 07.12.07   Nino   Rosemarie, 30.01.07   Irene 02.01.08   Sandra, 25.11.07   Funda, 28.12.07   Marie-Therese   Martina

Erika 25.11.07   Allison 20.12.07   Eva, 27.01.08   Irina, 28.12.07   Annika, 07.12.07   Tanja, 07.12.07

Yvonne 23.12.07   Holly   Stephanie 9.12.07   Claudia 18.01.08

Julia, 27.07.08   Hannah 9.12.07   —Ulli, 02.12.07   —Margret 13.01.08   Susann, 27.01.08 Letizia, 8.12.07   Kathrin, 28.11.07

Frederike, 9.12.07   Karin 03.02.08   Noor 07.12.07   Elisabeth, 22.11.07   Franziska, 5.12.07   —Nicole, 28.12.07   —Silas, 02.01.08   Marlo, 07.12.07

Mariann 30.01.08

—Wiebke, 1.12.07   Emanuell 02.01.08   —Claudia, 6.1.08   利権 (11.08)   _Martina, 1.12.07   Susann, 22.11.07   GINA, 28.12.07   Ian

—Harißo 9.12.07   ナミ子, 13.01.08   —Florence 02.01.08

—Andreas, 13.01.08
—Ana Cláudia, 5.1.08

—Laura, 26.12.07   —Felix, 13.01.08

—Leon, 13.01.08

                        —Linda, 06.01.08

— Caroline 02.01.08

                                                        —Elias, —1.02.08 —Carlos, 13.01.08

— Charlotte, 25.11.07

—Martin, 25.11.07

                                                                                    —Lukas, 25.11.07

1.01.08

— Sarah, 25.11.07   —Clea, 25.11.07

—Louise, 03.01.08

— Mia, 02.01.08

— Isaac, 07.02.08   ~JASPER, 28.1.08

_ Michael, 8.12.07

_ Nicholas, 26.12.07   _ Ingolf, 27.01.08   _ Jenn

_ Dominik, 03.01.08 _ Rudo, 13.01.08   _ Stefan, 6.1.08

_ Michael, 26.01.08   _ Hans 11.12.07   _ Dietmar 8.12.07   Ansgar 8.

_ Yoerg 2.12.07   _ Klaus, 27.01.08   _ Christoph 20.12.07

_ Felix 02.01.08   _ Tobias 10.01.08   _ Fabio, 27.01.08

_ Boris P. 30.11.07 _ Johannes, 18.02.08   _ Heribert _ MaRC, 12.12.07   _ Jürgen 28.12.07 _ Tobias 9.12.07 _ Hannes, 22.01.08   _ Leo 3.12.07

MIGUEL 11.12.07   _ Kristin, 6.1.08 _ Laura, 5.1.08 Claudius, 27.01.08 Fabian 28.12.07   Jan, 25.11.07 _ Brian 02.01.08   _ Martin 04.01.08 _ Bernard 03.02.08

_ Leonid   Philippe, 12.12.07   _ Ralph, 03.02.08   Fabian 24.01.08   _ Nicolas 21.11.07

nne, 8.12.07 Beppo 27.04 Olivier, 13.01.08 _ Franz 03.02.08   Hg-Jo 03.01.08   Rafael, 03.02.08   _ Alexand

_ Robert 9.12.07 _ Achim, 27.01 Bich, 27.01.08 Catharina 9.12.07   Ute, 28.12.07   Sisho 9.12.07   _ Detlev, 07.02.08 Markus, 07.12.07   _ Moritz 26.12.07   _ Lambi

_ Katrin, 27.01.08   _ Rüdiger, 07.12.07 _   Roland, 30.12.07 Markus, 03.02.08   Georg, 02.12.07   _ 19 _ ,25.11.07 Ann, 27.01. Hellmut, 26.12.07   _ phili

_ Ulrike, 24.11.07   _ Michael   Antonia 24.11.07 Daniel, 02.12.07   Christiane, 22.12.07 ROLAND ELSTNER 28.12.07   _ Dimitri _, 24.01.08 Stuart 27.01.07 Barbara, 25.11.07

_ Oliver, 26.12.07 _ Ines 03.01.08 _ Susanne, 23.01.08   Kaja, 07.12.07 _ Daniela 02.01.08   KONRAD 22.01.08 Andreas, 13.01.08   _ Dimitri _, 24.01.08 Tom 25.11.07 Max 28.12.07

_ Hans, 12.01.08 _ Heinz 22.01.08 Ignacio 27.01 Marie 27.01 Andreas, 07.12.07   Jeannine, 05.01.08 Florian, 1.12.07 Matteo, 02.01.08 _ Markus 6.1.08   07.02.08   MiCol

_ Matthias, 07.12.07   Aaron, 18.12.07   +Annika, 26.12.07 _ MARTINA, 13.01.08 Martina, 13.01.08 Fabienne 05.01.08 Rull, 07.12.07   _ Leonie, 9.12.07   Janina 07.12.07 _ Amelie, 6.1.08

Iring, 30.11.07   Sonja, 16.12.07 Nicola, 5.1.08   _ Jutta, 28.01.08   Christine 24.11.07 _ Caroline, 5.1.08   _ Mira   07.11.07 _ Linda 29.01.08   _ Nicola, 11.01.08

_ Benny, 07.12.07 _ Julia, 28.11.07   Sabrina, 07.12.07 Hm, 18.02.08 _ Alessandra, 03.01.08   Bopawa, 22.01.08   Gertraud, 22.11.07 Mizzi   Florian, 6.1.08   _ Rudolf, 24.11.07

_ Victoria 07.01.08 Georg, 22.11.07 _ ELKE 26.12. Miriam 25.11.07 _ Caro 15.01.08 Rita-Barbara, 24.11.07   Angelika 22.01.08   Simone 02.01.08   Natalia, 25.11.07 _ Verena, 30.11.07

Nicola 02.01.08 _ Giam-Piero, 24.11.07 _ Margrit, 26.11.07 Jean-Marc, 02.12.07 Jovana Isabell 07.12.07 _ Silke, 9.12.07   Jessi, 07.12.07   _ Januar, 21.12.07 Ulrike, 02.02.08   Sarazin, 21.12.07

Riki, 5.1.08   _ Christa, 8.12.07 _ Brigitta, 27.01 Daniela, 07.12.07 Noii 23.11.07   Karin, 22.01.08 Elisabeth, 27.01.08 Aaron, 21.12.07 _ Walter 16.01.08 _ Kathi, 07.12.07 _ Elisa, 02.01.08

Karin, 06.01.08   _ Ullo 3.01.08   _ Christa 03.01.08 Moui, 07.12.07   Charlotte, 25.11.07 Christine 17.01.08 Desiree 02.01.08 _ Maria, 9.12.07 _ Arzu, 12.01.08

Annili, 07.12.07 _ Lucia, 4.12.07 _ Helga 08.02.2108   Kirsten, 26.01.08 _ AHHA, 27.01.08   Franta, 30.01.07   Uli, 07.02.08   _ Annette, 6.1.08   _ Lea 12.12.07 _ Sabine D/

AnneH, 15.12.07   _ Silvie, 27.1.08 Ramona 11.12.07   Marij 11.12.07   02.12.07   _ Stefan, 07.12.07   _ Anna, 07.12.07 _ Ada, _ 18.02.08   _ Olga, 22.11.07

_ Anika, 03.01.08   佐奈江 2.1.2008   _ Brigitte 16.01.08   _ Jakob, 27.11.07   _ Leonie, _ 27.01.08   Gabriela, 22.01.08 Lisa, 07.12.07

_ Leonie, 25.11.07   _ Federica 02.01.08

                        _ Leslie, 25.11.07   _ Luisa, 30.12.07

          มาลี อำนวยสุข, 07.12.07 _ Monru Dee, 07.12.07

                                                                                                    _ Keua, 25.11.07

_ Ferdinand, 26.12.07

                                        _ Benedikt, 5.1.08

_ Amelie 1.1.08

                                    _ Moritz, 25.11.07

                                                                                  _ Fritz 2.12.07

    _ Kilian, 25.11.07   _ Luisa, 27.01.08

                                                                                          _ Béla, 24.

                                                    _ Willy 2.12.07

                                                                                  _ Ava, 13.01.08

28.12.07   _ Livia, 22.01.08

                        _ Jeremy Manó, 30.12.07

— Kai, 26.12.07

— Alexander 13.12.07
— Thomas, 06.01.08
— Walter, 6.1.08
— Sebastian, 29.12.07
— Jörg, 25.11.07
— SVEN, 04.12.07
— Michael, 07.02.08

— Martin 9.12.07
oni, 27.01.08
— Matthias, 26.01.08
ias 04.01.08
— André, 2001.08
— Holger, 6.1.08
— Robert, 13.01.08
Götz, 6.1.08
— Martin, 13.01.08
Natalia, 29.12.07
— Alexander, 05.01.08
3.01.08
— Stephanie, 2001.08
Joachim, 25.11.07
— Ulrich
Max 9.12.07
Teresa 9.12.07
Pel, 25.11.07
— Karsten, 13.01.08
Gunnar, 02.12.07
— Alexander
Gerd, 27.01.08
Jaime, 13.01.08
Nicola 04.01.08
Hanco 07.12.07
Rainer, 31.01.08
Martin, 13.01.08
07.02.08
Andreas
opher, 25.11.07
— Christoph, 9.11.07
— Eduardo, 12.01.08
Mark, 22.11.07
Antonio, 27.11.07
Donbard, 03.01.08
Antonio, 25.11.07
Jörg, 26.12.07
Berkin, 30.11.07
Hannes, 25.11.07
— Thom
ne, 25.11.07
— Atila, 15.12.07
Marc-André, 6.1.08
Sarah, 5.11.07
Isabella, 4.12.07
Udo, 30.11.07
22.12.07
— Thomas, 6.1.08
Werner, 13.01.08
Michael 9.12.07
Jörg, 25.11.07
Nirjan 9.12.07
Sonja, 18.12.07
Dirk 25.11.07
Piero, 16.12.07
Owians, 29.12.07
Peter, 6.1.08
Kerstin 8.01.2008
Sebastian 02.02.08
Jürgen, 06.01.08
Sabine 13.11.08
Julio, 02.01.08
Gabi, 15.12.07
Trina 26.12.07
Michael 9.12.07
Jonothan 05 Magnus 9.12.07
Rachel 9.12.07
Daniel, 30.12.07
Karoline, 25.
Matthias, Nica 20 9.12.07
Amelien, 27.01.08
Kathrin 01.02.08
Bitte, 22.11.07
Davide, 13.12.07
Antje, 01.02.08
Rainer, 01.02.08
— Luca 11.12.07
— Aline 28.12.03
Michael, 27.01.08
Teresa, 28.11.07
Karen, 30.12.07
Andrea, 22.01.08
Bettina, 10.01.08
Katharina, 25.11.07
Nicola, 8.12.07
Veronika, 07.12.07
Heinz, 03.01.04
Michael 9.
Christa, 6.1.08
Gabi,
Sigi, 17.01.08
Martin 9.12.07
Sarah, 6.1.08
Karin 9.12.07
Rüdiger
Francesco, 30.11.07
Gudrun, 22
Marlies 26.12.4
Edelgard, 16.01.08
I, 07.12.07
Ursu
01.08
— Jeannette, 25.11.07, 27.01.08
Maria
Laura, 30.07
Laureline, 5.12.07
Claudia, 6.1.08
Anni Hi, 10.02.08
Manuela, 04
Ugo, 09.08
Agata, 22.11.07
Sabine, 8.12.07
Ina, 6.1.08
Andrea,
Raphaela, 26.01.08
Uschi, 26.11.02
Janet, 28.11.08
Johanna 07.02.08
Himous 18.12.07
Carina, 07
Heike, 8.
Trina 22.01.08
Go, 6.1.08
Sigrid, 30.01.07
Sabine, 25.11.07
Patrick 07.12.07
Arth, 18.12.07
Renate, 4.12.07
Bärbel
Magdit 15.12.07
Eva, 11.12.07
Maya 03.01.08
Stefania, 19.01.08
Cornelia 24.11.07
Julia, 18.12.07
Claudio, 8.12.07
Claudia, 07.02.08
Raquel 04.01.08
Cora, 13.12.07
Lorena, 25.11.07
Charlotte 8.
Christelle, 25.11.07
Ol 28.12.07
— Gabi, 8.12.07
Marlies, 06.01.08
Fabrizio 8.11.07
Anne, 5.12.07
Teresa, 13.01.08
Estta 29.12.07
Andrea, 22.11.07
Laura, 07.12.07
— Andrea 13.01.08
Dvessi 27.12.07
Güli, 28.12.07
Ghada 04.01.08
Kaftra 2008
Karin 16.12.07
Uschi, 26.12.07
Paola
— Roxanne, 30.01.08
Annette 04.01.08
yela, 8.12.07
Irmgard, 2001.08
Helga, 15.12.07
Christiana, 22.01.08
Maria Sabina, 11.12.07
Letitia, 25.11.07
Eva, 27.01.08
Anna, 07.12.07
11.12.07
Annette, 25.11.07
— Stephanie, 26.12.07
Andrea, 8.12.07
Gudrun, 2008
Brigitte, 12.01.08
Ina, 01.02.08
Stephanie 05.12.07
— Monika, 13.01.08
— Inga, 25.11.07
Dani 2008
Inga, 24.11.07
Sylvia, 4.12.07
Lola, 03.01.08
Ute, 27.01.08
Jessica, 10.02.08
Zoe 16.01.08
Sabine, 06.01.08
cole, 07.12.07
— Heidi, 27.12.02
— Alison, 27.01.08
Ada — Gisella, 25.11.07
Johanna, 13.01.08
Nina 9.12.07
Susi 25.11.07
Annelies 9.12.07
ILENIA, 4.12.07
— Raquel, 27.01.08
Nadja, 4.12.07
Centa, 28.12.07
Bianca, 18.12.07
Pallavi, 30.01.07
Margot
— Leslie, 27.1.08
— Alexandra 8.02.2008

— Lita, 8.12.07

— Matthias, 9.12.07

— KiKi 26.12.07

07

2008

— Kena, 27.1.08

— Marianne, 5.12.07

— Noémie, 10.1.08

— Markue, 6.1.08

— Carla 26.12.07

— Uti, 07.02.08

— Hannes, 26.12.07
— VEIT, 12.01.08

— Alessio 4.12.07

— Alexander, 06.01.08

— Daniel 9.12.07   — Olaf, — 1.02.08   — Martin, 25.11.07

Bernd, 9.12.07 — Christiane — 1.02.08   — Daniel, 13.01.08   — Onnen, 6.12.07   Željko 02.01.08
          — Olivier, — 10.02.08   — Jonathan 24.11.08   Benedikt,
...ert, 13.01.08   — Ralf, 24.11.07   — Axel, 30.11.07   — Mathias, 03.02.08   Jean-Louis 02.01.08 — Michael, 13.01.08   — Andreas, 01.02.08
          — Philip, 27.01.08   — Ralf, 13.01.08   — Torsten, 26.12.07   — Peter, 01.02.08   Uwe, 6.12.07
...02.08   — Wolfgang, — 1.02.08   — Felix, 06.01.08   — Thimo, 03.02.08   — York 23.12.07
...s, 29.12.07   — Gabriele, 20.01.08   — Jean, 30.11.07   Halte 9.12.07   — Michael, 20.01.08   Daniel, 03.02.08   Peter, 16.12.07
          Peter 9.12.07 — Steffen, 26.12.07 — Christopher, 13.01.08   Jannis, 07.12.07   Bill, 02.12.07 — Dieter, 09.02.08 Hacca, 13.12.07   — Ewa 9.11.07 — Ghislain, 6.1.08   Florian, 25.11.07
...cello, 13.12.07   — Rolf, — 27.01.08   Rudolf, 02.12.07
— Marcus, 03.01.08   — Luca 11.12.07   Nana 9.12.07   — Eduard 15.01.08 — Andi 10.02.08   Boris, 19.01.08   Claudia 9.12.07   — Thomas, 11.12.07 — Fabrizio, 30.12.07   Andreas 12.04.08
— Pierre — 24.01.08   — William, 30.01.08 — Wolf, 13.01.08   Maximo, 25.11.07   — Neringa   Federi   — Jürgen, 22.01.08
...11.07   — Jürgen, 6.1.08   Barbara, 07.12.07   — Hans — 10.2.08   Sarah 2.12.2007   Corinna, 18.12.07   Heike 9.12.07   Karl, 01.02.08 Andreas, 02.12.07   Hauke, 25.11.07   Maximilian 27.01.08
          — Jürgen, 30.11.07   — EL JLKIN, 17.01.08   Nadja, 16.12.07   Krishn, 27.01.08   — Davor, 02.12.07   Natalie, 1.12.07   — Laura, 30.11.08   Karljosef Max, 28.11.07   — Corinne 9.12.07
...02.07   — Gerberg 11.12.07   Theresa 09.02.08   Dorit, 25.11.07 — Claudi,   Hubert, 07.12.07 — Jörn,   Marita 02.01.08 — Babette, 06.01.08 — Gesine 13.11.08   Christine, 28.11.0   Anna, 12.01.08   RHIAN
...i, 6.1.08   — Carlo 16.12.07   Lludso, 16.12.07   — Maria 09.02.08   Wilfried-Alois, 28.11.07   — Jose-Maria, 25.11.07   Roth, 10.2.08   Frauke, 03.01.08   Kurt 9.12.07 — Lara 23.01.08
...ula, 8.12.07   Andreas, 22.01.08   Marianne, 22.11.07   Matthias, 24.11.07   — Christian, 28.12.07   Bob 02.01.08   Ann 02.01.08 — Edeltraud   Joan 20.01.08   Mathilde, 1.12.07
...Lena 30.01.08   Lisa, 28.11.07   Sarah   Elisabeth, 16.12.07   — Eleonora, 30.12.08   Michi, 22.11.07   Sophia, 03.02.0   Franziska, 17.01.08   Charlotte   24.11.07   Gudrun, 30.11.07
...Sabine 22.01.08   Ramona 10.04.08   Rebecca 02.01.08   Elisabeth, 01.02.08 Joachim   — Clarize, 04.01.08 — Arndt   Daniel, 25.11.07   Ilaria 13.01.08   Felicia 03.01.08   Emma, 25.11.07 — Amber 03.02.08
...Joschi 08.01.08 — Ingeid, 6.1.08   Svea, 28.11.07   Claudia Maria 02.01.08   — Laura 06.01.08   — Silja, 02.12.07 — Luise 26.01.08   Bettina, 18.12.07   Maria, 15.01.08   Angelina, 18.12.07
          Astrid 11.12.07   — Ricarda, 30.11.07 — Katarina   Mia Melanie   Cynthia, 02.12.07   — Margarete 9.12.07 — Katrin, 20.11.07   Hemma, 16.12.07 — Ute, 13.01.08   Anna
          Steph, 18.12.07   Diana, 25.11.07   Fidelle, 15.12.07 5.11.07   Lisa, 18.12.07 — Margot, 26.12.07 — Yvonne, 18.12.07   Addie, 24.11.07 — Christina — 27.01.07   Sabrina, 18.12.07
...la, 6.1.08   — Patrick   — Felicia, 09.02.08   — Drote 29.12.07   Lisi, 22.12.0   — Cory, 30.12.07   Julia, 30.11.07   Catherine, 6.1.08   — Nancy, 02.12.07 — Magdalena, 20.01.08   Melanie, 18.12.07
Christ, 16.12.07   — Barbara, 21.12.07 — Ursel, 28.11.07   Andrea 9.11.07 — Sylvia, 30.12.07   Susanne, 12.12.07
          Diana, 24.11.07   Rossana 8.12.07   Marlies, 17.01.07   Ute, 23.11.07   Inge 9.12.07   Yvonne, 18.12.07 — Brigitte 18.01.08   Claudia 9.12.07
          — Brigitta — 10.2.08
— Waltraud, 28.11.07   — Gudrun 22.12.07 — Lisa, 06.01.08   — Ellen, 16.12.07   Mariella, 18.12.07   李立, 03.02.08   Joan, 20.01.08   — Katharina 27.01.08   — Gertra...
...t, — 10.02.08   — Eva 8.02.2008

                                                                      — Anneliese 9.12.07
                                                                                          — David, 06.01.08
— Magdalena, 03.01.08

...08   — Elisabeth, 25.11.07

          — Jonathan, 20.01.08

                                        — Elsa, 30.12.07   — Ella...

— Anna-Charlotte — 1.02.08

                    — Maximilian, 03.02.08

                              — Pauline, 30.12.07
          — Sarah 27.01.08

—Thorsten,– 10.2.08   _Nig, 27.01.08   —— Tobias, 07.02.08   —— Rouven 9.

s, 06.01.08   —Florian, 6.1.08   —— Siegward, 6.1.08
—— IVARS. 4.12.07   —Arndt, 06.01.08
                            —Martin, 23.12.07   —Luca, 05.02.08 ——Valentino, 27.11.07   —— Euäγγέλος, 27.11.07   —Franz, 12.01.08   _Tobias
—— RAINER, 8.12.07   —Philipp, 03.02.08   —Cornelius, 20.01.08   Heinz 2.12.07
—Andreas, 12.01.08 Bernd, 25.11.07   Rudolf 9.12.07 Maximilian, 27.11.07 —Sven, 06.01.08   Heide 11.01.
—Lukas, 6.1.08   —Christian, 16.12.07 Dietrich 06.02.08 Ronny 05.01.08 Max 9.12.07 —Matthias, 27.01.08   Rolf 05.01.08 Robert 9.12.07   Mirko,16.12.07 —Christoph, 27.11
12.07 —Stephan, 28.11.07 Philipp, 6.1.08   Iris 05.01.08 Michael, 22.11.07 —Simon 05.01.08 Walburga, 27.11.07
—Gregor, 24.11.07 —Brigitta 23.12.07   Marina 9.12.07 —Andreas, 03.01.08 —Jürgen, 6.1.08   Michael 9.12.07 Ingrid, 07.02.08 Ritzu 9.12.07   Raul, 21.12.07 Gabe 06.01.08 Geos   BRUNO,
—Manfred, 01.02.08 Markus, 22.11.07 —Gerd 6.1.08 Uel, 03.02.08 —Lene Lise 02.01.08 Regina 8.12.07 Udo, 24.11.07   Martin, 07.02.08   Anna, 01.02.08 Hein
—Jack 26.12.03 Bernd 04.01.08 —Efrat Jahr   Kaijii 6.1.08   Danni, 9.12.07 —Andrea, 06.01.08   Regina, 24.11.07 —Bernhard 07.02.08 Nick 18.12.07 —Andreas, 27.11.07
vlis, 10.2.08 Wiebke –Niebork 10.2.08 Annika 9.12.07 Dietter 9.12.07 Roswitha, 22.11.07 Daniel 9.12.07 Gert, 12.01.08 02.08 Ines, 11.1.08   Max, 11.01.01   Romolo 9.12.07
—Gintare 03.02.08 Sabine 26.01.08 Roswitha 2.12.07 —René, 15.01.08 —Eric, 24.11.07 Christina 9.12.07 Andrea, 03.02.08 —Sophia 17.11.07   Melanie 9.12.07
—Anne-Marie, 6.1.08 —Dana, 30.11.07 —Heiki, 06.01.08 9.12.07 —Barbara, 9.12.07 —Zit, 03.02.07 Friederike 1801 —Katharina,28.11 Eva, 07.02.08 Claudia, 24.11.07 —Rebecca, 03.0
—Isabel, 25.11.07 —Alisou,12.1.07 Rita, 02.12.07 —Tini,220—Manu, 11.01.08 Saskia 9.12.07 —Sabine 12.12.11 Brigitte, 9.12.07 Betta, 30.11.07 Sabrina, 30.11.07 Brigitte, 12.01.08 Dana, 26.11
—Magdalena 9.12.07 —Gudrun,20.01.08 Jasmin, 12.01.08 Alisa, 06.01.08 —Julika, 20.01.08 Tsabella 09.02.08   Jannika, 18.01.08 Tim, 01.02.08 —Matthias 9.12.07
—Gudrun 9.12.07 Kathrien, 02.12.07—Katrin   Christiane, 24.11.07 Irene 27.01.08 Sophia, 17.01.08   Tomas, 02.12.07 Lukas, 27.11.07 Friederike 26.12.07 Elena 9.12.07 —Eleonore 9.12.07 Andi, 25.11
—Julia,12.01.08 Doreen, 18.12.07 — Angelika, 06.01.08 —Krystyna, 06.01.08   Doris,09.02.08   Lise 9.12.07   —Barbara 9.12.07 Jenny 8.12.07   Margarete 09.02.08
15.01.08 —Sonja 15.01.08   Maria, 24.11.07   Ilenia, 13.12.07   Yasmina, 16.01.08 — Steffi 23.12.07 Waltraud 04.01.08   Ulanen 30.12.2007 Mariam, 15.01.08 Lindsay, 12.01.08   Babette, 06.01.08 — Vero
9.11.07 Bettina, 06.01.08 James 9.12.07   Natalia, 21.12.07   Nyil, 05.02.08   Lise 9.12.07   —Jeroen, 15.01.08   Christiane,09.02.08
4.01.08 —Barbara 30.12.07 Laura 23.12.07 Silke, 24.01.08   Rebecca, 30.12.07   —Estelle, 25.11.07   Dagmar, 6.1.08 Christine 9.12.07 —Vittoria, 20.01.08 Ani,
ria, 01.02.08 —Julia, 16.12.07 Ursula, 07.01.08 Luise 9.12.07 Elisabeth, 05.01.08 07.12.07 —Juana, 06.01.08 —Alica,09.02.08 —Letizia, 20.01.08   Simone 9.12.07
8.12.07 —Alessandra, 20.01.08   Laura, 09.02.08   —Sara 8.12.07 —Dana,16.01.08 —Mariana, 06.01.08   —Magdalena
—Amina 9.12.07   —Ho Ho, 6.1.08 —Susi, 06.01.08 Sabine, 6.1.08   Bärbel, 12.12.07

—— Liselotte, 25.11.07

                                                                                                                                        —— Hanza, 03.02.08

          —— christian 23.12.07

                    —David, 20.01.08

                                —Quentin, 20.01.08

                                                                                                              —Carlotta, 12.01.08

                                                                                                                              _Em

        —Charlotte, 06.01.08
—Oskar, 6.1.08

                                                                                      —— Jonathan 23.12.07

        —Katharina, 6.1.08

                                                              —Anton, 12.01.08

— Thorsten,— 10.2.08   _ Nig, 27.01.08   — Tobias, 07.02.08   — Rouven 9.12.07

.12.07   — Florian, 6.1.08
          — Arndt, 06.01.08   — Siegward, 6.1.08   — Franz, 12.01.08
          — Martin, 23.12.07   — Tobias, 03.01.08
     — Philipp, 03.02.08   — Luca, 05.02.08 — Valentino, 27.11.07   — Euàyyeλos, 27.11.07   — Hans, 24.11.07
Andreas, 12.01.08   Bernd, 25.11.07   — Cornelius, 20.01.08   Heinz 2.12.07   — Daniel, 30.12.07
— Christian, 16.12.07 Dietrich 18.02.08   Ronny 05.01.08 Max 9.12.07 — Matthias, 27.01.08   Rudolf 9.12.07 Maximilian, 27.11.07 — Sven, 06.01.08 — Heide 11.01.08 — Armin,–27.01.08
8.12.07 — Philipp, 6.1.08   Iris 05.02.08 Michael, 22.11.07   Simon 05.04.08   Rolf 05.01.08   Robert 9.12.07   Mirko, 16.12.07   Christoph, 27.11.07   — Jan, 06.01.08 —
23.12.07   Walburga, 27.11.07   — Michel,
     — Marina 9.12.07   Andreas, 03.01.08   — Jürgen, 6.1.08   Michael 9.12.07 Ritus 9.12.07   Raul, 21.12.07 — Gabe 06.01.08 Geos   Bruno, 16.12.07
8 — Markus, 22.11.07   — Gerd 6.1.08   Ben 18.12.07   Uli, 03.02.08 Ingrid, 07.02.08   Udo 24.11.07   Nick 18.12.07   — Martin, 07.02.08   Andreas, 27.11.07   Stan. 09.02.08   Thomas
     — Efrat Jaffa   — Roswitha, 22.11.07 — Andrea, 06.01.08   Bernhard, 07.02.08   — Anna, 01.02.08   Heiner, 11.01.08
04.01.08 Annika 9.12.07   Dieter 9.12.07   Regina 24.11.07   Gert, 12.01.08   Ines, 11.1.08   iiefo…D,08.02.08   Detlev, 22.11.07
11.07-Helmut   Roswitha, 2.12.07   — Rene, 15.01.08   Daniel 9.12.07   — Hans, 01.02.08   Andrea, 03.02.08   — Sophia, 27.11.07   Max, 11.01.08 Romolo 9.12.07   Melanie 9.12.07 — Michael 10.01.08   Frank
— Dana, 30.11.07 -Heiki, 06.01.08   9.12.07 — Barbara, 9.12.07   — Eric, 20.01.08   Christina 9.12.07   Claudia, 24.11.07 -Rebecca, 03.01.08 Zola, 16.12.07 — Max
— Alison, 02.12.07   — Tini, 22.01 09-Stephan,02.07 Tomas, 02.12.07   Lukas, 27.11.07   Friederike 1201 — Katharina, 28.11   Eva,07.02.08   Jenny 9.12.07   Isabel, 25.11.07   Steffi, 01.02.08 — Beate, 01.02.08
07 — Gudrun,20.01.08   Rita, 02.12.07   Olga, 18.12.07   Sabine 12.12.07 Brigitte, 9.12.07   Dutta,30.12.07   — Sabrina, 30.12.07   — Brigitte, 12.01.08 — Dana, 26.01.08   Angela, 22.11.07 — Jo
athrien, 02.12.07-Ketrin   Jasmin, 12.01.08 Elisa, 06.01.08 Julika, 20.01.08 Roswitha 25.11.07   Eva 23.01.08   Christa, 22.11.07 — Tim, 01.02.08 — Matthias 9.12.07   Julia 27.01.08 — Christine
     Doreen, 18.12.07   — Angelika, 06.01.08   — Irene 27.01.08 Sophia, 12.01.07 — Isabella,07.02.08   Elena 9.12.07 — Eleonore, 10.01.08 Wilma, 6.1.08   — Margarete,08.02.08   Ruth 23.12.07
— 24.11.07   Ilenia, 13.01.07   — Christiane, 24.11.07   Patricia, 22.11.07   Doris,09.02.08   Barbara 9.12.07 Jenny   8.12.07   Andi, 25.11.07   — Veronik, –27.01.08   Maxi
Johannes 9.12.07   — Jasmina, 16.12.07 — Steffi 27.11.07   Lise 9.12.07   Ulanon 30.12.2007 — Mariam, 15.01.08   Lindsay, 12.01.08   — Babette, 06.01.08   Kristina
.07   — Laura 23.12.07 — Silke,23.01.08   Miriam 05.01.08   Waltraud 04.01.08   — Jeroen, 15.01.08   Christiane, 02.02.08   Brigitte 9.12.07 — Bärbel 9.12.07   — Angel
ulia, 16.12.07   Ursula, 07.01.08   Luise 9.12.07 Elisabeth 02.02.08 02.12.07   — Rebecca, 30.12.07   Estelle 25.11.07 Dagmar, 6.1.08   Christine 9.12.07 — Vittoria, 20.01.08 — Ani, 11.01.08   — Wend
     — Laura, 09.02.08   — Sara, 8.02.07   — Juana, 06.01.08   Alica,09.02.08 — Letizia, 20.01.08   Simone 9.12.07   — Christine
— Mo Mo, 6.1.08 -Susi, 06.01.08   — Sabine, 6.1.08   — Dana, 16.01.08 — Mariana, 06.01.08   Alica,09.02.08   — Magdalena, 20.01.08
                                                                        — Bärbel, 12.12.07

               — Lisetotte, 25.11.07

          — christian 23.12.07   — Honza, 03.02.08

               — David, 20.01.08

                    — Quentin, 20.01.08

                                                  — Carlotta, 12.01.08

                                                  — Ema, 12.01.08

     — Charlotte 06.01.08

                              — Jonathan 23.12.07

     — Katharina, 6.1.08

                              — Anton, 12.01.08

HC, 23.12.07 —— Rainer, 24.11.07 — Tobias 16.01.08

— Mike, 25.11.07 — Carsten, 12.01.08 — Benjamin, 20.01.08
— Mike, 21.12.07 — Alexander, 20.01.08 —— Manfred, 12.12.07 — Sven, 27.12.07
07 — Tom, 23.07.08. — Markus, 6.1.08 — René, 13.01.08 — Nicolas, 6.
— Peter, 15.12.07 —— Estelle 9.12.07 — Joe, 3.12.07 — Verena 15.01.08 Heike, 6.1.
6.1.08 — Lisa, 11.01.08 — Melanie. 06.01.08 Johann, 15.01.08
Jacques, 26.12.07 —— Silvia, 26.01.08 — Jonathan, 13.01.08 — Johannes 13.12.07
— Ottmar, 6.1.08 —— Klaus, 27.11.07 — Klaus, 20.01.08 Marie-Ann
7 — Malgorzata, 6.1.08 — Anne-Katrin 12.01.08, 30.11.07 — Julia, 20.01.08 - Melinda, 20.01.08
David, 20.01.08 — Francesco, 9.12.07 — Kieran, 15.12.07 — Mathias 10.02.08 — Ute,
— Andreas, 10.2.08 —— Alexandra, 6.1.08
—— Mai 9.12.07 — Nico, 17.1.08 —— Petra 9.12.07 — Haide 10.01.08
Christoph, 27.11.07 —— Gabriela 9.12.07 — Bolo, 13.12.07 Brigitte, 06.01.08 — Sophia 19.12.07 — Fritz,
— Sonja 18.04.08 — Sonja 05.01.08 — Swetlana, 9.12.07 — Sven, 25.11.07 — Romina 16.01.08
— Carly, 5.1.08 — Inga 02.01.08 Susanne 9.12.07 — Suzanne 9.12.07
— Annunciata, 2008 — Lena, 20.01.08 — Alexander
5.12.07 — Helga, 6.1.08 — Zola 9.12.07 — Coco, 02.12.07 — Angelika, 12.12.07
— Julia-Renate, 22.11.07 — Barbara, 28.12.07 — Jacob, 5.1.08 — Brüni 26.12.07 - Lisa, 17.01
Hanna 9.12.07 — Ann-Britt, 6.1.08 — Angela, 15.01.08 — Renate - P.01.08 — Saskia, 13.01.0
Traud, 03.01.08 —— Valeska, 21.12.07 — Sabine 27.01.08 Kathrin, 28.11.07 - Heike, 27.12.07
03.02.08 Elizabeth, 6.1.08 — Christiane, 12.01.08 — Moni, 22.11.
— Anja, 10.2.08 —— Alina. 26.01.08 — Christine 10.7.08 — Daniel, 0
26.01.08 Rosemarie, 6.1.08
—— Cecilia 9.12.07

Liza 9.12.07 —— Barbara, 11.01.08

—— Riccarda, 26.01.08

— Juseppe, 13.12.07

— Kalvis, 29.12.07

— Hannes, 27.11.07

Philipp, 22.11.07
— Andy, 20.01.08   — André, 12.12.07   — Andreas, 27.11.07
— Peter 11.12.07   — Johannes, 27.11.07   — Lars, 03.01.08   — Rolf, 27.1.08 — Stefan, 27.1.08   Sebastian, 18.12.07   — Admir
— Mihael 06.01.08 Karl 16.01.08   — Arnim, 1.12.07   — Bekir, 27.11.07 — Florian, 6.1.08   Fabian, 27.11.07   — Benjami
— Feldinand, 09.02.08   — Falk, 26.01.08   — Sebastian, 6.1.08   — Marco, 18.12.07
— Gesine, 20.01.08   — Frank 9.12.07   — Annemieke, 24.11.07   — Markus 13.02.07
— ANJAN, 22.12.07 Vincent, 23.12   Korbinian, 24.11.07   — Hansjörg, 27.11.07 — Jörg 27.01.08   Matthias, 02.02.07
— Katja 9.12.07 Nicole, 30.11.07   — Martin, 16.12.07   Stefanie 9.12.07   — Stefan, 6.1.08   — Ricardo, 21.12.07
— Antoinette, 16.12.07   — Sophia, 20.01.08 — Yvonne, 27.11.08   — Peter, 13.01.08   Ute 17.01.07 Olivier   — Richard, 6.1.08   — Stefan, 20.11.08   — Marcus, 17.01.08   — Florian, 27.
— Caroline 10.01.08 — Margret 25.1.08   Anna 9.12.07   — Susi 10.02.08   — Benny, 12.12.07   — Michael, 27.11.08
— Mandi, 11.1.08 11.12.07   Christian 04.01.08 Ingrida 29.12.07 Babara 24.11.07   — Till, 16.12.07   LH21 07.02.08 Anton, 27.1.08   — Elisa, 25.11.07 — Kay, 17.01.08 Silvia, 25.11.07
— Gabi Daniela 9.12.07   — Julia 1.12.07   Isabella, 27.11.07   Alrun, 22.11.07 — Marion 13.01.08   Philipp, 12.12.07   — Andy, 12.12.07 — Andrea Christian
— 22.11.07 — Barbara, 03.02.08 — Elli 27.01.08 Martina 26.01.08 Nicola 15.01.08   — Claas, 6.1.08   Dong 9.12.07   — Johanna, 15.12.07   — Patricia — Caroline
— Juris 11.12.07 — Lid Wigs Lena 2.12.07 Anja 26.01.08   Leo 22.12.07   Irmi, 29.12.07   Betty 03.02.08 — Ilka, 6.1.08   — Christine
— Stefanie 20.01.08   — Iris 12.01.08   Amri 18.11.07 Wilhelm, 15.01.02 — Irmi, 27.1.08   — Tobi, 22.12.07 Marion, 6.1.08   Raffael, 27.11.07   Carmen, 16.12.07   — Ines
— 16.12.07   — Sabine, 4.12.07 Fi, 29.12.07   Pala, 24.11.07   Doris, 6.1.08 — Susanne 06.01.08   Rachel, 25.11.07   Karin, 22.01.08   Helga, 24.11.07 — Rolf 07.1.08 Anas Dorothea
— Carina, 13.01.08   Jessalyn 27.1.08 Daniela, 25.11.07   Nicole, 26.12.07   Amrei 02.01.08 — Kerstin 27.01.08   Ullrike 05.01.08   — Anette, 06.01.08 Angelika, 6.1.08
— Dieter, 26.12.07   — Christiane, 16.12.07 — Helen 30.11   Johanna, 12.12.07   — Carolin 27.01.08   Daniela, 27.11.07   Marianne 9.12.07   — Katl
— Irmgard, 17.01.08   — Heike 06.02.08   — Gudrun, 1.12.07   — Kathrin, 16.12.07   — Barbara, 26.12.07 — Barbara, 02.12.07
— 03.02.08   — Marianne, 22.01.08   Dora 18.01.08
— Veronika, 27.01.08   Christiane, 11.01.08   — Dagmar, 16.12.07   — Claudia, 27.11.07   — Silvi
— Regina, 20.01.08
— Franziska, 6.1.08   — Sophia, 26.01.08

— Liam, 06.01.08

— Pascal 06.02.08   — Magdalena, — 27.01.08

— Greg or 06.02.08

— Theresa — 27.1.08

— Christopher, 20.01.08   — Titus, 6.1.08

— Mathias, 28.12.0?

Gunnar, 27.11.07

Florian — 27.01.08

Simon, 6.1.08   Mark 27.01.08

— Fabian 12.0...

— Ansgar, 17.01.08

...as, 18.12.07   — Kurt, 27.1.08
...tian, 26.01.08 — Kurt, 27.1.08
— Gerard, 15.01.08   — Julius, 25.11.07   — Walter, 02.12.07   Hans, 6.1.08   — Manfred — 27.01.08   — Reinar, 02.12.07   — Bernhard, 27.11.07
— Werner, 20.01.08
Reiner 03.01.08   — Florian, 26.12.07   Maxim, 18.12.07   — Tobias 02.12.07 Alfred, 23.08   Jörg 9.12.07   — Sylvie, 28.12.07   — Jörg 07.02.08
Jörg, 02.08   — Dieter, 02.12.07   — Arne, 20.01.08   — Marianne, 28.11.0?   Olaf, 27.11.07 — Dominique — 27.1.08   Jakob, 02.12.07   Steffen, 2.2.08   Zoran 03.02.08   — Stefan 27.01.08   Paul 12.01.08 NORWAY
Johannes 20.12.07   — Jerome 27.11.08   — Joachim, 26.12.07   — Riccardo 02.01.08 Roberto 02.01.08   Helmar, 15.12.07   — Katja, 20.12.07   Christoph 29.12.07   — Isabell, 02.12.07 — Thorsten, 30.
Etienne — Jean-Marie, 25.11.07 — Nini, 23.12.07   — Jovana, 02.12.07   Angelo 02.04.08   Paul 22.11.07   Avdy, 16.12.07   — Georg, 03.01.08 Henning, 05.01.08
— Katya, 01.02.08   — Leena, 22.11.07 Rita 21.11.08   Johanna, 02.12.07 — Fabian 23.12.07 — Sascha, 20.01.08 — Dieter, 20.01.08 Wolfgang 9.12.07 Ekkehard 27.1.08 Maxim — 27.1.08 Mark 16.12.07 — Peter — 22.
— Manuel, 15.01.08   Donja, 28.11.0?   — Michael 23.12.07 — Nadja —, 27.1.08 Christian, 25.11.07   — Hélène — 27.01.08   Eva 25.11.07 Sandrine,
Oliver, 11.01.08   Gert 2.12.07   — Johannes, 15.12.07 — Sebastian 20.12.07 — Nadja —, 27.1.08 — Lila — 10.2.08 — Anne, 5.1.08   Simone, 23.01.08 — Mauro 02.01.08 — Claus 27.1.08 Christine, 20.01.08 Christine, 20.01.08 — Ricconald 29
— Christopher, 09.03.08   Katrin, 27.11.07   Reinhold 15.11.07 Heike, 25.11.07 Bärbel, 6.1.08   Ullo 17.01.07 Reinhard, 22.11.07   Heidi, 07.02.08 — Maike — 2
Wolfgang, 09.02.08   Pavel, 27.01.08   Stefani 3.12.07   Johanna, 30.07 Matthias, 5.1.08   Klaus 26.01.08   Ulrike, 27.1.08   — Jano,
Thomas, 18.12.07   — Gertrud 20.1.0? — Ernst, Reinhold 27.1.08   Bottina 9.12.07 — Thomas, 27.1.08 Stefan 22.07 Heidi 07.07 Dietmar, 26.1.
Pierpaolo, 02.11.0   Luka 03.01.08   — Stephan 27.01.08 ARMIN 23.12.07   — Karin, 23.01.08   Stefanie, 22.11.07   Debbie, 22.01.08   Stefanza 27.07   Elisabeth, 9.12.07
— Thomas 27.11.08   Jürgen, 9.12.07   Anna Maria 03.07 09.01.08 06.01.08 Antonio, 26.12.07 Hans 9.12.07 Attila, 25.01.08 — Samoli, 27.11.0
082.12.07   — Laura 02.04.08   Jutta, 6.1.08 — Rudolf 27.1.08   Bettina 27.11.07 Tobias, 25.11.07 Christian 26.1.07 — Sandra, 02.08 Zania, 24.07   — Samoli, 27.11.0
— Silke, 09.02.08 — Schrulli 27.11.0   Elisabeth, 16.12.07 Bärbel, 27.1.08 Sigrid, 27.12.07   Savda 16.12.07 — katrin 27.01.08 Kerstin, 23.11.07   Steff, 6.1.08   Theresa, 07   — Regine 16.12.07   — Co...
— Lisa, 18.12.07   Kicki, 30.12.07   — Soraya, 02.12.07   Shofag 22.01.08   Dagmar, 16.12.07 Sophia 27.01.08 Julia 9.12.07   Andrea, 13.01.08 — Henni, 22.07   — Johanna, 29.12.07 — Ivan,
Stefania 9.12.07   Gabriela, 25.11.07   — Josefina, 26.12.07 — Selvaggia 03.01.08   Guoda 9.12.07 — Sigrid — 27.01.08 Couny 6.1.08 Irma, 26.12.07   Christine 9.12.07 — Mirjam, 20.04.0? Felix, 05
— Ilona, 18.12.07 — Susanne 06.01.08 — Barbara, 27.01.08 — Anja — 02.08 Rehana, 02.12.07   — Heinrich 9.12.07   — Tanja 27.01.08 — Sigrid, 24.11.07 — Stefa...
— Susanne, 25.11.07 Wiebke, 12.08 Nora, 23.11.07 — katharina, 15.01.0? Christine, 18.12.07   — Johanna, 07.01.08 Quirioko 23.12.07 — Silvius 27.1.08 Florena 02.01.07 — Honi Ko 27.11.0?
Gitta, 02.12.07   青野, 30.12.07   Françoise, 1.12.07   田原, 30.12.07   — Hubert, 23.11.07   — Angelika, 02.12.07   — Nancy 2...
— Merlone — 10.2.08   — Karin — 27.1.08
— Myriam, 02.12.07

— Gisela, 1.12.07   — Uta, — 27.1.08   — Michel, 03.02.08   — Neda, 02.12.07   — Esther, 23.11.07 — Eric...
— Chris 9.12.07   Sabine, 05.01.08   — Marielle 03.01.08
— Yoko 26.12.07   — Karolina, 25.11.07
— Christian, 20.01.08   — Karin, — 27.1.08   — Legja, 02.02.07   — 真弓, 25.11.07
Janine, 18.12.07

— Charlotte, — 10.02.08

— Tobias, 20.01.08

— ALCIME 8.02.2008

— Theresa,

— Sebastian, — 27.1.08

— Uschi 16.01.08

— Farhad 27.01.08

——— Johannes, 27.11.07

— Sajena, 02.12.07

—— Ella, 27.11.07

— Linos, 30.12.07   — Elias, 30.12.07

— Jannis, 30.12.07   — Martin, 23.11.07

— Christoph, 03.02.08   — Adrian, 27.11.07

— István, 22.11.07   — Markus, 16.12.07   — Johan Fredrik, 27.1.08   — Thomas, 26.01.08   — Johannes, 27.11.07   — Manfred, 30.11.07   — John, 06.

— Moni 9.12.07   — Wilfried 9.12.07   — Matthias 02.12.07   — Ralf 9.12.07   — Alessandro, 5.
— MONT9.23.12.2007   — Lotz, 02.12.07   — Andreas, 09.02.08   — Tiago, 02.12.07   — Jean-Marc 28.12.07   — Ali, 13.01.08   — Josef 03.   — Kai 25.11.07
— Jens, 16.12.07   — Hein, 21.12.07   — Davyd 02.01.08   — Gerhard 22.11.07   — Peter, 27.11.07   — Peter, 02.12.07   — Isabel, 2
— Reinold, 28.11.07   — Maxi, 27.11.07   — Christoph, 27.11.07   — Klaus, 02.12.07   — Martin 23.12.07   — Martin, 17.01.08   — Willigan, 25.11.07
— Veronika, 24.11.07   — Thomas 9.12.07   — Ulrich, 25.11.07   — Lukas 05.01.08   — Stefan, 16.12.07   — Toni, 12.12.07   — Ewald, 16.12.07   — Anna 9.12.07
— Werner, 02.12.07   — Madeleine, 02.12.07   — Hannes 5.12.07   — Mathias   — Leonie 23.12.07   — Florian,
— Henrik, 03.01.08   — Robert, 07.12.07   — Arnold 26.12.07   — Beate Charlotte 5.12.07   — Werner 2.12.07
— Brigitte, 25.11.07   — Kathrin, 02.12.07   — Elisabeth   — Cornelia, 27.11.07   — Jason, 03.01.08   — Florian, 03.01.08   — Miguel, 06.04.08
— Ali, 02.12.07   — Lukas, 27.11.07   — Claire 27.01.08   — Anna, 06.01.08   — Karen 22.11.07   — Marko, 26.12.07   — Julia, 27.11.07
— Doris 9.12.07   — Daniela   — Doris, 24.11.07   — Ludger, 15.12.07   — Kathie 24.11.07   — Karoline 9.12.07   — Alex, 12.12.07   — Astrid,
— Lisa 16.01.08   — Beate, 26.12.07   — Renate, 22.11.07   — Esther 28.12.07   — Roland 22.01.08   — Anne-Sophie, 02.12.07
— Doris 24.11.07   — Liliane, 11.01.08   — Johann 23.12.07   — Audrey, 19.01.08   — Anna, 25.11.07   — Gaetano 9.12.07
— Carmen, 4.12.07   — Cora, 22.11.07   — Uta, 02.12.07   — Ingrid, 03.01.08   — Marlene, 28.12.07   — Renate, 02.01.08   — Paola 5.1.08   — Jetta, 02.02.08
— Giusi 26.12.07   — Gisele 15.12.07   — Judith, 15.12.07   — Christine, 27.12.07   — Maren, 27.12.07   — Deniz, 29.12.07
— Anorte, 23.11.07   — Rosmarie, 25.11.07   — Yvonne, 03.01.08   — Franziska, 24.11.07   — Stefania, 5.1.08
— Nil, 06.04.08   — Christine 27.01.08   — Laure, 26.12.07
— 22.12.07   — Karin, 23.12.07   — 02.01.08

— Petra 03.01.08   — Emily, 26.01.08   — Leon, 6.1.08

— Thimon 03.01.08

— Madita, 25.11.07

— Hannah, 20.01.08   — LiLith, 08.02.08   — Moema, 28.12.07

— Franziska 03.01.08

— Katharina, 27.1.08

— Julius, 16.12.07

— Leonard 27.01.08

— Astrid, 23.12.07

— James, 01.01.08
— Jelle, 29.12.07
— Uwe 9.12.07

— Marc-Etienne, 22.11.07

— Rainer, 20.01.08
— Marc, 20.01.08
— Günther, 09.02.08
— Carl 02.01.08
— Rolr, 12.01.08 — Jos, 20.01.08
— Hermann -, 27.01.08
FERMIN, 23-XII-07
— Rupert, 27.1.08
— Klaus, 6.1.08
— Frank 04.01.08
— Dennis 9.12.07
— Klaus 9.12.07
— Jan, 20.01.08

— Stefan, 27.1.08
— Sebastian 02.01.08
— Jörg, 26.12.07 — Thorsten, 10.02.08
— Anton, 17.01.08
— Ralph, 20.01.08
— Stephen, 16.12.07
Olaf, 16.12.07 — Toni, 27.1.08
— Benjamin, 6.1.08 Joachim, 22.11.07
— Anika, 02.12.07
— Willi, 1.12.07
— Lucca 03.01.08
— Thomas, 20.01.08
— Andreas 27.01.08
— Ewald, 20.01.08
Zwerinns 9.12.07 — Alexander 26.12.07
— Simon, 03.01.08
— John 04.01.08 — Sepp 9.12.07
— Basti, 27.1.08
— Christian 28.12.07
— Andreas 28.12.07
— Oliver 9.12.07
— Josef, 27.11.07
— Sebastian, 16.12.07
— Pavel 26.12.07
— Björn, 30.01.08
— Florian 10.01.08
— Paulemanne 22.12.07
— Till 04.01.08
Friederike, 1.12.07
— Chris 9.12.07
— Frank, 10.01.08
— Florian, 07.01.08 — Werner, 18.12.07
— Daniel, 2.12.07 — Gabin, 27.1.08
— Harald, 28.12.07 — Hans 27.01.08
— Henny, 02.01.08
— Silvia, 20.01.08
— Franz 07.01.08
— Laurent, 16.12.07
— Bernd, 26.01.08
— Regina, 7.2.08
Julia, 21.12.07
— Sofia 03.01.08
— Martin, 20.12.07 — Frieda, 20.1.08 Wolfgang, 26.12.07
Stephan 22.11.07
— Wolfgang, 17.12.07 — Edi, 12.01.08
— Hanssa 9.12.07
Sybille, 02.12.07
— Ulrike, 26.01.08 — Petr 27.1.08
Simone, 23.01.08
— Tomusz 2.1.08
— Bettina 27.01.08
— Berk 15.12.07
Alexandra 9.12.07
Jason, 29.12.07
— Simone, 03.01.08
Klaus-D. 31.12.07
— Tom, 25.11.07 — Bernhard, 27.1.08
Simon, 25.11.07
— Nadine, 20.01.08
— Andrea 04.01.08
Michael, 25.11.07
— Francesco, 05.01.08
Jochen 2.12.07
— Doris 9.12.07 — Info 0.2.08
Matz 9.12.07
— Ingo, 09.02.08
— Jighd 03.01.08 — Natacha, 16.12.07
— Till 30.01.08
Christiana 07.01.08 25.12.07
Erika 16.12.07 — Silja 27.1.08
Marie 9.12.07 — Stolts 27.1.08 Hansjörg, 22.11.07
— Margit, 20.01.08
Christiane, 22.11.07
— Jan, 15.12.07
— Susanne 27.01.08
— Stephan 04.01.08
— Astor 03.01.08
Birgit 9.12.07 — Eichhorn, 27.1.08
Martina, 23.12.07 — Linda 10.01.08
Natalia 9.12.07 — Fritz 20.01.08
Sabine, 02.12.07
— Kira 27.01.08 — Sandra, 30.01.08
— Alexandra 04.01.08
Julia, 13.01.08 — Ivan, 30.01.08
— Damien 26.01.08 — Leonore 26.01.08
— Wolgan, 21.12.07 — Ilse, 12.01.08
— Markus, 25.11.07
— Bettina 27.01.08
— FIKRI, 15.12.07
— Alexander 17.01.08
— Peter, 28.12.07 — Andreas 18.01.08
Chipra, 03.01.08
— Martin 22.11.07
— Christine 02.01.08 — Azad — Alfons 02.01.08 — Martin, 27.1.08
— Elke, 12.12.07
— Ake 1.1.08
— Liviana 03.01.08
— Armin, 30.01.08
— Lilia, 6.1.08
Beatrice 2.12.07
— Martin 04.01.08 — Birgit 9.12.07
— Eline 02.01.08
— Kerstin, 25.11.07
— Renate 02.01.08
— Gisela 9.2.08
— Francesca 03.01.08
23.11.07 — Lisan 29.12.07
— Wolfgang, 02.01.08 Fabian, 06.01.08
Anja 02.12.07 — Gabriele 23.01.08
— Simon, 03.01.08
— Valerie 02.01.08
— Annette 04.01.08 Anne 9.12.07
— Kirsten 02.01.08
— Thalek, 15.12.07
— Sophia, 20.01.08
— Johanna, 16.12.07 — Olga, 26.12.07
Anneliese, 18.12.07
— Renate 02.01.08
— Sarah, 31.01.08
Dagma, 03.02.08
Natalia 26.12.07 — Maria, 26.12.07
Eva-Maria 02.01.08
— Danielle 2.12.07
— Eva-Sabina 02.01.08
— Alessandra 23.12.07
— Edita, 11.01.08
Jacqueline 02.01.08 — Monika, 20.01.08
— Muriel 02.01.08
— Raúl 27.1.08 — Denise
Friederike 9.12.07
— Elsa 9.12.07
— Alice, 20.01.08
— Aurelia 31.01.08
Serenella 11.12.07
Patrizia 9.12.07
Eva 23.12.07
— Richard, 4.12.07
— Waltraud, 27.1.08
Caroline — 27.1.08
— Paulina, 27.1.08
— Max, 06.01.08
— Barbara 02.01.08
— Ulrike, — 27.1.08
— Angelika, 16.12.07
Jen, 23.12.07
— Justine, 17.01.08 Inga, 11.01.08
Anita, 21.12.07
Adriana, 21.12.07
— Luise — 27.01.08
— Valerie, 16.12.07
— Katja, 25.11.07
— Katharina 02.01.08
Susanne 9.12.07
Beatrix, 25.11.07 — Ursula 27.01.08
— Ilse, 02.12.07
— Tino, 15.01.08
— Renate 04.01.08 Fabienne, 15.12.07

— Tino, 08.02.08
— Irene 27.1.08
— Manuela, — 27.1.08
— Erica 03.01.08

— Viktor 27.1.08

— Johannes, 22.12.07
— Felix 03.01.08

— Lennard, 20.01.08

— Elisabeth — 27.1.08

— Vincent 02.01.08

— Theo — 27.1.08
— Carlotta, 25.11.07

—Marcell 02.01.08

—Christian, 17.01.08   —Tobit, 29.12.07   —Marcel, Nino Thomas,
                                                                    —Ge

— Wolfgang, 08.01.08   —— Max, 25.11.07 Joachim 18.04.08 —Julia 23.12.07 —Joem
— Arta 02.01.08   —Sandra, 13.01.08   —Simon, 22.01.08
— Claus 24.01.08
— Jeromin 24.01.08   —Reinhard, 11.01.08   — Dan, 27.12.07 —Steffen 29.12.07
— Nicki 31.01.08   —— Franz, 12.12.07   — Klaus, 26.12.07   —Peter, 11.01.08 —Antoine —27.01.
— Sven 22.12.07   —Tobias, 20.01.08   —Vladimir, 03.02.08 Torsten, 25.11.07   —John
— Thomas, 20.01.08   — Paul, 30.
                          — Deniz 9.12.07 —— Haus, 27.11.07 —Sigi, 6.1.08   —Sophia, 10.2.08
—Karla 21.11.07   —Aktan, 6.1.08 —   —Andreas, — 27.01.08   — Ismet 9.12.07 —Jan, 27.1.
                24.12.07   Rolando 11.12.07 —— WOLFGANG 22.12.07 —Ge
— Kattin   Götz, 25.11.07   — Sibylle, 30.12.07 —Rosa —27.01.08   An
— Gabi, 13.01.08 Mehmet, 6.1.08   —Julia, 6.1.08   ried, 02.12.07
              23.12.07   Bob, 15.12.07   — Desmond, 27.12.07 —Oliver   — Pe
— Lydia 22.12.07   —— Oda, 25.11.07   —Helmut, 08.02.08 Gökem 9.12.07 — Tessa 27.12.07 —Pia, 12.0
          Bastian, 29.12.07 —— Riitto 12.01.08 — 27.01.08   Evka, 23.11.0
—Robert 26.12.07   —— Yvette 2.12.07   — Leilah, 02.12.03 —Katja, 02.02.08 Marion 27.12.07
—Ellen 26.12.07   — Patricia 15.01.08   Eva, 01.02.08 —Sabine Sabine, 27.11.07
              13.01.08 —— Agnes —Roberto, 9.12.07 —Sylvia, 15.01.08   —Shengl
—Veronika 21.12.07 Günter, 16.12.07 —Barbara 07.02.08   03.01.08 —Sabino 23.12.07
                    —Ramona, 12.12.07   — Christel 1.1.08 —Radustina   15.12.0   Jenna;
              29.12.07 —Eva-Marie 11.12.07   Flavia, 09.02
—PETER 22.12.07 —Deniz 01.08 Graeve, 25.11.07 —Sandra 23.12.07   Andrea
                    —Gianluca 11.12.07 —Hildegard, 13.04.08 —Elisabeth, 9.11.07 Carola, 30.01.08 —Theresia, 10.0
— 23.12.07   —Patrizia 9.12.07 —Andrea 26.12.07 —— Suzanne, 30.01.08   Jok
                    —Christine 21.1.08
—— Swetlana 21.12.07   — Irmgard, 13.1.08 Elke, 16.12.07   —Ju, 29.12.07
—Nathalie 22.12.07   —SeLin, 15.12.07   —Irina 23.12.07   —— Ryne, 28
                                                          —Saskia, 11.01.08
                                                                    —— Elfi 08

                          —Lea, 27.12.07
—Mariane 1.1.08   —Reside, 6.1.08
                    —Nora, 27.12.07

—Dilara, 6.1.08   —Caroline, 12.01.08

—Damian, 16.12.07

30.12.07

— Kuni, 07.12

— Jonas 23.12.07

— Klaus, 28.01.08 Fabio, 15.12 07 — Helge, 6.1.08 — Christian, 15.12.07 — Moritz 10.02.08

Christian, 30.12.07 — Klaus, 03.02.08 — Frank, 22.11.07 — Florian, 15.12 07 — Markus 27.01.08 — Jonas

JÜRGEN. 18.12.07 — Sven 27.01.08 — Johannes 28.01.08 — Carl-Erik, 22.11.07 Paul 10.02.08 —

Conrad, 5.1.08 — Gernot, 12.12.07 — Richi, 29.01.08 — Alex 27.11.07 — Baird, 17.01.08 Thomas, 15.12.07 Jonathan, 24.11.07 — Otto, 28.11.07

Stefan, 25.11.07 — Rüdiger, 16.12.07 — Jens, 30.11.07 — Fabian, 3.02.08 Lars, 30.11.07 Michel Damme, 4.12.07 — Klaus, 26.11.07 Michael 01.04.08

Artur, 03.02.08 — Daniel, 28.11.07 — Tim, 02.12.07 — Anton, 16.12.07 Kai Philipp, 15.12.07 Christoph, 1.12.07 Marco, 29.12.07 Atilla, 25.11.07 — Michel 23.12.07

Geoff, 15.12.07 — Melanie, 30.12.07 — Kurt, 28.11.07 — Andreas 23.12.07 — Mario, 3.12.07 Andreas, 24.01.08 Jürgen, 6.1.08 27.11.07 Damian, 11.12.07 — Guido,

Thomas, 23.11.07 — Frederik, 06.07 Herald 27.01.08 — Egon, 28.11.07 — Willi 29.12.07 — Peter 0 27.01.08 Tom, 07.12.07

Andy 12.01.08 — Claudia, 6.1.08 Christoph, 23.11 Frank, 24.11.07 Nicolas, 28.11.07 — Julien, 8.12.07 Aljoz 9 12.07 Toni, 08.12.07

Anne 25.11.07 — Gosia 09.12.07 Mira 9 12.07 Philippe, 25.11.07 Katharina 9.12.07 Jörg 02.12.07 Chris 02.12.07 Fortunato, 25.11.07

Georg, 11.01.08 — Sebastian 27.1.08 Stefanie, 25.11.07 Alessio, 29.11.07 Peter 08.01.08 Willi 11.02.08 Veronika 20.01.08 Gabi 26.11.07 Michi, 22.01.08 Pascale, 18.12.07

Ton, 21.12.07 Alvaro, 15.12.07 Julia, 28.11.07 Mauro, 06.12.07 Fernando 15.01.08 Marcella 23.12.07 Christine, 29.01.08 Kristiani 25.11.07

Sergio, 16.12.07 Heike 27.01.08 Edgar, 15.12.07 BIRGIT 9.12.07 Francesco, 3.11.07 Daniela, 25.11.07 Petra, 28.11.07 ALEXANDRA. 18.12.07

Maria 1.12.07 Michael 3.12.08 Sophia 9.12.07 Gabi, 24.11.07 Karin, 17.01.07 Lous 23.12.07 Annett 20.01.08 ALEXANDRA. 18.12.07 — Heinz 27.11.08

Nicolien 28.11.07 Maria 27.11.08 Marion 08.12.07 Susanne, 23.11.07 Elaine 11.11.08 Ulrike, 25.11.07 Linda 9.12.07 Nicola 07.12.07

JULIA, 9.12.07 Stephanie 02.12.07 Sara, 8.12.07 Ann 26.01.08 Peter, 15.12.07 Sitti, 06.01.08 Solveig, 25.11.07 Ria 23.12.07 Ekkelard

Nico, 03.02.08 Janet, 27.01.08 Sandra 27.01.08 Juliette 9.12.07 Lena, 25.11.07 Justin, 25.11.07 Annette, 28.11.07 Elke, 24.11.07 Christian, 25.11.07

Tanja, 25.11.07 — Vicente, 28.11 Bettina, 6.1.08 Paul, 07.12.07 Christine 19.01.08 Cordula, 24.11.07 Alice, 02.11.07 Alice, 25.11.07 Renate, 07.12.07

Gregoria 13.01.08 — Piano 23.12.07 Lydia, 16.12.07 Irma 9.12.07 Sophia 9.12.07 Christine, 03.02.08 Maria 20.08 Alessandra, 16.12.07

Nike, 24.11.07 — Sofia, 20.01.08 — Ruth, 13.01.08 Eve, 27.01.08 — Andrea, 24.11.07 Louise 23.12.07 — Corrie 23.12.07 Dana, 02.12.07 Evelyn, 26.01.08

Anneliese, 23.11.07 — Valerie, 28.11.07 Georgia, 16.12.07 — Antonella, 28.11 — Alina, 02.12.07 Caroline, 27.01.08 Silvia, 8.12.07 Anna, 01.01.08

Julia, 06.01.08 — Estelle 27.01.08 — Bibiana, 10.02.08 — Sabine, 02.12.07 — Aurelie, 11.01.08 Sibylle, 03.02.08 Yesim, 24.11.07

Helga, 11.12.07 — Sabine, 02.12.07 素子 18.12.07 — 郁子 23.12.07 Hildegard, 08.12.07 Ilaria, 5.1.08

Claudia, 15.12.07 — Hildegard, 26.12.07 Florian 2.1.08

あやの, 18.12.07 — Fabian 23.12.07

— Marta, 27.1.08

— Anna-Maria, 12.01.08

— Victor, 16.12.07 — Federico, 5.1.08

— Lea, 3.1.08

— Felice, 28.11.07

— Markus, 16.12.07

— Artemis, 16.12.07

— Erato, 16.12.07

Antonie 27.01.08

— Nadja, 26.12.07

— Johanna, 27.1.08

Davide, 16.12.07

ard, — 27.1.08

— 试试 — 17.01.08

— Lola, 24.11.07

12.07

— Mao, 25.11.07

— Sebastian 23.12.2007

— Marcos 6.02

— Jost-H. - 8.02.08

— Carsten, 13.01.08   — Miles 02.01.08   — Andreas 09.12.07   — Markus, 02.12.

— Sal, 26.01.08

V. ,09.02.08   — BORIS, 27.12.07   — Felix, 27.12.07   — Holger. 11.01.08   — Ulrich, 25.11.07

S, 8.12.07   — Matthias, 25.11.07   — Petter, - 27.01.08   — Johannes. 06.01.08   — Michael, 13.01.08   — Magnus, 27.12.07   — Jimmy, 07.02.08

Ron, 11.12.07   — Kay-Bäll, 6.1.08   — Hans-Hubert, 3.01.08   — John, - 27.1.08   — Julius. 1.12.07   — Stephan, 6.01.08   — Rüdiger, 24.11.07   真善   23.

— Daniel, 15.01.08   Christopher, 02.12.07   — Heidi, 26.12.07   Philipp. 03.01.08   — Michael -, 27.01.08   Alexander. 22.01.08   — Willi 11.12.07   — Fini - 27.01.08

— Timm, 28.12.07   — Wolfgang, 08.01.08   Hans-Jürgen, - 27.1.08   — Stefan, 29.01.08   Martin, 16.12.07   Sebastian, 9.12.07   — Bettina, - 3.01.08   Carolin, 24.11.07   — Bernardo 6.02   Marco

— Matthias, 26.01.08   Klemens 9.12.07   Markus 5.1.08   Wolfgang, 28.11.07   — Philipp, 29.01.08   — Silas   Klaus, 15.12.07   — Andrey. 9.01.08   — Michael. 20.01.08   Zinus 1.1.08   — Christian, 01.

— Benjamin, 22.11.07   — Christiane 10.01.08   — Max, 03.02.08   Dom, 25.11.07   — Andreas, 29.01.08   Ellen. 02.02.07   — Wolfgang 11.12.07   Claude. 22.01.08   Aleksandra   Peter. 05.01.

Pac 9.12.07   Wolfgang, 02.12.07   — Kerstin, - 27.01.08   — Rebecca, 11.12.07   Christopher   Natascha. 25.1.08   Bertrand, 02.12.07   Helga, Dennis, 11.01.08   — Helene 18.04.08   Andrea, 24.11.07   Rüdiger, 12

1.02.08   — Michael 02.01.08   Bodo 10.01.08   Eva. 22.01.08   Nikolas, 13.11.08   stefanie, 11.01.08   Gabriel, 03.01.08   Jan. 28.12.07   Don, 07.12.07   — 田光

— Alexandro, 25.11.07   — Anni, 24.01.08   Herbert, 26.12.07   Monika. 07.02.08   Mette, 22.11.07   — Erin 25.11.07   — Andreas 26.11.   Elke 27.01.08   Sal Vo, 02.12.07   — Rinke, 07.12.07

30.12.2007   — Yll a, 15.01.08   Debora 8.12.07   Timo, 29.12.07   Sarah 22.12.08   Stephanie   Georgi, 24.11.07   Franziska, 15.01.08   — Carolin, 25.11.07   Lucia, 24.06.08   — Jim 9.12.07

07.12.07   — Andy   Jeanette   Christina. 26.01.08   Sabrina, 02.01.08   Sabina 30.11.07   Andrea, 9.12.07   — Christine,   Bettina, 6.1.08   — Carla, 02.12.07   Esther.   Melanie, 29.1.08

28.12.08   Dorothee, 24.11.07   Katharina 5.1.08   Martina   Maria, 24.11.07   Ulli, 02.12.07   Sil va, 29.11.07   Birgit, 22.11.07   Beatrice 26.12.07   Hilda, 26.12.07   — Nina, 6.1.08   — Sarah

— Sybille, 16.12.07   Yvonne, 29.12.07   Johannes   Sabine, 5.1.08   Ariane, 16.12.07   Catrin, 23.12.07   Berta, 16.12.07   Natalie, 24.11.07   — Patricia, 27.01.08   Josy, 25.11.07   Kirsten, 22.

08   Eva, 25.11.07   Sophie, 12.01.08   Kayniedner, 11.12.07   Nathalie, 02.12.07   Sylvie, 28.12.07   Ute, 16.12.07   АНЖЕЛИКА, 22.01.08   Hella 18.01.08   Gertraud, 22.01.08   Barbara, 24.11.07

5.1.08   Lilian 11.12.07   Shona   Alina, 20.01.08   Sabine, 16.12.07   Melody, 6.1.08   Anki, 25.11.07   Madhuri, 25.11.07   Vroni, 18.12.07   ISAELE, 10.01.08   — Tatiana   — Helga, 25.11.07

07.02.08   Michelle, 30.01.08   Roswitha, 28.01.08   Jane 27.01.08   Jen, 02.12.07   Claudia, 18.12.07   Isa, 18.12.07   — Regine, 06.01.08   小雨 30.12.07   Astrid, 11.01.08   Marina, 16.12.07

12.07   Anke, 02.12.07   — Sara, 16.12.07   Uschi, 27.01.08   Bentje 01.01.08   Jeanette 26.12.07   Manuela, 24.11.07   — Marina, 25.12.07   Marion   Christel, 29.01.08

5.1.08   — Eva 04.01.08   김준형 27.01.08   16.12.07   Ulrike, 07.02.08   — Eli, 27.01.08   — Stefanie, 02.12.07

Ristau, 16.12.07   — Doris, 23.11.07   — 于思森 20.01.08   Dani, 27.01.08   Inge, 23.11.01   Lyna, 05.01.08   Nina, 02.12.07   — Amanda, 04.01.08   김예지 27.01.08   尹
Margie - 27.01.08

— Felix, 03.02.08

— Justin, 16.12.07   — Chiara, 03.01.08   — Florian, 24.11.07

— Leoni, 1.12.07

— Hermine; 28.12.07

— Lasse, 30.12.07

— Cameron, 03.01.08   — Siegmund 30.12.07

— Elias; 28.12.07

— Carina, 16.12.07

— Amelie, 23.11.07

— Lara, - 27.1.08

— Leo - 27.01.08   — Bertille, 28.12.07

— Mateusz, 13.01.08

— Carlot

— Orlando 12.01.08

— Nick, 06.01.08

— Mat

— Damon 23.12.07

— CHARLIE 23.12.07

— Christian, 1.12.07

— Marc, 03.02.08

— Wolfgang, 25.11.07   — David, 02.12.07

— Inga, 24.11.07

— Simon, 2.2.08

— Alexander, 02.12.07

— Jayan, 25.11.07

— Luisa 04.01.08

— Santiago, 02.12.07

— Joaquín, 02.12.07

— Dominik, 25.11.07

— Daniel, 6.1.08   — Alexander 22/12/2007   — Sebastian, 05.01.08 _Michael j 27.12.07
— Steffen, 25.1.09 Franz, 11.01.08   — Christian, 25.11.07
— Sven, 03.02.08   — Volker, 25.11.07   — Denis, 26.01.08   — Maximilian peter felix 03.02.08
— Judger, 25.11.08   — Stefan, 06.01.08 – Edgar, 06.01.08   — Theo Stefan Thomas. 06.01.08
— Christopher, 08.01.08   Jess, 28.11.07   — Thomas, 30.12.07 — Thomas, 01.01.08
— Miquel 27.01.08   Ron, 11.01.08   Kevin, 22.01.08   — Till, 13.01.08   Fabian 04.01.08   — Josef, 22.01.08   Matthias, 9.12.07 – Peter, 31.01.08   — Christian, 03.01.08   — Ralf, 29.11.0
— John, 6.1.08   Tucker, 30.01.08   — Jörg, 15.12.07   Maurice, 1.12.07   — Jo 10.01.08   Basilio, 26.01.08   Johannes, 22.11.07 – Marc 26.12.07   — Bernt, 24.11.07   — Ingo
Robert, 8.12.07   Helmut, 18.12.07   — Alexander 25.12.07   — Augustin 29.12.07   Joachim, 25.11.07   Henry 03.02.08   Matthias, 28.01.07   Gregor, 26.01.08   — Daniel, 21.1.08
— Stefan, 25.11.07   franziska, 22.11.07   Rienk 16.01.08   — Lukas – 27.01.08   Michael 27.01.08   Hilke, 02.12.07   Matti, 07.12.07   Sarah 10.02.08   — Cornelia, 25.11.07
— Alex, 19.01.08   Barbara Kaufmann 25.11.07   Karr 02.01.08   Peter 27.11.07   Philipp 13.01.08   Reinhard, 15.12.07 – Anna 28.01.07   — Angela, 02.01.08
Michael, 12.12.07   — Barbara   Ingeborg, 15.12.07   Jerome, 02.12.07   Anne, 22.01.08   Isabell, 06.01.08 –, Cornelia, 06.01.08   Stephan 9.12.07   Wilfrid, 4.12.07
Valeri, 1.12.07   Charlotte, 26.12.07 – Kathi, 29.01.08   — Alberto, 24.11.07   Evi, 9.12.07   Louise 2.12.07 Valeria, 9.12.07   Lisa, 24.11.07 – Siri 28.11.07   Franziska, 24.01.08   Ute, 25.11.07
— Marc, 13.01.08   Benedikt, 5.12.07   Stephan, 22.11.07   Ludwig, 8.12.07 – Susanne 26.12.07   Maren, 28.11.07 – Tatjana, 05.01.08   Marie Luise, 22.12.07   Christiane, 29.11.07
— Natalia, 15.01.08   Melanie, 12.01.08   Karin, 15.12.07   Ans, 26.01.08   Christin, 25.11.07   Kristin 26.01.08   Julia, 18.12.07
— May 22.12.07   Sussan 01.08   Petra, 15.12.07   Eva, 25.11.07   Barbara 25.11.07   Margike, 24.11.07   Naima   Christin, 25.11.07   Annegret, 05.02.08   — Gabriel
Rosemari, 23.11.07   — Elena, 11.01.08   Nolke 15.12.07   Börbel, 02.12.07   Maria, 30.11.07   Berta, 4.11.07   Franciska, 25.11.07   — Tanja, 6.1.08   — Erika
Susanne, 22.11.07 Kat 11.01.08   Tara, 02.02.08   Valentina, 24.11.07   Rita, 8.12.07   Hanelore, 07.12.07   Sine, 25.11.07   — Juta, 9.12.07   — Elisa 9.12.07   — Julia
— Martha, 21.12.07 – Ricarda 18.1.08   — Verena, 29.01.08   — Julia, 13.1.07   Melanie, 02.12.07   — Antje 11.01.08   — Hildeg
Ingrid 02.02.08   — Susane 25.1.08   — Marie, 20.01.08   Dick 25.11.07   Ingrid, 06.01.08 –, Laura, 28.01.08   Katja 9.12.07   — Johanna 28.12.07 – Heidi, 03.02.08   Marina 02.01.08
— Renate 9.12.07   — Silvia, 24.11.07   Marie 18.01.08   — Gabriele 9.12.07   Marieluise, 11.01.08 — Giorgia   — Christiane, 24.11.07   — Giulia, 1.0
— Jara 9.12.07   — Karo 02.02.08   美保 23.12.07   Heide, 01.02.08   — Hannelore. 18.12.07 – Theresa, 12.01.08   Serena, 24
— 토현기 27.12.07   — 北、 18.12.07   Cati, 09.02.08   Christina 02.12.07   — Audrey, 02.12.07   — Emma 24.1.08 — Margarita 27.01.08   Bess, 18.
— Elisabeth 25.11.07   — Vida 02.01.08   — Παναγιώτα 30.12.07   상지 010.Feb.2008√   — Irene, 24.11.07   — Renate, 09.02.08   — Netsumi, 28.12.07
— Mayumee, 06.01.08   — Beate, 15.12.07   — Hannah 02.12.07   MarieU 03.04.08   — Amy, 20.01.08   Sieglinde, 22.11.07 – Σουλέλα 30.12.07   겨   夏未   — Noe, 02.12.07
— Christine, 6.1.08   — Susi, 03.02.08   — Marima, 25.11.07
— 야비기 27.12.07   — Ines, 03.02.08

— Lucas 26.12.07

— Kirsten, 05.01.08,

— Elin, 6.1.08

— Marlies, 24.11

— Michelle, 25.11.07

— Paul, 02.12.07

— Philipp, 25.11.07

— Michael, 03.02.08

achen 23.12.07
— Andi, 16.01.08
— John, 02.12.07
— Roger, 6.1.08
— Sebastian, 20.01.08   Stephane, 28.1…
— Денис, 26.01.08
08
Ferdinand, 23.12.07
— Stefan, 26.01.08   Jerome, 03.01.08   Fabien 29.12.07
— Norbert, 9.12.87   — Horst-Detlev, 13.01.08
— Tom, 30.12.07   — Niklaus, 29.12.07   — Manfred, 03.01.08   Gerd, 26.12.07   — Fritz 29.12.07   Florian, 16.12.07
— Ricardo, 30.12.07 — Klaus Werner 18.01.08   Florian 02.02.08   — Heinrich, 26.01.08
— Beate, 26.12.07   — Tim, 06.01.08   — Alex, 25.1.08   — Jesco, 23.12.07   — Paolino, 10.02.08   — Pedro, 06.01.08   — Andrea, 1…
k, 02.12.07   — Antoine, 23.11.07   — Vassilis, 1.01.08   — Erik, 28.12.07   — Angelos, 02.12.07   — Lutz, 25.11.07   Alex 12.01.08   — Manuel, 02.12.07
— Sebastian 9.12.07   — Stefan 09.02.08 Jorg, 30.11.8   — Oliver, 10.02.08   — Thomas, 27.11.08   — Istvan, 29.12.07   Katrin, 07.12.07   Fabio, 10.02.08
— Theo, 12.12.07   BEN. 03.04.08   Martin, 25.11.07   — Bruno, 02.02.08   Carlo, 24.11.07   — Bertram, 03.02.08   Irma, 1.12.07   STEFI, 09.12.07   Angela, 22.11.07
WERNER 23.12.07 — Maximilian 18.01.08   Ronald, 8.12.07 — Filippo 23.12.07   — Franziska 24.11.07   kathi, 31.01.08   Maria, 30.12.07   Ulrich, 30.01.08   Maximilian, 5.12.07
— Paul 23.12.07   — ANGELA. 4.12.07   — Dagmar, 26.01.08   — Julia 28.12.07   Marina, 26.01.08 Norman 14.12.07   Christoph, 22.01.08   Bernardo, 21.12.07   Martin, 28.12.07
net, 25.01.07   — Ernesto, 30.11.07   Gregor 13, 30.12.07   Auji 12.04.69   — Charles, 30.11.07 — Brigitte 18.01.08   Manfred, 5.12.07   Roman, 13.01.08   Steven 22.11.07   Eva, 16.12.07   Andrej 27.12.07
— Claudia, 04.01.08   Isabella, 25.11.07   Dave, 24.11.07 — Basti, 6.1.08 — LJUBA, 30.11.07 — Michael 09.02.08   Pepi, 02.12.07   Giulia, 02.01.08   Luca 02.02.08   CHARLY 8.12.07   — Laura, 28.12.07
— 22.11.07   — Dominik, 06.01.07   baby 04.01.08   — Christiane 9.12.07   Klaus 04.01.08 — Andrea 27.12.07   — Silvia, vaz 08   — Jochen, 20.01.08   Peter, 22.11.07 — Jean, 10.01.08   Helena 9.12.07   Gerd, 2.12.07   Kristine, …
— Rainer, 26.01.08   Helga, 29.11.07   — Angelika 09.12.07   Mea, 30.11.8 — Brigitte 29.01.08   Gertraud, 25.11.07   Lena 02.02.08   Sonja, 02.12.07   — Gergel, 24.01.08   Martin, 15.12.07   Daniela, 15.01.08
— SARAH. 18.12.07   — Heribert 18.01.08   Carol 09.12.07 — Katharina 06.01.08   Betting 29.11.07   Barbara 8.12.07 — Roland, 05.02.08   Frank, 6.1.08   Klaus, 25.11.07
e, 25.11.07   — Eva 09.02.08 — Geraldine, 4.12.07   — Andy, 24.11.07   Hans 9.12.07   Alexandra 1.01.08 Jasmin 9.12.07   Frank, 6.1.08   Maja, 26.12.07 — Elisabeth, 30.11.07
Bianca, 9.12.07 — Isabel 02.01.08   Ti, 22.11.07 — Meike 16.01.08   Krestina, 12.01.07 — Evgeni, 30.12.07   Poldi, 3.12.07   Kerstin, 22.11.07 — Julia, 11.12.07   Maria 9.12.07 Marie-Lou
Saskia, 9.12.07   CAMILLA. 18.12.07 — Marie 07.02.08   — Isabelle, 02.01.08   Alessa, 12.01.08 Ulrike 27.11.07   Christa, 25.11.07 — Dhara 02.04.08
Pietro, 25.11.07 — Morvi 8.12.07 — Mara, 30.11.07   Susanne 9.12.07   Andrea 24.11.07   Edith, 22.11.07   Anna 9.12.07 — Juli 16.01.08   Elisabeth, 28.12.07   Tiziana, 30.12.07 — Ema
Eleonora, 1.01.08 — Elisabeth, 09.02.08 — Gisi 22.01.08   Carina, 30.11.07 — Erika, 04.01.08 — Teresa 02.01.08   Sarah, 01.02.08   Anna, 15.12.07   Catalina, 13.01.08   Ka…
— Jessica, 29.12.07   — Helena, 06.01.08   Magdalena 02.01.08   Assaf 04.01.08   Aylin, 30.12.07   Lauren 11.01.08   Silvia, 25.11.07   Katharina 12.0…
— Carola, 31.01.08 — Brita 07.02.08   Julia 24.11.07   Omelia 22.12.07   Matthew 06.01.08 — Brigitte, 06.01.08   MEGHAN, 20.01.08 — Evi 11.01.08   Kitchony, 6.1.08   — Riki, 23.12.07   Mimi, 19.12.07 — Flora, 12.01.08
— Heidi, 18.12.07 — Evelin, 29.01.08 — Dory, 24.11.07   Andrea 9.12.07 — Nadine, 12.01.08   Angela, 25.11.07 — Jacquelen, 02.12.07 ⇒ Jacqueline, 02.12.07   Fabio, 1.01.08
— Helen, 28.12.07   — Cathrine, 21.12.07   Sarah, 5.12.07   — Anahita, 15.12.07   — Margit, 30.12.07 — Valeska, 6.1.08   — Katharina, 2…
— Claudia, 5.12.07   伊勢春., 06.01.08   — Dagmar, 28.12.07   Serena, 25.11.07   Patricia, 25.11.07
笑子, 06.01.08

—Sophia 04.01.08   — Melanie, 1.12.07
— Niklas, 13.01.08   — Laura 04.01.08

—Leopold 04.01.08

— Anne-Kathrin, 25.11.07   — Lisa, 25.11.07

—Ann-Sophie 28.12.07

—Theodor 06.01.08   — Veronika, 25.11.07

—Helena 9.12.07

— Stephan, 02.12.07

— Paula, 30.12.07

— Vincent, 07.01.08,

8.11.07
— Henning 9.12.07
— André, 06.01.08   — Christian, 06.01.08 — Thomas, 20.01.08
— Philippe, 24.11.07   Emanuele, 24.11.07
— Andrius, 1.01.08 — Florian 12.12 Jeplan, 1.01.08   — Morten, 2.12.07 — Benjamin, 03.01.08   Matthias, 25.11.07
— Alexys,   — Heiko — 27.01.08
1.01.08 — Bärbel, 9.11.07   — Peter 04.01.08   — Andreas, 16.12.07   — Alexandra, 25.11.07   Frank, 28.11.07
07 — Hansjörg 20.01.08   — Frank 22.12.07 — Michael, 28.12 Hartmut, 03.01.08   — Marke 9.12.07   — Constantin, 02.12.07   — Marc, 6.1.08   — Christian, 2.12.07
— Reinhold, 1.01.08   Matthias, 1.12.07 — Alex 27.11.07 — Natalia, 06.01.08   — Wolfgang, 11.01.08   Matschi, 27.11.07 — Sebastian, 02.12.07   Reinhard, 23.11
Cordula   Stephan, 26.12.07 — Josef, 5.1.08   Laura, 25.11.07 — Dannie 02.01.08   — Martin, 03.01.08   — Ludovic 10.02.08   Martin, 03.01.08   Philipp, 24.11.07   Christoph, 16.12.07   — Arwed, 28.12   Stefano
01.08 Manfred, 22.11.07 Tamara, 27.01.08 Markus, 02.12.07 — Hayley, 05.01.08   22.12.07 — Job 22.12.07 — Laurent, 25.01.08   Dana, 25.11.07   Karin, 3.01.08   Martin, 02.12.07   — Rainer, 02.12
— Sabine, 5.12.07   — Renaud, 24.01.08   — Joachim, 26.01.08   — Christopher, 5.11.07   Jochen, 25.11.07   Wulf, 05.01.08   Kerstin   Steffe, 16.12.07
Jakob, 30.11.07 — Laura, 25.01.08   Justine, 9.12.07 — Madlen, 18.12.07   Karl 5.12.07 ROMANA Sarina, 2.12.07   Reinhard 11.01.08   — Domiziano, 24.11.07   — Joe,
07 Lena, 03.02.07 Elisabeth 05.01.08   — Thomas, 02.12.07   Kristin 26.12   Franziska, 25.11.07   — Reinhard 11.01.08   Shenpen   Peter 02.01.08
Lisa, 1.12.07 — Heiner, 9.12.07   — Teresa   Wolfgang, 30.11   Groni, 07.12.07   AMANDIS, 9.12.07   Bärbel, 26.12.07   Petra 27.01.08
07.12.07 — Kathrin 28.11.a   — Caitlin, 05.01.08 — Laura 27.01.08   Karin, 22.11.07   Swantje, 6.1.08 — Brigitte 11.01.08   Shaun
Eve, 25.11.07   Gail 25.11 Helena, 24.11.07   Anna, 27.11.07   Margarita Bärbl, 27.12.07   Katharina, 25.11.07   Kathy, 28.11.07
Louis, 25.11.07 — Kath, 5.1.08   Gisela, 03.01.08   — Julia, 5.1.08 — Gudrun, 9.12.07   Kyra 25.11.07 Dorota   Susanne, 22.11.07   Sylvia, 02.02.08   Petra, 23.11.
02.01.08 — Margarete 26.01.07   Hanna 9.12.07 — Trisha 26.12.07 — Ruth, 26.01.08   Cornelia 15.1.08   Kathrin, 25.11.07   Franziska, 9.12.07   — Lena, 2.12.07   — Barbara 23.1
IVa, 25.11.07   Manuela, 5.11.07 — Marianne 30.11.07   — Gabi, 6.1.08   — Nadine 19.12.07   Manijeh 24.12.07   Doris 08.01.08   Joanna, 30.1.07 — Suzy, 05.02.08 Tu, 25.
12.01.08   Ursula, 4.12.07 — Renate, Khanh, 25.11.07   Kristýna, 23.11.07 — Bettina, 29.12.07   Mathilde, 30.01.08   Anna, 24.11.07 — Kristine, 02.12.07
Klare, 22.11.07 — Saskia, 19.12.2007   Maria, 25.11.07   Clara, 27.11.07   Monika, 30.01.08   Mari-Eve, 6.1.08   Lucia 04.01.08 — Vo kh 16.11.07 — Kri
Haja 5.12.07 — Zsofia 22.01.08 Lucia, 11.01.08   — Eva, 30.11.07   ZOE, 9.11.07   Janet 27.01.08   Heiko, 02.12.07   Jelena, 26.01.08   Katja, 10.01.08   — Sandra, 02.12.07
a, 27.11.07 — Alexandra 27.11.07 — Dominik, 03.02.07 Bärbel 08.02.08 Michele, 9.11.02   Ingrid, 23.11.07   Gisela, 24.01.08   Christina, 6.1.08   Sun Sook, 12.12.07   — Sus
— Bernadette 05.01.08   Fabiana, 25.11.07   Dairy 29.12.07 — 27.01.08 — Nina, 27.12.07   — Nicole 24.1.07   Rosanna, 9.12.07   Amira, 6.1.08
Christiane, 30.01.08   — Liliana, 9.12.07   — Claudia 28.12.07   Karine, 6.1.08   — Cuqui 9.12.07

— Martin, 29.12.07   — Yves, 20.01.08   — Volker 9.12.07   — ANTON, 29.01.08   — Ga
— Eberhard, 07.02.08   — Andreas, 22.12.07
Frank 27.01.08
— Philipp, 5.12.07
Franz, 25.11.07

— Nadine 12.01.08

— Maximilian, 06.01.08

— Laura 10.02.08

— Sophie 12.01.08

— Anna Lena, 24.11.07   — Jan, 25.11.07

— Georgios, 24.11.07   — Samuel, 6.1.08

— Sofia, 25.11.07

— Karl, 02.12.07   — Till, 25.11.07   — Paul, 27.01.08
                                                                                — John, 25.
                — Gilles, 9.12.07   — Christian, 29.12.07
12.07   — Festil, 06.01.08   Rolf, 22.11.07   — Jakob, 30.12.0
        — Florian, 23.12.07   Martin, 15.12.07   Markus, 25.11.07   Andreas, 06.07.08   Lenz, 29.12.07   — Andreas, 03.02.08   Markus, 09.02.08
John, 1.01.08   9.12.07   — Wibo, 30.12.07   Manfred, 02.02.08   GüntHer, 9.12.07   — Claudio, 1.01.08   — Clau
Markus, 9.12.07   — Alexandra, 06.01.08   Setina, 1.01.08   — Doris, 24.01.08   LEO, 18.12.07   — Dietmar
H9. 30.12.07   — Thorsten 27.01.08   THomas. 8.12.07   Konstantin 23.12.07   Everet, 2.2.08   Leo, 03.02.07   — Lusie, 25.11.07   Rolf, 03.02.08   Mark, 02.12.07
        — Axel, 22.11.07   — Reto, 06.01.08   Richard, 25.11.07   — Andreas, 04.01.08   Gerhard, 9.12.07   Achim, 02.02.02
        — Alphs, 02.01.08 Steffi 23.12.07   Dietmar 02.12.07   — Gavin, 30.11.07   Luca, 24.11.07   Annika, 09.02.08   — Christina, 05.01.08   Barbara   Philipp, 25.11.07
09.02.08   — Tomas, 13.01.08   Maximilian, 26.01.08   Christina, 07.12.07   Franz, 06.01.08   Karl-Eugen, 9.12.07   — Mehli, 22.11.07   Svetlana, 25.11.07
Bruno, 27.12.07   — Leo, 25.11.07   Hontz 9.12.07   — Lars, 06.01.08   EVA, 9.12.07   — Matteo, 11.01.08
Katharina 16.01.08   Kenneth, 16.12.07   — Florian, 22.11.07   Iva, 06.01.08   Adrian, 25.11.07   Denis, 1.01.08   Iris, 2001.08   Stephen, 27.11.07   — Michel   Clemens, 27.11.07 John, 15.01.0   Joh
— Rebecca, 25.11.07 Alvaro, 27.01.08 kim, 17.01.00   Paul, 25.11.07   — Daniela, 2908   Jürgen, 1.12.07   — 9.12.07   — Gaby, 24.01   Mortin, 8.12.07   Sonja, 05.01.08   Martina 01.02.08
— Paul, 1.01.08   — Heer 26.17.07   — Norbert, 02.12.07   — Carlo 27.01.08   Jothan, 30.01.08   — 22.12.07   Beate, 30.01.08   Renz, 9.12.07
— Christine, 05.07.07   — Marieluise, 26.07   Frey, 20.72   Pad-   Francisca, 26.12.07   Greta, 24.11.07   Tiffany 29.12.07   Pierluigi   Fran 02.12.07   Wolfgang 9.12.07   Karo, 11.01.08
— Alex, 25.11.07   — Andrea, 26.11.07   Lilli, 25.11.07   Lisa 06.01.08   Harja 100708   Tarsma, 02.01.08   Anna, 9.12.07   Vikiff 02.01.07   Alexey, 27.11.07
Konstanze, Jan.08   — Hannah 16.01.08 Hamed, 02.12.07   Evi, 05.1.08 Hannelore, 22.11.07   Marcio 25.11.07   — Johann, 6.1.08   Claudia 16.01.08   Wolfgang, 03.02.08   Sabrina, 27.11.07 Polli, 25.11.07   Eicher
Maximilian, 25.11.07   — Maximilian, 5.12.07   Christine 17.01.08   Christine, 25.11   Kersten, 25.11.07   Christ 9.12.07   Rebecca, 31.01.07   Katariua, 6.1.08   — Nina, Nicole, Anna
9.12.07   — Daniela, 17.01.07   Luise, 26.12.07   Rosella 9.12.07   — Kerstin, 05.01.08 Walter 16.12.07   Anke, 25.11.07   Burgi   Elizabeth 23.12. 12
        — Christel, 26.01.08 Charmmi   MARINA, 29.01.08   Gloria, 24.08   Rebecca, 16.12.07   Ursula, 26.01.07   — Vanessa, 24.11.07   Emanuel 27.01.08
— Annika, 15.12.07   — Alexander, 06.01.08   Juli 20.01.08   BriH. Main, 02.12.07   Jüta   Kevin, 28.11.07   — IIJIMA.T 29.11.07   Claudia, Jörg   Paulina, 4.12.07   H
2.11.07   Andree-Anne, 6.1.08   Sech, 24.11.07   Clémence, 27.12.07   — Kirsten, 06.01.08   1.12.07   — Georg, 22.01.08   Pedro, 9.12.07   — Lea 01.01.08   Lisa, 30.01.08   Claudia, 25.11.0
        — Véronique, 8.12.07   Freike, 8.12.07   Franziska 16.01.08   Pavle, 9.01.02   Joha 27.01.08   — Christine 22.12.07
ine, 25.11.07   — Luise 05.01.08   Elli   9.12.07   Mirjam, 06.01.08   Sabine, 25.11.02   Theresia, 9.12.07   Bene Cisa, 02.12.07   — Louise, 2.12.07   — 真実 23.12.07   Claudia,25.11.0
9.12.07   — Mohila, 02.12.07   Praaw 25.11.07   — Christine 18.01.08   Elisa, 1.01.08   Mario 27.01.08   Gisela 08.01.08   — Maipn 23|12|07   柏 23.12.07   — Ana, 11.01.08   Cothrin, 24.
Carolo, 17.01.08   — Kortrin, 15.12.07   Maria, 9.12.07   — Ela, 04.01.08   Dorothea, 9.11.07   Suzanne, 05.01.08   Birgit. 22.11.07   ガシ 17.01.08   — Sara, 01.01.08
                — Tatjana, 05.01.08   Mara, 26.12   Natascha) 28.12.0   Magdi, 30.12.0   — Eva, 03.02.08   — Konstantina, 03.02.08   — Doris,
                        — Lisbeth, 22.11.08   IIJIMA, 29.11.07   Elena, 24.11.07   奈□ 9.12.07   — Gabriele 18.01.08   Valentina, 24.11.07
        — Caitriona, 24.01.08   JE.Kim, 10.02.08
                — Mone, 02.12.07   — Jernej, 8.12.0
                — Tobias 27.01.08   — Dakila, 9.12.07   — Ludowika — 27.01.08   — Roso — 27.01.08
                                — Oliver, 26.12.07   — 将太 23.12.07

— Hannes, 25.11.07

                                                                                — Hannah,

        — Lina, 2.12.07   — Ja
                — Agnes, 12.02.08

— MIRIAM, 23.12.07   — Daniel, 01.01.08   — Felix 27.01.08   — Sven 27.01.08

                        — Julius, 6.1.08

— Viktoria — 27.01.08

                — Merct, 17.01.08

                                                        — B Zac, 02.12.07

‒ Rudolf, 20.01.08

__Patrick, 25.11.07

1.07
                                                                        __ Wolfgang, 02.12.07
                                                        ‒ Kuri, 9.12.07 ‒ Jörg, 8.12.07
‒Karl-Friedrich, 30.01.08 __ Stefan, 9.12.07   __ Dominique, 05.01.08   __ Alexander 23.12.07   __ Nils‒27.01.08
                                                            Christian 24.11.07
dia, 25.11.07 __ Andreas, 09.02.08   __ Pascal, 9.12.07   Günter, 25.11.07 ‒Matthias, 06.01.08 ‒ Caroline, 1.01.08 Johann 9.12.07
                    Karl-Heinz   Gabriele, 29.12.07 ‒Manfred 1.1.08   HeiKO, 9.11.07   ‒Thomas‒10208 ‒Marcus, 06.01.08 __Philipp-Maximilian
__ Natalie, 25.11.07   Michael, 1.01.08 Roland, 24.11.07 ‒Tim, 07.02.08 Gisela, 15.12.07   __ Walter, 23.11.07 Oliver, 20.01.08 Uli 25.11.07
    __ Martin, 28.11.07 Felix, 03.02.08 Kevin, 20.01.08 __ Marovela 02.01.08 Karl-Georg, 25.11.07   Thomas, 26.01.08
       __Andreas, 17.01.08 __ Renate, 02.12.07   Thomas 10.01.08   ‒ Thomas, 06.01.08   Mateusz, 02.12.07   __Manfred, 6.1.0
__ Udo, 02.11.07   Torsten, 02.12.07   Helmut, 02.12.07   Kathrin, 30.11.07 ‒Joachim, 16.12.07   ALEXANDER, 8.12
im, 4.12.07   __ Salvatore, 9.11.07 Toni, 17.01.08   ACHIM, 9.11.07 22.01.08   Getti, 8.11.07 Martina, 16.12.07 Regina, 8.12.07
nu, 24.11.07 ‒Hans Peter, 9.12.07 ‒Ilya, 05.01.08 Steffi, 25.11.07‒HeiKo,05.11.08 Stephan, 02.12.07 ‒Martin, 28.1.08 ‒Thomas, 24.01.08 ‒Marion, 06.01.08 Angelika, 27.0
ristoph 18.01.08 ‒Monika, 02.12.07 Werner, 02.12.07 __ Wolf, 22.12.07 Elia, 9.12.07 Andrea, 26.12.07 Franz, 03.02.08 sven, 02.12.07 Elke, 04.02.08 Dirk, 02.12.07 Richard, 26.01.08 Sylke, 22.11.07
Patricia 8.12.07 ‒Katharina, ‒27.01.08 Sabine, 25.11.07 ‒Franziska, 06.01.08 Ines, 03.02.08 Gill 15.12.07‒Tina 27.01.08   Sybille ‒27.01.08   Görli, 16.12.07 Anne 07   Dagmar 23.12.07 Stef
Leila, 9.11.07 __ Sabine, 02.12.07 Giucia 8.12.07 Frithjof, 6.1.08 DANi, 8.12.07 Eva, 9.12.07 Stefan, 1.12.07 Christian Michael, 26.01.08 Paulina, 16.12.07 Ursula, 15.01.08 Ramia 9.12.07 Sonja, 3
DVARDO 20/12/07   Eva, 22.11.07 ‒Gitta, 11.01.08 Kurt, 24.01.08 Sophie 13.12.07 Beate 04.01.08 Ulrike 6.1.08   Nicole, 30.11.07 __ Anna 10.01.08   Sonja, 25.11.07‒LENI, 2
uri 28.11.07 __Peter, 9.12.07 Marie, 9.12.07 Marie-Luise, 06.01.08 Sandra, 25.11.07 ‒Keschu, 26.12.07 Lara 23.12.07 Nina 15.12.07 Andina ‒27.01.08   Eva 5.12.07 Elfriede, 11.01.08 INGE. 8.
Astrid, 03.02.08   MANFRED, 20.01.08 Alexa Charlott‒Sysanne 22.12.07 Mona, 27.01.08 Sabine 9.11.07 Ulrike 24.01.08 Donata, 25.11.07‒Andrea Jaana, 06.01.08 Anette, 17.01.08 Tatjana, 25.11.07 Chiaro
chael, 21.12.07 Anna, 25.11.07 ‒Hana, 9.12.07 Holga, 02.12.07   Nikos, 23.11.07   Tina, 9.12.07   Susanna 11.01.08 KATHRINA, 8.12.07
nika, 26.01.08   Takuya, 02.12.07 Leonard, 25.11.07 PERRINE, 8.12.07 ESV 02.02.08 Eva, 25.11.07 Laura, 27.01.08   Paola, 23.11.07   Jovana 02.01.08 Sue 16.12.07
Kate, 25.11.07   ANNA, 20.01.08 Brigitte 18.01.08 Ingrid, 16.12.07 ‒Britta, 03.02.08 ‒Ilona, ‒2k.07 ‒Renate, 25.11.07   Paola, 23.11.07 Hildegard 09.02.08 Maria, 25.11.07 Gaby, 22.01.08
Peachy, 30.12.07   Doris, 02.02.08   Doris, 24.11.07   Christina 02.01.08   Anthi, 25.11.07   肖健云 9.12.07   王弥, 22.01.08 Rita, 6.1.08   ‒Christina, 03.02.08 Aida
08   Yvonne, 25.11.07   ‒Emilia 24.1.08 ‒Anais, 9.12.07 ‒Duygu, 03.02.08 Leo, 06.01.08   Regine ‒27.01.08   Georgia, 07.
__Simone, 16.12.07   Passon, 03.02.08   Pilar 9.12.07
9.12.07   __Tadeja, 9.11.07   ‒kiri 24.01.08   __Marianne, 9.12.07 ‒Regina, 1.12.07 __Majt, 9.12.07
   __王 22.12.07   __ Hiroko, 02.12.07   ‒Michel, 06.01.08

                                                                                                    ‒Flora, 25.11.07

6.01.08   Constantin, 19.2.08 ‒Aaron, 02.12.07

               __Selina, 26.12.07   __ Jenne, 25.11.07

nik, 06.01.08

                                __Irina; 28.11.07

__Nikolas, 6.1.08

                                __Luis, 06.01.08   ‒Frieda, 06.01.08

            __Alida; 28.12.07

                                                                                              __Oscar, 17.01.08

— Roberto, 06.01.08   —— Claudio, 23.11.07

— Ulrich, 1.01.08

                                                                        -Dieter, 06.01.08

2.07   — MARTIN, 27.12.07   Daniel, 25.11.07   — Dieter 02.01.08
— Gottfried, 16.12.07   — Simon 27.01.08   — Michael, 03.02.08
,27.01.08 — Hakon, 6.1.08 — Tobias, 27.01.08 — Robert, 06.01.08 — Stephan, 06.01.08   — Thomas, 07.02.08   — Antta
— Max, 16.12.07 — Gernot, 23.01.08 — Arno, 09.02.08 — Sven 06.01.08 Jonathan, 25.11.07   — 9.12.07   — Alexandria - 27.01.08
8.12.07 — Andreas, 25.11.07   — Jan-Willem, 24.11.07   — Dieter, 26.1.08 — Florian, 6.1.08 NRN, 8.12.07   — Alexandria - 27.01.08   — Chri
  — Günther, 02.12.07   — Jonathan, 17.01.08   Christian L, 21.11.07 — Martin, 06.01.08 Simon, 28.11.07   — DIETER, 8.12.07   — Chr
02.12.07 — Stefan, 27.01.08   — Christof, 9.12.07 — Basti, 29.01.08   — Djamila, 9.12.07 — Manfred 27.12.07 — Uli, 27.01.08 Andrea, 23.11.07 — Helmut, 9.12.
  — Daniela, 16.12.07 — Isa, 28.12.07 Matthias, 17.01.08 Roland, 29.12.07   — Norbert, 25.11.07 — Marlen 27.02 Stefan, anon. Andrea, 23.11.07   — Iván, 06.01.08
Sascha, 9.12.07 — Hubert, 02.12.07 — Peter - 27.01.08 Julian, 8.12.07 Mario 27.01.08 02.12.07 — Wolfgang, 26.01.08 Manfred, 24.11.07 Alexandra, 8.12.07   — Georges, 29.12.07
Christian, 9.12.07   — Joana, 02.02.08 — Renate, 6.1.08 — Werner, 16.12.07 Pablo, 02.02.08 — Judy, 06.01.08 — Claus, 06.01.08   — Walther, 06.01.08 — Viviane, 17.01.08   — Wolfgang, 08.01.08   — Kirst
, 03.02.08 — 29.01.08   — Hani, 13.01.08
,5.1.08 — Hans-Rainer, 22.11.07   Peter, 26.12.07 — Carolin, 06.01.08 Rainer, 9.12.07 Ulrike, 09.12.07 Vreni, 09.12.07 Inga, 23.12.07   jSigune, 25.11.07 — Ralf - 27.01.08   — Max
Karl-Heinz, 07.02 — Birgit, 30.11.08 — August, 29.12.07 Barbara, 26.07.08 Italia, 25.12.07 Dieter 27.01.08 9.12.07 — Annabella, 27.11.08 Tobias, 15.12.07   Sanni, 17.01.08
— Harald, 06.01.08 Yvonne, 08.12.07 — Carlo, 10.1.08 — Giancarlo, 18.12.07 Andrea, 24.11.07   Jasmin, 28.11.07 — Anja, 06.01.08 Theresa, 03.02.08 Nadine, 28.11.07   — Jenk, 9.12.07 — Johanna, 16.01.08 Henrike, 15.12.07 Birg
— Anja, 7.12.07 — Brigitte, 03.02 — Tilia, 02.12.07 — Babette, 06.01.08 Marc, 12.01.08 Anita, 23.11.07   Sophie, 9.12.07 — Zoi, 17.01.08   — Günther, 24.11.07   — Doris, 09.02.08 Michelle 21
— Jörg, 24.11.07   Anne, 27.01.08 — 20.01.08 — Julia 06.01.08 FABIO 09/17/07 — Angelica — Güvolo, 16.12.07 Michael, 27.01.02 Alessandro, 29.12.03 — Swane, 6.1.08 — Sabine, 06.01.08   — Ellen 27.01.08
23.12.07 Monica, 26.01.08 — Hanni, 06.01.08 — ASTRID, 29.01.08 JOJO 23.12.07 — GIUSEPPE 27-12-07 — Patricia, 6.12.07 — Sandra, 24.01.08 Klaus 29.01.08 Paola, 24.01.08   Arne, 25.11.07 — Ilse, 11.02.08 — Eva, 06.01.08 Melanie, 28.11.07 — Susanne
la, 25.11.07 — Katja, 29.12.07 — Ueli, 12.01.07 — Patricia, 02.12.07 Tatjana, 16.12.07 — Ilse, 22.01.08 — Filip, 8.12.07 Felicitas, 16.12.07 23.03.02.08 — Femke, 05.02.08 — Eeka, 03.02.08 — Nicole
mla, 21.12.07   Ursula, 25.11.07   JUTTA 27.12.07 — Rosemarie, 05.02.08 Geraldine, 25.11.07 Karin, 06.1.08 Edita, 11.01.08 Daniela 27.12.07 Barbara, 7.12.07 Marianne, 24.1.08 Anita, 9.12.07 Christian, 26.01.08 GISELA
12.07 — Anna, 18.01.08 — Tanja, 27.01.08   — Katharina, 13.01.08   — Anne, 24.11.07   — Natalie, 11.01.08 — Walter, 15.12.07 Michaela Sab
  — Adelheid, 15.12.07   — Marie-Laure, 25.11.07 — Laura, 27.01.08 IRA, 27.12.07 — Lotte 24.12.07   — Sandra 27.01.08   Vittoria, 25.11.07   — Doris, 16.
rtraud, 22.08 — Julia 02.02.08 — Claudia 27.01.08   Tanja, 27.01.08 KERSTIN 23.12.07   — Judith, 02.12.07   瑞祺, 9.12.02 — Christiane, 11.01.08   — Maria, 24.
rtraud, 25.11.07   — Lillian, 17.01.08   — Julia 10.01.08   — Geli, 06.01.08 — MARGARITA, 29.01.08   — Ana, 06.01.08   — 가가, 2
  — Anne, 23.11.07   Elisabeth, 07.02.08   — Naara, 06.01.08
Anna, 25.11.07   — Ulla, 02.12.07 — Stefanie, 15.12.07 — Juana, 25.11.07   Monika, 25.11.07 — Zijing, 6.1.08 — Janina, 1.12.07
                — Marisa, 06.01.08
        — Irmgard, 09.02.08 — Alessandra 23/6/07   — Leonhard, 06.01.08   — Flora, 25.11
— Natalie 27.01.08   — Raffaella - Raffaella, 29.01.08

                    — Katharine 29.01.08   — Viktor, 30.12.07

        — 옥구, 06.01.08

                                                                        — Lola 29.01.08

        — Lucie, 25.11.07

— Kai, 5.1.08

                        — Celeste, 25.11.07   — Josephine, 25.11.07

11.07   — Laura, 06.01.08

        — Max, 27.01.'08

                — Martin, 06.01.08
— Ula, 5.1.08

        — Lia, 27.01.'08

                                                                                — Luc

— Finnole, 06.01.08

Thomas, 2.12.07

Hanke, 09.02.08

Wolfgang 06.01.08   Florian, 6.1.08   Frank 27.01.08   Johannes 27.01.08   Vojta, 23.11.07
Peter, 18.01.08   Ermacora 27.01.08   Rüdiger 27.01.08   Jens, 29.
toine, 03.02.08   Torsten, 30.12.07   Wolfga
Joël 23.12.07   Guido, 29.12.07   Evan, 15.12.07   Thorsten, 03.02.08
                                                       Jörg 2.12.07   Meloozina, 13.12.07
ristian, 25.11.07   Stefan, 25.11.07   Humberto 30.12.07   Mirza, 30.12.07   Maxel, 16.12.07   Michael, 01.01.08   PETER, 29.07
07 Wilfried 27.01.08 Linus 27.01.08 Holger, 22.11.07   Jochen 27.01.08   Peter, 02.01.08   Igor 13.01.08
Irmgard, 18.01.08   Niki 08.01.08   Oliver, 06.01.08   Peter, 02.01.08   Theresa   Michael, 30.01.08   Manfred, 02.12.07
18.01.08 Tammo Simona, 15.12.07 Anton 12.12.07 Jürgen 27.11.07 Ellen, 30.12.07 Sylvia, 16.01.08
Klaus, 25.11.07 Andy 27.01.08 Jürgen M. 26.12.07 Racine 2.12.07 Ursula, 02.01.08 Angelika, 21.11.08 Jessika, 05.01.08 Jolande 9.12.07 Florian, 21.11.07 Sonja,
sten, 02.12.07 Chaco, 16.12.07 Reinhard 30.12.07 Marc 2.12.07 Thomas, 16.12.07 James, 13.01.08 27.01.08 Angela, 02.12.07 Michael, 01.02.08
rieke, 24.01.08 Frank Myrese 24.01.08 Damien, 9.12.07 Ercan, 03.02.08 Stephanie, 22.01.08 Tobias, 30.01.08 Thomas, 15.12.07 Roland, 16.12.07 Tina, 6.1.08 Pejo, 4.12.07
aximiliane, 21.11.07 Cali, 02.12.07 Christopher 24.12.07 Corinne, 1.12.07 Hildegard, 02.12.07 Peter 27.01.07 Ursula, 07.02.07 Petra Sophie 27
agit, 6.1.08 Philipp, 16.12.07 Marc 30.08 Françoise 27.01.08 Sabine 30.08 Sabrina 25.11.07 Christian 25.08 Gerte, 01.02.08 Claudia 10.08 Ilona 23.11.0
3.12.07 Jessica 27.01.08 Stefan 6.1.08 Andrea, 25.11.07 Corinne, 30.08 Sabine, 2.12.07 Helena 17.11.08 Tijana 02.04.08 Bergd 27.01.08 Andreas 04.01.08 Tanny 27
NARJES 25.11.07 Linda, 25.11.07 Birgit 25.12.07 Stefan, 29.08 Kay, Ulla, 15.01.08 Juliane 28.08 Constanze, 16.12.07 Franco 2
3.12.07 Renan, 26.01.08 Heidi, 6.1.08 Regina, 22.01.08 Shaunna 27.01.08 G+L 9.12.07 Illi, 27.12.07 Marina 27.01.08 Julia, 25.11.07 Cecilie, 25
ssa, 25.11.07 Gisela, 5.1.08 Sarah, 25.11.07 Jasmin 08.08 Fryni 25.11.07 Iris 27.01.07 Anna, 05.01.08 Nicole, 16.01.08 39.7.5.07.12.07 Rosie, 19.05
ve, 29.12.07 Dieter, 6.12.07 Marion Anita 06.01.08 Sofia 27.01.08 Horst 16.12.07 Anna, 23.11.07 Manfred, 16.12.07 Anja, 07.08 Paul, 24.11.07
le 2.12.07 Nadia, 25.11.07 Maura 27.01.08 Gabi 23.12.07 Stefanie 30.08 Heide, 25.11.07 Karin 30.08 Natalya 16.12.07 Otto 6.108 Katharina 02.01.08
Regina, 17.01.08 Gerda, 22.01.08 Renate 07.01.08 Alexandra 30.08 Kathrin 6.108 Christina 2.12.07 FRANZISKA 8.07 Christian Silvia, 15.12.07
ine 11.12.07 Andrea 30.08 Katie, 15.12.07 Audra 27.12.07 Maximiliane 25.12.07 SoVi 26.12.07 Hannah, 16.12.07 Florian, 30.01.08 Annemarie 08.08 Andrea, 15.12.07 Anike, 02.01.
a, 22.01.08 Dagmar 16.12.07 Julia 30.08 Katharina 30.08 Brigitt 19.01.08 Sarah 30.08 Michaela, 28.12.07 Bregu 27.01.08 MARIAN DL. 18.12.07 Judith 01.01.08 kar
6.12.07 Vera 12.01.08 Ergi 22.11.07 Karin, 01.02.08 Siglinde 22.11.07 Vera, 23.11.07 Christina, 6.1.08 EvČa, 23.11.07 Beatrice 27.01.08 PETRA, 25.11.07
24.01.08 Noelia, 07.11.07 Lena 12.01.08 Angelika, 28.11.07 Andrea, 16.12.07 Marina, 11.08
26.12.07 David, 30.12.07 Elisabeth, 22.11.07 Marie, 02.12.07 Liljana 08.01.08 李平 6.1.08 Maggie, 6.1.08 Verena, 11.1.08 KATHI, 27.01.08 He
                                 ORSOLYA, 15.12.07 INGRID 8.12.07 Radka, 23.11.07 Christine, 04.01.08 Michèle 9.1.
11.07 Vincent 27.12.07 Covadonga, 02.12.07 Jana 18.12.07 Maxi-Marie, 14.01.08 Ifa, 6.1

                                                         Eva, 20.01.08   Tim, 03.02.08
                                               Rebecca, 27.01.08

Daniel 23.11.07 Giorgio 23.12.07
Ferdinand 27.12.07   Julian, 16.12.07

                                                      Fiona, 03.02.08

Dennis 23.12.07

Leo, 22.01.08   Gregor, 25.11.07

LUKAS 23.12.07

CLEMENCE, 25.11.07

Julie, 25.11.07
ucka, 9.12.07   Luis, 22.01.08

— Hannes, 06.01.08

— Jannis, 05.01.08
— Francesco, 15.12.07

— Janez, 05.01.08
— Gerd, 27.12.07

— Ferdinand, 25.11.

— Carlo, 03.02.08
— Lorenz, 18.12.07.   — Jörg, 08
— Lars, 29.11.07
— Max 23.12.07

Jiří, 23.11.07 — Martin, 11.01.08
— Wolfgang 04.01.08 Georg, 2.12.07 — Markus, 16.01.08   — Markus, 16.01.08   — Hugo, 23.11.07
Nikač, 23.11.07   — Nils, 27.12.07 — Radu   — Catrin, 22.11.07   — Clemens 16.12.07
Harry, 03.02.08   18.01.08   Ralf, 07.02.08 Lucas, 06.01.08
Andreas 02.01.08 — Dino, 09.02.08 Alfred, 27.01.08 Bernd, 15.12.07   Hugo 09.02.08   Christoph — Daniel, 25.11.07 — Urs, 30.2.07   — Dieter, 28.11.07   — Tob
— Andreas, 9.12.07   Charlotte, 01.02.08   — Frank, 06.01.08   — Ursula 16.01.08   Axel, 25.11.07   — Thomas, 16.01.08
— Wolfgang 26.01.08   Alexandra 16.12.07   — Frank, 22.11.07   — DAVID 23.12.07 1.12.07 — Adalbert 10.01.08   Axel, 25.11.07 — Karin, 15.12.07   — Sina, 25.11.07
Katinka, 30.11.07 — Luk... Clarka, 23.11.07   Fabian 25.11.07 Hubert, 25.11.07   Anka, 27.01.08 JeanLuca 11.12.07 — Sonja — Ralph, 9.12.07 — Wolfgang 8.01.08   — Joachim, 16.12.07
23.11.07 — Filippo, 29.12.07 Paula, 2.12.07 — Trix, 29.2.07   Jürgen, 15.12.07 — Sandra, 06.01.08 Sabine, 03.02.08 Heurike, 6.1.07 — Hansjürgen   Manfredo 01.12.07   — Ulrich, 18.12.07 — Marina,
Saša, 05.02.08   Ulla, 27.12.07 Susanne 03.02.08   Eva 16.12.07   Maximilian, 25.11.07 Claudelle, 15.12.07   Katrin, 07.12.07 — Morgan, 03.02.08
Jiří, 16.12.07 — Ney   Jana 02.01.08   — Anika, 6.1.08   Armando   Jana 27.07.07   Bazem 26.01.08 Josef, 01.02.08   — Brenda, 29.12.07 — Ursula, 6.1.08
— Hirjam 02.01.08 — Karin, 05.01.08 Fred, 15.12.07 Alboin 6.1.08   Heike, 1.12.07 Doro 6.1.08 Sabrina 04.01.08   Alexandra 23.12.07 — Alenka, 06.01.08   Ernst, 28.11.07 — Frida, 07.01.08 Die
Friederike 04.01.08 Rajče, 23.11.07 — Karolina 04.01.08   — Fedor, 24.01.08 — Leon 29.01.08   Zoe 15.12.07 — Friedemann 30.1.07 — Carolin 27.01.08 Christina 04.01.08 — Sabine, 03.02.08   — Anna 02.01.08 — Günther, 29.
16.01.08 — Christina 06.01.08 Helga, 25.11.07 — Till, 06.01.08   Dirk, 25.11.07 — Ralf 16.01.08   Marika, 12.01.08 — Karin 10.01.08 — Ulrike, 15.01.08   Ute, 23.11.07 Gude, 08.12.07   — Georgia, — Marina,
Felix, 6.1.08 — Annegret, 11.01.08 E 26.01.08   Nora, 25.11.07 — Dorothee 29.12.07   Isabel, 25.11.07 — Conny 6.1.08 — Rebecca 15.01.08   — Sophie, 19.01.08 — Bärbel, 02.12.07
01.08 — Gabriele, 02.12.07   — Bärbel, 30.01.08 — Helga, 06.01.08 Justine, 06.01.08   Diana, 15.12.07   Karel, 26.12.07 — Julia 02.01.08   Moni
02.12.07 Anita 01.08 — Ricarda, 27.01.08 Lind, 25.11.07 Claire 16.12.07 Christina 02.02.08 — NICOLE, 29.01.08 — Simone, 30.01.08   Kathrin, 1.12.07 — Dominika, 25.11.07 — Paola, 14.12.07 Berta 26.01.08 Stefanie, 15.12.07
01.08 — Aideen 14.12.07 — Johanna, 11.1.08   Alison, 15.12.07 — Fabienne, 05.01.08 Brigitte 01.02.08   Ester, 16.12.07 — Constanza 23.04.08 — Annette 27.12.07   Dolores, 29.12.07
11.01.08 — Nati, 11.02.08 — Haike, 03.02.08   Sally, 29.12.07   — Monika, 02.12.07 — Shana 25.11.07 Alessia 26.01.08   Monika, 29.12.07   Larissa, 24.11.07   Jens, 11.12.
— Duck-Hee Kwon 25.11.07   JITKA, 23.11.07 — BARBARA, 29.01.08 Stephanie, 17.01.08   — Franziska, 06.01.08   Tina, 16.01.08
5.11.07   Daniela, 25.11.07   Jessica, 06.01.08 — Brigitte, 06.01.08 — Jane — 27.01.08   Sara, 27.11.07   MENINA ⬜
— Helen, 6.1.08   Christiane, 25.11.07   Anne-Marie, 1.12.07   Ashley, 06.01.08   Sisa, 6.1.08
25.11.07 — PATRICIA, 29.01.08 Amy, 25.1.08   Camila, 25.11.07   — Vanessa, 26.01.08
30.01.08 — Jonas 27.01.08 — Katalin, 16.12.07 — Felix, 27.12.07   — Maximilian, 09.02.08   — Helena 24.01.08   — Helga, 06.01.08   — Rafaela, 03.02.08

— Adrian, 09.02.08

— Yu-Gyeong Chun. 25.11.07   — Rommy, 03.02.08   — Nils, 25.11.07

— Jennystar. 2008.2.6.

— Jonas, 16.01.08

— Ada, 27.01.08

—Hannes, 06.01.08

8   —Jannis, 05.01.08   —Janez, 05.01.08   — Ferdinand, 25.11.07
Ti', 23.11.07 —Martin, 18.01.08   —Francesco, 15.11.07   -Gerd, 27.12.07
                                                                                    —Carlo, 03.02.08   —Jörg, 03.01.08
—Wolfgang, 04.01.08 — Georg, 2.12.07 —Markus, 16.01.08   —Markus, 16.01.08   —Lorenz, 18.12.07.   —Lars, 29.12.07   —Dr
—23.11.07   —Nils, 27.12.07 —Radu   18.01.08   Catrin, 22.11.07 —Clemens 16.12.07   —Jugo, 23.11.07   —Max 23.12.07   —Tobias, 25.11
02.08 —reas 02.01.08 —Dino, 09.02.08 Alfred, 27.01.08 —Rolf, 02.02.08 Lucas, 06.01.08   Petra, 07.02.08
—Andreas, 9.12.07   Charlotte, 01.02.08   Bernd, 15.12.07 —Jugo, 09.02.08 Christoph —Daniel, 25.11.07 —Urs, 30.12.07   —Dieter, 28.11.07   Fadi, 22.
—Wolfgang, 26.01.08   Alexandra, 16.12.07 —Frank, 22.11.07 —Frank, 06.01.08 —DAVID 23.12.07 1.12.07 —Ursula 16.01.08 Axel, 25.11.07 —Martin, 15.12.07 —Thomas, 16.01.08 —NORBERT,
Jana Luk30 Vondrka, 23.11.07 —Fabion 25.11.07 Hubert, 25.11.07 —Anka, 27.01.08 JeanLuca 11.12.07 —Sophia Adalbert 10.01.08   0202.08   Ralph, 9.12.07 —Wolfgang, 08.08 —Sina, 25.11.07 —Kerlheir
03.01.08 Filippo, 29.12.07 Paula, 2.12.07 —Trix, 29.12.07 Jürgen, 15.12.07 —Sandra, 06.01.08 Sabine, 05.02.08 Heurike, 6.1.07 —Hansjürgen 10.01.08   Manfredo, 02.12.07 —Ulrich, 18.12.07 —Marina, 06.01.08 Roman, 29/01
iris, 16.12.07 —Ney Ulla, 27.11.07 Susanna, 03.02.08 Jana 02.01.08 Anika, 6.1.08 Tana, 27.07.08 Maximilian, 25.11.07 —Claudette, 15.12.07 —Hilde, 02.01.08 Katrin, 07.12.07 —Morgan, 03.02.08 Elisabeth,
Ro...e, 23.11.07 Bärbel, 15.12.07 Heike, 1.12.07 —Armando 15.12.07 — Alexandra 23.12.07 —Alenka, 06.01.08   Brenda, 29.12.07 —Ursula, 6.1.08   Dieter, 9.12
—Annette, 06.01.08 —Karolina 04.01.08 Monik... —Fedor, 24.01.08 —Leon, 29.01.08 Dero, 6.1.08 Sabrina 04.01.08 Friedemann Jonas —Carolin 27.01.08 Christina 04.01.08 Kristina Haus Ernst, 28.11.07 —Frida 02.01.08 Anna 02.01.08 —Günther, 29.12.07
Gabriele, 02.12.07 Eva 27.01.08 Dirk, 25.11.07 —Ralf 16.01.08 Zoe 15.12.07 —Isabel 23.01.08 Orianna, 25.11.07 Gabriele 9.12.07 Sabina 02.02.08   Julia, 23.11.07 —Petra 06.01.08 Antje, 11.
—Annegret, 11.01.08 Helga 21.11.07 —Tit, 06.01.08 —Rose, 18.12.07 —Marita 06.01.08 —Karin 16.01.08 Ulrike, 15.01.08 —ALEX, 29.07.08 Gyde, 08.12.07   Georgio, 09.01.08 Marina, 29.01.08 Hanna, 06.01.08 Nicole,
—Esra 02.01.08 Enza 02.01.08 Barbara, 25.11.07 Dorothee 29.12.07 —Isabel, 25.11.07 —Conny 06.01.08 Rebecca 06.01.08 Ute, 23.11.07 Karen, 26.12.07 Julia 02.01.08 Sophie, 19.01.08 —Baibel, 02.12.07 Gudrun, 04.02.08
Gabriela, 02.12.07 —Marina, 06.01.08 Partha, 17.01.08 Claire 14.12.07 Christina 01.02.08 NICOLE, 29.01.08 —Simone, 30.01.08 Kathrin, 1.12.07 Dominika, 25.11.07 An-Kathrin 06.01.08 —Nicole, 4.12.07 Vera, 24.01.08 Monika, 28.11.
—Aideen 14.12.07 —Ricarda, 27.01.08 Rosalind, 25.11.07 —Alison, 15.12.07 —Fabienne, 05.01.08 Brigitte 01.02.08 Alessia, 26.01.08   Haidi, 03.02.08 —Ester, 16.12.07 —COSTANZA, 29.01.08 Stefanie, 15.12.07   Eva, 6.1.08
08 —Haike, 03.02.08 —Johanna, 11.1.08 —Sally, 29.12.07 Monika, 02.12.07 —Shana 25.12.07 Monika, 29.12.07   —Annette 24.12.07 —Dolores, 29.12.07 —Sabine, 30.
uck-Hee Kwin, 25.11.07 Heike, 6.1.08 JITKA, 23.11.07 —BARBARA, 23.01.08 Stephanie, 17.01.08   Larissa, 24.11.07 —Jens, 11.12.07 —M
—Daniela, 25.11.07 —Jessica, 06.01.08 —Brigitte, 06.01.08 —Jane —2701.08 Sara, 27.11.07   —Franziska, 06.01.08   —Tina, 16.01.08   —Waltraud,
6.1.08   —Christiane, 25.11.07   —Anne-Marie, 1.12.07   Ashley, 06.01.08   Sisa, 6.1.08   —MENINA MANTEPA 30.12.07
— PATRICIA, 29.01.08 —Filip, 25.1.08   —Camila, 25.11.07
—Katalin, 16.12.07   —Felix, 27.12.07   — Helena 26.01.08   —Helga, 06.01.08   —Vanessa, 26.01.08
—Jonas 27.01.08
                        —Maximilian, 09.02.08

                        —Adrian, 09.02.08
                                                                                                        —Lea,

                                                                                            — Rafaela, 03.02.08

        — Yu-Gyeong Chun, 25.11.07   — Rommy, 03.02.08
                                                            — Nils, 25.11.07
—Jennystar. 2008.2.6.

                                    —Jonas, 16.01.08

— Ada, 27.01.08

— Wolfgang, 30.11.07
— Johannes, 20.01.08

02.12.07   — Julius, 23.12.07   — Michael, 6.1.08   — Christian, 29.01.08
                                        — DAVID, 23-12-07
                                  — Uli, 16.12.07   — Bernd, 20.01.08
                                        — Jonas, 19.01.08   — Torsten, 13.01.08
.01.08   — Armin, 15.12.07   — A.01.08 Pablo, 23.11.07   — Andreas, 2.12.07   — Matthias, 07.0
. 06.01.08   MAYtén — Wolf, 07.02.08   — Günther, 06.01.08 — Denver, 13.1
ico, 15.12.07 René, 15.12.07   — PETER 27.12.07   — Oliver 6.02.08
— Max. 26.01.08 — Hubertus, 09.02.08 02.12.07 — Manfred, 5.1.08   — Hansjörg, 21.12.07   — Kim,
hold, 30.11.07   — Ernst, 29.12.07   — Kerstin 02.01.08 — Sylvie, 16.12.07 Tamar, 03.02.08
na, 24.01.08 Julia, 03.01.08   Stefan, 16.12.07 - Jochen, 06.01.08 — Heike, 25.11.07 - Heidrun, 28.12.12
ristina, 02.12.07 - Xavier,   — Stefan, 6.1.08
Gabriela 04.01.08   — Dennis, 24.11.07   — Margot, 29.11.07
— Thanos, 28.12.12   — Wolfgang — 27.01.08   — SIMONE, 29.01.08   Tessa, 22/12/07   ___
— Robert, 25.11.07   — Felicia, 25.11.07 _ Kiril - 23.12.07.
Erich, 23.12.07 - Antje, 06.01.08   Caro   — Diana, 16.01.08   — Manula, 2.12.07
.01.08   — Ilie, 19.01.08   Henriette, 16.12.07   Doris 23.12.07   — Wolfgang, 29.1
esso 02.12.07 Bianca, 02.12.07 - Elisabeth, 29.12.07   Antonia 09.02.08 Johanna, 16.01.08   BARBARA 8.12.07
KATHERINA 4.12.07 — Selina, 19.01.08 — Jennifer 20.12.07 Carolani, 25.11.07   — Sabrina 02.01.08
— Annette 07.02.08   — Elisabeth 29.12.07 Antonia 23.12.07 — FERNANDA, 26.01.08 Anna, 11.01.08
07 - Marita, 30.12.07 Ulrike, 09.02.08 Gabriela, 5.1.08   — Caroline, 11.01.08 — Lena 23.12.07
.08   — PIA, 29.07.08   — Inge, 03.02.08 Vivien 24.11.07
— Ingrid, 5.12.07   — Инка, 23.12.07   — ELISABETH, 8.12.07   — Claudia 25.11.
— Phan, 16.12.07   — Aulceika, 27.11.07 - Babette, 28.12.12 — Eva, 6.1.08   — gergana 23.12.07 - Maggie
.08   — Gile, 07.02.08
                                        — RADKA, 23.12.07

          — Jasper 10.02.08

- Graciella, 06.01.08

— THOMTOM 4.12.07

— THEO 23.12.07

—— Martin, 07.12.07

JULIAN, 29.1.08

— Micha, 25.11.07
— Jens, 08.01.08
Frank, 26.12.07
Glenn, 27.01.08

— Holger, 02.12.07
— Hans, 27.01.08
— Thomas 18.01.08
— Klaus, 12.11.08
Rainer, 25.11.07 — Thomas 25.11.07
— Sebastian, 16.01.08
— Mark, 30.01.08

— Sebastian, 20.01.08
Moritz, 02.12.07
— Isabel, 1.12.07
— Oliver, 16.12.07
— Christian, 27.01.08
— Daniel, 18.12.07
— Hermann, 25.11.07
Peter, 12.02.0

— Stephan, 27.01.09
Florian, 02.12.07
— Felix, 8.12.07
Philipp, 6.1.08
Klaus, 25.11.07
Martin 23.12.07
Alexandra, 6.1.08
Thomas, 18.12.07
— Stefan, 7.12.07
— Mitch, 6.1.08
— Rudi,
— Markus, 27.01.08

— Benjamin, 26.01.08
— Stephen 18.01.08
Franz 04.01.08
Ursula, 3.01.08
Dieter, 03.02.08
— Francesco, 01.01.08
Kirsten, 3.12.07
— Mira, 06.01.0

16.12.07
— Sandra 23.12.07
— Michael, 2.12.07
— Victor, 9.12.07
Katarzyna 27.01.08
Marie-Christin, 22.11.07
Rudolf 05.01.08
Constantin, 5.12.07
— Eva, 6.1.08
— Christoph,

— Gerald, 06.01.08
— Renate 27.12.07
— Johanna, 6.1.08
Lara, 6.1.08
— Jesse,
Jörg 12.08
Joscha 2.12.07
Günther, 27.01.08
Edwardo, 05.02.08
Bahriye, 1.12.07
Isabela, 6.1.08
Siegfried, 22.11.0

— Michael 26.12.07
— Elena, 07.12.07
— Barbara, 13.01.
— Thomas Oliver, 25.11.07
Clara 16.01.08
Franzi 27.01.08
Matilde 18.01.08
Thomas, 18.12.07
DGM 04.01.08
Gerd, 30.12.0

— Elke, 22.11.07
— Hamid 10.01.08
— Radka, 13.12.07
— Lena 27.01.08
Sandra, 25.11.07
Julia 05.01.08
Zosha 23.12.07
Philipp, 16.12.07
Lidwina, 19.01.08
— Sebastian, 18.12.07
Julie, 2.12.07
Franziska 27.01.08

— Nike, 19.12.07
— Maccha, 06.01.08
— Yunsook, 29.12.0
Kiwi, 23.11.08
Isabel, 8.12.07
Claudia, 27.12.07
Billy, 24.11.07
Patrice, 26.12.07
Gisela 8.12.07
ShivaPriya, 05.01.08
23.12.07
Baptist 27.01.08

— Lucie, 30.12.07
— Kirstin 10.01.08
Hermann, 06.01.08
Hanna 23.12.07
Stefanie 18.02.08
Roswitha, 25.11.07
Miri, 20.01.08
Renate, 23.11.07
Korinna 25.11.07
Christine,

— Kathrin, 06.01.08
— Monika, 25.11.07
Denis 19.01.08
Barbel 04.01.08
Celine, 23.12.07
Lukas 04.01.08
Eva, 25.11.07
Elisabeth 27.01.08
Eleonora, 06.01.08
— Ulrike, 2.12.07
— Nina,

— Anna, 06.01.08
— Jesus 02.12.07
Brigitte 04.01.08
Franziska, 30.11.07
Alessandro, 78.12.07
— Lawren, 06.01.08

— ANA-LUISA, 29.01.08
— Teresa, 02.12.07
— Kirsten, 2.12.07
Christa, 03.02.08
Michaela 29.12.07
Julia 25.01.08
Christina, Hedi, 12.01.0

— Julia, 24.11.07
— Luis 02.12.07
— Maja, 26.01.08
— Anna, 11.01.08
Liane, 06.01.08
Davit 23.12.07
Megan, 02.12.07
Georgie, 8.12.07
Nataly

— Cécile, 27.12.07
— Irmgard, 23.12.07
— Xenia, 07.12.07
Sharon, 06.01.08
Federica, 01.01.08
Maria, 5.12.07
02.01.08

— Franckie, 29.01.08
— Chantal 10.02.08
Petra 25.01.08
Karin, 19.01.08
Monica, 25.11.07

— Almara, 01.08
— Gabriela Amelia 8.12.2007
— Valentina, Luciana, 15.01.08

— Michaela, 03.02.08
— Linda, 20.01.08
— Marianna, 26.12.07
— 미진, 27.01.08

—— Paul

— Lucas, 27.01.08

— Da

— Jakob 27.01.08

— Georg, 25.11.07

4.11.07 Stefan, 27.01.08   — Reinhard. 07.02.08   — Robert, 9.12.07   — Jean-Luc, 25.11.07
                                                        — Thomas, 16.01.08

Dietrich, 06.01.08   — Ramūnas, 01.02.08   — Klaus, 30.01.08   — Karsten, 27.01.08 Artur, 03.02.08 Randy, 05.01.08   — Johannes 10.02.07
— Tobias, 6.1.08 Kevin. 18.12.07 — Hannes, 02.01.08 Nicolas, 24.11.07 — Erik, 30.12.08 — Maurizio, 06.01.08 — Gérard, 24.11.07 — Michael, 27.01.08 Steffen, 28.01.08
a, 27.01.08 Wolfgang, 02.12.07   — Axel, 19.01.08   — Thomas, 02.12.07 — Florian, 27.01.08   Ulrike, 16.12.07   — Stephan, 15.12.07 — Ulf, 27.01.07
25.1.08 — Christina, 27.01.08 Hans — 27.01.08 — Parsel, karl, 02.12.07   Kent 22.12.07   — Johnas, 15.12.07   — Jan, 30.12.07 — Alex, 06.01.08   Martin,
30.01.08 Marco, 05.01.08   Danijel   Michael, 13.01.08 Max. 18.12.07 Billa, 6.1.08   Anna, 25.1.08 Hannah.07.02.08 Jan,01.02.08   Angelika, 02.12.07 — Evgenia,11.01.08 Robert, 25.11.07   Gise
er, 02.12.07 — Marco, 05.01.08   — Ansgar, 19.01.08   Bruno, 02.12.07   Sandra, 29.12.07   — Andreas Franz, 9.12.07 Alexander, 27.01.08
TED, 27.07.08   — Jens, 28.11.07 Johanna, 24.12 Marc-André 24.11.07 Florian, 29.12.07 Harald, 02.12.07 — Fredrik, 25.11.07 — Thilo, 30.11.07 — Urban, 15.12.07   Uwe
25.11.07 Kaselan,   Astrid, 28.11.07 Ulrike, 22.12.07 — Joachim, 2011 Roland, 22.11.07 Neike-27.01.08 Ciprian, 05.01.08 Sven, 30.12 Judith, 22.12 Thomas,   Beatrice,27.01.08
Leanie, 24.11.07 — Jutta, 27.12 9.12.07 Eleonora, 01.02.08 Christine, 27.01.08   — Nico, 24.11.07 — Agnes   SM.07 Katie 27.01.08 Peter, 27.01.08 Peter 27.01.08
Ingrid, 27.01.07 — Susanne, 20.01.08 — Grant, 06.01.08 Simone, 27.01.08 Pamela, 22.11.07 Irmin, 07.02.08 Claudio, 30.12 — Max, 16.12.07 Peter, 05. Martina, 25.11.07 Alex, 01.01.08 Beate,
Michaela, 02.12.07   Astrid, 02.12.07 — Valérie, 6.1.08 Robert 16.01.08 Karina Carlos, 30.12 Sylvin, 30.12 Erich, 02.12.07 Kurgi, 06.01.08 — Bruni, 12.01.08 Rüdiger, 22.01.08 Sara,
— Giuseppe, 01.01.08 Leigh, 06.01.08 Und 25.11.08 Asia, 29.12.07 Sabine, 02.12.07   26.12.07 — Rebecca, 15.12.07 — Stacey Leigh, 22.12.07 Bernd, 25.11.07 Carly, 27.01.08   Alida, 16.12.07
stine, 15.12.07 — Doro, 24.11.07 Christine, 05.01.08 Claudia, 01.02.08 Gregor 30.12 — Annette, 12.01.08 Magrit 27.01.08 la, 02.12.07 Simona 01.02.08 Sergei, 06.01.08 Sylvia, 02.12.07 Verena
01.08 Franziska, 25.1.08 Daniel, 9.12.07 Hilariu,   Sarah, 1.12.07 Monique, 22.11.07 Ningxia, 01.01.08 Regine 27.01.08 Doris, 16.12.07 — Helene, 30.11.08   Max
m, 28.11.07 Ture 27.07.08 Monika, 02.01.08 Natalia 27.01.08 04.12.07 — Saskia, 18.12.07 Karolina, 29.12.07 — Tina, 16.12.07 Juan, 6.12.07 Sonja, 25.11.07 Silvana, 03.02.08 Susanna, 30.12 Helga,
Monika, 24.11.07 — Lisa 21.01.08   — Sondra — 27.01.08 — Sonja, 27.12 — Katja, 25.11.07 Margarita, 28.11.07 Monika, 05.01.08 Herbert, 25.11.07 Eva, 25.11.07 Nicole,
1.08 — Isabel 22.01.08 Helga, 24.11.07 — Petra, 22.11.07 Mariana, 27.01.08 — Raquel, 02.12.07 — Maricó, 01.01.08 — CHARLOTT, 11.01.08 — Sandra 9.12.07 Doris, 02.12.07   Nazli, 22
Margot, 16.12.07 — Manuela, 30.12.07   Judith, 01.02.08   — Marlene, 11.01.08 Kyoko
— Celeste, 30.12.07 — Marie-Madeleine, 18.12.07 Jakin 29.01.08 — Melissa, 27.01.08   Geri, 02.12.07 — Laura, 16.12.07 — Maco (Maria Constanza), 29.01
— Alysia, 01.01.08 — Henriette, 27.01.08 — Aida, 11.01.08 — Marzena, 30.12.07   — Joseph 9.12.07   Minako
— Laura, 25.11.07   — Jet, 30.12.07
1.08   — Micheza, 25.11.07   — Irene, 20.01.08   — Iain 9.12.07   — Thea 9.12.07
                — Bettina, 02.12.07   — Bernadette, 25.11.07

— Chio!, 29.01.08

                                                                        — Michael, 13.01.08

                — Sara 18.01.08   — Xaver. 27.01.08   — Thomas, 6.1.08   — Mala, 02.12.07

                                                            — Leeela, 02.12.07

                                                                        — Anaïk

                                                                        — Eivor 18.

— Eisur 18.01.08

                                            — Ariadne, 27.01.08

                                                            — Béla, 25.

        — Carla, 02.12.07

_Jecob, 05.01.08

_Wolfgang, 27.01.08
_Paul, 1.12.07
.11.07   _Thobias, 03.02.08   _Horst, 25.11.07
_Heiner, 24.11.07   _Rolf, 02.12.07   — CHRISTIAN, 28.01.08   _Thomas, 27.01.08 —Alexander, 13.01.08
_Przemek 12.01.08   _Jürgen, 06.01.08 _Georg, 01.02.08   _George, —31.1.08   _Florian, 25.11.07 Roland, 24.11.07
—Thomas, 16.01.08 _Lars, 27.01.08   _Oliver, 24.11.07   _Frank, 8.12.07   Maximilian, 27.01.08 _Michael, 30.12.07   _Martin, 29.12.07   _Sebasti
_Christoph, 22.01 Dörer, 25.11.07   —Tobis, 01.01.08 _Nico, 05.02.08 —Christoph, 25.12.07   Ivan, 02.12.07 Andreas, 6.1.08   _Ralf 27.01.08   Ra
rtin, 24.11.07   Richard, 25.11.07 —Barsikarcsi, 06.01.08   _Christina, 6.1.08   —Martin, 18.12.07 Holten, 25.11.07   _Karsten, 1
_Gisela, 03.02.08 _Christine, 06.01.08   _Amadeus, 16.12.07   _Udo, 0.01.08   —Amy, 29.12.07   Helmut, 5.1.08 —Knut, 30.12.07   —Adonis, 06.01.08 —Silvio, 27.01.08   —Frauke, 06.01.08 —Jörgen, 26.01.
Drago, 16.12.07   Kerneels, 21.12.07   _Jörg, 15.12.07   _Joda, 25.11.07 Mirjam 24.11.07   _Ingrid 18.01.08   _Christian 27.01.08 _Emelie, 3.— Thomas, 29.12.07 Andre, 25.11
Uwe, 25.11.07   _Zane, 24.11.07   Max. 5.1.08   _Hans, 03.01.08   Enneli 25.11.07 Christine, 25.11.07 _Roberto, 26.12.07 _Lars, 25.11.07 _David, 16.12.
phie, 30.12.07 _Uli 04.01.08 Marina 15.12.07   Sabine, 27.01.08 _Maria, 21.12.07   Peter, 21.12.07 _Georg, 22.11.07 Przem 06.12.07   _Martin
07 _Isabelle 08.01.08 _Stephi 08.01.08 Kristina 25.11.07 _Angelika, 31.12.08 —Winnie 12.01.08 _Judith 18.01.07   Nicolao 04.01.08 Jika 5.12.07 Barbara 25.11.07 David Christina 25.11 Kost
12.07 Mirja   Marco 30.12.07 —Kristina, 20. —Hana 27.12.07 —Johanna, 13.01.08 —Peter-Klaus 26.01.08 Roberta 04.01.08   Hildegard, 05.01.08 Helga 27.01.08 Christoph. 27.01.07 Kost
ara, 25.11.07 —Cadi, 30.12.07   Regina, 02.12.07 —Carina, 30.12.08 —Henni, 21.12.07 Fiore 27.01.08   Anna-Leona, 25.11.07 Lisa 21.12.07   Moshe 2.12.07   Omyma 2.12.07   Francisco, 6.1.0
—Maja, 22.01.08 —Daniel, 5.12.07 Andrea 22.01.08   Kathrin, 25.11.07 Lettie, 21.12.07 Maria, 25.11.07 Laura, 30.12.07   Ute, 03.02.07   —Yvonne 01.01.08 —Debbie, 24.01.08 —Eva 27.01.08 Nelly, 16.0
Mareike   Leonie 27.01.08 —Laurane, 5.12.07   —Eike, 2.1.07 —Martina, 05.02.08 —Cornelia 03.01.07 Brigitte, 25.11.07 —Michaela, 28.12.07 Sybille 21.12.07 Susanna, 30.1. —Marie, 03.02.08
Madalena, 25.11.07   Sybille, 25.11.07 —Stavroula, 01.01.08   Tillis, 26.12.07 Ulla 27.01.07 —Carmen, 29.12.07 —Sarah, 01.01.08 Zoja, 01.01.08 Jessica, 25.11.07 —Willi, 28.12.07   —Fr
Helga, 01.01.08   Anka, 5.1.07   Ariana, 25.11.07   Klaud, 25.12.07 —Angela, 02.12.07   Susanne, 8.11.07 —Inge, 01.01.08 —Marysya, 30.12.0
Beate, 30.01. Rosi, 02.12.07 Jim, 27.01.08 —Nina, 24.12.07 Berta, 21.12.07 —Regina 23.12.07 —Annette, 06.01.08   Rebecca, 02.12.07 —Tana, 01.01.08   —Alex
1, 22.11.07   —Nancy 27.01.08 _Anna-Sophie, 23.11.07 —Susie, 01.01.08   Sabine, 25.11.07 —Nadine, 27.01.08 —Sari, 16.12.07   _Karin 04.01.08   _Alex
Yoko, 02.12.07   —Mariella, 30.11.08 —Lucca, 13.01.08 Dani, 29.01.08   Veronika 29.12.07   Beate, 16.12.07 —Steffi, 30.12.07 _Judith 28.11.07 —Anna 8.12.07 Bettina, 27.01.08
29.01.08   —Melina, 25.11.08 Monika, 22.11.07   —Masumi, 02.12.07 —Gisela, 06.01.08 Michael 01.02.08 Ursula 02.12.08 —Suher, 27.01.08
aako, 02.12.07   —Helena, 06.01.08   —Zara, 26.12.07   —Christine—27.01.08   —Eva 29.01.08

_Gabriele, 25.11.07   —kiki, 02.12.07   —Daniela, 01.01.08 Panu 9.12.2007 _Ines, 27.01.08 _Chatarina, 25.11.
_Linola 09/12/07   —Antonia, 01.02.08   Nozomi, 02.12.07   _Rudi, 0.
_Carolin, 27.01.08   —Simon, 0

—Chiara, 6.1.08

—Sophie, 29.12.07

— Louisa, 02.12.07   —Philipp, 25.11.07

—Selina, 8.12.07

—Cornelius, 01.02.08

- Anna, 13.01.08

Amaik, 25.11.07

vor 18.01.08   —Hugo, 30.12.07

—Carolin, 13.01.08

—Robin, 27.01.08

—正则 13.01.08

a, 25.11.07

Mirco, 25.11.07 — Johannes, 27.12.07 — Alfonso, 01.01.08 — Robert, 25.11.07 — Sönke, 30.12

Karsten, 24.11.07 — Helge, 09.02.08 — Ben, 1.12.07 — Stefan, 30.12

Ingolf, 22.11.07 — Johannes, 03.02.08 — Markus, 27.01.08 — Alexander, 25.11.07

Till, 25.11.07 — Michael 04.01.08 — Kay, 03.01.08 — Alexandar, 27.01.08

Florian, 06.01.08 — Rainer, 6.1.08 — Michael, 27.1.08

Filip, 03.02.08 — Jan, 30.12.07 — Timo, 03.02.08 — Manuela, 02.12.07 — Frank, 25.11.07

Ben, 05.01.08 — Christian, 28.12.07 — Damon, 25.11.07 — Bettina, 25.11.07 — Jan, 11.12.07 — Rainer, 03.02.08 — Carsten, 13.01.08 — Daniel

Mike, 25.11.07 — Petra, 09.02.08 — Jens, 16.12.07 — Jan, 27.01.08 — Rachel, 13.01.08 — Martin, 27.01.08 — Christiane, 22.11.07 — Paul, 27.1.08

William, 16.12.07 — Martin 26.12.07 — Malin, 25.11.07 — Daniel, 24.11.07 — Tomaso, 25.11.07 — Ronni, 25.11.07 — Rolf

Sven, 09.02.08 — Christian, 27.01.08 — Alfredo — Klaus, 25.11.07 — Andreas, 4.12.07

Matthias, 18.12.07 — Steffen, 02.12.07 — Christiane — Jutta, 06.01.08 — Jackie, 05.01.08 — Thomas, 27.01.08 — David, 25.11.07 — Kristina

Lutz, 05.01.08 — Christina 23.12.07 — Maja, 09.02.08 — Tanja, 02.12.07

Susanne, 27.01.08 — Franz 08.01.08 — Stefan, 09.02.08 — Lothar, 24.11.07 — Fabian — Monika

Julia, 25.11.07 — Ulrike, 25.01.08 — Julien, 25.11.07 — Franziska, 11.12.07 — Andrea — Elena, 27.01.08 — Rita, 25.11.07 — Christel, 9.12.07

ANDREA, 6.01.08 — Helge, 1.12.07 — Claus — Elena, 06.01.08 — Natalija, 27.01.08 — Caryn, 05.01.08 — Sophie, 5.12.07 — Sabine, 22.12.07 — Gisela

Anita, 25.11.07 — PETER, 4.12.07 — Sabina, 27.01.08 — Saran, 12.07 — Eva, 25.11.07 — Nicole 25.11.07 — Markus — Arminos, 18.12.07

RIKE 23.12.07 — Minetta, 08.01.08 — Gina — Anna — Michi — Elena, 27.01.08 — Carmen, 25.11.07

Silvia, 25.04.08 — Brita, 1.12.07 — Carolin, 25.11.07 — Klara, 22.11.07 — Anja, 25.11.07 — Marina — Christiane, 18.01.08 — Laontine

Kathryn, 23.11.07 — Alisa, 22.11.07 — Babette — Judith, 08.01.08 — Nina, 18.12.07 — Lisa, 22.01.08 — Jennifer

Annette — Antje, 02.12.07 — Dorothea, 5.08 — Esther, 02.12.07 — Miriam 02.11.07 — Stephani, 29.12.07

Wibke 02.12.07 — Dorothee, 9.11.07 — Andreina, 01.01.08 — Christoph — Agnes — Saskia, 03.01.08

Jane, 27.01.08 — Lilli, 27.01.08 — Patti, 27.01.08 — Birgit, 15.12.07 — Angela, 27.01.08 — Barbara, 06.01.08 — Gabriela, 27.1.08 — Sophie, 03.02.08 — Madeleine

Dea, 24.11.07 — Jenny 29.12.07 — Rosina, 06.01.08

Brigitte, 06.01.08 — Patricia, 16.12.07 — Ingrid, 06.01.08 — Steffi, 29.01.08 — Melanie, 5.12.07 — Miyuki, 27.1.08

Nicole, 30.12.07 — Ella, 07.12.07

Laura, 5.12.07 — Andrea, 30.12.07 — 03.02.08 — 27.01.08 — Carolin, 27.01.08 — Lissy, 24.11.07 — Helena, 25.11.07

Ania, 25.11.07 — Brooke, 16.12.07

Matti, 25.11.07 — Lukas, 25.11.07

Richard, 16.12.07

Valentin, 27.01.08 — Yassina, 25.11.07

Luise, 29.12.07 — Sophie, 27.01.08

Charlotte, 25.11.07

Helenmay, 27.01.08 — Alexander, 25.1

Clemens, 03.02.08 — Moritz, 27.01.08

Christopher, 06.01.08 — Anna, 25.11.07 — Jonas, 25.

Pauline, 25.11.07

Lionel, 25.11.07

Gustav, 27.1.08

Sophie, 1.12.07

—Jecob, 05.01.08

—Wolfgang, 27.01.08   —Mirco, 25.11.07   —Johannes, 27.12.07   —Alfonso, 01.01.08
—Paul, 1.12.07   —Karsten, 24.11.07
—Thomas, 27.01.08 —Alexander, 13.01.08   —Francesko, 25.11.07 —Till, 25.11.07 Ingolf, 22.11.07   —Markus, -27.01.08   —Helge, 09.0
                                             —Wutsch, 25.11.07   —Florian, 06.01.08   —Johannes, 03.02.08   —Kay, 03.01.08,
and, 24.11.07   —Sebastian, 25.11.07   —Rainer, 6.1.08   —Filip, 03.02.08   —Michael 04.01.08   —Michael, -27.1.08
—Martin, 29.12.07   —Rainer, 30.01.08 —Varena, 25.11.07   —Ben, 05.01.08   —Christian, 28.11   —Damon, 25.11.07   —SEUNG-IL CHUNG
—Ralf 27.01.08   —Karsten, 1.12.07 —Dimitri, 06.01.08   —Mike, 25.11.07   Petra, 09.02.08 Jens, 16.12.07 Jan, 27.01.08   —Bettina, 25.
—Holten, 25.11.07   Simon, 23.12.07   —William, 16.12.07   —Martin 26.12.07   —Rachel, 13.
—Silvio, 27.01.08 —Frauke, 06.01.08 —Jörgen, 26.01.08 Christian, 27.01   Babette, 25.11.07 —Peter, -31.01.08   —Malina, 25.11.0
—Christian 27.01.08 Emelie, 31.12 Thomas, 29.12.07   Jasck-27.01 Roland, 06.01.08 Julio, 13.01.08 Matthias, 18.12.07 Sven, 09.02.08 Jana, 6.1.08 Michael b, 03.02.07 —Christian,
25.11.07 —Roberto, 26.12.07 —Lars, 25.11.07 —David, 16.11.07   Simone, 24.11.07   Shane, 3.12.07   —Lutz, 05.01.08 Christina 23.12.07 Stefan 09.02.07 Jutta, 06.01.08 —THOMAS, A
org, 22.11.07 Pizza B 06.12.07 —Martin, 05.01.08 Samantha 23.12.07 UteDahli, 25.11.07 Sandra, 27.04.08 Julien 25.11.07 Lothar, 24.11.07 Jackie, 08 01.08
Barbara, 25.11.07 David Christina, 25.11.07   —Peter, 26.01.08   Susanne 27.01.07 Luther, 25.11.07 Verena 09.02.08 Franziska, 11.12.07 —Dro 26.12.07 —Andrea
Helge, 27.01.08 008.01.08 —Christian, 27.1.07   Gerard, 23.12.07   Julia, 21.11 ANDREA, 6.01.08 Helge, 1.12.07 Claus 8.01 —Marseille, 04.01.08
he 2.12.07   Omyma Roxika, 25.11.08 Nelly, 16.07 Evelin, 25.11.07 Amita, 25.11.07 Via, 22.06 PETER, 4.12.07 Sabina, 27.01.08 —Elena, 06.01.08 Natali 22.27.01.08
—Yvonne, 01.01.08 —Debbie, 24.01.08 —Eva 23.01.08 Konni, 03.02.01 Torild 25.11.07 Lisalotte 25.11.07 RIKE 23.12.07 Minetta, 06.01.08 Gina 23.11.08 Andrea 06.01.08 Eva, 25.11.07 Nico
—Sibylle, 22.11.07 Daniela, 25.11.07   Marie, 03.02.08   Anita, 25.11.07 Carina 01.08 Cathrin 25.11.07 Jessica, 23.0 Erhard Britta, 1.12.07   —Carolin, 25.11.0 Klara, 22.1
essica, 25.11.07 —Willi, 28.01.08 Friederike, 25.11.07 —Nora, 01.01.08 Ina, 06.01.08 Petra, 27.01.08 Kathryn, 23.11.07 Tanja, 30.12 Alisa, 22.11.07 —Babette, 27.01.08 Claudia 27
—Inge 01.01.08 —Rebecca, 02.12.07 —Jana, 06.01.08 Valeria, 6.1.08   Pasquale, 01.01.08   —Antje, 02.12.07 Dorothea, 5.12.07 Esther
—Sari, 16.12.07 —Karin 04.01.08 —Alexandra, 1.12.07 —Arlette, 9.12.07 Anna 16.01.08 5.12.07 —Wibke 02.12.07   Dorothee, 9.11.07 —Andreina, 01.01.
—Anna 9.12.07 Bettina, 27.01.08 06.01.08 —Renate, 28.12.07 明日香 06.01.08 Lilli, 27.01.08 Patti 27.01.08 Katja, 1.02.08 Christine, 20.08 Klaus
28.11.07 —Gisela, 06.11.08 Michael 27.01.08 Ursula, 03.02.08 —Valentina, 6.1.08 Carina 01.08 呵呵, 25.11.07   —Dea, 24.11.07   —Birgit, 15.12.07 Angela, 27.01.08
02.12.07 —Eva, 29.01.08   Hildegard, 25.11.07   —Patricia, 16.12.07 —Ingrid, 06.01.08   —Steffi, 29.01.08
01.08   —Brigitte, 06.01.08   —Nicole, 30.12.07   —Ella, 02.12.07   —Melanie
—Pom 8.12.2007 Ines, 27.01.08 —Chatarina, 25.11.07   —Auréa, 5.12.07 Laura, 5.12.07 —Andrea 30.12.07 전석, 03.02.08 —莫红, 27.01.08   —Miyuki
—Rudi, 02.12.07   —Doca, 29.01.08   Ania, 25.11.07   —Brooke, 16.12.07   —Carolin, 27.01.08
—Lidio — 27.01.08   —Matti, 25.11.07 Lukas, 25.11.07
—Simon, 02.12.07   —Richard, 16.12.07

—Johannes, 02.12.07   —Luise, 29.12.07   —Sophie, 27.01.08

—Sophie, 29.12.07

—Clemens, 03.02.08   —Moritz, 27.01.08

Hugo, 30.12.07   —Christopher, 06.01.08   —Anna, 25.11.07
—Carolin, 13.01.08

—Sophie, 1.12.07

__ Robert, 25.11.07   — Sönke, 30.12.07   _ Rob -, 27.01.08   _ Olaf, 25.11.07   Fred, 25.11.07   — Volker, 9.12.07

                              _ Stefan, 30.12.07   — Heiner, 27.01.08   Nikos 29.12.07   Massiomo, 25.11.07   — Michael, 28.11

_ Alexander. 25.11.07
      __ Alexandar, 27.01.08   _ Norbert, 25.11.07   – Ingo, 06.01.08   Christophe, 19.01.08   — Jürgen, 25.11.07
                                              — David, 13.01.08   — Markus 05.01.08 Arno, 16.12.07   Georg 03.02.08   — Michael, 6.1.08
.02.08 — Manuela, 02.12.07   — Olivier, 6.1.08   – Ronald, 06.01.08   _ Guido 3.12.07   — 13.12.07 Michael — Roman 01.08   Michael, 24.11
12.07 — Sandra, 13.01.08 — Thomas, 25.11.07   — Klaus, 30.01.08   Andrea, 16.12.07   — Fritz, 13.08.08   — Gerhard, 06.01.08
 — Rainer, 03.02.08 — Carsten, 13.01.08 — Danijel, 30.01.08 Ramsi, 02.12.07 Catherine, 5.1.08 Thomas, 07.02.08 — Chris, 21.12.07 — Cyrille, Henning, 28.1.08   Ralf, 25.11.07 Oliver, 25.11.07 –
01.08 — Christiane, 22.11.07 — Paul, 27.1.08 Andreas, 02.12.07 — Wolfram, 27.01.08 BEATE 24.11.07   — 25.11.07 — Ulrike, 06.01.08 — Susanne, 13.01.08 Pablo 29.12.
24.11.07 — Ronni, 25.11.07   — Ralf, 27.1.07 — Seppel, 29.12.07 Elise, 01.01.08 Irene, 02.01.08   Mei Ying, 25.11.07   _ Lukas, 3.12.07 Adam 29.1
omaso, 25.11.07 — John, 21.01.08   Kenny, 06.01.08 — Seamus, M.01.08   Theo 01.08   Christine,
       Klaus, 23.1.07 Steffen, 25.11.07 Günter, 24.11.07   ANDREAS Manfred, 25.11.07 Werner, 27.01.08 Benjamin, 21.12.07   Amit, 03.02.08 Franziska, 25.
   David, 30.01.08 — Mark, 26.12.07 Michaela, Janna, 30.12.07 Bene, 01.08   — Harald, 20.08 Agate, 5.12.07 Wolfram Pessa, 25.11.07 Lisa, 24.11.07 Robert, 21.12.07 Melanie
 — Julia, 06.01.08 Kostas 29.12.07 Christel, 9.12.07 Katrin, 25.11.07 — Fabio, 25.11.07 — Claudia. 06.01.08 Simon, 18.12.07 Janick, 13.11.07 – Nici, 30.11 Tanja 27.01.08 — Katha
      — Corrinna, 01.08 Sabine, 22.11.07 — Anja 01.08 Heidi, 25.11.07 Julia, 25.11.07 Annette 24.11.07 Nicko 29.01.08 16.12.07 — Anke, 16.12.07 Johanna, Christina, 26.12.07 —
   Sophie, 5.12.07 Sabine 27.01.08 Gisela, 27.12 Edit 27.02.08 Nina, 18.12.07 — Greg Liana, 27.1.07 Juan F, 18.12.07 Deaa hanit, 02.12.07 Laura, Jenny, Amt, 25.11.07
  Arruños, Virginie, 5.12.07 – Julia 30.12 Gitta 27.1.08 Oliver, 02.12.07 – Ignacio, 06.01.08 Seu, 2.1.08 Jörg, 30.1.08   — Felix, 12.12.07 Carolin, – Julia, 11.01.08
25.11.07 Carmen, 24.11.07 Leontine, 13.01.08 Christina, 15.12.07   Alexis, 5.12.07 – Lisa   Nicolas, 5.12.07 Ethel 05.01.08 12.07   08.01.08   – Beatrix 3.12.07
 — 18.12.07 — Lisa, 27.01.08   Jennifer. 25.11.07   Joachim, 03.02.08 Daniela 27.12.07 — Ellen, 27.01.08 Ana, 27.01.08   Ursula 02.02 Mariella, 25.11.07 Ol 03.02.08 — Francesca
  — Miriam 02.11.07 — Stephani, 29.12.07   — Christina, 30.01.08 VINCE, 9.12.07 Shanti, 03.02.08 Dana, 25.11.07 — Nastaran, 06.01.08   Pia, 24.11.07 — Marina, 25.11.07 Po
Mattiu, 2.12.07   — Sophie, 03.02.08   Madeleine, 01.01.08 Annie, 5.12.07 05.01.08   Tana, 25.11.07 Eva, 12.01.08   Casa, 5.1.08 Jelena, 16.12.07 — Gerlinde 2
 — Jenny 29.12.07   Betty, 29.12.07 Deike, 16.12.07 Verena, 9.12.07   Simon, 05.01.08 Veronica, 25.11.07
                        — Rosina. 06.01.08   Gülay, 27.01.08   Haeer, 1.12.07   — まり子, 18.12.07   Katharina, 25.11.07

            _ Helena, 25.11.07   _ 28.12.07   — Marisa, 27.01.08
07
                                         — Lina, 07.02.08   — 涼子 23.12.07   — Sarah, 27.12.07   — Lenny, 27.01.08   — Kasta
— Valentin, 27.01.08 — Yassina, 25.11.07   — Olivia, 24.11.07   — Tabea, 25.11.07

                                                                                       — Leon, 13.01.08

                                                        — Jana, 27.01.08

                                                    – Leonhard, 13.01.08

— Helenmay, 27.01.08   — Alexander, 25.11.07

                                                                        _ Andrian, 27.11.07   — Andy 27.11.07

                    — Jonas, 25.11.07

— Pauline, 25.11.07

                              – Josef 06.01.08

                                                                                                                                                    —Leoni

— Gustav, 27.1.08

                                                                                                                                          — Holly 23.12.07

07

_Andreas, 9.12.07   —Christian; 28.12.07   —Arnd 10.01.08   —Peter, 06

…hael, 28.12.07   _Dominik, 25.11.07   _Rita 2.12.07   _Joben, 27.01.08

—DANIEL, 20.01.'08   —Wolfgang, 1301.08   Paolo, 02.12.07 —Sebastian 04.01.08   —Sebastian, 29.11.07

_Thomas, 27.01.08   Francesco, 03.02.08   —Volker 18.01.08   —Sven, 30.0.07 —Oscar,-08.02.08   —Jonas, 25.11.0

…6.1.08   Karl Heinz,-080208   —Mac 2.12.07   —Josef, 06.01.08

…24.11.07 —Uli 23.12.2007 —Xaver, 13.01.08   Giacomo, 9.12.07   _Alban, 9.12.07   —Alexander, 24.01.08 Can, 15.12.07 —Roland, 27.0

…06.01.08   —Ben.-27.01.08   Constan   05.12.07   Katharina, 11.01.08   Brando, 11.11.08   —Patrick, in 08   _Nick, 05.01.08 —Nicholas, 1

…07 —Bernd 23.12.07 —Oliveri   Marc, 27.11.07   Manfred 23.12.07   Birgit, 2701.08   Tatsuo 達男, 25.11.07 Konstantin, 10.208 —Titus, 05.01.08   Christian, 27.01.08   —Marc, 16.12.07   —Dominik, 27.07.08

…lo, 29.12.07   Eva 9.12.07 —Rutwin, Jan 08 —Jeffrey   Jean-Pierre, 25.11.07 —Wolfram 28.12.07   Adli 24.11.07   Thierry, 25.11.07   —Peter, 06.01.08   Birgit. 29.11.07 _Ralf,

…Christine, 25.11.07   —Britta, 9.12.07 —Margareta, 12.01.08   —Jonas-0201.08   Margaret, 25.11.07 Peter, 05.01.08 Juri, 15.12.07   Hannes, 24.01.08   Alex, 25.11.07 —Ursel-020208 Marcel   —Simone 02.01.08

…9 Franziska, 1008   —Antje, 23.11.07   Karolina, 9.12.07 —Maurizio, 27.12.07   Elena 9.12.07   Laurentiu, 25.11.07   Marco, 22.04   Andre   Gerhlin   9.12.07   Pierce, 22.11.07

…12.07   —Melanie,   —Martin, 29.12.07   Jordi, 24.11.07 —Julie, 13.01.08   Eai, 24.11.08 —Markus, 22.01   Carola, 22.11.07   May, 30.01.08 Johann- Hierrich 02.12.07   Sophie, 25.11.07   —Ma

…11.07 _Alexandra, 25.11.07 —Marcel 24.01.08 —Rene, 20.01.07   Norbert, 22.12.07   Christine 02.01.08 Heike, 9.12.07   Reiner 05.01.08   18.01.08 —Xenia 04.01.08 —Michael, 19

…07 —Katharina,   Felix, 25.11.07 —Jerome, 05.01.08   Cyrielle, 5.12.07   Einste, 25.11.07   Andrea 05.01.08   Flo, 25.11.07   Ikpa 27.01.08   Caroline 9.11.07 BИКТОР БАРКАР, 27.1

…26.12.07 —Heidi,   Carola   —Fritai, 27.01.08   Frederic, 25.11.07 Martina   Cornelia, 25.11.07 Beatr.   Christa, 05.01.08   11.12.07   Thea, 2

…25.11.07 —Fritti,—27.1.08 —Aldona,   —Gisela, 27.12.07 —Gerda, 20.01.08   Miriam 27.12.07   Grea 24.01.07 —Claudia, 10.01.08   Salam, 02.12.07   —Markus, 4.12.07

…3.12.07   Christina, 25.011.07 —Fabian,-21.01.07 Nicole 25.11.07   Doris   9.12.07 -Nicole   Marine, 5.12.07   Thomas 05.01.08 Anke 04.01.08   Mira, 27.01.07 —Rachael   Dau

…Simone, 02.12.07 —Kati,04.01.08 Gabriela, 02.12.07 —Natascha, 30.11.08   Marga, 03.01.08   Wiebke, 06.01.08 Friederike, 25.11.07   Gudrun, 25.11.07   Tereza, 03.02.08

…12.07   Kathia, 05.01.08   Malvina, 5.12.07 —Heidrun, 29.12.07 —Shay, 28.01.08   Jule, 24.01.08   Conny, 23.01.07   Erica, 5.1.08   Ewelina, 08

…ncesca, 24.11.07 _Silke, 27.01.08 —Stephan   Anne 9.12.07 —Figen, 05.02.08   Rita, 22.11.07 Andrea, 25.11.07   Erica, 22.11.07 —Jane, 24.01.08   Magdalena 08.12.07 —Jordina 04

…11.07   Paula, 25.11.07   —Caroline, 15.12.07   Anna, 05.01.08 —Viktoria, 24.01.08   Magalie 03.02.08   Anna-Maria, 05.01.08 —Diane, 5.12.07

…nde 23.XII '07   —Helga, 24.11.07 —kristiane,-27.1.08   Sally, 24.01.08   Caroline, 02.12.07   Célia, 5.12.07 —Clémentine, 5.12.07 —Mar

…25.11.07   —lapuca, 08.01.08 —Blanca,-27.1.08   Gesine, 25.11.07   Elodie, 5.12.07   Iuge, 29.12.07 —Elisabeth, 05.01.08   Andrea, 24.11.07

…Živa, 16.12.07 —Rose-Marie,   Teajala, 16.12.07   —Luzia 29.12.07   Ula, 27.01.08   —Daniela, 21.08   —Brita, 28.12.07

…25.11.07   —Susonne,-24.01.08   —Daniel 23.12.07   —Leander, 25.11.07   —Elpino, 27.12.07

—Nora, 2.2.08   —Simon; 27.12.07   —Martin, 03.02.08

—Lea, 2.2.08   —David, 02.02.08

—Kastania; 28.12.07   —Rafael 27.12.07

07   —Adrian, 25.11.07   —luis,-10.2.08

—Luisa, 9.12.07   —Sabrina; 28.12.07

—Alvaro 22.12.07

—Leon, 27.11.07   —Simone; 28.12.07

—Carolin, 27.11.07

—Arianna, 16.12.07   —Jan Miguel, 27.11.07

—Luis, 25.11.07

—Leonia 06.01.08   —Frederic, 25.11.07

—Mirella,-27.1.08

—Lanfranco, 03.01.08

—Jens, 25.11.07

—Markus, 03.02.08 Giuseppe 2.01.08

—Jörg, 4.12.07

Christian, 25.11.07   Felipe, 02.12.07   —Sebastian, 25.11.07   —Matee j, 04.01.08
Markward, 02.12.07 —Volker, 9.12.07   —Tommy, 9.12.07   —Travis, 26.12.07   Jan, 23.11.07
—Rolf, 05.01.08   —Fabian 02.01.08   —Claus, 19.01.08   —Frank, 01.11.08
—Guillaume, 5.12.07   —Jeremy, 24.01.08   Stephan, 25.11.07   —Yanitopios, 05.01.08   Metin, 27.01.08   —Reinhard 27.01.08
—Jonathan, 24.01.08   —Michael, -10.2.08   —IVAN, 6.01.08   —Petra, 03.02.08   Vitek, 16.12.07   —Reiner 03.02.08   —Marc, 01.01.08
—Javier, 11.01.08   15.12.02 Andy, 26.09   RADEK, 9.12.07   —Jørgen, 02.12.07   Christoph 05.02.08   —Thomas 06.01.08
—Felix, 9.12.07   Günter   —Beat, 06.01.8   —Georg, 16.12.07   Margit, 27.01.08
—Göfe, 24.01.08 —Paolo, -27.1.08   —Markus, 22.11.07   —Elisabeth 05.01.08   Benedikt 03.02.02   Benjamin, 5.12.07   —Aline 27.01.08   Hans-Joachim, 25.11.07 Thomas, 25.11.07   Charly, 05.01
—Phillph, 12.01.08   —Ralf 19.01.08   Rostislav, 27.01.08
—Karl, 17.01.08   —Jon. 25.11.   Ratja, 27.01   Fedso, 16.12.07   —David 22.12.07   Kurt 8.12.07   Kerstin 19.01.08   Richard, 16.12.07 —Eric, 26.12   Elisabeth 25.11.07   David, 24.11.07   —Irene, 03.02.08
—Ralph, 24.11.07   Bernol 25.11.07   PETER 21.11.07   Rita, 03.02.08   Margin 01.01.08   Telena 05.01.08
Andrea, 9.12.07   Klaus, 9.12.07 —Thomas, 16.12.07   Roman, 02.01.08   BIANCA 23.12.07   Silvia 25.11.07   Claudia, 3.11.02
—Jürgen, 02.12.07   —Manfred, 19.01.08 —Lara, 02.03.08   Rainer 25.11.07   TOM, 9.12.02   Marco 15.12.07   Agola, 16.12.07   Anna 27.01.08   Ellen, 16
—Jana, 29.01.08   —Jochen, 13.01.08 —Johannes, 17.01.08   —Andi   —Govanni 9.12.07   Susanne, 02.12.07   —Ann-Kathrin, 06.01.08   —Francesco 01.01.08   Ramona 22.01.08   Rafael 25.11.07   Florian 06.01.08   Jenifer, 02.12.0
—Ebbe 23.12.07   Friedrich, 07.12.07   —Dominic, 03.01.08   Tobias 25.11.07   Milena, 15.01.08   —Anida 25.11.07   Petra, 03.02.08   MARTIN, 9.12.07   —Walter, 26.12.07
Lisa, 25.11.07   Annette, 22.11.07   Christl, 01.01.08   Sara, 30.12.07 Anna, Beate 25.11.07   —Julia 9.22.07   —Anna, 21.11.07   Joelle 2.2.08   Petra, 18.12.07   Caroline, 05.0
—Lajos 02.02.08   Tina, 16.12.07   Siaron 12.12.07   —Martd 08.02.08   —Verena, 01.01.08   Irmi, 15.12.07   Christina, 25.11.07   Lisa, 24.11.07   Mira, 16.12.07
Hildegard, 24.11.07   Alexandra, 26.01.08   Carmen 25.11 Sabine, 25.11.07   —Fransbodot 25.11.07   —Alessio 10.01.08   Roland 25.11.07 —Daniela 26.11.0   —Sebastian, 2
Karin, 25.11.07   Ina-Fatuma 25.11.07   Brigitta 2008   —Erno, 16.12.07   —David 79 Francesca 05.01.07   —Katya 01.01.0 Irene 10.12.0   Beatrix 03.01.08   Liliana 02.12.07 —Irma, 05.0
—Anne 24.01.08   —Ursula 06.01.08   —Minh, 05.01.08   Anna 8.12.07   Silvia 27.01.08 16.12.07   Katarina, 24.11.07   Irmgard, 24.01.08   Mokeko 02.12.07   Elise 26.12.07   Andrea, 25.11.07
—Ingrid 02.01.08   —Isabella, 24.11.07   —Stella, 01.01.08   —Tina, 16.12.07   Barbel, 25.11.07   Eliane, 9.12.07 —ANNE 03.02.08   Ana, 16.12.07   —Erika, 03.02.0 —Michaela, 11.12.07   Jeniece, 26.12.0
a*08.12.07   —Linda 8.Dez 07 —Ana, 11.01.08   Dorin, 25.11.07   —Jasmin, -24.01.08   —Manuela 2.12.07   —Nadja, 30.12.07   Eve, 22.11.07 —Valentino, 27.1.08
—Laura 23.12.07   —Thu, 06.01.08   —Gundi, -27.1.08   Ingrid 2.12.07   —Franziska, 27.01.08   Simon, 02.12.07   浩美, 25.11.07
—Lissy 08.01.08   Kate, 25.11.07   —Valerie, 02.12.07   —Anna Maria, 9.12.07   Monika, 11.01.08   AnnaLisa, 02.12.07   —Andras 03.01.08   Patricia, 31.01.08
—Janine, 24.01.08   —Vernanda 23.12.07   —Marietta 2.12.07   —Marianne 11.12
—Thereso, 27.01.08   —Johanna, 06.01.08   —Marina, 30.12.07
—Sandra

—Matija, 16.12.07

—Minh-Tam, 03.02.08   —Elena 03.01.08   TIM, 9.12.07

—Jade 03.01.08

—Sandra, 16.12.07

—Tamaja, 16.12.07   —Livia, 03.02.08

—Daniel-Luca, 25.11.07

on, 16.12.07

—Lola, 25.11.07

—Willi, 02.12.07

—Isabelle, 30.01.08

— Ekkehart, 8.12.07

— Reinhard, 05.01.08

— Bharath, 9.12.07
— John, 29.01.08   — Maximilian, 03.02.08   Michael, 24.11.07
— Hans, 9.12.07   — Udo, 27.01.08   — Oliver, 25.11.07   — Sigurd, 03.02.08
— Tobias, 30.01.08   — Michael, 22.11.07

— Wessel, 15.12.07
— Bastian, 01.02.08
— Bernard, 08.01.08
— Alois, 13.01.08   — Christian, 03.02.08
— Brit, 9.12.07   — Simon, 13.01.08   — Stefan, 25.11.07
— Dominique, 16.12.07

03.02.08 Boris, 8.12.07
07 — Guido, 18.12.07 — Michael, 03.02.08 — Micha, 25.11.07   — 28.01.08   — Diego, 06.01.08   — Stephan, 9.12.07   — Jürgen, 9.11.07
— Walter, 05.01.08   — Verena, 27.01.08   — Matthias, 25.11.07   Gerhardt, 25.11.07   — Peter, 25.11.07   Albert, 24.11.07 Dieter, 03.01.08   — 23.11.07   — Axel, 22.1
Michael, 25.11.07   — Heike, 16.01.08   — Katja, 13.01.08   Benjamin, 25.11.07   — Andrej, 16.12.07   Heinz, 9.12.07   — Vincent, 9.12.07   Grego
Derwin, 03.02.08   — Stephane, 9.12.07   Wolfgang, 24.11.07   Viktoria, 06.01.08   — Matthias, 22.11.07   — Tim, 22.12.07   — Hans-Heinrich, 16.12.07   Jörg
— Uta, 03.02.08   — Greg, 25.11.07 — Bernhard, 24.11.07   — Jeremy, 01.01.08 — Philip, 23.8.07   — Olga, 03.01.08   — Selman, 02.01.08 Markus, 07.02.08 — Helmut, Angeli, 16.02.08
— Annetta, 30.01.08   Heidi, 8.12.07 — Michael, 16.01.08   Annette, 07.12.07   Marina, 03.01.08   Jan-Oliver, 25.11.07 — Hermes, 26.12.07   Andreas
— Stefan   — Austin, 05.01.08   Jacqueline, 06.01.08   RUDI, 9.11.07   Marie, 01.02.08 — Eva, 02.02.07   Adrian, 08.01.08   Regina
— Rosa, 02.02.08 Claudia, 25.11.07   Ditmar, 24.11.07   — Marion   — Julia, 4.12.07   Sascha, 03.01.08   Veha, 16.12.07   Charlsen, 25.11.07   Matthias, 22.11.07 — Lisa, 14.12.08   Dominik,
Beate, 13.01.08   02.12.07 — Myriam, 9.12.07   Gabriele, 26.12.07   — Ulrike, 07.12.07   — Joachim   — Ilse, 16.12.07   — Angela, 26.01.08 Susanne   Maria, 25.11.07
— Anna, 19.12.07   — Katarina, 25.11.07   Karin, 02.12.07   Sabine, 27.01.08   Lore, 25.11.07   — Myriam   Brigitte, 9.12.07   Heidi, 5.12.07
— Petra, 22.11.07   — Johanna, 15.12.07   Rita, 25.11.07   — John   08.12.07   Renate, 22.11.07   — Katharina   — Anita, 25.11.07 Gisela, 03.01.08   Rita, 25.11.07 Charlotte
— Katarina, 25.11.07   Edeltraud, 24.11.07 Michael   — Claudia, 05.01.08   Nicholas, 04.01.08   — Ingrid   — Radmila, 13.01.08   Matthes, 19.01.08   Miguel
Kasia, 16.12.07 — Ariane   Ruth, 08.12.07   Lisanne, 26.01.08   Andri, 06.01.08   — Goldie, 25.11.07 Marina   — Barbara, 25.11.07 — Sascha, 29.12.07   Angela, 24.11.07 Irma
Heidi, 25.11.07   — Kohei Omori, 18.12.07   Romy, 9.12.07   Holga, 03.12.07   Andrea, 27.01.08   Petra, 16.12.07 Vanessa, 08.01.08   Frank   Angela, 24.11.07
— Felix, 17.01.08 — Ingrid, 27.01.08   — Elisabeth, 29.12.07   Sissi, 16.12.07 — Alexandra, 25.11.07   Barbara, 16.12.07   Brigitte, 05.01.08   — Lucy
23/12/07   — Regina, 9.12.07   Sabrina, 02.01.08 lodge, 25.11.07   Marlene, 24.11.07   고운, 12.01.08   — 25.11.07   — Susanne, 01.01.08   — 24.11.07   Doris, 15.12.07 Stefan
— 恵美, 25.11.07   — Simona, 04.01.08   — Netta, 16.12.07   09.02.08 Heimba, 02.12.07   — Teresa, 16.12.07   Felizitas, 23.01.08   Benedicte, 25.11.07
— Antonie, 27.12.07   — Luise, 27.12.07   — Claudia, 23.11.07   — Simon, 26.01.08 Gabriel, 25.11.07
dra 18.01.08   — Maria Julia, 04.01.08   Marianna, 04.01.08   — Theodore, 02.01.08   — Monica, 30.12.07

— Theresa-Maria, 25.11.07   — रोज़ा, 31/11/07   — Severin, 13.01.08   — Vera, 13.01.08

—Elias, 25.11.07   — Sophie, 02.12.07   — Tabea, 27.01.08

— Lilly, 06.01.08

— Severin, 27.01.08

— Emmelie, 15.1

— Maximilian, 01.01.08

—Lutz, 02.02.08

—Erwin, 25.11.07
—Tobias 21.12.07
—Daniel 04.01.08
—Oleg, 31.1.08
—Sebastian, 29.0
—Michael, 29.12

—Voss 05.01.08

...an, 3.12.07
—Fabio, 23.11.07
—Jörg 9.12.07
—Magnus, 24.11.07
—Robert, 25.11.07
—Andreas, 01.02.08

—Axel, 16.12.07
—Peter 23.11.2.07
—Sepp, 07.12.07
—Klaus 02.12.07
—Michele, 03.02.08
Klaus, 01.12.07

Dima, 02.01.08
Vladislav, 01.02.08
Wolfgang, 03.02.08
Luis 22.12.07
—Jörg 19.1.08
—Reinhold, 26.02.08
Jeff, 22.12.07
Klaus, 29.01.08

Christoph, 25.11.07
—Andreas 18.01.08
Uzi 27.01.08
Žiga, 16.12.07
Michael 9.12.07
Frank, 26.12.07
Georg, 16.12.07

—Dana, 06.01.08
Christian 27.01.08
Koen, 4.12.07
Werner, 22.12.07
Rudolf, 9.12

Pader, 25.11.07
Karl, 5.12.07
Wolfgang, 25.11.07
Volker, 11.12.07
Thomas
Nicole, 03.02.08
Leandro 9.12.07
Sarah 25.11.07
Roman, 25.11.07
Marcus 03.02
Niky, 21.11.07
Angelika

Sebastian, 02.12.07
—Tobias 13.01.08
Christian, 8.12.07
Frank, 3.12.07
Oliver
Josef,
Nina, 23.12.2007
Ivan, 24.11.07
Katharina

—Linda, 15.12.07
Swen, 24.11.07
Sabine 25.11.07
Luka, 16.12.07
Keienke, 4.12.07

Irsa, 8.11.07
ZAKARIA 25.11.07
Hary 05.01.08
Gustav 25.11.07
ROMAN, 21.11.07
Hans 12.01.08
Inge, 29.11.07
Lothar, 19.01.08
Sigi, 22.11.07
Bea, 25.11.07
Paco, 03.02.08

Niklas, 25.11.07
Rita, 02.02.08
Juliana, 16.12.07
Tadea,
Christiane, Caroline,

Jessica
Juliana, 25.11.07
Elka, 23.11.07
Gabriele, 9.12.07
Nina, 23.12
Andrea 03.01.08
Etala, 25.11.07

Helmut, 25.11.07
Monika, 25.01.08
Elizabeth
Alexander 9.12.07
Beata, 05.01.08
Tony, 25.11.07
Tanja, 25.11.07
Eva, 26.12.07
Greta, 01.01.08
Nickol, 25.01.08
Susanne, 22.

Anneke, 25.11.07
Alice 25.11.07
Klara, 16.12.07
Mathieu
Eva, 5.12.07
Katharina, 22.11.07
Jérôme
Jutte 25.11.07
Brigitte, 25.11.07

Ursula 9.11.02
Desirée
Laura, 25.11.07
Sofie, 24.11.07
Annette 22.11.07
Marion 30.01.08

Ilario
Stini, 9.11.02
Kim, 29.11.07
Judith
Alison, 11.12.07
Claire, 22.08
Fabian, 18.11.07
Ursula,
Bojusch, 02.12.07

Nora 17.01.08
Stephanie, 9.11.02
Haike, 9.12.07
Dora, 16.12.07
Zoi, 4.12.07
Irmi 11.12.07
Isabel, 25.11.07
Sara, 25.11.07
Franciska 8.01.08
Elaine,

Herta, 03.01.08
Monika, 21.11.07
Hilde, 22.12.07
Marcella, 03.01.08
Silvia, 15.12.07
SARAH, 5.12.07
IKUKO
Helga, 6.1.08

—Heekyoung, 09.02.08
Lori, 03.01.08
Sandra, 25.11.07
Margat 15.12.07
Lalla, 01.01.08
Annika — 27.01.08

—Linda, 02.12.07
Haruka, 4.12.07
Hagen, 03.02.08
Özlem, 02.02.08
Pachi 27.01.08

—Renate, 29.12.07
—Johanna, 03.02.08
23.02.08

—Monika, 30.12.07

—Sonja, 06.01.08
—Juba, 04.01.08

—Adrian, 02.02.08

—T.Sonia, 02.02.08

05.01.08

—Elena 02.01.08

—瀚文, 02.02.08

——Carmina, 25.11.07
—Luka, 25.11.07

—Marvin, 13.01.08
—Magdalena, —27.1.08

—Claudia 02.01.08
—Emma

—懷文, 03.02.08
—Luis, 25.11.07

—Doria, 03.01.08

—Aurelia, 30.12.07
—Che

—Sasa, 06.01.08

———Tori, 1.12.07

—Letizia, 30.12.07

_ Günter 10.02.08

_stian, 29.12.07   _ Robert, 25.11.07
_el, 29.12.07
_ Ingo 27.01.08   _ Kurt, 6.12.07   _ Marcus, 03.02.08
                                   _ Fabian, 8.12.07   Karl-Heinz, 25.11.07 _ Ralf, 8.12.07
_ Michael, 01.02.08   _ Višnja, 19.01.08   _ Norbert, 8.12.07   _ Alfred, 12.01.08 _Christoph
Marc, 25.11.07 _ Jochen, 30.01.08   _ Andrik, 28.01.08   _ Marc, 21.12.07   Chris 23.12.07 Chris, 25.11.07   _ Peer, 05.0
_ Ruth, 25.11.07   _ Wolfgang, 03.01.08 _ Paul, 13.01.08 _ Paris 23.12.07 _ Waldemar, 8.12.07   _ Wolfgang, 26.12.07 _ Georg
_ Felix, 1.12.07   _ Heinrich 21.11.07 Florian, 25.11.07   _ Luis, 07.02.08   _ Peter, 6.1.08 _ David, 28.12.07   _ Klaus 8.12.07   Philipp 27.11.07 Hannes
_ Dan, 26.12.07 _ Josef, 02.12.07   Taco 04.01.08   Axel, 13.01.08 Verena, 25.11.07   _ Simon, 15.12.07   _ Roland, 26.12.07   _ Klaus, 15.12.07
_ Franz-Xaver 18.12.2007 _ Michael, 26.12.07   _ Jörg, 21.12.07   _ Florian, 8.12.07   _ Bill, 16.12.07 _ Sergey 3.02.08   _ Elke, 29.12.07   _ Sab
Paul 8.12.07   _ Javerio, 01.01.08 _ Peter 27.07.07   _ Sebastian, 12.12.07   _ Olivier, 30.01.08   _ Eric, 23.11.07   Philipp 24.1.08 _ Anna, 08.01.08 _ Uli, 27.01.08
Angelika 2.12.07   Achim, 24.11.07   Nikola, 16.12.07 _ Christian 27.07.07 _ Johannes 24.11.07 _ Berno, 11.11.08 _ Florian 13.01.08   _ Jürgen 16.01.08 _ Gerhard, 30.11.08   _ Tobias, 13.01.08
arina, 16.12.07   Michelle 16.01.08 Rainer, 22.11.07   _ Nicole, 02.02.09   Tewelde, 24.011.07 Ellen, 8.12.07   _ Wolfgang 31.07   Rainer 8.12.07   Florian, 25
_ Alex, 30.12.07   Kathrine, 25.11.07 Vineta 6.12.07   Claus 25.1.07   Elisabet, 25.11.07 Uta, 23.11.07   Christa, 18.01.08   Maria for 2.08
Gertrud, 29.11.07   Pierre 29.12.07   Ben 17.01.08   Ruzica, 25.11.07
Gertrud, 24.11.07   Jose, 26.12.07   Anne 8.12.07   Michel, 16.12.07 Felix, 29.12.07 Barbara 22.11.07   Jana   Theresia, 07.12.07   Jessic
Volker 4.12.07   Carolin 03.01.08 amara, 9.12.03 Johann, 27.11.07 christel 17.01.08   Anna, 01.12.07 Ulrike 27.11.07   Julia, 02.01.08   Verena, 21.11.07
Maryann 23.01.08   Andreas, 27.01.07   Anna, 15.12.2007 Gabi, 24.12.07 Nina 8.12.07   Mechthild, 25.11.07   Elisabeth, 13.12.07
Helle 25.11.07   Kathrin 22.11.07 Wim 23-12-2007   Diana, 12.12.07   Annemarie, 21.11.07 Johanna Lena 25.12.07 Vixi 8.12.07   Baudetta, 25.11.07 Beatriz, 05.01.08 Jörg, 26.12.07   Nina, 25
Eva 12.01.08   Melanie, 03.01.08   Nadine 25.11.07   Concetta, 25.11.07
Svenja, 25.11.07   Louise, 5.12.07   Jessica, 1.12.07   Sabine 02.12.07   Melanie 23.12.07   Nienke, 8.12.07 Simone, 18.12.2007
Nicola, 8.12.07   Danute, 16.12.07   Sarah 02.01.08   Anneliese 03.01.08   Marion 23.12.07   Mapileva 30.12.07
Katrin, 1.12.07   _ Loisi, 8.12.07   Sandra 13.01.08   Katrin 8.12.07   Evelyn 03.12.07   _ Marion 23.12.07 _ Gusti 11.12.07
Katrin, 1.12.07   _ Silvia, 03.02.08   Ana, 07.12.07   _ Antonia 27.12.07   _ Angela, 28.12.07
Elaine, 8.12.07   _ Corla, 24.01.08 _ Hannah 23.12.07   _ Lucie 02.02.2008   _ Nicole, 20.01.08 Marianne, 13.01.08
_ Jasmin, 26.01.08   _ Lucas, 30.12.07   _ Valentina, 30.12.07 Kate, 16.12.07 _ Muriel 28.12.07   _ Donatella, 28.12.07   _ Theresa, 30.01.08   Sabine, 8.12.07   _ Ana, 23.11.07   _ Julie, 5.12
_ Eva 11.12.07   Gitte, 1.12.07   _ J17 10.01.08   Rossella, 1.12.07   Debora, 07.12.07   _ Renate, 26.12.07   _ Ingeborg 8.12.07
_ Tina 27.01.08   _ Brigitte 01.01.08   _ Abeer, 02.12.07   Jana 8
_ Tobias, 10.01.08   _ Lieselotte, 11.01.08   _ Edda, 5.12.07
                                   _ Tracy, 24.11.07   _ Franca, 30.12.07   _ Re
                          _ Quirin, 27.1.08
_ 7.07&H, 23.07.08.

                           _ Ulrich, 09.02.08   _ Karl, 26.12.07
_ Eva, 30.12.07

     _ Pia _ 27.01.08
                                                              _ Luis, 30.12.07   _ Arthur

                                                                 _ Paul 30.12.07

                                                                                                                                    _ Anna, 26.12.07

                    _ Lisa, 19.01.08

_ Emma, 25.11.07

_ Charlie, 25.11.07

_ ShuLien, 8.12.07

                           _ Sara, 30.12.07

                       _ Konstantin, 09.01.08

_ KOH 航, 4.12.07

                                                                                    _ Rebecca, 25.11.07

– Alexander, 02.02.08

__ Rupert, 25.11.07
__ Peter, 9.12.07   – Michael, 13.01.08

__ Thomas 16.01.08
__ Klaus, 29.01.08   Ansgar 03.01.08   – Jörg, 30.12.07
efan, 25.11.07   __ Jan, 30.11.07   – Fabian, 6.1.08   Andreas, 24.11.07   Jörg, 26.12.07 – Armin, 11.01.08   __ André, 25.11
nnes, 03.02.08 Jaap, 2.12.07 – Markus, 27.01.08   M? 09.01.08   – Wout, 26.12.07   __ Roland, 27.
ael, 05.01.08 Vit, 02.12.07 __ Nicole, 19.01.08   – Manfred, 01.01.08
tmut, 13.12.07 Jan, 03.02.08 Tilman, 16.12.07 – Fédéric, 24.11.07   Florian 24.11.07   Erhard, 24.11.07 – Eric 02.01.08   Christian, 9.12.07
lwin, 05.01.08 Vit, 02.12.07 Ulrich, 23.11.07 – Vincent, 05.01.08   – Guido, 12.08   Jean-Matthieu 14.12.08   Ingo, 22.01.08   – Andreas, 11.01.08
Andreas, 07.02.08 – Pia, 20.11.08 Peter, 9.12.07 Jenny, 16.12.07 Matteo, 30.07   Appin, 25.11.07 Jeu, 24.11.07   Thilo, 30.01.08   Richard, 25.11.07   23.11.07 – Peter 20.01.08
Vasje, 02.12.07 – Knud 26.12.07 Geoffrey, 9.12.07 Adrian, 16.12.07   Erich 10.01.08
Dominik, 01.02.08 – Winfried 28.12.07   – Dom 29/2.07   Adrian, 16.12.07   Jopi 22.01   Nick Andersson, 02.11.07   Corina, 26.12.07 – Heike 11.01.08
ot, 13.01.08 – Markus, 03.02.08   Stefan Jan,   Patrick, 11.01.08   Didi, 24.11.07   Ione, 22.12.07   URS, 15.12.07 – Wilfried, 29.11.07   Frederike, 29.11.07   Paul, 26.
Aaron, 9.12.07 Manuel 27.01.08 Robert 25.11.07 Frank, 03.02.07 Christoph, 24.11.07   Christoph, 25.11.07   Giovanni, 11.12.07   Paloma, 9.12.07
3.11.07 – Nina, Maren 23.03.07 y, 25.11.07 André, 28.11.07   GIANLUCA 9.12.07   Birgit 9.12.07 Francine, 2.12.07   Peter 26.12.07
ZAFER, 28.11.07 Arnaud 22.01.08   Adam, 11.11   christian 29.12.07   Gottfried, 21.11.07 – maria 02.12.07   Herre, 5.12.07 – Edda, 9.12.07 – Jean-Claude, 16.12
Hassen, 25.11.07 Britta, 25.11.07 Grazia, 7.12.07   Cloe, 5.12.07 Irmi, 20.01.08   Kirsten, 05.02   Lisa, 16.12.07   Theophile, 5.12.07 – Angela Tan
Martin, 25.11.07 Christine, 9.12.07 Take, 02.12.07 Sandra, 8.12.07 Christian, 11.08   Tanja 19.12   Roswitha to piota, 25.11.07 Jana 23.11.07   Janine   Manola, 03.02.08
LISA, 24.11.07 Jake, 02.12.07 Simon, 13.12.07   Steffi, 25.11.07 Gino 12.07   Susanne 23.11.07 – Charlotte Joanna, 25.11.07
Ulla, 15.12.07 Jonas Anina 27.11.07   Brigitte, 26.12.07 Dorotea 24.11.07   Andra 1.12.07 Anna 17.12.07   Alice, 5.12.07 – Lydia Jutta, 25.11.07
Barbara, 9.12.07 Edouard, 5.12.07 Gerlind, 23.11.07 Kristin 25.11.07 Lucile, 5.12.07   Anne, 07.12.07   Jutta, 25.11.07   Kirs
David, 24.12.07 – Jeanne, 21.08 Libby, 02.01.08   Renate, 15.12.07   Petra, 27.11.07   Tomik   Simona, 6.12.07 – Christiane, 28.11.07   Olga, 11.01.08
Carla, 22.11.07 – Inge 26.01.07 Leni, 25.11.07 – Kay Lavinia 25.11.07 Florian, 21.11.07   Rosaria   Ina, 25.11.07 Cathleen, 02.11.08   Danielle, 01.02.08
Jutta, 27.01.08 Carolyn, 10.2.08   – Gerda, 27.12   Anna, 30.11   Bärbel, 06.01.08   Max   24.1.08   Fridel, 27.01.08 Christine 21.12.07 ELisa, 29.12.07 Villy, 9.12.07
Regina, 9.12.07 Valeska, 02.12.07   Luisa, 02.12.07   Ji-Yeun, 16.12.07
Helga 04.01.08 Kerstin, __ Polly, 25.11.07 Chazal 09.01.08   Cathy, 9.12.07   Natalie, 30.12.07   Klara, 9.12.07   Eva,
– Beate, 24.11.07 Erna, 09.02.08 Ambra, 03.02.08 30.11.07   – Elisabeth 24.1.08 – Sybille, 10.2.08   VERUSCHKA 17.01.08 – Melanie, 11.01.08   Ines, 08.02.08   Georgia, 9.12.
Lise, 5.12.07 Maria Jesus, 28.01.08   – Patricia, 11.01.08   Vecihe, 24.01.08

iovanni, 07.12.07   – Gertrud, 5.08   – Felicia, 15.2.08   Martina 12.02.08
                   – 純子 29.12.2007   Plamenka, 02.12.0
                                – Evgenio, 28.11.07   – Lukas, 02.12.07   __ Leoni, 25.11.07

                       __ Ferdinand 4.12.07

                                                              – LAUren, 15.12.07

        __ Clemens 9.12.07   – Nicola 27.01.08
                                                                              – Winvent, 02.12.07
– Heinz 19.07.07   – Karen, 03.01.08
                        – Jonas 27.01.08

                                      – Sam, 15.12.07
                                          – Jakob, 17.01.08

                                                              – Norah, 09.2.08   – Emilia, 16.12.07
                 – Ida, 2.2.08

                                  – Tobias, 13.01.08
                      – Timon, 16.12.07

– Paula, 26.01.08

      – Fredirik, 15.12.07

                                              – Joseph, 13.01.08

1107

— Benedikt, 02.0

— Michael, 13.01.08

— Mihael 1.1.08

— Jörg, 30.12.07

— Holger 14.12.07   — Hugo, 23.07.08.

— James, 16.0

—— Andre, 25.11.07   — Walter 24.1.08   Joachim, 30.01.08   — Falk, 11.01.08

— Christoph, 26.01.08   — Frieder, 26.12.07

— Roland, 27.01.08   Ina, 25.11.07   — Albert, 06.01.08   Adriano, 6.12.07   — Tom, 15.12.07   — Benedikt 02.01.08   — Felix, 06.01.08   — Thierry, 8.12.07   Rudi, noch   — Jürgen, 25.11.07

Eric 02.01.08   — Manfred, 01.01.08   JULIAN, 28.12.07   Boris, 13.12.07   — Johannes, 01.02.08   — Christian, 27.11.8   Ignaz, 28.11.2   Eva, 16.12.07   — Jacques, 14.07.08   Uwe, 03   — Alessandro 13.11.

01.08   — Christian, 8.12.07   — Tobi, 26.12.07   — Rolf, 05.01.08   Mattihas, 24.11.07   — Tristan, 11.01.08   Klaus, 24.11.07   — Marco, 28.11.07   Götz, 9.01.08

— Andreas, noch   — Peter 20.01.08   — Alessandro, 6.12.07   Nigel, 24.01.08

— Bruno, 23.11.07   Bill, 24.11.07   Arina, 24.11.07   — Gerrit, 06.01.08   Detlef, 07.12.07   — Jean, 29.12.07   David, 03.02.08   Alvise 02.01.08

— Erich 10.01.08   Jekatarina, 26.01.08   — Katharina 04.01.08   Nicolai, 25.11.07   Daryl, 6.1.08   Tajaro — Ruprecht, 2

— Corina, 26.12.07   — Heike, 01.01.08   Ann, 24.11.07   Manfred 9.12.07   Christoph, 03.02.08   Alfred, 25.11.07   Helmut, 31.01.08   — Stefan, 15.12.07   ROBE

Dieter, 26.01.08   Uli, 05.01.08   — Jürgen, 16.12.07   — Sascha, 31.   Achim, 02.02.08   Thomas, 21.1.   Benjamin, 26.12.07   08.02.08

— Freederike, 29.11.07   — Paloma, 9.12.07   Paul, 26.01.08   Angela, 25.11.07   — Uwe, 25.12.07   Joachim, 10.01.08   Frank, 24.11.07   — Janke, 2.12.07   — Elena, 26.11.02   — Barbara   Judith, 25.11.07

— Edda, 9.12.07   — Jean-Claude, 16.12.07   — Christian 24.11.07   Matias, 25.11.07   Martin, 05.01.08   — Anne-Sophie, 30.11   Danielle, 07.02.08

— Theophile, 5.12.07   — Ingela   Tanya, 9.12.07   Silke, 05.01.08   Kari Katarina, 25.11.07   Regine, 21.12.07   Nina, 15.12.07   Sandra   Silvia, 19.11.07   — Angelica, 01.02.0

— Jürgen, 22.11.07   Trish, 16.12.07   Niklaus 26.12.07   Sofia 23.12.07   — Hans   Chris tian, 24.11.07   Hans-Georg, 23.22.11.07   Petra, 16.12.07   Jo, 13.12.07   Mateo, 28.11.07   Gesine, 23.11.

— Joanna, 23.11.07   Gabriela, Erika   Stella 05.01.08   Daniela, 26.12.07   Bianca, 22.11.07   Ilse, 07.12.07   Gaia 28.11.07   Sebastian   Therese, 25.11.07   JOHN 23.12.07

— Jona, 16.01.08   Hyo-Young, 8.12.07   Barbara   Ulrike 23.11.07   — Bianka, 26.12.07   Stefanie, 23.12.07   Luka, 9.12.07   — Lisa, 22.11.07   Ulrike

— Jutta, 25.11.07   Kirsten, 24.11.07   Heike, 07.12.07   — Anna, 11.01.08   Theresa 25.11.07   — Alex, 24.01.08   — Mara 14.12.07

— Olga, 9.12.07   Mary, 01.02.08   Juliane, 25.11.07   Kristalina   Raphaela, 23.11.07   Iris, 27.11.   Katja, 15.01.08   Goduca, 28.01.08   Angie, 25.11.07   — Kathleen, 6.1.08   Bianca

— Montse, 70.07.07   Danielle, 01.02.08   Joanna, 9.12.07   Theresa   Celia, 02.12.07   — Bettina, 11.01.08   Elfride, 25.11.07   Hans, 13.01.08   ELENA, 23.12.07   Barbara

Sebastian   Yevgeniya, 05.01.08   Magali, 5.12.07   Julia, 4.12.07   — Inge, 13.12.07   XJ 10.01.08   Cecilia, 4.12.07   Claire, 5.12.07   Bartolomeo   Regina   Eli

— Elisa, 29.12.07   Villy, 9.12.07   Verena, 18.12.2007   — Jette, 13.12.07   — Bert, 05.01.08   Rosanna, 6.12.07   Stefano 28.11.07   Nadia, 25.12.07   Gabriella, 6.12.07   Amandine, 02.02   Sonia, 31.01.08   VERONICA, 24.11.07   Gio

— Klara, 9.12.07   Eva, 24.11.07   Marina, 18.12.2007   Lydia 11.01.08   Helga, 12.01.08   EDMEE 19.01.08   06.01.08   Ursula, 16.01.08   Gerda, 16.12.07   Marga, 30.01.08

— Georgia, 9.12.07   — Miriam 6.02.08   Agnes, 9.12.07   Margarita, 30.01.08   FEDERICA 28.11.07   Domen, 9.12.07   Solenn, 5.12.07   — Julinda, 16.

— Annette, 06.01.08   04.01.08   — Gabriele 29.12.07   — Renate, 02.02.08   Silvia, 22.12.07   — Alessandra, 03.01.0

— Martina — 12.02.08   Coco, 16.12.07

— Plamenka, 02.12.07   — Franziska, — 24.01.08   — Jamile, 20.01.08

11.07   — Veronika 6.02.07   — Laura 27.01.08

— Anne-

— Paul, 05.01.08

— Ellen, 26.12.07

— Nicola, 12.01.08   —— Daniel, 27.11.07

— Vincent, 02.12.07

—— Marlene, 27.11.07   —— Trystan, 27.11.07

— Fanny, 27.01.08

09.2.08   — Emilia, 16.12.07

— Zoe, 16.12.07

Joseph, 13.01.08

— Philipp 23.12.07

— Sienna, 01.01.08   — Am

John, 22.11.07

— Rolf, 16.12.07

— Lars, 23.11.07

Siegfried, 6.12.07

Alfons, 02.01.08

08— Patrick, 25.11.07 — Karl, 22.11.07 — Korbinian, 29.12.07
Gero, 16.12.07
Jan, 22.01.08
Benedikt, 01.07
Jens, 13.2.08
Daniel, 05.01.08

Sabine, 02.02.08 — Christoph, 8.02.08 — Max, 5.12.07 — William, 29.12.07
Wolfgang, 30.12.07 — Martin, 31.12.08 — Jochen, 20.01.08 Georg, 24.11.07

Hermann, 29.11.07 — Kay, 23.12.07 Wulf, 17.01.08 — Annette 19.1.08 Erich, 08.01.08 — Ulrich, 4.12.07 Christian, 26.12.07 Robinzky, 6.12.07 Jürgen, 02.01.08 Wolfgang, 6.12.07

Max, 13.12.07 — Joost 01.01.08 Hans, 2.12.07 — Abud, 13.01.08 Reinhold, 16.01.08 Franck, 27.07.08 Christian, 30.11.07 Louis-François 23.12.07 Tobias, 26.01.08 Thomas, 1.12.07

te, 22.12.07 ALAIN-17.01.08 Heineke, 26.01.08 Sepp, 07.02.08 Marka, 19.01.08 Felix, 16.12.07 Ditz, 22.12.07 Beck, 22.01.08 Nitti, 1.12.07 Jos, 01.02.08 Luca, 03.01.08

alter, 6.12.07 Oliver, 05.02.08 Max, 23.11.07 Isabel, 8.12.07 G.ovanni, 23.11.07 MIHA Petra, 26.01.08 Daniele, 05.01.08 Stefan, 18.11.08 Christian, 29.11.07

Sebastian, 01.01.08 Markus, 6.1.08 Martin, 26.01.08 Heike 24.1.08 Matthias, 16.12.07 Rainer, 09.02.08 Viktor 27.11.07 Hias, 05.01.08 Roberto, 15.12.07 Ulrich, 30.11.07 Josef, 01.08 Tine,

Barbara, 9.12.07 Thomas 19.01.08 Antonio, 28.11.07 Andreas 22.11.07 Tom 02.01.08 Alexander, 23.11.07 Peter, 04.01.08 Heinrich, 26.12.07 Norbert, 02.01.08 Wolfgang, 27.11.07 Sandra, 4.12.07

Friedrich, 23.11.07 Julia, 30.01.07 Hiro, 24.11.07 Lyonne, 05.01.08 Ludmila, 23.12.07 Vittoriomaria, 28.11.07 Hila, 27.11.07 Sus

fsgang, 23.11.07 Christue, 16.12.07 Joost 29.01.08 Werner 11.01.08 Gilla, 6.12.07 Moses 27.12.07 Angela, 6.12.07 Edith, 11.12.07 Noel 27.01.08

07 Jana 03.01.08 Helmut, 25.11.07 Daniela, 8.12.07 Margit, 30.01.08 Leonie 23.12.07 Renato, 09.02.08 Sylvia, 30.1.07 Harald, 04.01.08 Erda 26.11.07 Wilhelm, 27.11.07 Elisabeth, 28.11.07

Marten, Valentina Julia, 01.08 Iris, 23.11.07 Günter Sandra Nina, 6.12.07 Yopa 08.02.08 Djoeke, 4.12.07 Sarah, 26.11.07 David, 23.11.07 Gabi, 26.12.07

Heidi, 16.12.07 Sophia, 17.01.08 Luitgard 28.11.07 Mona 02.02.08 Toni Maria, 23.11.07 Pia 27.01.08 Christine, 5.12.07 Claudia

Kevin, 13.01.08 Stephan, 12.01.08 Keji, 18.01.08 Valentina, 23.11.07 Angela 22.01.08 Sosi 26.01.08 Axel, 07.02.08 Sonja, 16.12.07

Aude, 25.11.07 Raphaela, 13.01.08 Sigrun, 09.02.08 Doris, 27.11.07 Elfriede 12.01.08 Maria, 23.11.07 Elisabeth, 28.11.07 Elisa, 28.11.07

te, 23.12.07 Julia, 26.12.07 Life, 02.12.07 Gertraud, 6.12.07 Brigitte, 5.12.07 Dietmar, Alwyn, 6.1.08 Verena, 11.2.07 Véronique, 12.01.07 James 29.12.07 Robert,

Maria, 25.11.07 Karla 28.11.07 Mina 8.12.07 Lisa, 24.11.07 Andrea, 16.12.07 Joseph 19.01.08 DaMi, 25.11.07 Doris 02.12.07 Dragica, 24.11.07

Hanne Brigitte, 17.01.08 Fan, 8.12.07 Suse, 16.12.07 Elke 18.01.08 Anna 12.01.07 Michael, 02.01.08 Johana, 05.01.08

5.12.07 Josain Casper 23.12.07 Margit, 26.12.07 Sylvia 29.12.07 Jasmin, 5.12.07 Andi 12.07 Siegfried, 02.12.07 Evi, 11.01.08 Marlene, 2.12.07

11.07 Bartolomeo, 03.01.08 Hanna 18.01.08 Tamami 24.11.07 Sarah 04.01.08 Tara 16.02.07 Daniela, 26.12.07 Eva 30.01.08 Andrea 27.01.08 Carmine, 07.12.07

Deggarit, 8.12.07 Alice 23.11.07 Alice 18.01.08 neko, 24.11.07 Joelle, Jana, 03.01.08 Avva, 18.12.07 Judith, 05.01.08 Emanuela 10.01.08 Lisa, 24.1.08

Gabriele 18.01.08 Simona, 12.01.08 Sarah 27.01.08 Enrica, 02.01.08 Christoph, 03.02.08 ILSE, 17.01.08 Arijana 15.12.07 Katja, 09.02.08 Karpira 18.12.

wrence, 23.12.07 Sissi, 23.11.07 Irina, 27.02.08 Erika 16.01.08 Lucia, 30.01.07

her, 8.12.07 Avja 29.12.07 Alima, 26.12.07 Leonie 27.01.08 Ilse, 26.12.07 Markian, 31.1.08 Moritz,

Marilyne, 13.12.07 YISCA, 24.11.07 Camille, 02.02.08 Kristina, 15.12.07 Beatrice, 28.11.07

Leonard 20.01.08

Leslie 27.01.08

Laura, 31.01.08

Louise 28.11.07 Elisabeth, 02.01.08 Joshua, 26.12.07 Sophia, 02

27.01.08 Nicole, 13.01.08

Michelle, 13.01.08

Justine 28.11.07

anda, 02.02.08

Florian, 6.1.08

Aurelian, 16.

Hanna, 6.01.08

Elan 16.01.08

Max, 12.01.08

Marlene, 10.2.08

John, 22.11.07
Rolf, 16.12.07
— Tunoqaü 03.12.07
— David, 13.01.08

Korbinian, 29.12.07
Siegfried, 6.12.07
Lars, 23.11.07
Alfons, 02.01.08
—Stephan, 20.01.08
Roman, 13.01.08
— Jan, 22.01.08
Gero, 16.12.07
Benedikt, 21.12.17
— Lars, 02.02.08

— Max, 5.12.07
William, 29.12.07
Jens, 13.2.08
Daniel, 05.01.08
Engelbert 23.01.08
Horst 23.12.07
Michael
.1.08
Erich, 08.01.08
Ulrich, 4.12.07
Wolfgang 30.1.08
Martin, -31.1.08
Jochen, 20.01.08
Georg, 24.11.07
Axel 16.01.08

Reinhold, 18.01.08
Franck, 27.01.08
Christian, 26.12.07
Robinzky, 6.12.07
Louis-François, 23.12.07
Jürgen, 02.01.08
Wolfgang, 6.12.07
Thomas, 1.12.07
— ΛΑΚΙΣ — 28.11.07
Peter, 13.01.08
Simon, 16.1.
Max 12.0
Marius, 19.01.08
Felix, 16.12.07
Christian, 30.11.07
Ditz, 22.12.07
Stefan, 8.01.08
Beate 22.01.08
Tobias, 26.01.08
— ΠΟλιτυμη —28.11.07
Alexander, 16.12.07
王, 23.11.07
Stefan, 11.1
gmund, 23.11.07
MIHA 8.12.07
Petra 26.01.08
Daniele, 05.01.08
Helmut 08.02.08
Stefan, 03.01.08
Willi, 1.12.07
Luca, 03.01.08
Werner, 21.12.07
DoSia — 28.11.07
Christa 27.11.07
Marco, 25.12
Giovanni, 23.12.
Klaus 02.02.08
Christian, 29.11.07
Josef, 02.02.08
Linda, -31.01.08
Peter, 13.01.08
Tobi
Meike 24.1.08
Mathias, 16.12.07
Rainer, 08.02.08
Ursel, 27.11.07
Ilias, 05.01.08
Peter, 16.12.07
Ioannous Ba... 28.11.07
Patrick, 27.11.07
Andy, 24.11.07
28.11.07
Andreas 22.11.07
Heinz, 30.12.07
Roberto, 15.12.07
Wolfgang, 27.11.07
Tina, 22.11.07
Karin 05.01.08
Mouro, 02.12.07
Daniele
Francesco, 01.08
Neil, 5.12.07
Werner, 19.01.08
Dietmar
Alexander, 23.11.07
Heinrich, 26.12.07
Ulrich, 30.11.07
Sandra, 4.12.07
Carla, 24.12.07
Hiro, 24.11.07
Iyonne, 05.01.08
Ludmila, 23.12.07
MBO 23.01.12
Angela, 6.12.07
Vittoriamaria, 28.11.07
Nico 28.12.07
Eric, 15.01.08
Susanne 02.12.07
Robert 23.11.07
Ann
Margit, 30.10.07
Leonie, 23.12.
Zilla, 6.12.07
Sylvia, 30.11.07
Noël 27.01.08
Hila 27.11.07
Susanne 02.12.07
Alessandro 05.01.08
Petra 02.07
Mary, 1
23.11.07
Sandra,
Nina, 6.12.07
Harald 04.01.08
Edith
Hyllyeme 29.12.07
FadaReb, 12.12.07
Sonja, 16.12.07
Maria-Gracia 01.12.07
Rosa 03.01.
Sophia, 17.04.07
Luitgard 28.11.07
Monika 03.02.08
Djoeke, 4.12.07
Wilhelm, 6.12.07
Sarah
David, 23.11.07
Gab. 26.12.07
Sonja 15.12.07
Otto, 27.11.07
stephan, 25.11.07
Valentina, 28.11.07
Toni
Maria, 23.11.07
Pia 27.11.07
Christine 5.12.07
Claudia
Ursula, 5.12.07
Brigitte, 5.12.07
Doris, 27.11.07
Sevi, 26.01.08
Elisabeth, 26.11.07
Elisa 28.11.07
Robert, 23.11.07
Tim, 23.11.07
Edith, 05.02.08
life, 6.12.07
Alessio, 28.11.
Lisa 14.12.07
Andrea, 16.12.07
Verena, 4.12.07
Veronique, 12.12.07
Joseph, 19.01.08
Angelika, 16.12.07
Siegfried, 02.12.07
Dragica, 24.11.07
Angelika, 22.12.07
Heide 16.04.08
Claudia, 6.12.07
Sachiko 15.12.07
Sylvie 29.12.07
Andi 12.01.07
Michael, 02.01.08
Johana, 05.01.08
Laura, 18.02.08
Lieselotte, 4.12.07
Benedicte 28.11.07
neko, 24.11.07
Jasmin, 5.12.07
Gulyum 29.12.07
Anja
Daniela, 26.12.07
Eva 06.01.08
Carmine, 07.12.07
Marlene, 2.12.07
Coco, 16.12.07
EMI 09.12.2007
Angela, 02.01.08
Japan, 03.01.08
Elena, 03.01.08
Joëlle
Jana, 16.12.07
Judith, 05.01.08
Emanuela 10.01.08
Lisa 24.1.08
Anna, 18.12.07
Christine, 22.01.08
Elisabeth, 29.11.
Sarah 27.01.08
Enrica, 02.01.08
Christoph, 03.02.07
ILSE, 17.01.08
Arijana 18.12.07
Ingeborg, 27.11.07
Helen, 14.12.07
Moritz
Katja, 09.02.08
Kampira 18.12.07
Hinka 29.01.08
Maiko 04.01.08
辰子 14.12
Leonie 27.01.08
Erika 16.01.08
Lucia, 30.12.07
Kristina, 15.12.07
Beatrice, 28.11.07
Ilse, 26.12.07
Moritz, 03.02.08
Hermine, 4.12.07
Emely 1.1.08
Markian, 31.1.08
Katharina, 03.02.08
Camille, 02.02.08
Natascia, 03.01.08
Simon, 13.01.08
Sara, 03.01.08

08
— Christoph, 13.01.08

Laura, -31.01.08

Louise 28.11.07
Elisabeth, 02.01.08
Sophia, 02.01.08
Joshua, 26.12.07
Nicole, 13.01.08

Susanne, 02.01.08

Michelle, 13.01.08
Clemens, 16.12.07

Justine 28.11.07

Nelly, 30.11.07

Florian, 6.1.08
Aurélien, 16.12.07

— Ella,

Max, 12.01.08

— Marlene, 18.2.08

_ Enrico, 16.12.07   _ Michael 6.02.08

_ Karl-Heinz, 30.11.07 _ Michael, 05.01.08   _ Jeroen, 30.12.07 _ Wolfgang, 19.01.08
_ Florian 24.1.08   _ Fish 12.01.08   _ Matthias, 09.02.08
02.08   _ Tony, 13.01.08 _ Artur 12.01.08   _ Zwicki 16.12.07
_ Sevag, 5.12.07 _ Karl, 02.01.08   _ Harry 03.02.08   _ Mattia, 22.1.1   _ Johan, 05.01.08   _ Nathan 10.02.08 _ Jesse, 11.01.08   _ Duma 11.01.08
_ Hugo, 30.11.07   _ Julia, 13.01.08   _ Nigel 22.12.07   _ Alexandros, 21.12.07 _ Simon, 28.12.07   _ Daniel 23.12.07 _ Chris B.R.O.   _ Steffen, 13.12.07 _ Farhad, 08.01.09
13.12.07   _ Dieter 1.12.07   _ Volkmar, 17.12.07 Katja, 16.12.07   _ Joachim, 17.12.07   _ Katja, 16.12.07   Shpresim, 25.11.07 _ Tobias, 03.01.08 _ Rolly, 10.2.07
_ Antonio 17.01.08   _ Carlo, 16.12.07   _ Julian, 13.01.07   _ Willi 12.01.08 _ Martin 10.02.08   _ FRANZ 11.2.08
_ Victor, 02.01.08 _ Bruno, 15.11.07 _ Ian, 26.01.08 Markus, 23.11.07 _ Michael, 02.02.08 _ Günther, 21.12.07   _ Kostas 6.12.07 _ KRIS 23.12.07 _ Ernesto Pablo _ Klaus, 5.11.07
_ Adriano, 23.11.07   _ Mathias, 28.01.08 _ Dirk, 13.12.07 _ Davide 28.12.07   _ Frank, 4.12.07   Robert   _ Maximilian, 2.11.07 _ Peter 03.01.08 _ Hanna 08.01.08
_ Christoph, 0.12.07   _ Eckart, 24.11.07   _ 13.12.07 _ Martin 05.02.08   _ Tanja 1.12.07   _ 10.01.08   _ Zbigniew, 13.12.07 _ Michael 23.12.07
_ Emanuele, 28.11.07 Balthasar   _ 15.12.03   _ Sylvia, 30.11.07   Elli, 19.01.08   _ David, 6.12.07 _ Christine 61.08
13.12.07 _ Sebestian, 23.12.07 _ Athenais 12.01.07 _ Jahnke, 07.01.07   _ Johanna, 13.01.07   Eleni, 6.12.07 _ Reinhold, 30.12.07 _ Claire 12.1.07 _ Franz 04.02.08
_ Elke, 28.11.07 _ Stephanie, 16.12.07   _ Santa, 03.02.07 _ Hermann, 13.01.08 _ Heinrich 4.01.07 _ Eva 23.12.07   Daniele, 28.11.07   Kristina, 23.11.07 _ Sara, 20.01.08
B, 27.11.07   _ Tani 2.12.07   _ Julia, 25.11.07   _ Zwi, 21.12.07   _ Manuel, 25.11.07   _ Tony, 15.01.07 _ Michaela 19.12.07 _ Ross 27.11.08 _ Sebine 23.12.07
_ Philipp, Kayo   _ Kora, 16.12.07   _ Dora, 03.02.08   _ Marlen   _ Andreas 10.01.07
_ Sabine, 6.12.07   _ Ulrike 08.01.08 _ Tanja, 28.11.07   _ Julia, 13.01.08   _ Viola 2.12.07   _ Gabriele, 13.01.08 _ Lisanna, 1.12.07 _ Magic 14.01.08
07 _ Rosmarie, 27.11.07   _ Sabina, 13.01.08   _ Christine 15.12.07 _ Betina 23.12.07 20.12.07   Xplorewa, 1.,16.12.07   _ Carmen, 26.12.07 _ Alessandra, 13.01.08
_ Jenna, 26.12.07   _ Paolo 03.01.08   _ Boo, 02.03.08 Steffi, 3.01.07   _ Vanna, 13.01.08   _ Kelly, 10.11.07   _ LINA, 26.01.08 _ Regi, 30.12.07 _ Heidi 03.01.08
_ Lili, Steeof   _ Daniela 20.01.08   _ Regina, 12.01.07   _ Anna, 05.01.08   _ Eleonora, 28.11.07   _ Rosa, 26.12.07 _ Heidrun 04.01.08
_ Anna, 20.01.07 _ Konrad, 07.12.07   _ Davide, 28.11.07   _ Katja, 10.01.08   _ Upuna 11.01.08 _ Elisabeth, 19.01.08
_ Elena, 26.12.07 _ Julie 0.01.08   _ Anastasia, 6.12.07   _ Jenny, 13.01.08   Mechthild, 07.12.07   _ Irene, 13.01.08   _ Akakia, 29.12.07   _ Maria, 26.12.07 _ Julia, 26.12.07   _ Valentina, 12.12.07   _ Judith, 16.01.08 _ Willi, 19.01.08
_ Maike, 24.11.07 _ Barbara, 26.01.08   _ Jacqueline, 3.12.07   _ Erna, 17.01.07 _ 02.12.07 din _ Angela, -08.02.08 _ Fiona 23.11.07
_ Beate, 6.12.07 _ Maria, 6.12.07   _ Christine, 13.01.08   Susanna, 28.11.07   _ Natalia, 11.01.08 _ Heidrun, 06.01.08
Lia, 6.12.07 _ Svenja 2001.08   _ Elfriede, 13.12.07   _ Roswitha, 30.12.07   Giada, 28.11.07   _ Lirh, 03.02.08
Tam, 03.02.08 _ Venessa, 12.12.07   _ Atamayka, 30.12.07

_ Roberta, 28.11.07   _ Joshua 6.01.08   _ Виктория, 11.01.08

n 12.12.07

Lena, 30.12.07

_ Elise, 16.12.07

_ Hugo, 30.12.07

_ Emily, 13.01.08   _ Emilia, 30.12.07

_ Paulina, 16.12.07

_ Natalie, 30.12.07

26.12.07   _ ЮЛЯ 11.01.08

_ Sarah Zoe, 31.12.07

_ Luc, 13.01.08

                                                _ Lampros, 13.01.08

_ Arlind. 28.11.07

Works in order of appearance

Across that Place, 2008
Fictional letter addressed to Roman Ondák
from the no longer existing Canal Zone in Panama
Detail of the installation

Passage, 2007
One-day event at the restaurant Anzengruber in Vienna
Chocolate bars, silver foil

Measuring the Universe, 2007
For the whole duration of the exhibition, museum attendants
offer to mark the height of exhibition visitors on the gallery
walls along with their first name and the date on which the
measurement is taken.
Performance and installation at Pinakothek der Moderne,
Munich, DAAD Gallery, Berlin and Museo de Arte
Contemporánea, Vigo

Pocket Money of My Son, 2007
Coins, shelf made from a section of a table

Concealed Episode, 2007
Nelson sitting in a small airplane and circling above Miami
shortly before he jumped on South Beach.
Behind-the-scenes photograph

Concealed Episode, 2007
Nelson Perez, a parachutist of a Cuban origin and a Miami
resident, was invited to simulate an escape from Cuba by a
parachute jump on South Beach in Miami.
Video

His Affair with Time, 2003
Colour photograph from a series of two

Lucky Day, 2006
Adam counting coins before they were thrown by Pablo
into the fountain in Santiago de Compostella.
Behind-the-scenes photograph

Good Feelings in Good Times, 2003
Staged queue in front of the entrance to the Old Parliament
building in Wellington
Performance

My Winter Shoes Rest in Summer, 2007
Shoelaces from the artist's winter shoes tied together and
suspended from a ceiling
Installation DAAD Gallery, Berlin

Two Mars Stories, 2004–2006
Press release from NASA's Kennedy Space Center
Detail of the installation

Remote Journey, 2008
The interior of an airplane was drawn by Ondák's relatives
according to his description. He then added to the drawings
by drawing himself sitting in one of the seats.
Drawing from a series of ten

Spirit and Opportunity, 2004
The surface of Mars reconstructed on the basis of images
published in newspapers and magazines.
Detail of the installation, Kölnischer Kunstverein, Cologne

Failed Fall, 2008
In the month of February, the floor of the Winter Garden in
Sheffield – a greenhouse full of evergreen plants – was filled
with autumn leaves collected from trees around the city
during the previous autumn.
Installation Winter Garden, Sheffield

Room Extension, 2000
Wooden platform, cut-out opening in a window pane, string
stretched between the wall inside the room and the façade
of the opposite house
Detail of the installation, Kunsthof, Zurich

Big Bang, 2006
Colour photograph

Across that Place, 2008
An event of stone skimming organized with a group of
volunteers at the Panama Canal.
Various documentary photographs and fictional postcards
addressed to Roman Ondák from the no longer existing
Canal Zone in Panama

Measuring the Universe, 2007
Installation Pinakothek der Moderne, Munich

Concealed Episode, 2007
Video still

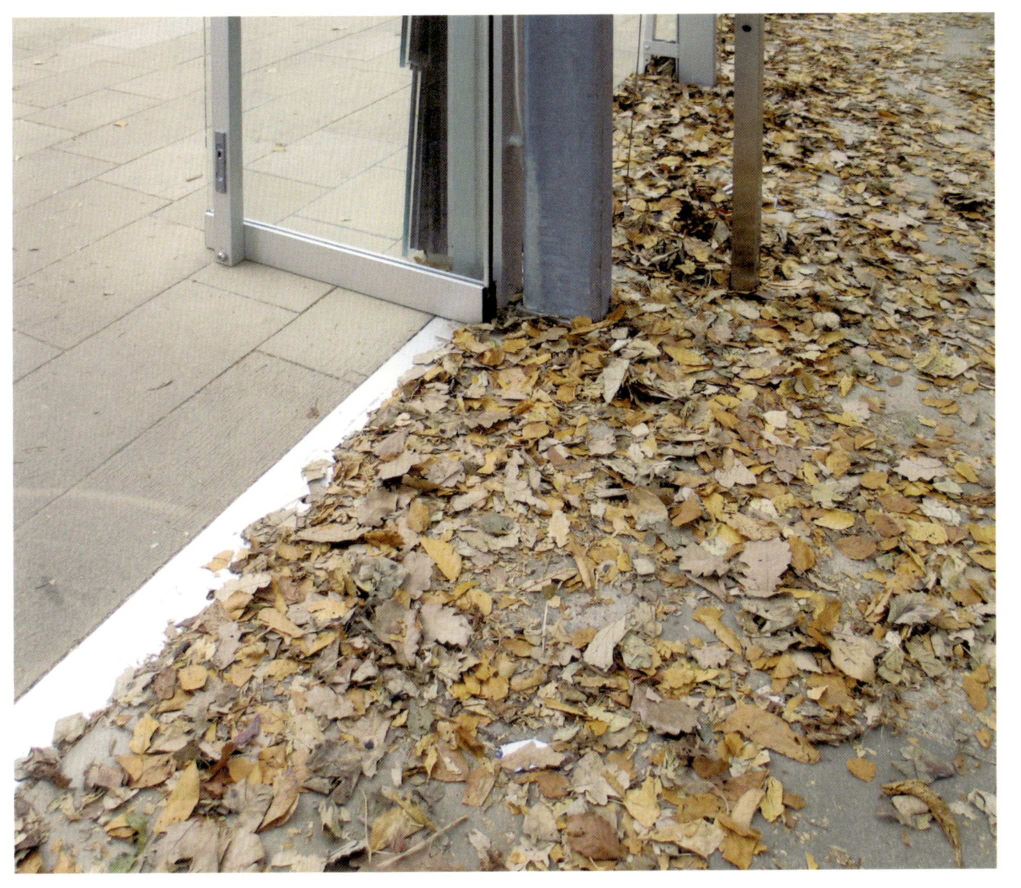

Credits

Across that Place, 2008
Courtesy 8. Panama Biennale, Panama
Photos: Walo Araújo, Francisco Barsallo, Roman Ondák

Passage, 2007
Courtesy of the artist
Photo: Roman Ondák

Measuring the Universe, 2007
Collection Pinakothek der Moderne, Munich;
MoMA, New York
Views of the exhibitions:
Roman Ondák, My Summer Shoes Rest in Winter, Pinakothek
der Moderne, Munich, photos: Ernst Jank, Haydar Koyupinar,
Roman Ondák
Roman Ondák, Measuring the Universe, DAAD Gallery,
Berlin, photos: Nadine Dinter
The Museum as Medium, Museo de Arte Contemporánea,
Vigo, photos: Enrique Touriño

Pocket Money of My Son, 2007
Courtesy of the artist
Photo: Roman Ondák

Concealed Episode, 2007
Courtesy of the artist
Photos: Stacen Berg

His Affair with Time, 2003
Courtesy of the artist

Lucky Day, 2006
Courtesy of the artist

Good Feelings in Good Times, 2003
Tate Collection, London
Photo: Roman Ondák

My Winter Shoes Rest in Summer, 2007
Courtesy DAAD Gallery, Berlin
Photo: Roman Ondák

Two Mars Stories, 2004–2006
Courtesy of the artist

Remote Journey, 2008
Private collection, Munich

Spirit and Opportunity, 2004
Courtesy Kölnischer Kunstverein, Cologne
Photo: Roman Ondák

Failed Fall, 2008
Courtesy Sheffield Contemporary Art Forum
Photos: Roman Ondák

Room Extension, 2000
Courtesy Kunsthof, Zurich
Photo: Roman Ondák

Big Bang, 2006
Courtesy of the artist

Biographies

Roman Ondák is an artist living and working in Bratislava.

Bernhart Schwenk is a chief curator for contemporary art at Pinakothek der Moderne in Munich.

Jeanine Griffin is a curator at Site Gallery, Sheffield.

Tim Etchells is an artist and the director of the performance group *Forced Entertainment*, based in Sheffield.

Magali Arriola is an art critic and independent curator living in Los Angeles.

Colophon

Roman Ondák
Measuring the Universe
Bawag Foundation Edition, volume 9

Editor
Christine Kintisch, Bawag Foundation, Vienna

Curator Bawag Foundation Edition
Brigitte Huck

Concept
Roman Ondák

Authors
Magali Arriola, Tim Etchells, Jeanine Griffin, Bernhart Schwenk

Translation
Elise Feiersinger

Copy editing
Jill Winder

Graphic design
MVD Austria/Michael Rieper, Christine Schmauszer
Roman Ondák

Scans
Spinner, Bratislava
Typocon, Bratislava

Print and binding
REMAprint, Vienna

ISBN
978-3-03764-024-1

Printed in the EU

BAWAG FOUNDATION EDITION

The BAWAG Foundation Edition is a series of artists' books
in the context of the exhibition programme of the BAWAG
Foundation, Vienna. It's a portable exhibition space and a
medium of communication between artists, their work
and the public.

Also published in this series:
Florian Pumhösl, *Champs d'Experience*, 2002
Einar Thorsteinn/Olafur Eliasson, *to the inhabitants of space
in general and the spacial inhabitants in particular*, 2002
Marko Lulic, *Tesla 21*, 2003
Elke Krystufek, *The Rich Visit the Poor, the Poor
Visit the Rich*, 2004
Cerith Wyn Evans, *The Curves of the Needle*, 2005
Christian Philipp Müller, *Portrait of the Museum
as a Chair*, 2006
Anette Baldauf/Dorit Margreiter, *The She Zone*, 2007
Josef Dabernig, *Handwritten Copies.....*, 2008

BAWAG Foundation
Foundationsquartier
Wiedner Hauptstrasse 15
A-1040 Vienna
T +43 (0) 1 504 98 80 – 38
foundation@bawag.com
www.bawag-foundation.at

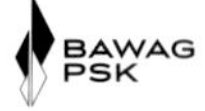

CHRISTOPH KELLER EDITIONS

Published in a limited print run, this series of artists' books and
conceptual art publications, edited and selected by Christoph
Keller, aims to explore the bandwidth of artistic book making and
the mediation of contemporary art in the printed format of the book.

Other titles in this series:
Emmanuelle Antille, *Tornadoes of My Heart*, 2006
Helen Mirra, *Cloud, the, 3*, 2007
Jonathan Meese & Slavoj Zizek, *Ernteschach dem Dämon*, 2007
Peter Piller, *Teilzeitkraft*, 2007
Mungo Thomson, *Negative Space*, 2006
Stuart Bailey & Ryan Gander, *Appendix Appendix*, 2007
Peter Piller, *Nijverdal/Hellendoorn*, 2007
Matias Faldbakken, *Not Made Visible*, 2007
Johannes Wohnseifer, *Werkverzeichnis 1992–2007*, 2007
Archiv Peter Piller, *nimmt Schaden*, 2007
Mai-Thu Perret, *Land of Crystal*, 2008
Julien Berthier, *Nothing Special*, 2008
Archiv Peter Piller, *Zeitung*, 2007
Michael Stevenson, *Celebration at Persepolis*, 2008
Jonathan Monk, *Complete Ilford Works*, 2008
Zilla Leutenegger, *Zilla und das 7. Zimmer*, 2008
Aglaia Konrad, *Desert Cities*, 2008
Jeanne Faust, *Outlandos*, 2008
Loris Gréaud, *Cellar Door*, 2008
Claudia & Julia Müller, *Habitus vs. Habitat: Primaten*, 2009
Boris Groys & Andro Wekua, *Wait to Wait*, 2009
Korpys/Löffler, *Die Sehnsucht nach Glück …*, 2009

Published by:
JRP|RINGIER
Letzigraben 134
CH-8047 Zurich
T +41 (0) 43 311 27 50
F +41 (0) 43 311 27 51
info@jrp-ringier.com
www.jrp-ringier.com

JRP|Ringier books are available internationally at selected
bookstores and the following distribution partners:
Switzerland: Buch 2000, www.ava.ch
France: Les Presses du réel, www.lespressesdureel.com
Germany and Austria: Vice Versa Vertrieb,
www.vice-versa-vertrieb.de
UK and other European countries: Cornerhouse Publications,
www.cornerhouse.org/books
USA, Canada, Asia, and Australia: D.A.P./Distributed Art
Publishers, www.artbook.com

For a list of our partner bookshops or for any general questions,
please contact JRP|Ringier directly at info@jrp-ringier.com, or
visit our homepage www.jrp-ringier.com for further information
about our program.